67-24005 (12-20-67)

Spain: the Vital Years

spain:

PHILADELPHIA AND NEW YORK

LUIS BOLIN

THE
VITAL YEARS

Foreword by
SIR ARTHUR BRYANT C.B.E.

J. B. LIPPINCOTT COMPANY

To the Youth of Spain
*in the hope that they will forgive all
and forget nothing*

Foreword

by Sir Arthur Bryant C.B.E.

Today air travel has made Spain one of the world's most popular holiday resorts. Thirty years ago she was the scene of an internecine conflict which, exceeding in scale and intensity every other in history except the American Civil War, aroused in countries elsewhere the most violent partisanship, much of it based, as we are beginning to see, on an illusion. Presented in the Press and on political platforms as a heroic struggle for liberty by an oppressed people against a treasonable clique of military adventurers, reactionary aristocrats and corrupt priests sustained only by Moorish mercenaries and Italian and German fascists, the real nature of the Spanish Civil War was almost completely misunderstood. That it was heroic was true enough; there was never—on both sides of the barricades—a more valiantly fought and more desperate struggle. That foreigners—Italian, French, German, British, Russian, particularly Russian—intervened in it was only too true. But none of them got anything out of it except burnt fingers, save possibly Britain whose official rulers at least genuinely tried to limit foreign intervention and may thereby have helped, however fortuitously, to strengthen Franco's resolve to remain neutral in the fateful years 1940-2, when his intervention on the side of his fellow dictators might well have proved disastrous. The truth, as this book makes clear, is that the Spanish Civil War was a purely Spanish affair in which a great people, passionately and tragically divided by beliefs and circumstances whose origins lay deep in their past, fought one another to resolve those differences and find, through suffering and sacrifice, a common denominator for their future. It is part of the irony of things that today, after a generation of what to its critics seems merely a repressive Fascist dictatorship, so many of the things for which the best of the defeated and divided men of the Left were striving have been achieved and a new propertied lower middle and working class is emerging. Nor has this been wholly accidental; before he assumed command of the forces in revolt against a government which was failing in its fundamental tasks of preserving public order and justice, Franco was known as a man of liberal sympathies and an advocate of social reform. Nor was it only, as is generally supposed, a minority of Spaniards who rose against what seemed to them chaos; within fifteen months of an apparently forlorn and doomed rising, 600,000 Spaniards, the overwhelming majority of them volunteers, were fighting for the Nationalist cause against 450,000 for the Republican. By the end of the war there were a million of them.

This study of the Spanish Civil War from the Nationalist side has been written by the man whose courage and initiative at a decisive moment of his country's history probably tilted the scales which, at whatever cost to a divided and embattled generation, saved Spain from becoming, like Russia and China, a Communist country and another prison-house for the human soul. His opening account of his secret flight from England in a chartered plane to ferry the soldier who was to become Spain's man of destiny from the Canaries to Morocco is as exciting as a John Buchan story. I hope his book will do something to enable readers everywhere to realize the background to the tragic events of thirty years ago and to understand the cause for which at least one-half of the Spanish people, and that the most disciplined and cohesive part, were prepared to give their lives.

ARTHUR BRYANT

Contents

CONTENTS

CONTENTS

APPENDIXES

Maps

Illustrations

Acknowledgements

The author wishes to thank all those who have helped him in the preparation of this book, especially Lt.-General Don Antonio Barroso, General Franco's G.S.O. 1 for military operations in the field during the Spanish Civil War, later Army Minister in Madrid, and the Historical Archives of the Spanish General Staff, for the figures quoted in Parts II, V, VI and VII, and in Appendixes II and III, most of which have never been published before; to Lt.-General Don José Cuesta, late Chief of the Spanish General Staff, and Don Antonio Olmedo, for information, privately given in the first case, or contained in their book on General Queipo de Llano; to Don Fernando M. Castiella, Spanish Minister for Foreign Affairs, for permission to reproduce the documents in Appendix V; to Generals Franco and Millán Astray, for references to their works on the Spanish Foreign Legion; to Don Melchor Fernández Almagro and Ambassador Manuel Aznar, for information contained in their books on the Republic and the Military History of the Civil War respectively. Also to Francisco Vázquez Maure (Ingeniero Geógrafo) of Madrid, for all the maps contained in this book, and Kit Talbot for the jacket photograph.

The author also wishes to thank the authors and publishers of the following works for permission to reprint copyright material. *The Thirties: A Dream Revolved* by Julian Symons, Cresset Press; *The Spanish Civil War* by Hugh Thomas, Eyre & Spottiswoode; *Laughter in the Next Room* by Sir Osbert Sitwell, David Higham Associates; *Study of Communism* by J. E. Hoover, Holt, Rinehart & Winston; *Spanish Rehearsal* by Sir Arnold Lunn, Hutchinson; *La Revue de Paris* for permission to quote from an article 'Liberalism and Communism' by Don Gregorio Marañón; *Homage to Catalonia* by George Orwell, Martin Secker & Warburg; Standard Telephones and Cables Ltd for permission to quote from an article 'Spain: Genius, Faith, Glory' by Murray D. Kirkwood; *The Tablet* for permission to quote from a review of G. L. Steer's *Sealed and Delivered*.

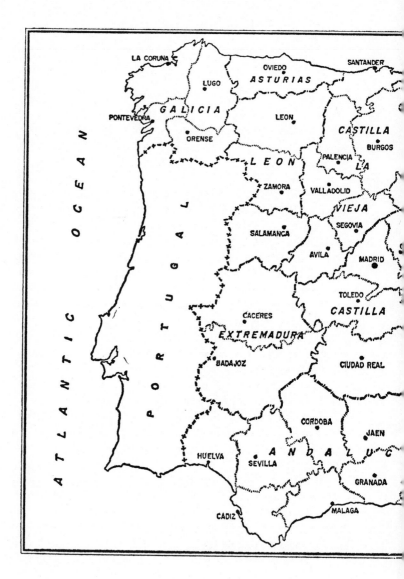

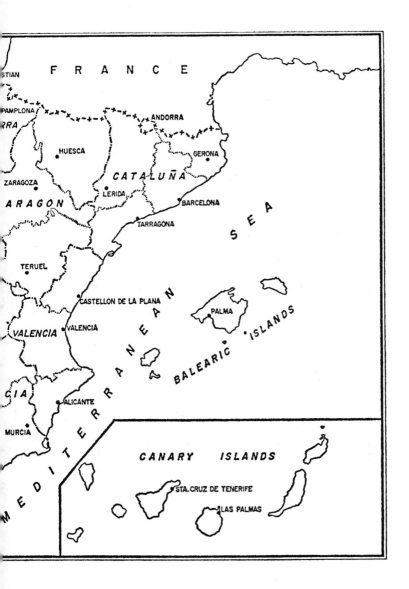

Introduction

I am a Spaniard who has spent half of his life in Spain, the other half in Britain, the United States and France, three countries which I know well and love next to my own. I have written this book in English, my mother's native tongue, to record and explain for my British and American friends what I saw of the Spanish Civil War and of the events that led to it. I hope that what I say here may also become accessible to my French friends. To obtain the necessary perspective I have stepped back in history and described some of the conditions which prevailed in my country during the quarter of a century that preceded the Civil War. I have written in the first person when referring to events which I had some part in or witnessed, and narrated other events which are relevant to the story as a whole and of which I received first-hand information at the time when they occurred.

I have seen England and France not only in peace but at war, and this is why this book includes some references to my experiences as a War Correspondent with the British and French troops in France. I give a picture of Spain in the first decades of the present century and a brief comment on the discovery and initial development of the Americas. The war in Spanish Morocco, which influenced not only the general trend of Spanish politics for almost eighteen years but later developments as well, is the subject of a brief chapter. A longer chapter is devoted to the Spanish Republic. Most of my book deals with the Spanish Civil War.

The Black Legend that was woven around Spain in the sixteenth and seventeenth centuries obscures the truth about that country. Spanish reticence and apathy have contributed to a situation which Salvador de Madariaga had in mind when he wrote on page 37 of *Spain: A Modern History* (Jonathan Cape, London, 1963), that 'It has become customary to sum up the history of Spanish creative effort in America in three hasty generalizations: cupidity, cruelty, and ignorance.' As regards cupidity, Madariaga recalls that 'while these conquerors conquered by themselves, none conquered for himself'. Of Spanish conduct towards the Indians he says, 'Both in theory and practice, Spain was in advance of the times. The crown established legal freedom for all the Indians, and allowed slavery only in the case of cannibals and natives who resisted evangelization.' As for ignorance, the main effort of the Conquistadores, Madariaga says, 'was in the realm of enlightenment. The first Bishop of Mexico founded a college for Indian noblemen in order that they should be in a position to teach the native language and ways to Spanish monks and priests who came over to catechize the New World—an example of the spirit in which the immense civilizing work of the Spaniards in America was carried out. The Spaniards founded and maintained universities in New Spain (Mexico), Santo Domingo, Cuba, New Granada (now Colombia), Peru, Chile, the viceroyalty of La Plata (now Argentina), and part of Bolivia. More attention was paid to elementary schools than was the case in the metropolis (a clear case in which religious zeal had happy effects).' My own comments on the subject are in pages 66 to 70 of this book.

The differences which split the Western world at the time of the Counter-Reformation, when the Star Chamber was also active, were responsible for distorted accounts of the Spanish Inquisition. Its Protestant historian, H. C. Lea, was strongly biased against Catholicism, but he accused Juan Antonio Llorente, an unfrocked priest connected with the Inquisition who later wrote its annals, of gross exaggeration in his estimate of the number of its victims. According to Lea, Llorente's total of 31,912 victims executed between 1480 and 1808 was an 'extravagant guess'. Many of those who write with justified horror of the Inquisition have condoned the infinitely worse horrors perpetrated in Communist countries, or those that were enacted in Spain, on the Republican side, during the Civil War. The *Manchester Guardian*, a paper consistently friendly with the Spanish Left and whose correspondent visited Madrid in 1937, stated that the official records of those massacred in that city reached the appalling figure of 35,000 in less than a year.

Foreign opinion about the Civil War was influenced not only by the Black Legend but by the halo with which the Spanish Republic surrounded itself in other lands, where it was looked upon kindly in wide circles and the initial announcements of its leaders stimulated confidence and high expectations. True, when the Monarchy fell there was room for improvement in Spain, and the Republic was not sparing in its promises. But it did not live up to them. Few abroad realized the manner in which it governed the nation, fewer still understood the gravity of the circumstances which led to civil war, and, later on, even fewer saw the differences between the ways in which one side and the other conducted the war and ruled the territories under their respective control. Also, in 1936–9 Great Britain and other European and American countries were beginning to think in terms of the coming world conflict. The fact that Hitler and Mussolini helped the Spanish Nationalists was a cause of great and perhaps natural prejudice in those countries, though it should be noted that those who criticized us for accepting Hitler's help saw nothing strange in the acceptance of Stalin, who had invaded Poland with Hitler, as their ally in World War II. When men are fighting for all that is dear to them they accept help from wherever it comes. But the loose habit of referring to all authoritarian regimes other than the Communist as 'Fascist' made it hard for people to appreciate the vast differences that separate the Spanish Falange from Nazism. Nor did they read the lessons of the Requeté's closeness to the Falange. Had the latter been Nazist it might have forced Spain to enter the war on Hitler's side, but it would never have been allied to the Requeté in the Civil War or later. The Spanish Blue Division which fought on the Russian Front during the Second World War did not set out from Spain to help the Nazis. Its sole purpose was to fight Communism, which in the Civil War had done its best to defeat the Nationalists.

In English-speaking countries Catholics supported the Nationalists because for them the issues were crystal clear, but they were far from being our only supporters in these countries. Dean Inge—the Dean of St Paul's—appeared on English platforms defending our cause, and Sir Henry Lunn, a prominent Methodist, was a member of the Friends of Nationalist Spain Committee, whose chairman, Lord Phillimore, rendered great service to the same cause. So did Douglas Woodruff, the editor of the *Tablet*. Sir Martin Melvin, the proprietor of the *Universe*, was told by Mr Neville Chamberlain that had it not been for the Catholics he might have had to blockade the Nationalists and intervene against them. Jacques Maritain had some reason for crossing the Atlantic to tell American Catholics to stay neutral, but he refrained from crossing the Pyrenees to visit the two sides into which Spain was then divided and find out for himself whether Catholics in other countries should stay neutral or not. Once France was at war Maritain's

3

delicate prejudices against accepting help from undesirable dictators disappeared. He welcomed Stalin as enthusiastically as he condemned some of our people for accepting Hitler.

Elsewhere in this book I mention the names of some of those who supported the Nationalist cause in Great Britain during the Civil War. There were others. Gabrielle Herbert served on an ambulance which was often under fire and ran her own hospital on the Aragon Front. The late Cecil Gerahty and Roland Winn, the present Lord St Oswald, were frequently with me on the various fronts, gathering material at the risk of their lives to write objectively about the campaign. Practically on the scene when Toledo was taken was Aileen O'Brien, an Irish girl whose greatest effort on our behalf was made to prevent two shiploads of ammunition from leaving an American port for Red Spain. Miss O'Brien personally spoke on the telephone to every Catholic Bishop in the United States and begged them to request their parish priests to ask all members of their congregations to telegraph in protest to President Roosevelt. As a result of her efforts more than a million telegrams were received at the White House, and the munitions never reached their destination. Some time after this an attempt on Miss O'Brien's life was made at Los Angeles; when she opened the door of her room in response to the buzzer a shot embedded itself just over her head. Incidentally, my own life was threatened in Los Angeles in the year 1949. Speaking in Spanish over the telephone, a man referred to the part which I had played in the Civil War and announced that he would shoot me if I did not leave at once. I answered something unprintable and left a week later without hearing further from my caller.

The Spanish Civil War was an occasion for widespread displays of what Sir Arnold Lunn called 'selective indignation'. The same Socialists who objected rightly to the persecution of Jews and Socialists in Germany remained silent when thousands of nuns and priests and even larger numbers of private citizens were butchered in Red Spain. In 1934, the *New Statesman* enthusiastically supported armed revolt against a legal Spanish Government which was of a mild conservative hue. But it denounced General Franco and the Nationalists for armed revolt against a Left-wing Spanish Government. And it enthusiastically supported an armed revolt by Communists against the legal government of Greece. In the United States and England great play was made with the fact that there were only two Communist deputies in the Spanish Cortes. Later it has become known that

Moscow usually works through people who, like Fidel Castro, do not call themselves Communists at the start. Others in the United States saw the Spanish issues clearly, among them H. E. Knoblaugh, who published a book on the Civil War, *Correspondent in Spain*, London, 1937, after following it from the Red side, and William Carney, who wrote from Madrid for *The New York Times* and whose articles on Republican excesses made history for that paper.

Not all of those who fought for the Republicans were Communists. Though led by Communists, most of the men in the International Brigades were not Communists. Some were inspired by the same high ideals which the Spanish Republic had proclaimed at its advent and failed to honour from the start. Members of the Lincoln Brigade offered their lives gallantly, for a wrong cause, as did a son of Clive Bell, whose father, a sensitive art critic, I frequently saw in London during the twenties. But though countless numbers of those who died for the Republic were not Communists, I have used the terms 'Red' or 'Reds' repeatedly in my book because (a), on the Republican side uniforms had a red star to denote officer's rank; (b), the Communist salute was given—and returned by Mr Attlee when he visited Spain during the Civil War; (c), the hammer and the sickle were daubed in red in Republican towns; and (d), Communists were running not only the Army but everything else in the Red Zone when the war came to an end. Spanish people on both sides called them 'Reds', and they themselves used the term 'Red' to denote their affiliation. On the Republican side there were so many parties that a simple term became expedient to identify their members adequately. It was easier to refer collectively to the 'Reds' than to mention in turn Republican Action, the Socialist Party, the Workmen's Party for Marxist Unification (P.O.U.M.), the Radical Sociality Party, the Catalan Left, Galician Separatists, Basque Nationalists, the National Confederation of Workmen (C.N.T.), the Iberian Anarchist Federation (F.A.I.), the Workmen's General Union (W.G.T.), the Unified Socialists Youth Organization, and the Communist Party, to name but a few of those which together headed for chaos. But in my book I have also used the term 'Republican' on many occasions.

I hope that what I have written may help to clear up misunderstanding and contribute to strengthen the good relations which now exist between Spain and the peoples of the West.

PART I

CHAPTER ONE

A Call from Biarritz

One Sunday, towards the end of May, 1936, my wife and I took our five-year-old boy, Fernando, to spend an afternoon in Reigate with a young friend of his, the son of Emilia and Carlos González. Carlos belongs to the family that produces González Byass sherry in Jerez de la Frontera, the only place in the world, incidentally, where genuine sherry is made. His feelings about the Spanish Republic were similar to my own, and we had expressed them the year before at the Ibero-American Benevolent Society's annual dinner at the Savoy Hotel in London, an event usually attended by a large and distinguished gathering. On this occasion the Ambassador of the Spanish Republic had been in the chair. Carlos and I had acted surreptitiously and discreetly to substitute the Republican colours which decorated the room with those of the former flag of Spain, and to replace the Republican hymn played at the end of the dinner with the strains of the Spanish Royal anthem, somewhat to the discomfiture of our principal host—the late Ramón Pérez de Ayala, a famous novelist and, personally, as likeable a man as ever had the misfortune to represent a disastrous government in foreign parts.

Another guest at Reigate that day was the late Conde de los Andes, also a native of Jerez de la Frontera and a discerning judge of good food, vintage wines and *flamenco* dancing and singing. Paco Andes, a Cabinet Minister with Primo de Rivera, was now a frequent companion of the late King Alfonso. We were sitting in the garden. The children were splashing in a shallow pool nearby, and the afternoon was one of those that make Surrey so lovely in springtime. Before we left, Andes drew me aside and said, 'Something is brewing in Spain. No date has been fixed, but something is bound to happen soon. Are you willing to act?'

I was more than willing, and I said this to Andes and expressed the hope that General Franco would direct the rising. He was a military leader in whom I had full confidence. Like myself, thousands of Spaniards were awaiting action which to be decisive would have to be quick and determined; for, if attacked, the Popular Front, unlike King Alfonso in 1931, was sure to arm its adherents and call out the Army, now largely commanded by Left-wingers. Good leadership on our side was vital, and the best man we had was General Franco, who would have to lead whatever troops could be made available the moment the rising broke out. The struggle was sure to be hard.

Already the situation in Spain was causing concern in other lands. English papers were full of it. At Mass on Sunday, 5 July, Father Martindale, the Jesuit preacher, had referred to the Spanish troubles in his sermon at Our Lady of Victories, a church we attended regularly in Kensington, not far from our house in Hornton Street and from Fernando's kindergarten at the Convent of the Assumption, where my mother had been educated. After lunch that same day I had gone to a small meeting at which two Spaniards, fresh from Madrid, spoke of the chaos in which my country now found itself. When I returned to Hornton Street, my wife, Mercedes, raised her eyes from the book she was reading and, in a casual tone, said: 'Juan Ignacio has called you from Biarritz. He will telephone again later.' Juan Ignacio was the Marqués de Luca de Tena, publisher of *A.B.C.*, the Madrid paper for which I was London correspondent, and a bitter opponent of the Republic. Somehow I felt that the hour had struck, and without thinking twice I rang up Juan de la Cierva, my best friend in London at the time.

Years before, La Cierva had invented the autogiro, predecessor of modern helicopters. To complete his invention and patent it in England he had founded the Cierva Autogiro Company, with which Lord Weir, a prominent leader in the British industrial field, was closely connected. The Autogiro Company of America, with Harold Pitcairn in charge, had its headquarters at Philadelphia. In 1936, La Cierva had developed the autogiro to the point that it could take off and land vertically, hover, deliver or pick up parcels tied to a string, and accomplish much else which no ordinary plane could do.

La Cierva and I would occasionally fly an autogiro to a friend's house in the outskirts of London, land on the lawn, and skim back over the Thames to the experimental field where a small hangar housed the machines. We had driven there one day with King Alfonso and his son, Prince Juan de Borbón, later Count of Barcelona and heir to the Spanish throne. Both had tried the autogiro and greatly enjoyed their experience. La Cierva's father was one of the King's ablest Ministers and the only Cabinet member who, in the crisis that brought about the fall of the Monarchy, stood up against Republican demands. His son's experiments in aviation had been encouraged from the start by King Alfonso.

Juan de la Cierva, a brilliant scientist and a fine aviator, was also my baby daughter's godfather. We saw each other constantly. He had rooms in Half Moon Street, off Piccadilly, where he would lock himself up for days and work at problems of torque and propellor pitch with a radio by his side blaring out classical music, the sound of which, he explained, kept his mind from straying while he worked. It was not easy to prevent it from wandering, for he was as concerned as I was with the trend of events in Spain. If what we both hoped for came to pass, his father and his brother Ricardo might soon find themselves in grave danger. La Cierva's fears were not unfounded. His father died two years later in Madrid, in the Legation where he sought refuge during the civil war from enemies bent on his destruction, and Ricardo was shot earlier in that city after being recognized by a Customs official as he was about to leave Spain. My friend, Juan de la Cierva, was killed in an aeroplane accident at Croydon, on 9 December 1936, while on a wartime mission personally entrusted to him by General Franco.

That evening—5 July—I rang up La Cierva and told him that Luca de Tena was calling me from Biarritz and that it looked as if Spain might be on the verge of revolt. We had to meet for a talk without delay. La Cierva was dining with Lord Weir's brother, James Weir, and he gave me a telephone number which I was to use if my premonitions proved correct.

Two hours later, Luca de Tena came through from Biarritz and went straight to the point. 'I want you to charter a seaplane in England,' he said, 'capable of flying direct from the Canary Islands to Ceuta, in Spanish Morocco. Get an ordinary plane, if no seaplane is available, but make sure it's the best. A Spaniard called Mayorga, who works at Kleinwort's, the banking firm in the City, will give you the necessary money to pay for the flight. Act quickly. Your plane has to be in Casablanca next Saturday, 11 July. Tell the pilot to stay at the Hotel Carlton there and await the arrival of an agent who will use the password *Galicia saluda a Francia*—Galicia salutes France—and give him further instructions. He may have to go on to the Canaries, pick up a passenger, and fly him to Ceuta. To identify this passenger the pilot should visit a doctor called Gabarda, who lives in Tenerife, at Viera y Clavijo, 52, give the password to the doctor and say "the plane has arrived". Should no agent turn up at Casablanca by 31 July, the pilot will return to London without calling at the Canaries. Don't waste time. Good luck to you!'

While Luca de Tena spoke I had been making notes feverishly. From the garden, where our daughter, Marisol, lay in her pram, playing with the fading sunlight that filtered through the trees, my wife had come in to join me. Now she was asking questions by my side. I needed her advice and assistance, so I told her all I knew, my hopes and my fears, and from that moment she became one of the most valuable aides the Spanish movement had in London.

I had to rely also on Juan de la Cierva, for my mission was in many ways beyond me. I knew nothing about planes or pilots, nor had I flown since the days when I was War Correspondent with the British Army in France. La Cierva, on the other hand, had all the necessary contacts in the flying world and could help me in a thousand ways. He was about to finish dinner the second time I called him that evening; an hour later he was with us in our sitting room, discussing the possibilities over a whisky and soda. There was little likelihood, he told me, of getting the seaplane we needed. Some navies had seaplanes, but there was none for hire in the open market. This meant that we would have to get along with the usual type of aircraft. La Cierva knew the leading man in the field of flying insurance, and because insurance rates depended at the time not only on the merits of a plane but on those of the man who flew it he felt confident of obtaining reliable information concerning whatever plane I could manage to find, and its pilot. He undertook to inquire about a machine capable of flying to Spain and French Morocco, with long hops between the various landings.

Two other points were settled between us that night. Luca de Tena had merely requested me to charter a plane, but the expedition needed a leader, able to decide what to do and when to do it. The venture could not be entrusted to a man we did not even know. One of us, La Cierva or myself, would have to be in command from the start. I was all for La Cierva, who was far more at home in the air than I was, and I also felt that if I stayed at home my English newspaper contacts might prove useful when matters came to a head in Spain. La Cierva thought otherwise. Should he suddenly take off on a mysterious flight to the south, our enemies might get wind of his departure, and his eventual arrival in the Canaries would also arouse suspicion. Because of this, La Cierva remained in London, and I took charge of the flight.

Understandably, Luca de Tena had called me from Biarritz. It was difficult for him to speak openly from his summer residence in San Sebastian, where the Spanish police would have easily overheard his instructions. Had the French police listened in? The Popular Front Government in France was on excellent terms with the Popular Front Government in Spain. Did they already know our plans? To change them I called Biarritz and asked Luca de Tena to lunch the following day at Maxim's in Paris. La Cierva attended the lunch in my place just in case somebody happened to be on the look out for me. It was time to start putting others off the scent.

No names had been mentioned over the long distance telephone, but the three of us knew that the mysterious passenger who might have to be picked up in Tenerife was none other than General Franco. The whole object of the flight was to land him safely in Ceuta. In the Canary Islands he was a virtual prisoner of the Republicans, who could easily intercept him should he sail on his own for the Peninsula, like Morocco several days away by sea from the Canaries. Only a plane could provide him with the initiative and freedom of movement essential to outwit our enemies at the start.

Alone in my room that night, the grim consequences of a possible failure began to weigh upon my mind. We were on the eve of a tremendous revolution, which General Franco would lead if I managed to play the role that had been assigned to me. The slightest slip on my part could be fatal, but the success of my venture might well be the spark that set off civil war in Spain. I was morally prepared for all that was involved in civil strife. I knew that only force could now save my country, and that the alternative to force was Communism and chaos. For years I had awaited this hour. Then I thought of my mother, of my brothers and sisters, of the dangers that would threaten them if violence was let loose in Spain. Any attempt to warn people there of what was about to happen would give the show away. How could I be convincing without revealing part of our plans, the rest of which somebody might possibly guess? It was appalling to think that if I kept silent thousands might run the risk of being murdered, but there was nothing that I could do, and though the perilous position of my family and my friends filled me with anguish, the one dominating fear in my mind was that the plot might fail, for then the whole of Spain would be doomed. In five days I was to be in Casablanca, where I might have to spend three lonely weeks waiting for an agent with a password, or for an order to return to London. Meanwhile there were many details to work out, much to arrange, and very little time in which to do it all.

On Monday, La Cierva's first reports were not encouraging. No seaplane was to be had in the entire European continent, and no land plane that we might charter could fly direct from the Canaries to Spanish Morocco, for the distance was too great. This was indeed a setback. Risky as intermediate stops between the two points might be on the way out, with Franco on board they would be fraught with the gravest danger. To make matters worse, there was no landing strip in Ceuta; only a lot of water in the harbour on which our elusive seaplane could have settled had we been able to find it.

I spent part of the day attending to my passport, and that same evening La Cierva flew off to Paris for the meeting with Luca de Tena. Before leaving he told me that Olley Air Services at Croydon had the right plane for our purpose, so, early the next morning, I went to Croydon for a talk with Captain Olley. What I said sounded fishy to my ears, but the Captain seemed to take it naturally. I had 'urgent business' in Portugal and in French Morocco; once there I might have to fly 'as far as Dakar', possibly also to the Canary Islands. My trip was sure to be a lengthy one, three weeks or more, and I needed a plane capable of covering long stretches without refuelling, and a first-class pilot, the best he could provide. I was due in Lisbon soon, and wished to avoid any stops in Spain. How anxious I was to avoid them, or why, was something which Olley did not perhaps realize.

He took me to a shed, where I saw several planes, and pointed out one which, he told me, was exactly what I needed—a de Havilland

Dragon Rapide, registration number G-ACYR, with two brand new Gipsy Wright engines. It looked all right, was identical with the Prince of Wales's Dragon Rapide G-ACTT, and was ready to start at a moment's notice. The cabin could accommodate six, besides the pilot. Everything seemed reassuring, but the deal could not be completed till La Cierva returned from Paris. He was due back at any moment, so I withheld my decision and retraced my steps to meet him in London.

What La Cierva told me about his talk with Luca de Tena set my heart beating faster. There was widespread support for a national rising in Spain, but the odds against us were tremendous. The attitude of the Army, especially in large towns and cities, was more than doubtful. Our main asset was the forces in Spanish Morocco, which General Franco was expected to lead the moment he landed from my plane.

Two Blondes and a Trustworthy Fellow

La Cierva thought it unwise for me to leave for the Canary Islands as the sole passenger of a seven-seater Dragon Rapide, in which the only other occupants would be members of the crew. What excuse could I give, if questioned, for travelling alone by such a costly means of transportation? Our enemies were sure to be on their guard, and would be watching Franco closely. There was also a possibility that I might be recognized in the Canaries. While on an official tour of the islands in the late twenties, as Regional Delegate of the Spanish Tourist Board, I had been repeatedly interviewed and my photograph had appeared in the local papers. Only a few weeks before, as I left Brompton Oratory one Sunday, a casual visitor from Tenerife had singled me out from the large crowd and recalled our meeting in Icod, a small place on the island of Tenerife where he had been town councillor when I visited it in 1929. If suspicious, the Reds might destroy the plane. It was my business to see that nothing happened to the Dragon Rapide before it left the Canaries with Franco.

'Why not take a blonde with you,' ventured La Cierva; 'the more glamorous the better?' Not noticing the expression on my wife's face, he added, 'Take two blondes and another fellow. Make it look like a party, like two couples having a good time. Nothing would seem more natural. It would throw dust in other people's eyes and be a lot safer.'

It was now 8 July. Three days later I had to be in Casablanca. Where was I to find my three fellow passengers? Mercedes volunteered to come with me, and suggested the name of a friend who could act the part of second girl, but the risk was too great, and I wanted no one on board with even a remote idea of our ultimate objective. The passengers I needed, besides being willing to fly with me to the unknown at a moment's notice, had to be unaware of my political views and, if possible, of my existence.

Douglas Jerrold, the writer and editor of the *English Review*, was lunching with me at Simpson's the next day. I told La Cierva to join us, called the restaurant, and booked a corner table where the three of us could talk freely. When we got there it was late. Every corner table was occupied; two jovial Englishmen were drinking soup at the one I liked best, but they agreed to move the moment I asked them.

'Why all this fuss?' Douglas inquired as we took our seats. When the waiter had left I replied to his question. 'I am in a fix,' I said. 'I need two blondes and a trustworthy fellow willing to fly with me next Friday to an unknown destination on the West Coast of Africa.'

A flash of amusement lit up Jerrold's eyes. 'What are you up to?' he asked.

'I can't say more.'

'Not another word?'

'Not one.'

For what seemed like an age Douglas remained silent. Finally he mentioned the name of a retired Naval officer.

'Anybody else?'

'There are others. Yeats-Brown, for instance. But he's away.'

I had met the author of *Bengal Lancer*, and agreed he might be the man I wanted. Roast lamb was being served, and I poured claret into our glasses.

'What about Hugh Pollard?' said Jerrold, thinking aloud. 'He's a retired Army major, a hunting man, an expert on fire-arms, a regular contributor to *Country Life* and very much your way of thinking. He'll do.'

'Where can we find him?'

A messenger-boy was summoned, and Jerrold wrote down the name of his friend and a telephone number in Sussex. 'Tell the operator it's urgent.' Pollard was soon on the line. After some moments, during which La Cierva and I barely exchanged a word, Jerrold returned to our table, a broad smile on his face. 'Hugh will see us this afternoon,' he announced. 'I think he's your man. I have told him to keep his head under a cold-water tap till we get there.'

'What about the blondes?'

'He says Dorothy will come.'

'We need another,' I insisted.

'Don't be impatient, old boy. It has taken me fifteen minutes to find you a willing traveller and one blonde. We're not doing so badly.'

We were doing rather well. Jerrold was not only a wizard, but the essence of tact and discretion; the connection between my mysterious trip to 'West Africa' and the most likely outcome of recent events in Spain must have been obvious to him, yet he had made no reference to the general purpose of my flight. What more could I ask? We understood each other perfectly. In my place, I thought, he would have been as reticent as myself. Never had I had greater proof of friendship, nor has service ever been rendered to another man and his country with less self-interest or in a more gracious manner.

At three o'clock that afternoon La Cierva brought his car to Eyre and Spottiswoode's, the publishers, where Jerrold had an office. We started immediately, and tramlines and buses were soon left behind. The country looked beautiful, and the sight of flowers and a warm sun filled me with confidence and joy. Once we found the other blonde, everything was going to be all right.

We drove fast through deserted lanes, and eventually our car turned into a carriage-drive that led to Whitelands, Pollard's home in Midhurst, Sussex. The garden was a mass of colour and as inviting and restful as an English garden can be early in July, when June has been kind and sunny. From behind a tall hedge came the sounds of young people, playing tennis under a pale blue sky.

I shook hands with Major Pollard in a long, dark, panelled room filled with Jacobean furniture, the severity of which was somewhat tempered by the sight of a few decanters surrounded by glasses on a large walnut table. We spoke of the loveliness of the flowers that summer, and of the weather, which was undoubtedly fine. I had come to talk of war in an atmosphere of great peace. Pollard poured out a drink for each of us and another for himself, took his glass in his hand, and after strolling once around the room, turned to me and said:

'I understand you have a proposition to make.'

'That is so,' I answered, clearing my throat. 'I would like you to fly with me, the day after tomorrow, to a spot on the West Coast of Africa. To complete our party we need two attractive and glamorous young ladies. Can you help me to find them?'

I could hardly have made a more preposterous request to a man I had never seen in my life. Smiles broke out on the faces of the two friends who had brought me there to meet him, but Pollard did not move a muscle. Middle-aged, with an air of reassurance and an intelligent look in his eyes, he was obviously a fellow who could cope with anything that came his way.

'Could you clarify your invitation,' he asked me, 'or illuminate, however slightly, the object of the flight? It all sounds rather mysterious.'

'I agree,' said I, 'but there is nothing more that I can add, except that what I have in mind is something to which, if you only knew it, I think you would not object on principle. The trip will, I trust, be a pleasant one, and you and the young ladies who might honour us with their company will be my guests the whole way there and back. I promise to take care of everything.'

'Our insurance policies included?' Pollard inquired anxiously. 'I have a wife and family. One must think of these things.'

I hastened to explain that insurance policies for one and all were a part of my invitation, and Pollard, without putting down his glass, began to pace the room again. Only for a moment, though; quite soon he turned to me, and, with a charming smile, said:

'I'm on!'

At last the basic deal was settled, but the matter of the blondes brooked no delay. When I ventured a tactful reference to this, Pollard merely repeated what he had said to Jerrold over the telephone. Dorothy would come.

'Have you spoken to her?' I asked.

'No, but she's sure to come. Just now she's in London, saying good-bye to a boy friend who is also off to some wild place. I think we can count on her.'

'Even so,' I urged, 'we need another girl. Forgive me for being insistent, but we are due in Casablanca four days from now.'

Pollard was not unresourceful. 'Diana might be persuaded, provided she likes the idea. She's my daughter, you know. Let me talk to her mother.' As the Major left the room the three of us glanced at each other. Things were moving a good deal faster than we had dared to hope earlier that day.

'How does he impress you?' asked Jerrold.

'I like him,' I said; 'he makes up his mind quickly.' The door opened, and Mrs Pollard, a charming lady with typically English good looks, shook hands with us and remained talking a few moments. Soon after this Diana came in. Blonde, attractive, and as alert as her father, she seemed delighted with the idea of a summer holiday in an unknown part of the world. Indeed, so pleased was she that she could barely speak. 'Daddy tells me that you, I mean, that we ... Thanks very much. It's too wonderful for words! I can hardly believe it!'

Neither could I. Now all we needed was Dorothy. According to Pollard she was also a blonde, two or three years older than Diana, with pleasant looks and a not too inquisitive disposition. To meet her before returning to London we adjourned to a pub conveniently situated near the railway station, where we consumed pints of bitter ale while talking about passports, visas, insurance policies and suitable places for a summer vacation on the West Coast of Africa. The train carrying Dorothy Watson finally steamed in. Her appearance justified all that Pollard had said, and her willingness to fly with me to the unknown seemed greater, if possible, than that of her friends. The party was now complete; only some details remained to be settled. Pollard suggested I should lunch with him the following day. 'It will give us a chance to get better acquainted,' he said. I accepted his invitation as readily as he had accepted mine.

The next day—Thursday, 9 July—I collected at Kleinwort's, a banking firm in the City, the £2,000 which had been provided to cover the cost of my flight and incidental expenses. As arranged, Señor Mayorga handed me the crisp white notes without asking any questions, but there was an anxious look in his eyes, and a feeling of near panic seized me the moment I pocketed the money. What if it were stolen? I had to have cash. Cheques were no good for spot payments such as I would have to start making in the immediate future, but our whole plan could be shattered by a theft, possibly the outcome of a plot, a first move on the part of our enemies should they have overheard Luca de Tena's instructions from Biarritz. I jumped into a taxi, took the money home and hid it carefully. The next few days, if I went out with any part of it in my pockets, my wife kept close to me whenever we got into a crowd.

At lunch with Pollard in the Savile Club we spoke of everything except the matters that were uppermost in our minds. My recently acquired travelling companion told me something about himself. He was an expert on fire-arms, liked to live in the country, and preferred to be driven in a car rather than drive it. On my part I outlined some of my own background. In a purely detached manner we referred casually to our flight, which Pollard begged me to postpone for one more day. He and the girls had to do a little shopping and get their passports and visas in order for the journey. To comply with his request was not difficult, for, at the earliest, my plane would not be ready to leave before Friday evening or Saturday morning.

After lunch I went to Croydon and concluded my deal with Captain Olley. First I paid for the trip, thus applying a considerable part of my funds to the purpose for which they had been assigned. My arrangement with Captain Olley entitled me to take a full load of passengers from London to Casablanca, stay there until 31 July, or spend part of the time in the Canaries, where a more pleasant climate could be enjoyed. As an alternative, we could go to Mallorca, Tripoli or the Riviera. The option was left to me. Also, on the way out or back the Dragon Rapide would land wherever convenient.

So far everything had run smoothly, but now Olley mentioned something which left me wondering and somewhat perturbed. 'This is not an ordinary trip,' said he. 'There's no need to tell me what is really in your mind, but I have a feeling that it may involve risks not covered by the usual kind of policy. Because of this, I must ask you to assure me that the plane will be used exclusively to transport you or such people as you may authorize to the places listed in our agreement. Should it be destroyed or damaged as a result of events not normally included in routine insurance, you yourself would meet the loss up to an amount not exceeding £10,000.' This was a great deal of money at the time, but I wrote down my signature without a tremor. What else was I to do?

'Could I meet my pilot?' Olley pressed a button, and Captain Cecil W. H. Bebb entered the office where we were talking. Young, freckled and red-haired, with blue eyes and winning smile, from the start his looks inspired me with a feeling of confidence that was not unfounded. Bebb, during World War II, was personal pilot to Air Chief Marshal Sir Arthur Sheridan Barratt, Commander-in-Chief of the Royal Air Force in France. Later he became chief test pilot to one of the companies of the Hawker Group; today he holds a high executive post with British United Airways. Throughout our flight he was magnificent. He and I agreed to have the plane ready at 7 a.m. on Saturday and try to reach Casablanca that same day—the date appointed for my arrival there. A competent mechanic would fly with us, tune up the engines before each lap and carry out minor repairs. However, it was proving difficult to enlist the services of an equally competent radio-operator. None of Olley's men was free.

'I do not personally know the chap I have in mind,' said Olley, 'but his references seem all right. If he's as good as the other two, you'll have no cause to grumble.'

The news was disquieting, but what troubled me most were Olley's hints about the real object of my flight. Was his scent for the unusual as keen as all that? Did he suspect more than I had told him? Even so, I thought to myself, he won't go out of his way to alert others.

Thursday I devoted entirely to completing my own arrangements for the trip. My passport had expired, and I had to get a new one at the Spanish Consulate. I knew the Consul-General, Don Luis Calderón, a career diplomat whose personal sympathies were on our side. But certain members of his staff were not to be trusted, and there was a chance that it might prove difficult to get my papers in order, for my hostility to the Republican Government was a matter of common knowledge. Anything could have happened; a delay at this moment would have been fatal. To my great relief, the vital document was delivered to me without a question or the slightest hitch.

On Friday morning I went to the Carmelites in Church Street, not far from my house in Kensington, and made my peace with God. If my life was necessary for the success of our cause, I was ready to offer it. That same day La Cierva came to my house for lunch and agreed that all we could do was to face the more disturbing points of my chat with Olley, but when I mentioned the guarantee I had signed, his reaction was typical of him. 'Let me speak about this to the Duke of Alba,' he said. We went to Claridge's, where the Duke was staying. He shared our belief that revolt was the only course now left to save Spain from ruin, and approved the idea of my flight. Alba also thought it essential that Franco should lead the movement. 'This time,' he said, recalling Sanjurjo's rising, 'there must be no mistakes.' La Cierva then spoke of the guarantee I had signed, and I felt relieved and grateful when they each undertook to cover one-half of my responsibility.

Juan de la Cierva gave a farewell party for me that night and invited friends of his to dine and dance with us. It was the last evening I spent with him in London, the last of many we had enjoyed there together during the preceding years. Not once did we mention my journey, nor did any of those present have an inkling of the circumstances in which I was about to leave London. To explain my absence, Mercedes would say that I was taking a brief holiday near Oslo with a friend. Weeks elapsed before the truth was discovered, and though most people understood the reasons for our secrecy, some felt I should have taken them into my confidence. The passing of the years has not helped me to share their point of view.

CHAPTER THREE

The Hazards of a Day

My wife and I rose early on the morning of 11 July; we were up by five. I loved our house in Hornton Street, where we had lived some of our happiest years and from which, every afternoon, my boy had gone with his Scottish nanny to sail his boats on the Round Pound and play near Peter Pan's statue. I never saw that house again; it was destroyed in the Blitz during World War II. Before leaving for Croydon, Mercedes woke up the kiddies. Neither of us knew when we would be together once more, or where. The morning was grey and dull. Suddenly, everything seemed purposeless, drab, and flat. Marisol was five months old, and Spain had known no peace since her birth. She looked lovely as she slept, her head a mass of fair curls. Fernando was almost six, and when I took him in my arms he said, 'Why must you go away, Daddy, why?'

La Cierva came to breakfast, and it was barely 6 a.m. when the three of us set off for Croydon. When we arrived there, while Mercedes met Pollard and the girls, my friend and I stayed in the car; we had something to say to each other, and we both thought it wiser to avoid being seen together at that moment. Then I embraced my wife with a leaden heart and walked towards the plane with the rest of the party. The adventure had begun. Bebb sat me next to him. Pollard was on the opposite side from me, with the girls behind and the mechanic and the radio operator in the two remaining seats. Our first stop was to be at Bordeaux, where Luca de Tena awaited me with the final instructions for my trip. Four hours later, after flying across the Channel and over rain-drenched apple orchards in Normandy, we got to Bordeaux in a torrential downpour, our wheels splashing up water as we taxied to the main building. In London I had been counselled to feign surprise on meeting Luca de Tena, but my pretence at astonishment was effortless, for he was not alone when I saw him. He had brought along four mutual friends whom I liked and three of whom I did not expect to see. Talking to him in public was a risk that could not be avoided, but to be met by a group of Spaniards, all of them known for their Monarchist and anti-Republican feelings, was another matter. The blondes saved the situation. My Spanish friends were quickly briefed, and soon they were chatting to the girls as if they had come expressly to meet them. At lunch the crew of the plane had their own table; the blondes and the boys made merry with Pollard at another; I sat at a third with Luca de Tena and the late Marqués del Mérito, who had come to join our party and fly with me as far as Casablanca. From there Mérito would proceed to Tangier and purchase a small plane which Franco would perhaps need to reach a wide plateau in Spanish Morocco called Llano Amarillo, near a cedar forest in Ketama where the Foreign Legion awaited his arrival to start the revolt against Madrid.

Pepe Mérito, an experienced pilot, had assumed another name for the whole trip and held a Bolivian diplomatic passport which his father-in-law, Simon Patiño, the tin millionaire, had thoughtfully provided from the Legation of which he was the head in Paris. To make room for Mérito in the Dragon Rapide I dispatched our mechanic to Toulouse, where he could board a passenger plane to Casablanca, Bebb having assured me that his services would not be really necessary before the long hop from the African Coast to the Canaries. And, in accordance with a code which we had prearranged in London, I sent a cable to my wife, saying: SOUTH AMERICAN BUYING TANGERINES. It meant that Mérito was on the Dragon Rapide and would continue to Tangier as arranged.

The Bay of Biscay was calm and blue near Biarritz, St-Jean-de-Luz and San Sebastian, playgrounds of my youthful days clearly visible from our lofty perch, but around Bilbao great banks of clouds obscured the mountains, and Bebb flew so high at my instigation that a thick layer of ice soon covered our wings. The aircraft staggered along carrying its extra load of ice and barely maintaining flying speed, with Bebb working hard at the controls and the radio officer calling ground stations frantically for assistance. True to form, we got no answer. High over the plains of Castile we emerged from those lovely cloud formations and Bebb dived his aircraft through a hole in the sky, to shed the ice at warmer levels and ascertain his position. Everything below us looked alike, and though the radio officer fiddled with his knobs he failed to give us the necessary navigational assistance. We were utterly lost over the vast Spanish plateau, red, green and yellow in the blinding sun of that July afternoon. Beautiful as they were, to land in one of those plains was the last thing that I wanted.

I heard Bebb cursing the radio operator, sweat pouring down his forehead. Ahead of us and far to the right loomed the outline of the Naranco de Bulnes, crowning tip of the Picos de Europa range and home of chamois and brown bear. Strong, unsuspected winds had taken us west instead of south-west. We searched for landmarks that might indicate our position, finding none, though we flew low enough to read the meaningless names of isolated railway stations. To my dismay, Bebb finally turned his plane towards the Parma airfield at Biarritz. There we landed, refuelled, and set off with Mérito beside the pilot, a new set of Michelin road maps in his hands. Bebb had now decided to fly in sight of the ground without assistance from his radio officer, who had apparently drunk too much claret at Bordeaux. The lap was a long one, there was no end to the Spanish landscape, and the scenery in Portugal consisted of low hills devoid of airstrips. We looked vainly for Braganza, our tentative destination for a first landing on Portuguese soil, and with no fuel reserve headed for the town of Espinho, while beads of perspiration—an ominous sign—sprouted again on the pilot's brow. 'I may have to pancake on one of those hills,' he gasped eventually, hating the idea as much as I did, for even if we came down safely it would have been beyond his power to get the plane off the ground. Every minute seemed an eternity, every mile seemed like two. Would we make it? Bebb nursed his engines for maximum range, until, suddenly, as if in a dream, we saw the sea before us, its shining expanse lit up by the rays of the setting sun, with Espinho dead ahead. 'It's a military airfield,' shouted the pilot, 'but there's no alternative. We must come down.'

We landed. A gust of the same stiff breeze that had battled our progress for hundreds of miles hit my lungs like a tonic. We had flown over ten hours since leaving London, but Spain was behind us, and I waved my hand joyfully at two Portuguese soldiers and a corporal who were walking towards the plane. When they spoke, my spirits fell. By coming down without permission in a military field we had committed a grave offence. Our plane was confiscated, and we were all placed under arrest. Hard as I tried to explain that we would have crashed had we not landed there, the corporal was adamant, nor did he waver before the sight of brand-new English bank-notes. His duty was to report us to his lieutenant, and he was resolved to carry it out.

The sun dissolved into the Atlantic, the impasse remained obdurate, and the lieutenant finally appeared. His view of the situation was not lenient. We would have to be taken to Oporto, twelve miles north of the airfield and the one place where we could be adequately dealt with. As we passed through Espinho, the local fire brigade was celebrating its annual fiesta, and the entire town was rejoicing with its members. Combined with the charm of my two blondes, the event made a suitable impression on the lieutenant, who promised to release our plane next morning and accepted my invitation to dinner.

Seasoned travellers are familiar with the feeling of survival that marks the end of a hazardous flight. We shared it that day; it had not been uneventful, and though we had failed to reach Casablanca, the fact made little difference to the substance of our plans. Tomorrow we would get there. Now we were gathered for dinner at the Escondidinho, 'The Little Hidden One', a famous restaurant in Oporto where sea-food is comparable to that served in Galicia, and where delicious Portuguese wines, unknown in other lands, are as good with fish as with meat. I could relax. Bebb was a fine pilot, and his Dragon Rapide had fulfilled my expectations. The plains of Castile were a memory of the past. Dorothy and Diana, though a prey to air-sickness during bumps, had saved us at an awkward moment. Pollard had anchored serenity to his outlook and proved indifferent under strain. Mérito was my safety valve. We shared jokes in Spanish and entrusted our secret thoughts to each other. And though Port is even better in England than in its native land, that night it helped me to sleep.

At Lisbon, on Sunday morning, we landed on the Alverca field near the Tagus, and when the car we had summoned turned up, Mérito and I set off with the girls and Pollard, leaving Bebb and the radio operator to look after the Dragon Rapide.

Our travelling companions wished to see the city, but Mérito and I had business to attend. We had to find General Sanjurjo, considered by many as the real leader of the revolt, and inform him about our flight and its purpose. Sanjurjo, who was living quietly with his wife and a young son in a small hotel in Lisbon, was out when we called to see him. Nor was it possible to trace him in Estoril, sixteen miles away, whither we drove fast in his quest after being told that we might find him there. To Lisbon we returned through a maze of narrow streets—the fine road from the Portuguese capital to Estoril had not yet been constructed—entreating our driver to waste no time. We had none to spare if we were to sleep that night in Casablanca.

The keen-sighted Mérito was the first to spot the General as we crossed his car in a crowded street. We doubled on our tracks in hot pursuit until Sanjurjo saw me and pulled up in response to our appeals. A hurried talk in a deserted alley sufficed to tell him what we knew. Confident and enthusiastic with regard to our revolt, he showed no ambition for leadership, but he attached the utmost importance to my flight. It was vital, he said, that Franco should reach Morocco quickly. His youth and capability, he insisted, were essential for the success of our cause.

The completion of formalities at Alverca gave me the opportunity I needed for a chat with my English companions before we got to Casablanca. Should Mérito and I be arrested there, as might well happen if the two Popular Front Governments had agreed to thwart our movements after hearing about them, the whole plan would fall to pieces. I took Pollard by the arm and started to pace with him in the hot sunshine. 'Should I leave you suddenly at our next stop,' I said to him, 'take the plane to the Canaries with the rest of the party except Mérito, who must go to Tangier on his own. From Las Palmas, where you will land at Gando airport, proceed by sea to Santa Cruz de Tenerife and find some pretext to visit a doctor called Gabarda, who lives in that city at Viera y Clavijo, 52. Say to him "*Galicia saluda a Francia*; the aeroplane has arrived." Once this is done, you and the girls may like to stay for a few days on some island before sailing back to England.'

Pollard's sole concern was to get my instructions right. Without asking a single question he copied them carefully in a small notebook, jotting down the password in phonetic spelling, which I dictated to him. Then he pondered for a moment. 'I think we ought to disguise this,' he said at last, 'for it contains a valuable clue. Let's assume that my health is poor, and that I am constantly on the move. In such a case it would be natural for me to have the names and addresses of doctors in various lands. And, in this way, the significance of Dr Gabarda's name and address would not be so apparent.' So we invented a doctor in Munich, another in the Riviera and a third in Rome, all of whose imaginary names and addresses were carefully jotted down, and I left Major Pollard much pleased. I had finally entrusted him with a part, at least, of my secret.

It was now Bebb's turn. To him I mentioned nothing of the password or of Gabarda's existence. All I said was that he might have a different set of passengers for the return journey from the Canaries—I had to tell him that we were going there—which Pollard would help him to identify. Again I did not mention Franco's name, or the fact that Spain was on the verge of a revolt. Even more unconcerned than Pollard, Bebb simply said 'Right-o!' and moved off to board the plane.

For a while our flight towards the African continent was bumpy, but the air became smoother over the sea. The afternoon was hot. South of Portugal we flew close to the Spanish coast. Far down in the water I could see the thick outline of the huge 'almadraba' nets, used by the fishermen of Huelva and Cadiz to catch tuna by the hundred. I also saw the village of Palos, the incredibly humble starting point for the discovery of America; the tiny monastery of La Rábida, where Columbus planned his voyage; the tall monument to his memory, presented to General Primo de Rivera by an American sculptress, Mrs Harry Payne Whitney, in a ceremony which I had attended when Spain lived peacefully under the King; the vast Coto de Doñana, one of the finest wild-life refuges in the world, owned partly by Pepe Mérito, where I had shot duck three years before; and the wide stretch of the Guadalquivir river, running into the sea at Sanlucar. South of this, the deep indent of the Bay of Cadiz and the narrowing gap of the Strait of Gibraltar, with ships funnelling in and out of its swift currents and Cape Espartel jutting into the Atlantic, west of Tangier.

The Hotel Carlton in Casablanca was not in the same class as former or present Carltons in the Haymarket or in Cannes, nor could it stand comparison with the Ritz-Carlton in New York, but its depressing appearance and shady atmosphere seemed to protect us against the risk of recognition, and the lady at the reception desk, due possibly to force of habit, evinced no interest in our identities. It was easy to conceal my Spanish passport under the heap of similar documents which my British companions dumped before her, so I seized the opportunity of becoming Tony Bidwell, a native of London, England. My change of name and nationality was duly inscribed on a printed form, and I notified it accordingly to my imperturbable friends.

Hugh Pollard drew me aside. 'I can't stand our radio operator,' he said; 'I don't trust him an inch. Let's get rid of him. Bebb will find the islands all right without that bastard's help. Why not pack him home? I'll see to everything; my Consul will send him back on a tramp steamer and it won't cost you a penny.' Good old Pollard! I never saw the radio operator again, nor did I hear another word about him.

CHAPTER FOUR

The Hour of Decision

On our way back from lunch next day, Mérito bought a newspaper. In large headlines on the front page I read: CALVO SOTELO MURDERED IN MADRID, and knew that we had to act, now or never.

At 3 a.m. that same day—13 July—the door-bell had rung at Calvo Sotelo's apartment in Madrid, a large flat in the Calle Velázquez, situated in one of the principal residential districts of the town, where the leader of the opposition to the Republican Government had spent the previous day, a Sunday, with his wife and children. A frightened maid had opened the door and seen three men in plain clothes, escorted by uniformed police. 'We have orders to search this place,' they had told her. Calvo Sotelo, a black dressing gown over his pyjamas, expressed surprise on hearing the reason for their visit. From an open window he called to a couple of policemen, on duty below. 'Are these men genuine members of the force?' he asked. 'Yes, sir,' came the answer. 'They're all right.' The apartment was searched. Nothing was found except a flag with the old Spanish colours, which the visitors tore to shreds.

'You must come with us to headquarters.'

'I will do no such thing. I am a member of the Cortes, and you cannot detain me without the Chamber's permission.'

'You are not being detained; you are simply wanted for questioning.'

'At this hour of the night?' An argument ensued, and Calvo Sotelo went to the telephone. As he was about to raise the receiver a smiling, fair-haired civilian seized the cord and wrenched it from the wall.

'In view of this I refuse to move before daylight.'

'You will come with us now!'

'But I don't even know who you are!'

One of the civilians produced his identity card. He was a captain in the Civil Guard, and his name was Fernando Condés. 'That's different,' the Rightist leader said. 'I won't be long.' Four men watched him while he dressed. With tears in her eyes, his wife begged him not to leave. 'Don't worry, darling,' her husband told her. 'I'll be back soon.'

An open police wagon—No. 17—with four rows of seats, had drawn up before the house. Patrols were detaining automobiles, questioning occupants, re-routeing them through other streets. Condés hesitated a moment and took a seat next to the driver. The Monarchist leader sat in the third row between two uniformed policemen; behind him was the smiling gunman, Cuenca. As the wagon picked up speed, Calvo Sotelo's wife fell to the floor of the balcony in a dead faint.

The truck raced through the deserted Calle Lista. Cuenca stood up, and resumed his seat as Calvo Sotelo turned slightly in his direction. 'Shall I shoot?' he asked the man next to him. The third civilian nodded and pointed upwards with his finger. Cuenca took careful aim at his victim's neck and fired twice in quick succession. Calvo Sotelo's body gave a jerk, fell heavily on one of the policemen, and slid to the floor of the truck. The driver braked hard, but when his passengers shouted at him he sped to the gates of the nearest cemetery, where the corpse was dumped on the pavement.

All news of the crime was suppressed by the Government, but there were too many witnesses, too much evidence, too many known facts, and these spread like wildfire through the city. A huge crowd attended the burial. As the coffin was being lowered into the ground, the Royalist deputy Goicoechea said: 'We do not offer to pray for you. We beg you to pray for us, and we solemnly swear before God to follow your example, to avenge your death and to save our country.' Two days later Count Vallellano, another Monarchist deputy, declared before a packed Chamber that Calvo Sotelo's death was a State crime, planned and executed by agents of the Government in power. To the Republican majority in the Cortes, Gil Robles said, 'His blood is on your heads. You will never rid yourselves of its stain!'

The telephone message which I had received in London from Biarritz on 5 July instructed the pilot of the plane to proceed to Casablanca and wait there for the arrival of a secret agent, who would identify himself by giving the password *Galicia saluda a Francia*, and point out the next step to take. Should this messenger fail to appear before 31 July, I was to fly back to London in my plane. In Bordeaux, Luca de Tena had confirmed these instructions personally without altering them in any way. We had reached Casablanca practically on time—on 12 July instead of 11 July—and that very night Calvo Sotelo, the leader of the Opposition to the Government, had been murdered in Madrid. This event had changed my entire outlook. It was now or never. I had to send the plane to Franco without awaiting further orders. To request them over the telephone would have been foolish; in 1936 all telephone lines in Morocco, Spain and France were controlled by Popular Front Governments, French or Spanish. And it seemed futile to wait until 31 July, as I had been told to do, for the arrival of a secret agent who in all probability would now never turn up. Matters had reached a head in Spain, and there was reason to believe that the movements of those who wished to leave the country were already being subjected to restrictions. The plane had to be dispatched to the Canaries, where Franco needed it urgently, as soon as possible, and without waiting for anything or anybody.

Mérito would proceed to Tangier, as arranged, and purchase the small plane which Franco might eventually need to fly from Tangier to Llano Amarillo, the plateau in Spanish Morocco where the Foreign Legion awaited the General and where my own plane was unable to land for lack of a suitable airstrip. At the same time Mérito would ascertain, with the help of reliable friends in Spanish Morocco, if there were other places where the Dragon Rapide, with Franco on board, could if necessary land on its return flight from the Canaries without being intercepted by our enemies. For this landing there were four possible choices in Northern Africa: Tangier itself, with an international, neutral airport, and the three military airfields in the Spanish Zone —Laraiche, Tetuán, or Melilla. Whichever one of these four offered greater guarantees of safety had to be our choice. On the flight from the Canaries intermediate stops would be possible at Agadir or Casablanca, both in French Morocco, but the final landing constituted a problem. For the moment nobody knew where it could be effected. It might even have to be made in Spain or Portugal. Mérito had to clear up these points and transmit the resulting information to somebody who, in turn, would pass on the news to Franco and Bebb at the crucial moment, telling them where to go for the final landing. We had to be careful; there was a risk that those on board the plane might be shot at sight when they set foot on the ground. Action was imperative, but secrecy and caution were also vital.

It soon became apparent that I myself would have to remain in Casablanca while the Dragon Rapide flew to the Canaries and Mérito played his part in Tangier. Nobody else was available in Casablanca to establish the necessary liaison with Mérito, and somebody had to meet the plane with the required information when it arrived there with Franco on board. Consequently the Dragon Rapide had to fly from Casablanca to Las Palmas, in Grand Canary. As soon as it landed there Major Pollard would carry out the instructions which I had given him before leaving Lisbon and continue to Tenerife. Somehow or other he would establish contact with General Franco and put him in touch with my pilot, Captain Bebb. On its return to Casablanca I would board the plane and fly in it to its final destination to make sure that my mission had been accomplished.

The quandaries which faced me in Casablanca on 13 July 1936 were typical of those that confronted active participants in the events immediately preceding the nationalist rising which broke out in Spain that year. Few of us had a definite plan to carry out; the leaders of the revolt had to rely on the initiative and resourcefulness of each and every one of those to whom they assigned a specific role with a clearly-marked objective. There were no detailed instructions; there could be none, for it was impossible to foresee the course of events in each case, and it would have been too risky to try to adjust action all over the country to definite, well-thought-out plans, which might fall to pieces if anything unexpected arose. Even so, little by little the whole picture before me began to take shape. The idea of remaining alone in Casablanca while my friends flew to their various destinations seemed depressing, but there was no alternative. All things considered, the best way to disguise the purpose of the Dragon Rapide's flight to the Canaries was to allow it to land there with a British crew, a group of British passengers, and no Spaniards on board. Provided it worked well, this simple stratagem might throw our opponents off their guard.

Mérito and I made up a simple code in French, English and Spanish, to be used by both of us whenever he called me from Tangier. Bebb, on his side, assured me that he could find his way to Grand Canary without the assistance of the radio operator, who had been discarded and sent home. Little as I liked the idea, Bebb was going to make a

34

stop in Cape Juby, a Spanish military outpost on the edge of the Sahara, to refuel before his final hop across the sea to the islands. And although I wanted him to leave on the morrow, he needed a whole day in Casablanca to overhaul his engines. In the course of a chat with Pollard I completed the necessary arrangements for the role he had to play in the Canaries and for his return trip to England, which he and the girls kindly agreed to undertake after spending a week or so on a beach.

Later, while Mérito and I were talking quietly in my room, two trustworthy friends called us from Biarritz. They wished to make sure that we had not forgotten the password, which they carefully repeated over the wire; they wondered whether I had memorized correctly the doctor's address in Tenerife, which they considered important, and re-stated. We reassured them, and rang off.

Monsieur Mouchenino, an Algerian of ample proportions who ran the airfield at Casablanca with a genial disposition, welcomed us heartily when I arrived with the party for their take-off. Reluctantly I said good-bye to my friends. All of them had acted their parts wonderfully, and the girls had played theirs despite an occasionally patent disinclination for air travel. So charming were they that Mouchenino could not make out why I stayed behind. 'Two young ladies as attractive as these two, and you do not fly with them? I do not understand.' I repaid his interest with a hundred francs, advised my friends to do the same, and returned to my dismal hotel in Casablanca.

I missed my companions. No longer was I one of a group, possibly the guest of an Englishman who had chartered a plane for a pleasant trip. If questioned, there was nothing to warrant my presence in Casablanca, where I had registered as a British subject while holding a passport issued in Spain. My tremors were not allayed when, after lunching at a small restaurant in the centre of the town, I found that I was being followed; a fellow who could easily have passed as another secret agent was shadowing me, not too discreetly, from the other side of the street. When I paused to admire the view, he also paused, sometimes slipping into a doorway for shelter. When I stopped to look at a shop-window, he did the same. Once, after turning a corner, I entered an apartment house and waited, but he also waited until I came out, which was soon, for I had nothing to do inside. So I dived into my hotel and remained there; and that night, for dinner, I contented myself with a sandwich and a glass of beer. I felt safer under cover.

Meanwhile, as I was to learn eventually, Pollard and the girls had reached Cape Juby in my trustworthy Dragon Rapide. Earlier, Mérito had landed in Tangier. The arrival of two blondes at a lonely Spanish outpost on the fringes of the Sahara caused a flutter among the men of the garrison, who had not seen a white woman for months. Fowls were sacrificed, and a sumptuous repast was prepared. Officers polished up their English or talked by sign to Dorothy and Diana. Pollard received every mark of consideration, and the plane was scrutinized and admired. Every assistance was given to the pilot while he plotted his course for the next lap, but the officer commanding the outpost performed his duty. Shortly after the Dragon Rapide landed, he dispatched a message by radio to the Minister of War in Madrid, informing him that a British plane had called at Cape Juby without requesting permission to do so, while on a pleasure trip to the Canary Islands. Had I been on board, the fact would have been mentioned in the message, and its more probable implications would not have passed unnoticed. As it was, all the Minister of War did was to cable the Military Governor of the Islands—General Franco—instructing him to detain the Dragon Rapide on arrival, pending clarification of the circumstances in which it had landed at Cape Juby. On account of their nationality, the cable pointed out, those on board the plane were not to be molested. They were British, and therefore above suspicion.

Late in the afternoon of the day on which it left Casablanca and called at Cape Juby—Wednesday, 15 July—the Dragon Rapide reached the airport of Gando, on Grand Canary, one of the two larger islands in the archipelago. Gando, in 1936, was the only safe airport in the Canaries. There was a small runway on Tenerife, the other large island, a short distance from General Franco's headquarters as military governor of the entire area, but it was frequently shrouded in fog, and Bebb disliked the idea of calling there.

Immediately after landing at Gando, Pollard and the two girls went to Las Palmas, the capital of Grand Canary, and took a small steamer for Santa Cruz, the capital of Tenerife. At this point I should perhaps remind my readers that while in Lisbon I had warned Major Pollard that if I left the party at Casablanca, he might have to sail from Las

Palmas to Tenerife and visit a doctor called Gabarda, who lived at Santa Cruz. The purpose of this visit, I explained to Pollard, was to announce that the aeroplane had arrived, but before saying this he had to give the doctor the password that would accredit him as a friend. In Casablanca, at the airport, I had repeated these instructions to the Major and begged him to carry them out.

Pollard and the girls had a rough passage on their way to Tenerife, but though it was 7.30 a.m. when they got there they went straight to see Dr Gabarda. A sleepy-eyed nurse was handed a message, written in French, stating that a mutual though nameless friend had sent the Major to the doctor, and that Diana, the Major's daughter, was unwell. Gabarda did not keep them waiting long. When he appeared, Pollard, with a courtly bow, said to him, 'G-a-h-l-e-e-t-h-e-a s-a-h-l-o-o-t-h-a a-h F-r-a-h-n-t-h-e-a,' using the phonetic spelling to which I had resorted in Lisbon, while writing out the password for his benefit. To the Major's surprise and distress, Gabarda, instead of giving him a pat on the back and taking him into his confidence, said testily, 'This is a nursing home, not a place for the delivery of cryptic messages. If your daughter is ailing, let her state the symptoms of her malady. Otherwise kindly leave me to my work.'

Pollard felt discomfited, but the doctor's attitude was understandable. A man of neutral views in politics, Gabarda had been chosen by our side to serve as the recipient of messages the meaning of which he was totally unable to penetrate. He had been selected to receive them because nobody connected him with a possible plot against the Republican Government, nor did anyone suspect that messages sent from Madrid by people who used imaginary names to transmit them were being relayed by the doctor, as a personal favour, to youthful members of General Franco's military entourage in the Canaries. Valentín Galarza, a staff colonel and main pivot of the conspiracy in Madrid, where the Republicans arrested him during the Civil War without ever discovering who he was—he had adopted another name for his patriotic activities, and though he lost half his weight in prison, other inmates there helped him to keep his identity secret and live to be Minister of the Interior under Franco—was frequently telephoning to say, 'The crops are coming on finely. We may have to start reaping them soon. Saturday might well be the day,' or words to that effect. Occasionally a casual acquaintance at Franco's headquarters would call on Dr Gabarda and inquire whether his bailiff had reported anything about the harvest.

Everything ran smoothly, and in due course Valentín Galarza concluded that the mild Gabarda was the right man to receive the vital password with the news that my plane had reached the Canaries. But the doctor had wearied of this nonsense, and when an affable Englishman, instead of asking him to take his blood pressure, declared that a group of Spanish provinces saluted France—'*Galicia saluda a Francia*'— he concluded that he was being made the victim of a hoax and addressed his visitor in plain terms.

Pollard retained his self-control. 'My dear sir,' he cried, 'I may be at a loss for the exact meaning of this message, but I have reason to suspect its importance. The plane has reached Gando. Should anyone wish to see me, I shall be at the Hotel Pino de Oro.' Shortly after this a young officer, wearing plain clothes, called on Major Pollard and fired a volley of questions at him. 'Can the plane fly direct to Spanish Morocco? Is the pilot quite reliable? When will he be ready to leave?'

The only man who could have supplied the answers to these questions was Captain Bebb, who had stayed in Grand Canary with the Dragon Rapide. It was Thursday, 16 July; the rebellion had been fixed for the 18th. There was no time to lose, and Franco decided to act the moment he heard that a plane had arrived with an Englishman on board who knew the password. Franco had sufficient power to act, for he was Military Governor of the territory, and the first thing he did was to isolate the island of Tenerife from the rest of the world. Telephone and telegraph lines were silenced and taken over by the army officers acting under Franco's instructions. The movements of ships were temporarily restricted. Martial Law was proclaimed; order was enforced with a firm hand; the Civil Governor of the province, who represented the Government, was arrested and confined. To allay suspicion, General Franco, after taking control in Tenerife, cabled the Minister of War in Madrid and reported that he was sailing for the nearby island of Grand Canary to attend the funeral of a former Foreign Legion comrade, General Balmes—the same officer who, in October 1934, had successfully fought the Reds in Asturias— accidentally shot while practising with a pistol in Las Palmas, to which city he had been relegated by the Popular Front a few months before. Needless to say, Franco did not tell Madrid that he had published a manifesto in Tenerife, calling upon the population to rise against the Republican Government, nor did he explain that once he had done the same in Grand Canary he would fly to lead the rising in Spanish

Morocco. But before leaving Santa Cruz, the General booked passages on a French steamer going to Le Havre for his wife and his only daughter, the present Marquesa de Villaverde, then a child eight or nine years old, who, the previous week, had almost been kidnapped by Red hoodlums near the house where she lived with her parents.

On the same 16 July I spent a long and lonely afternoon at the airport in Casablanca, where, to avoid being shadowed in the city and also for want of a better place, I had set up my headquarters for the day. At nightfall I returned to my hotel and stayed there. In due course, Mérito rang up to say that citrus fruit trees look promising in Northern Morocco. What he really meant was that Tangier seemed to be the mostly likely place for our landing after the Dragon Rapide and Franco had picked me up in Casablanca.

On the afternoon of this day, while Bebb was having a siesta in his hotel room at Las Palmas, a pleasant-looking fellow turned up and introduced himself to my pilot as a member of the garrison. Why had Bebb landed in Cape Juby without permission, the fellow asked? Because he was unaware that he needed permission, answered Bebb, who was then told that a general called Orgaz wished to see him. Did he know the church of San Agustín? Bebb had never heard of this church. Did he know the Cathedral? Yes, it had been pointed out to him while he strolled through the town the day before. 'Be there at 3.30. You will be asked to ride in a car. Please accept this invitation.'

The ride was uneventful, and the car finally stopped at the gates of a well-appointed house where Bebb was introduced to General Don Luis Orgaz, a close friend of Franco who had also been relegated to the Canary Islands by the Popular Front. Orgaz, a ruddy-faced soldier with a kindly smile and a genius for organization, became one of Franco's ablest assistants during the Civil War; besides commanding army forces on various fronts he set up the military academies which trained fifty thousand second-lieutenants for leadership and action on the field. Now he wanted to know whether the plane which had landed at Gando was the one which Franco awaited. The fact that Bebb did not give the password perplexed and troubled Orgaz, who, with the aid of an interpreter, requested the pilot of the Dragon Rapide to explain the reasons for his presence in the Canary Islands. All that Bebb could, or would, tell him was that the Dragon Rapide had been chartered in London by a wealthy client who had left for Tenerife the night before, saying that he wished to study tomato-growing in that island. Bebb made a good impression on General Orgaz, who requested him not to mention their conversation to a soul. However, by order of Orgaz, it was duly reported in Tenerife to General Franco, who at this time had good reason to suspect that Bebb's Dragon Rapide was the plane chartered for his trip to Spanish Morocco.

Franco landed on Grand Canary on Friday, 17 July, and before attending General Balmes's funeral, as announced, he adopted measures to take control of the island, as he had done on Tenerife the previous day. This, in Las Palmas, was less easy. The local Civil Governor, an able and determined Republican, was on his guard. He immediately called out a company of Shock Police and ordered them to resist any attempt on the part of the Army to proclaim Martial Law. Fighting broke out in the city, and for part of the day the issue was in doubt. Supported by a majority of the population, the military soon gained the upper hand; the Civil Governor lacked moral force and armed support to uphold the cause which he defended. But his action, and incipient strife, had the effect of delaying, however briefly, Franco's departure for Morocco. A soldier first and foremost, the General did not relish the idea of leaving the island of Grand Canary behind him before it was totally subdued. Instead of starting on the 17th for Morocco, as he had planned to do, he remained in Las Palmas until the next day, the day appointed for the rising, when total control of the islands finally fell into his hands. This afforded the British Consul in Las Palmas sufficient time to visit Franco and request the release of my plane, which according to him had been chartered by Major Pollard, a British subject. Franco, though fully aware by now of the reasons for the Dragon Rapide's arrival in Gando, told the Consul, a friend of his—they had met frequently at the Golf Club, where the General was learning to address the ball and picking up some English on the side—that he was considering the matter and hoping to release the plane soon. Before doing so, however, he had to receive a detailed report on the case 'from his legal advisers'.

That same afternoon a colonel called on Bebb, gave the password, which was all Greek to my pilot, and handed him a piece of screwed up paper with the words 'Take these two fellows to Mutt and Jeff.' Jeff, the colonel explained, was the Marqués del Mérito, and I was Mutt.

Attached to the small piece of paper was one half of a Spanish playing card. The other half would be presented to Bebb by the man who was to fly with him from Grand Canary to meet Mutt and Jeff somewhere in Morocco—presumably in Casablanca. The final preparations for the flight were completed that same evening, during a conference held at General Orgaz's villa near Las Palmas. Major Pollard, who had just returned from Tenerife, attended this meeting and listened while a fresh volley of questions was fired by the Spaniards at my pilot. Why couldn't Bebb fly straight to Spanish Morocco? Could he not carry the necessary fuel in extra tanks? Would his plane reach Agadir, three long hours away from Grand Canary? Was it in really good shape? Bebb replied satisfactorily to these questions, but more than his answers, his confident manner and his reassurance told General Orgaz and his aides all that they wanted to know. Their final report was favourable. It was decided to use my plane. Before dusk fell that evening, Franco knew he would be able to leave for Morocco the following morning.

Friday, 17 July, was an anxious day for me at Casablanca. It was my third day alone in that city. I could not use the telephone to find out what was happening, and the lack of news was beginning to weigh on my mind. More than once I wondered whether I had done the right thing in staying behind when the Dragon Rapide left for the Canaries without anybody on board who even knew of General Franco's existence or of his presence in the islands, of the reasons why the plane had to go there, or of the fact that a rebellion was brewing against the Popular Front Government in Madrid. Pollard must have suspected something, but no reference to the matter had passed between us. I was glad that I had given him the password. His knowledge of it constituted conclusive evidence of his connection with the right people. I felt that he would use it properly and get in touch with Dr Gabarda, as I had requested him to do.

My stay at Casablanca, I reflected, had been enforced by circumstances beyond my control. Much as I would have liked to fly with my friends to the Canaries, I had had to stay behind, to maintain contact with Mérito, and to establish the best place for Franco to land after the plane returned to Casablanca. What I did not know was that, had I landed with the others in Cape Juby, my presence on the Dragon Rapide would have been interpreted by the Republican authorities in Madrid and in Las Palmas as an indication that the machine was being used for subversive purposes. The plane could have been destroyed, or damaged beyond repair. With British passengers and a British crew as sole occupants of a British plane, this contingency was out of the question. Indeed, the arrangements which I hesitatingly made decided the success of my flight. As if to reassure me, while dusk fell on the airport at Casablanca, where I had again removed myself with my scant luggage in case the plane dropped suddenly from the skies, Monsieur Mouche-nino brought me a cable. It had been forwarded from my hotel in accordance with my instructions. Dated in London, it bore no signature and only contained three words: FATHER LEAVING TOMORROW. The message seemed mysterious, but it had been jointly dispatched, I eventually learnt, by my wife and La Cierva, who had heard from Captain Olley that Bebb was starting the next day on his return flight to Casablanca.

I slept rather better that night.

The morning of Saturday, 18 July—the day chosen for the rising—was a busy one at Las Palmas for some people. General Franco wanted to settle everything on Grand Canary before boarding the plane for Morocco; his colleagues wanted to make sure that his flight would be a successful one, and they also wished to join him as soon as they could; Bebb spared no pains to get his plane and its two engines in proper working order to cover the shortest possible course from Gando to Agadir. Pollard, whose knowledge of the password had won for him the confidence of his new acquaintances, enjoined Bebb to mistrust anyone who might attempt to board the plane without handing him the other half of the playing card, one-half of which Bebb already had in his possession.

Early that Saturday morning Mérito called me again on the telephone, and, somehow or other, managed to tell me that the day for the rising had dawned and that the place for the final landing was Tangier. My excitement knew no bounds. I packed up my bags, settled my hotel bill for the third time, and set off for the airport, where I now felt confident that Franco would arrive in the course of the day. The car that drove me was large and roomy, and it had a capable driver, so instead of dismissing it I told the man to wait and order his lunch at my expense. Mouchenino had said that it would take Bebb at least six hours to fly from Gando, and another hour to refuel at Agadir. Unless they left quite early, dusk might fall at Casablanca before my friends arrived. This meant that they would have to stay for the night and postpone their final landing for the morrow, a prospect which I did not like. Many Spaniards had settled in Casablanca; quite a few had served or lived in Spanish Morocco. Some of them might be old soldiers from the Foreign Legion who would recognize Franco, if they saw him. More than any doubts about their loyalty, what concerned me was an outbreak of enthusiasm on their part. Sooner than allow the General to face it or run the risk of being spotted by a foe, I decided that we would spend the night together in a small hotel on the outskirts of the town. I therefore adopted the necessary measures for this purpose, without giving any names except the one which I was using to conceal my identity in French Morocco.

At one o'clock that afternoon, the faithful Mouchenino brought me a message from the control tower of the airport at Casablanca. It said: *'Avion G-ACYR prêt a partir'*—'G-ACYR plane ready to leave'. The capital letters were those I had read, so many times now, on the fuselage of my Dragon Rapide. The message was dated at Las Palmas. I had only a few hours to wait.

That morning, before this message was dispatched, one of the men who had questioned Bebb the previous day called on him at his hotel in Las Palmas. He had been sent by General Orgaz and wore the uniform of a captain. He told Bebb that the plane was due to leave at noon, or possibly later, for Agadir and Casablanca, and that the time had come to drive to the airport. The ride was a long one. On the way they saw civilians, posted at every corner, ready to quell any trouble that might arise. They were riding in a military car, driven by a soldier, and, as they passed, the civilians raised their hands to indicate that all was well. On the more important cross-roads they saw a small show of force, made up of Civil Guards and police, who saluted as they drove by. Bebb could not help being impressed by these precautions, which, he mistakenly concluded, had been taken to protect whoever his passenger on the plane might turn out to be. It was obviously a person of importance.

In reality they had been adopted to outwit any who might entertain the idea of making an attempt on Franco's life during his long ride to

Gando. The situation in Las Palmas was under control, but not to the point at which the police and the military could feel sure that no such risk existed. Grand Canary had its share of anarchists and extremists, and the road to Gando passed through some of the shabbier quarters of the town. Consequently, every precaution was openly taken along this route, but Franco did not follow it. Instead, he went to Gando in a motor-boat, which he boarded on a lonely stretch of shore near Las Palmas. Gando is close to the open sea; there being no jetty there, the General, to reach the airport, had to wade up to his knees in water. Once he stepped on dry sand he strode towards the plane that awaited him, held out his right hand to Bebb and said, '*Soy el General Franco*'— 'I am General Franco'. There was no need to show Bebb the other half of the playing card. One look at the General was enough for the pilot to know that the passenger whose hand he had clasped was the man he had come to fetch from London.

An older man, and a younger one, boarded the plane with the General. It was two in the afternoon when the Dragon Rapide took off for the African coast, and five o'clock before it reached Agadir after a smooth flight which almost became eventful when they landed. Close to where they came to a stop in the Agadir airport, three Spanish military planes had pulled up to refuel—Republican planes from Cape Juby, manned by the same officers who three days before had so cordially welcomed Pollard and the girls, and who were now on their way to fight for the Popular Front in Spain. It is not known whether the officers in question saw the Dragon Rapide. They probably did. The idea of boarding it to greet the girls may have crossed their minds, but Franco spotted their planes in time and waved Bebb on to the opposite side of the little airfield—the proper side for civil aircraft to refuel—thus avoiding the danger of recognition and its possible consequences.

Saturday was a holiday in Agadir, and two hours elapsed before the Dragon Rapide could resume its flight to Casablanca. More than once, while waiting for it at the airport there, I caught myself reading my detective novel upside down. Local flying fans had brought friends and families to watch while they performed their antics in the air. I was perched on a high stool at the bar when a Frenchman, rather like the one who had shadowed me some days before in Casablanca, pointed to a copy of *La Dépêche Marocaine* and said: 'Have you seen the news? Revolt has broken out in Spanish Morocco.' I glanced at the paper, showing as little interest as I could in its contents, and read that in Melilla, in the Eastern Zone of the Spanish Protectorate, a group of officers had risen against the Republic. Just below this item there was a smaller one, saying, 'General Franco has been summoned to Madrid from the Canaries, and is now on his way to suppress the rising.' 'It will not last long,' my new friend assured me. 'These Spaniards are not capable of fighting.'

I agreed, though the news was only partly true. The rebellion had been set to start on the 18th, both in Spain and in Spanish Morocco, but a leakage in their plans had forced certain units in Melilla to rise against the Government the day before. The report that Franco had been called to Madrid lacked substance, as I well knew. The Government released it to confuse others, and at the same time asserted that most army units and all important cities in Spain were on their side, a ruse which succeeded in deceiving many, in that country and abroad.

Another Frenchman came up to me, drew his glass close to mine and, with an ingratiating smile, asked: 'Do you speak Spanish?' 'I'm afraid I don't,' I replied in French. 'That's odd,' he said, 'extremely odd.' 'Why should it be odd?' I inquired, adding, 'after all, I'm an Englishman.' 'Even so,' answered the fellow, 'Englishmen like yourself usually speak Spanish.' I shrugged my shoulders, but things were getting too hot for my liking. The French Deuxième Bureau was obviously on my heels.

Dusk had fallen, and local flying fans and their best girls were now wending their way home. I was alone with Mouchenino, my heart filled with anxiety. What if Bebb missed the airport? Would he make it at night without a radio operator? The day seemed endless, and my taxi driver was getting impatient. It was 9.15 when I heard the roar of a plane, and moments later I saw its lights, green and red, flashing in the dark towards me. The runway lit up, and the Dragon Rapide disappeared in the horizon to lose height and turn before it landed. Suddenly, the lights on the airstrip blacked out. While my imagination ran wild, a handy electrician climbed a ladder and repaired the damage —a fuse. Bebb's plane reappeared, this time much lower, and soon it was taxiing towards the spot where I waited, with Mouchenino at my side.

Two men I had never seen before set foot on solid earth. A third passenger followed them. It was General Franco. He was wearing a dark suit and a grey hat with the brim turned down over his forehead.

The General saw me, smiled, and held out his hand. As I clasped it, I whispered, 'Remember that I am English and speak no Spanish. We'll talk later.' Franco's first concern was about the usual formalities, but there were none to be accomplished, for both Police and Customs officials had left the airport an hour before. All authority there was was now vested in my friend Mouchenino. Spurred by kindness or the prospect of further tips, he agreed to leave routine matters for another day.

A Spanish diplomat, José Antonio de Sangroniz, later Ambassador in Rome, had lent his passport to General Franco, whose photograph was now substituted for the picture originally pasted on the document. The other two passengers carried their own identification papers. One of them was Lieut.-Col. Francisco Franco Salgado, a cousin of the General and a former comrade of his in the Foreign Legion. The other, a flying officer whose name I never caught, had filled a vacant seat on the plane to replace Bebb in the event of an improbable emergency. The four of us sat in the open air and requested unlimited ham sandwiches and iced beer, the only fare available at this late hour. Bebb and the mechanic did the same at another table, and the taxi-driver was urged to curb his restlessness with the prospect of double pay.

We ate ravenously. Franco's cousin feared that it might be unwise to stay that night in Casablanca. Why not go on to Tangier or fly to Laraiche, a port on the western shores of the Spanish Moroccan Protectorate, where he knew that the officers could be trusted? After speaking to Bebb, we turned down the idea. Dangerous as it was to remain in Casablanca, it might be even worse to attempt a night landing on an airstrip which, for all we knew, had no lights. At that moment Mouchenino called me to the telephone. It was Mérito. Speaking in French, he said, '*Il n'y a pas de mandarines*'—'no tangerines', which meant that there was nothing doing at Tangier. Turning to English, he exhorted me not to miss a tea-party arranged for the following day. I accepted his invitation. The 'tea-party' meant 'the place with two t's'— Tetuán. Tangier had had to be scrapped, Mérito told me later, because a group of paid assassins were waiting for us there with pistols and submachine guns. I gave this message to General Franco, and we agreed to make the final landing in Tetuán, as early as possible the following day.

My new friends, I told the good Mouchenino, were business associates of mine, due in Portugal early the next day. After leaving them in Lisbon, the plane would take me on to the Canaries and pick up

Pollard and the two girls, one of whom, as he well knew, I longed to see. Because of these reasons, none of which was true, we had to leave at five next morning. Any possible reluctance on the part of Mouchenino to the idea of rising at such an hour was softened by a couple of one hundred franc notes which at my suggestion Bebb dropped into his palm, as a reward for helping us to push the plane into its hangar.

Finally, to the surprise of the driver, who had given up all hope of seeing us, we piled our luggage and ourselves into the waiting taxi and the six of us set off for a secluded hotel near the coast, where I had planned to spend the night. When we arrived there a big party was in progress. The hotel was crowded with dancing couples and officers in uniform. I urged everybody back into the car and proceeded to a shabbier place, some miles away, explaining that my friends were tired and wished to sleep, far from the noise of a blaring band.

I promised our driver a bonus if he woke us up at four, and distributed the rooms which a drowsy manager allotted to my party. Franco and I shared one, a small, grey room with two beds and a bathroom, his cousin and the air force captain took another, and Bebb, who had registered us cryptically *en masse,* occupied a third with his mechanic. The bill, including early coffee and toast, was settled in advance, and I retired with the General for the heart-to-heart talk I had so long awaited about his hopes and plans in that supremely critical hour for Spain. We each had a bath before slipping into our narrow beds, and Franco shaved off his moustache, to alter his appearance however slightly. Neither of us could overlook the possibility of an ominous knock at the door.

Our conversation lasted until two. The General is a good talker, and that night he was irrepressible. He continued to talk even when I turned off the lights and told him that I was falling asleep. He was then forty-three years old, well-proportioned and good looking. As now, his large brown eyes were the most arresting feature on his ever-inquiring face. A passionate wish to serve Spain inspired him. He was determined to make up for the years of misery and oppression which his countrymen had suffered under Republican rule. His hard military training stood him in good stead, and his one ambition was to serve. All his thoughts were for the people. He wished to improve the lot of the working man and the position of the middle classes, both of which had so many times been deceived by Republican promises, to increase their living standards and provide their sons with opportunities for education and advancement. He wanted to develop housing, industry, and agriculture. Franco knew that law and order would have to be enforced with a firm hand throughout the country, but he did not think this would be difficult, after peace had been restored. Much as Spain would have to change if the nation was to progress, he also knew that the fundamental traditions of Spanish life had to be upheld.

The General had no illusions about the possibility of gaining a swift victory over the Popular Front. The odds against us were too great. He saw no chance of winning in the majority of the more important cities, and considered that Madrid, Barcelona, Valencia and Bilbao, amongst others, would be lost to us at the start, for our partisans, though numerous, could do nothing against the rabble, whom the Government was sure to arm, or against the strong Army forces led by Left-wing officers who had replaced those loyal to our cause. He was also doubtful about the Navy; it had been drenched with extremist propaganda, and he feared that some non-commissioned officers and seamen would turn on their officers and massacre them. So black was the picture which he painted that at one moment I asked whether we could win. His reply carried such force and conviction that throughout the war, even in its darkest hours, my faith in victory never wavered. 'In the last resort we would take to the hills,' he answered, 'and from there carry on the kind of guerilla warfare at which my men excel. The enemy could never beat us. But we shall not have to do that. We have ideals, faith and discipline; our opponents lack all this. It may take longer than most people think, but in the end we are certain to win.'

Franco had done his utmost to prevent civil war, both while in Spain and from his remote post in the Canary Islands. He told me about the message which, some time before, he had addressed to the head of the Republican Government in Madrid, warning him of what might happen if those in power did nothing to combat the violence and oppression to which the Spanish people were being ruthlessly subjected. His words had been treated with contempt, and now the nation was rising, with part of the Army, to fight for its liberties and overthrow a government which for years had been driving it to ruin.

CHAPTER FIVE

Flight into History

Many times that night, in the two brief hours during which Franco and I remained silent, I heard the roar of cars approaching our hotel and wondered whether it would be followed by the sound of voices, inquiring after our whereabouts. At last there was a violent knocking on the door of our room; my restless taxi-driver, possibly anxious about his fee, had come to wake us up. We took ten minutes to dress, and half that time to swallow our breakfast. We longed to be on our way. Dawn was breaking when we reached the airport, where Mouchenino was already bustling around. The gates of the hangar slid heavily on their metal wheels. We saw the Dragon Rapide, itching like a falcon for the air. We pushed it outside. It took Bebb only a moment to get the propellers spinning. As we waited for the engines to warm up, Mouchenino spied a distant group, walking towards us in the morning haze. '*Filez vite!*' he said to me; 'they are policemen and Customs officials who will surely make a nuisance of themselves. Get into your plane and fly!' It was five o'clock. His advice seemed sound, and I estimated its value at something like five hundred francs. Our plane rose quickly from the ground and departed without leaving any trace in Casablanca. Fate and Mouchenino had treated us kindly.

We sped high over lowlands the lushness of which contrasted with the barren, mountainous country allotted to Spain in the Protectorate under its care. Franco was silent now, and hardly a word passed between the rest of us. We had been on our way for about an hour when the General, reckoning that we were over the Spanish Protectorate, opened his suit case, discarded the dark grey suit in which he had travelled from the Canaries and changed into his khaki uniform. A lump rose in my throat when I saw him wind around his waist the scarlet, gold-tasselled sash which in the Spanish Army constitutes the most distinctive symbol of a General's rank. This was it. In his usual quiet and unassuming manner he had attired himself to take command of the forces that awaited his arrival. Years were to elapse ere he donned civilian clothes again.

Before the white walls of Tetuán appeared in the far distance, the glare of the sun, shimmering on Mediterranean waters, indicated that our flight over French and Spanish Morocco was coming to an end. We had crossed a wide expanse of land. Yebel Musa and Yebel Tarik loomed up on the western horizon, each on one side of the Straits of Gibraltar as if guarding the gates between the Mediterranean and the Atlantic. Below us were the black hills of the Beni Hozmar tribesmen, who had been so persistent in their attempts to raid the city during the not-so-remote days of a war which had contributed much to Franco's training and military efficiency. The peaks of the Gorgues range, scene of fierce fighting in the past, rolled out towards our left. Behind the lovely Moorish town of Djebel Dersa and its fortress, a relic of ancient times, extended a protecting arm. To the north was Rio Martin, with its array of tents on the summery, deserted beach. We were about to land. I moved up to Bebb and told him, 'Circle once over the airstrip, as low as possible. If I say "Up!", get away as quickly as you can.' None of us knew yet what had happened the previous night at the airport or in the city of Tetuán.

Franco was the first to reassure us. Five or six officers in uniform were

---

THE FLIGHT OF THE DRAGON RAPIDE
(Notes from the Log of Captain C. W. H. Bebb)

		Dep.		Arr.	Flying Time
11.7.36	Croydon–Bordeaux	07.15	–	10.30	3.15
11.7.36	Bordeaux–Biarritz	11.45	–	14.45	3.00
11.7.36	Biarritz–Espinho	16.45	–	20.15	3.30
12.7.36	Espinho–Alverca	09.00	–	10.10	1.10
12.7.36	Alverca–Casablanca	16.15	–	19.45	3.30
15.7.36	Casablanca–Cape Juby	07.55	–	11.50	3.55
15.7.36	Cape Juby–Las Palmas	13.30	–	14.40	1.10
18.7.36	Las Palmas–Agadir	14.05	–	16.55	2.50
18.7.36	Agadir–Casablanca	18.55	–	21.00	2.05
19.7.36	Casablanca–Tetuán	05.00	–	07.00	2.00
19.7.36	Tetuán–Lisbon	09.00	–	11.00	2.00
20.7.36	Lisbon–Biarritz	12.40	–	16.25	3.45
21.7.36	Biarritz–Marseilles	09.55	–	12.15	2.20

lined up in a row, standing near the main buildings. As we taxied towards them, he leaned over Bebb's shoulder and spotted a well-known face. '*Ahi está el Rubito!*' he cried. He had seen an old comrade, a veteran commander of the Moorish Regulars, Lieut.-Col.—eventually General—Sáenz de Buruaga. All was well.

The officers saluted and stood at attention, and Franco shook hands with them and asked for news. The situation in Spain was uncertain. Tetuán was calm, but the previous day it had been necessary to storm the airfield, where Republican troops had made a stand while our men surrounded and attacked buildings, the walls of which bore much evidence of shell bursts. The Moors were quiet. The Grand Vizier had rallied openly to our side, a good omen for the immediate future. While the General talked to others I went to Bebb and clasped him in my arms. 'One day you'll know what you have done,' I told him. 'There are no words to thank you.' When I presented him with a small token of my gratitude, Bebb smiled and said, 'You're ruining me! This is just what I needed to get married.' Franco was calling. 'It seems that a Moorish *harka*'—an irregular contingent, made up of native levies—'has taken up a threatening attitude at Wad-Lau, a few miles from here. Could your plane bomb it?' Bebb was not reluctant. 'I like your friend, and I'll do anything for him. If this is an anti-Communist stunt, count me on your side.' But as I walked back to rejoin the General I remembered my agreement with Olley. 'The pilot has no objection,' I said to him, 'but this plane has been chartered for certain purposes, and bombing is not one of them.' 'In that case I would like it to bring General Orgaz from the Canaries,' said Franco. 'I need him here.'

My Dragon Rapide had been hired for a trip the greater part of which was now completed. Another flight to the Canaries and back implied considerable mileage and at least sixteen hours in the air. Who would cover the expense? I mentioned this to Franco and pointed out that it looked as if we were short of planes. 'Where can we get them?' asked the General. 'The French must be ruled out,' I said, 'their Popular Front Government is sure to supply the Spanish Republic with any planes they can spare, and Russia is already sending arms and equipment to our opponents. In England I might perhaps do something, but so could Juan de la Cierva, who is in London. In Germany I don't think I'd be of much use; I can't speak the language. But I could make myself understood in Italy. Shall I go there?'

It was decided that I should fly to Italy, with a stop in Lisbon to see

General Sanjurjo and inform him of Franco's arrival in Tetuán. 'Could you write out something for me?' I asked Franco. 'It might be as well to carry some sort of credentials.' He called for a piece of notepaper and wrote down with a firm hand: 'I authorize Don Luis Antonio Bolin to negotiate urgently in England, Germany or Italy the purchase of aircraft and supplies for the Spanish non-Marxist Army. TETUÁN, 19 JULY 1936. *The Commander-in-Chief*, FRANCISCO FRANCO.' 'What kind of aircraft and supplies?' I asked, and the General added a footnote in pencil: '12 bombers, 3 fighters, with bombs (and bombing equipment) of from 50 to 100 kilos. 1000 50-kilo bombs and 100 more weighing about 500 kilos.'

A long caravan of cars followed Franco to the High Commissioner's headquarters in the city. Moorish troops lined the road at wide intervals and presented arms as we passed; a group of officers awaited Franco before the gates leading to the Alta Comisaría. Outside, in the Plaza Mayor, Spanish civilians and Moors cheered him on with great fervour. Once inside the building, the General lost no time in addressing his comrades. In brief, soldierly words that did not lack eloquence he explained his reasons for rebelling against the Government of the Popular Front. He spoke to their minds and to their hearts, and I saw evidence of deep emotion amongst them. When he referred to the present ignominious state of affairs and the depths to which the Reds had lowered Spain—'We can no longer hold our heads up and feel proud of being Spanish'—the intensity of his feelings dried up his throat, and he tapped the floor with his foot for some seconds before being able to continue.

Then he entered the stately office which a High Commissioner appointed by the Popular Front had occupied until the previous day. He beckoned me to follow, and I remained with him a few moments. Staff officers hurried in and out, carrying papers and delivering messages. Information concerning the march of events in Spain began to trickle in. The door opened again and Captain Marín, a young officer in the Engineers, appeared with a telegram in his hand: CEUTA REPORTS THAT SPANISH NAVAL SHIPS ARE ACTING SUSPICIOUSLY NEAR THE HARBOUR. THEY PERSISTENTLY CROSS ITS ENTRANCE AND FAIL TO ANSWER OUR SIGNALS. The significance of the message was clear: the ships in question had sided with the enemy. Unless we could sink them or drive them away it was going to be difficult to land our forces on Spanish soil, for we had lost command of the sea in an area that was vital to our interests.

Franco remained impassive. 'Order our batteries at Ceuta to fire a shot across the bow of any ship that behaves suspiciously,' he told Captain Marín; 'if she doesn't reply, tell them to sink her.'

It was almost nine o'clock, and I had been in Tetuán two hours. I requested permission to leave. General Franco granted it with a smile.

Some time later, at the height of the Spanish Civil War, Major-General J. F. C. Fuller, the distinguished historian and military critic, came from England to visit our Front. He said to me: 'Aren't you the chap who arranged General Franco's flight to Morocco from the Canary Islands, at the outbreak of the War?'

I said I was.

'Good staff work, that,' said General Fuller.

I was pleased with the compliment. My part had been a small one, and at the start I had been anxious, but long before our flight was half-way through, after seeing how easily the obstacles which we encountered were overcome and how unexpected hazards dissolved and disappeared almost miraculously, I had known that it would turn out well. And long before we made the final touch-down in Tetuán something told me that there was no real reason for my hair to go on getting whiter. Everything was going to be all right.

PART II

CHAPTER SIX

Clouds on the Spanish Horizon

A man must have sufficient cause to abandon his wife and children and embark on a mission the outcome of which may bring tragedy to all around him, including himself. The cause that sped me on my way to Morocco when I set out from London in the summer of 1936 was the imminence and inevitability of civil war in Spain. For years, then, civil strife had been brewing in my country. It was now on the point of breaking out. The fate of Spain as a nation hung in the balance. In the struggle to decide it I was anxious to do what I could. Perhaps the gravity of the situation which existed will become more apparent to my readers if I describe, however briefly, the chain of events that led up to the Spanish Civil War. Only by doing so is it possible to provide the historical perspective without which there can be no proper understanding of the nature of that conflict.

Early in 1919 I had left London and returned to Madrid. I had been away for three years, reading for the Bar at the Middle Temple or following the fighting in France as a War Correspondent attached to the British Forces in the field. I had witnessed many battles from the trenches or from the air and become familiar with large stretches of Allied lines from the Channel to the Forêt de Rheims. Once in Spain, when I tried to tell my countrymen about foreign parts and their wars, I found that Spanish people had made up their minds about the events which had changed the history of the world. Though interested in the issues at stake, they clung to their convictions and, true to form, paid little attention to the first-hand reports which an eye-witness tried to give them.

Spain was enjoying a brief period of prosperity. Her rulers had been wise enough to keep the nation out of the war. Their policy, criticized by victors and vanquished alike, each of whom would have welcomed Spain as an ally, was justified by national interests, for she had no direct concern with the quarrels being resolved on the battlefields of Europe. Trade had been brisk, the economic situation had improved, the peseta stood at a premium with most European currencies, French francs and sterling included. In Madrid the 1919 season was brilliant, and sumptuous banquets, attended by royalty, took place in the Embassies of the victorious nations or in stately mansions decorated with paintings and tapestries fine enough to ornament the Prado.

Two clouds overshadowed the horizon: political instability at home and intermittent strife in Morocco. Elections were indecisive, no government retained power more than a few months, and Cabinet Ministers were rarely in office long enough to achieve results. The wealth amassed during the preceding years had produced visible benefits without raising popular standards of living. Most of the resources available were used to finance the war in Morocco, where Spain was fulfilling international agreements shouldered reluctantly and somewhat rashly thirteen years before.

Unrest and intrigue in the old Sheriffian Empire had long threatened the peace of the world. By the Treaty of Algeciras in 1906, and a complementary agreement signed in 1912, Spain and France had undertaken to keep order in two unequal territories—unequal in size, in resources, and in political possibilities—into which Morocco was divided when the French and Spanish Protectorates were established. Geographically, Spain was closer to both areas than any other European nation. Historically, Spain and Morocco had common ties that could be traced back for twelve hundred years, during a third of which time, or more in some cases, the former had exercised sovereign rights, never surrendered, over a few small islands close to the African mainland on the Mediterranean, and in Ceuta, Melilla, and their respective hinterlands, also on the northern Moorish coast. Now her obligations were vital and urgent. She could not afford to ignore them, hard as they might be to fulfil.

In the partition that took place when the two Protectorates were outlined, France secured the lion's share and an easier and more rewarding task. Every important town, the Sultan's capital included, was entrusted to her care, thus providing her with a sphere of influence that extended to a sovereign who was more than a nominal ruler. The most fertile lands in his domains and the peacefully inclined populations who tended them were given over to France; under the masterly hand of General Lyautey they were speedily settled and developed by industrious French colonists. Allotted to Spain were four towns of minor importance and a stretch of arid, mountainous territory, representing one-twentieth of the Empire's total area and fiercely defended by warlike tribes who opposed every move made by the newcomers.

Spain had lacked, when Morocco was partitioned, statesmen and diplomats capable of influencing the issues. To equal the work being accomplished in the French Zone she needed a colonizer of Lyautey's stature and opportunities for immigrants of her own race, such as those who for many years have demonstrated their ability in the Spanish-speaking countries of America, or those who helped to open up Algiers. But not even Lyautey and his settlers could have made much out of the stony expanses covered with prickly pear, behind which rebellious natives took cover and fought the Spaniards with skill and determination. The Moors had readily submitted to their French masters, but in the Spanish Zone their warlike spirit was kept aflame by quantities of arms and ammunition, smuggled without too much difficulty over the French-Moroccan border, or, even more easily, from Tangier, an enclave in the Spanish Protectorate with a port on the Strait of Gibraltar and privileges that stemmed from a special status, ideally devised to promote intrigue in neighbouring areas. Contraband became a flourishing business, hard to suppress, fostered at times by political ineptitude in Madrid, and with complicated ramifications.

In their attempts to subdue Morocco, successive Spanish governments had fluctuated between policies alternately warlike and conciliatory. Military leaders on the spot trimmed their predecessors' plans and attacked, or made peace, according to their own judgement or to instructions issued by the Cabinet from Madrid. For ten years the tide of war had alternately surged and ebbed around Tetuán and Laraiche or in the barren lands between Melilla and Alhucemas Bay. Raisuni's warriors, well equipped and encouraged from Tangier, harassed vital communications with Ceuta. The eastern zone of the Protectorate had seen occasional fighting since 1909, when General Pinto's sallies towards Nador and Mount Gurugú met with stiff opposition on the outskirts of Melilla. On no part of the ground that stretched for over 200 miles between that city and Tetuán had Spain succeeded in setting a firm foot. Campaign followed campaign. War was never directed against the Sultan from the Spanish side; its purpose was simply to quell revolts which since time immemorial have broken out in these territories against the effectiveness of his rule, and to enforce it, under the terms of the treaties to which he was a party, in the different zones under Spanish protection. The war was draining national resources. When it died out in the Riff it flared up in Djebala or spread from there to the hills behind Arcila, Laraiche and Alcázarquivir. Casualties mounted, and fighting in Morocco became increasingly unpopular in Spain.

Such was the situation when I arrived in Melilla and found, contrary to current reports in Madrid, a fine spirit among the troops, and a confident civil population. Both were striving to honour international obligations, the importance of which few among them were able to comprehend. In Spain not many understood the temper that inspired her troops and none imagined that their younger leaders were learning lessons which would be of supreme value to the nation when the hour of her greatest crisis came.

Not only Morocco but Spain itself was then a mystery for most, a fabled land unknown even to many of its leaders, the majority of whom contented themselves with playing at local politics in the capital. In great tracts of the country the ways of life and the ideas of the twentieth century had not yet started to penetrate. There had been no industrial revolution, nor had prodigious sources of wealth been brought to light. Few had ever heard of the inevitability of progress, or of its indefinite nature. Railway trains wended their slow, voluptuous, smoky way over mountains and wide plains where shepherds, young or old, leaned heavily on their staffs and watched their flocks. Time had stopped still, and the only evidence of its passing was the unsightly maze of cables that occasionally stretched between the eaves and gables of ancient houses, stately churches and proud castles.

When I toured Spain in the early twenties, a rare achievement at that time, I found the roads deserted and better on the high, stony plateaux than on the fertile plains. However, it was not the state of the roads that kept some of my friends from driving on them; rather was it their apathy about anything devoid of an obvious bearing on their everyday lives. When Spain passed from a comparatively recent era of exploration and endeavour—at the close of the eighteenth century her mariners were discovering and naming large stretches of coast in Southern Alaska—to an age of renunciation and disillusionment brought about by the loss of her last colonies on the American continent, many Spaniards gave up all interest and curiosity for matters which they considered extraneous to their personal comfort and well-being. No longer did windmills taunt Don Quixote. He was back from his sorties, and the key had turned seven times in the lock that closed the sepulchre of the Cid.

For years, now, contacts between cities and rural areas had been scant; few among the wealthy troubled to become acquainted with the country which was their home. Time had widened the breaches between the humdrum haunts where they aired to little cliques their prejudices or their indignation at the shortcomings of others, and the vast expanses of Spanish soil which held horizons wide enough to harbour fresh desires and memories that might have stirred new dreams. Rural estates, barely cultivated, replete with game, and crying out for reafforestation and husbandry, remained untended, unhunted and alone, in the minds of their owners too far from Madrid (though at most only a few hundred miles away) to warrant an occasional visit and the drudgery involved in looking over this season's crops and yesteryear's accounts. Condescending and patronizing with their agents, who profited and grew rich at their expense, they spared few thoughts for the welfare of those who tilled the soil and found it hard to make up for the meagreness of their wages. Had they ventured out more frequently their experience would have been rewarding, for themselves and for those who worked for them, even after routine softened the tang of the unknown. The land was varied and beautiful, and under the sun's caresses it basked in weather that was almost perfect for at least two-thirds of the year. Those who lived in it were an intensely human people, and their loyalty to the ideal of service had endowed them with the manner of true *señores*.

The aspect of the countryside and of the towns and villages on my way changed with every stage of my journey of exploration, but I saw no fine *palazzos*, no elaborate *châteaux*, no country seats or baronial homes; there has never existed in Spain a taste comparable to that which flourished so exuberantly in France, in England, and in Italy for spacious residences and gardens, notable for their sumptuous features or for the lavishness of their ornamental displays. The outstanding efforts of architects and of those who directed them during the thirteen centuries that have witnessed the flowering of Spanish art were inspired by religious ideals or by military requirements of a defensive nature. Because of this, the milestones of Spanish history are starkly recorded by the castles, ramparts and fortifications that stemmed hostile incursions of feudal lords and Moorish chieftains, or by the churches, monasteries, and cathedrals that expressed the spiritual fervour of the people and their rulers.

Artistically, the medieval Spaniard rarely erred. His work reflected an instinctive sensitivity for the best and an ability to achieve it, maintained later in accordance with well-grounded rules and traditions. If sometimes his craftsmanship was at a loss, for lack of knowledge or of technique, his warlike or spiritual zeal was never wanting. Christian churches were constructed in Spain long before the advent of the Romanesque style. The earliest known monuments of Spanish Christian art were built in the Vizigothic era, far from the more frequented paths of contemporary civilization and culture; they are few and widely distributed, and they date from the sixth and seventh centuries. During the eighth century, when the reconquest of Spanish territory from the Moors had barely started and while the Christians were continually fighting the infidel and striving to repel him farther south, a special style of architecture was evolved in the Kingdom of Asturias, which the Moslems failed to occupy entirely. It conformed to a blend of predominating influences, local tendencies, and Byzantine art. The small but graceful churches erected in accordance with its rules, also few in number, and likewise preserved throughout the years by that very isolation which is one of their most striking features, are all in the vicinity of Oviedo. They bear witness to the spirit which inspired the reconquest of Spain from the Moors, and are deeply moving today.

Christian art surged to the fore in Spain whenever there was a respite in that struggle. The Romanesque style spread east from Navarre to the Mediterranean and west to Santiago de Compostela, where it produced the Pórtico de la Gloria, its supreme achievement in any part of the world. At the time of its advent, the Spaniards had conquered a wide strip of land that ran, roughly, from Oporto to Barcelona, with a loop to the north above Saragossa which the Moslems held for some time. Within this restricted space, Romanesque art, known as the

Norman style in England, flowed like blood through a vein in territories wrested from the infidel only a few years before. Its principal channel was the road followed by devout European pilgrims through Roncesvalles and Pamplona to Compostela—'Santiago's Way', the *Camino Real* of the Middle Ages—but the fervour that impelled it extended to places as remote as Tahull and Erill, villages of the Noguera Ribagorzana valley situated in what is now the province of Lérida and deeply ensconced in the heart of the Pyrenees, where it is doubtful if the Moors ever set foot.

From the Vienne, the Rhine, and the Arno, new architectural orders came to Spain and advanced south to the border line with Islam. But at no time did a style, however successful in other lands, set a fashion strong enough to sweep before it the resistance which a race as independent as the Spanish opposes to foreign trends. It took time for Gothic art to break through the barriers of the Romanesque, but when it finally triumphed it produced in an incredibly short period great cathedrals and other works that testify not only to its durable popularity but to the perfection which it attained in a land which adopted it reluctantly. Later, Spain remained loyal to Gothic influences long after the Renaissance had triumphed in other nations; not until Ferdinand and Isabella freed Andalusia from the Moors did new cathedrals conform to this style. And while Renaissance art prevailed in the rest of Europe, Spaniards in the New World reverted to their beloved Gothic or evolved their own Baroque while transplanting their faith so zealously that in the eighteenth century alone they erected in Mexico 8,000 churches and chapels.

Time had stood still for centuries in the plains and the mountains on my route, where churches and castles were the most conspicuous and constant landmarks, but in some provincial towns a wind was blowing that heralded changes in the political and social field. A rich history also lies buried in medieval quarters of Barcelona, where I spent some months in the early twenties. From the heights of Tibidabo, on the outskirts, there is a splendid view of modern districts with well-aligned streets, shops and restaurants, leafy parks, wide avenues, and distan factories beyond which blue waters lead to Sitges, Majorca, and the Costa Brava, legendary playgrounds of the Catalans. Flowers and pedestrians fill the Ramblas, where birds, caged or free, trill as lustily as the divas and tenors who delight or infuriate discerning audiences in the Liceo, one of the finest opera houses in the world.

But in Barcelona, when I first knew it, professional agitators, recruited in foreign countries or in Spain, tormented the city with subversion and unrest. Its wealth and its industries had made it an ideal target for anarchists and labour bosses, who organized strikes with impunity and shot down employers or other workmen who opposed them. Some years before, Barcelona had been the centre of operations for Ferrer, a demagogue who talked of progress and liberty and instigated the attempt against King Alfonso and Queen Victoria on the day of their wedding in May 1906, when several people were killed. Barcelona was the scene of the so-called 'Bloody Week' in 1909, and it was there that men of the Garellano Regiment mutinied in 1917 when about to embark for Spanish Morocco. It was to Barcelona that the murderers of Don Eduardo Dato, a man of moderate Liberal tendencies and a competent Prime Minister, fled in March 1921, after shooting him dead in Madrid on the 8th of that month as he drove from the Cortes to his home. A few days later, between Saragossa and Barcelona, I was stopped at rifle-point by civil guards on the look-out for the killers. The assassin principally responsible for the crime escaped to Russia, where he was fêted like a hero.

In Barcelona, for years on end, citizens in fear of their lives hired gunmen for their protection or clutched a pistol to forestall a likely murderer. Life was a nightmare for most people. One evening I entered a popular café and found its occupants pale and jittery after seeing a customer shot dead while sitting quietly at his table. Against this state of terror the Government, the police and the Law Courts were powerless. Judges and jurors were intimidated and, if necessary, killed. Obvious culprits, after being identified and arrested, were tried and set free. The penalty for denouncing a killer was death. Any representative of the central power who dealt or attempted to deal justly with the guilty parties was denounced in the press and ejected from his post. But grievances were rarely redressed.

Moral chaos and industrial paralysis were not the sole consequences of anarchy; the discontent felt by all classes stirred up separatism throughout part of this region. Spain had many loyal subjects in Catalonia, but local politicos were playing up self-government and free determination, popular catchwords since the signing of the Treaty of

Versailles. According to them, a break with the central authority constituted the best panacea imaginable for the ills and maladies of a troubled era. The craze for autonomy flourished in an area that produced much wealth, paid high taxes, and believed itself in a position to remunerate adequately those who might lead the breakaway from Spain. The tendency spread like wildfire though the inevitable consequence of autonomous government in Catalonia would have been a high tariff clamped by the rest of the nation on Catalonian products.

This state of affairs threatened to contaminate other parts of the country. Together with the failure to pacify Morocco, it contributed decisively to the end of democracy and parliamentary government under the Spanish monarchy, to introduce dictatorship under General Primo de Rivera, and, eventually, to create in the whole of Spain a situation which led to civil war in 1936.

CHAPTER SEVEN

A Mission to America

In 1920, after some months as Press Attaché to the Spanish Embassy in London, I joined the Secretariat of the League of Nations. I was the first Spaniard to work for the League, in London and later in Geneva, and in 1921 I was appointed to form part of a two-headed mission to South and Central America, made up of another Member of the League's Information Section and myself. We left Europe in July and returned to Geneva three months later. What I saw in the course of my travels taught me much about my own country.

People in certain nations entertain vague ideas about others. I myself have been shown an apple and asked, with a benevolent smile, 'Do you have these in Spain?', as if Spain were a mysterious and exotic land, hovering on the equator. On another occasion, while I was on my way to the Argentine, a fellow-traveller begged me to look up a friend in Colombia, as if Buenos Aires and Bogota were as close to each other as Manhattan and the Bronx. Occasionally someone inquires whether it is difficult for a Spaniard to understand the language spoken say, in Mexico or Chile. When I explain that a modern Spaniard, unless dumb or hard of hearing, has no language problem in those countries, my inquirer seems loath to believe me. At the back of his mind he may incline to think that it would be all to the good if an influence distrusted from early youth were finally eradicated from the soil of the Americas. There is nothing surprising in this. In three out of every four cases, he has been throughout his life a victim of misrepresentation.

'That we have not given justice to the Spanish pioneers is simply because we have been misled,' wrote Charles Lummis in 1893. 'They made a record unparalleled, but our text-books have not recognized the fact. The Spanish pioneering of the Americas was the largest and longest and most marvellous feat of mankind in all history. It was not possible for a Saxon boy to learn that truth in my boyhood; it is enormously difficult, if possible, now.'

Research and travel have contributed to light up the picture which English textbooks, as Lummis points out, distorted during the nineteenth century. The fact that Spain brought her religion and her culture to both American Continents, one hundred years before any other nation thought of doing so, has been systematically played down by her detractors. Progressive writers, their imagination spurred by the strictures which Fray Bartolomé de las Casas, in his fanatical zeal for the Indians, heaped upon the Conquistadores, are fond of harping on their faults, less ready to extol their virtues.

At no time during their protracted domination of the American continent did Spaniards proclaim their superiority over other races. When they first landed they did not announce themselves as the salt of the earth, nor as a product of God's own country. Alonso de Ojeda, who set foot in the Antilles the year 1509, addressed the Indians thus: 'God our Lord, who is one and eternal, created heaven and earth and one man and one woman, from which you, we, and all those who have been or will be in this world, descend.' The echo of Ojeda's words resounded over America. Repeated by the Conquistadores, they were preached to the natives by missionaries who helped to pacify and civilize. They embodied the faith of a nation and inspired her unique contribution to the history of the human race; they explain why Spain succeeded in incorporating the peoples she subdued to the Catholic faith. Nothing similar to this had ever been accomplished elsewhere, before or since. England, France, Holland and the United States opened up vast territories in their time without absorbing into their respective and considerable civilizations the races that inhabited them—Hindus, Berbers and Arabs, Malays, Indians and Negroes. Their approach to the problem was not the same.

No nation save Portugal—and Portugal was united to Spain during a vital period of her history—has acted in full accordance with Spain's belief that all men are equal because they possess an immortal soul, capable of salvation, and the free will to determine its destiny. This principle does not imply that all men are equally capable, physically and intellectually, or that they possess the same degree of political acumen. But it contains an alternative to Communist doctrine and it is accepted today by close to five hundred million Catholics and respected and reverenced by countless others who do not share their faith.

What Spain proclaimed in America was nothing less than the fundamental dignity of man and his freedom to do good, irrespective of race or colour. The Laws of the Indies, enacted in Spain or in her possessions beyond the seas and enforced there by Spanish rulers, prove that Spain practised what she preached. They are preserved in their original form in the Archives at Seville, and remain, hand-written on seventeen million documents, for all to see. No comparable body of legislation can be found anywhere else, and, because of these laws and of the spirit that inspired them, native races of pure or mixed blood now number millions in South and Central America, and, like the Spaniards themselves, occasionally rebel against those who forget their essential equality and their inherent dignity as men.

In the eighteenth century, when the Bourbons succeeded the Habsburgs on the throne of Spain, and *fleurs-de-lys* replaced the two-headed eagle on the Spanish escutcheon, the trends of thought and doctrines which brought about the French Revolution were introduced into the Peninsula and transplanted in due course to America, where they corrupted local forms of government and stirred up an unrest that came to a head when Napoleon invaded Spain. Aimed not so much against the basic features of Spanish rule, which many cherished and wished to preserve, as against the ideas now tainting it and which had already triumphed in France, that unrest helped to sever the bonds between Spain and her overseas possessions.

Today it is not yet easy, even for an objective and impartial student, to unearth the basic facts about Spanish action in America. They lie buried in the trash that has been piled high upon them by writers who have succeeded in spreading their opinions over most of the world. Spanish passivity and her aloofness and indifference to alien trends of thought are partly to blame for this, but she can hardly be held responsible for the manner in which the truth about her past has been, and is, misrepresented and hidden by others. Our contemporaries are continually exhorted to believe that the Conquistadores were fiends unparalleled in history; that credit for the discovery of America, or for the early civilization of practically the whole continent, does not belong to Spain; that although the discoverer himself, and, after him, his sons and their descendants, spelled their name 'Colón', *Columbus* is the proper way to write it; that San Salvador, the first land which Colón discovered in America, should really be known as Watling Island; that it was not Juan Sebastián de Elcano who first circumnavigated the world; and that anyone who speaks of Spanish America stamps himself as a reactionary.

Again I quote from Lummis: 'the greatest of English textbooks does not even have the name of the man who first sailed around the world (a Spaniard), nor of the man who discovered Brazil (a Spaniard), nor of him who discovered California (a Spaniard), nor of those Spaniards who first found and colonized in what is now the United States, and . . . it has a hundred other omissions as glaring and a hundred histories as untrue as the omissions are inexcusable.' 'The Spanish,' Lummis recalls, 'were not only the first conquerors of the New World, and its first colonizers, but also its first civilizers. They built the first cities, opened the first churches, schools and universities; brought the first printing-presses, made the first books; wrote the first dictionaries, histories and geographies, and brought the first missionaries; and before New England had a real newspaper, Mexico had a seventeenth-century attempt at one. One of the wonderful things about Spanish pioneering was the humane and progressive spirit which marked it from the first to last. Histories speak of that nation as cruel to Indians, but the record of Spain in this respect puts us to blush. The Spanish Legislation on behalf of the Indians everywhere was incomparably more extensive, more comprehensive, more systematic and more humane than that of Great Britain, the Colonies and the present United States all combined. It gave the Spanish language and the Christian faith to a thousand aborigines, where we gave a new language and religion to one. There have been Spanish schools for Indians in America since 1524. By 1575 —nearly a century before there was a printing-press in English America —many books in *twelve* different Indian languages had been printed in the city of Mexico, whereas in our history John Eliot's Indian Bible stands alone; and three Spanish universities in America were rounding out their centuries when Harvard was founded. A surprisingly large proportion of the pioneers of America were college men; intelligence went hand in hand with heroism in the early settlement of the New World.' Adolph F. Bandelier, the well-known American historian, has this to say about the book in which the above statements were published: '. . . the estimates and statements embodied in this volume are strictly true, and I hold myself ready to defend them from the standpoint of historical science.'

Such were my reflections as I sailed across the South Atlantic on my way back to Europe. I had been in seven of the eighteen Spanish-speaking nations of America; also in Brazil, which thanks to Portugal speaks Portuguese. During my travels I had discovered, not the remnants of a remote and almost extinct culture, 'presumably' of Iberian origin, but lasting evidence of the permanence and vitality of the civilization introduced by those countries into a new world. I knew now that Spain had not only built Gothic churches in Mexico, and Renaissance and Baroque churches in both American continents—the United States are far from being a barren field in this respect—but laid down in them the fundamental principles of Christianity and taught these principles in Universities opened by Spaniards in Lima and in Mexico City one hundred years before any other nation ever thought of doing the same in any part of the entire American continent. In most places I had been in, the most vital, industrious and fruitful element was the Spanish colony—the Spaniards of today, who were also among the most influential and prosperous in every walk of life. Spanish missionaries were still active in the cities and jungles of the countries I had visited. And though there were differences, not always subtle, between the language spoken by some of their inhabitants, and Castilian Spanish, they were perhaps not as noticeable as those which exist today between English of the 'U' variety, as spoken in Mayfair or in Melton Mowbray, and English as it is spoken in Brooklyn or in a Lancashire factory. The Spanish one reads in the better newspapers of Central and South America is often—not always, for Spanish-American writers succumb occasionally to the devastating influence of Yankee slang—as good or better than much of what is written in Spain itself.

So, while the *Massilia*'s log piled up knots on its way back to Europe, I reflected on the nature of the task carried out by Spain in areas she had done so much to civilize, and wondered whether Canning had acted with statesmanlike foresight when he brought in the Old World to redress the balance in the New; whether the disciples of Monroe had shown real vision when they used his slogan to sweep away the remnants of one of the most stabilizing factors in the American continent; and whether the United States, which without understanding Spain will be hard put to understand Spanish America, would not be well advised in its own interest to promote Spanish culture within the Union, transforming what is now a mere trickle into a considerable flow of immigrants from Spain. In any case, I had learnt something new and was beginning to feel that perhaps my journey had not been a total waste of time.

CHAPTER EIGHT

General Primo de Rivera's Rise to Power

I was in the Pyrenees near Gavarnie, high above Lourdes and Cauterets, when the first news of Primo de Rivera's *coup d'état* reached me. It was 14 September 1923; his accession to power, destined to change the history of Spain, had taken place the day before. Primo, at the time Captain-General of Catalonia, had persuaded King Alfonso to rid the nation of a system of government that prevented politicians, possibly more powerless than inept, to rule the country efficiently. Throughout his reign, until that moment, the King had acted as a constitutional monarch. The people had gone to the polls, and though elections lacked sincerity, the results of the elections had shaped the decisions of the Crown. Successive Cabinets had faithfully reflected the people's will, all parties had won a chance to govern, and every alternative within the regime had been put on trial. The game had been played according to its rules, but the rules of the game failed to work properly in Spain. King Alfonso gave in to Primo because he had no other choice. A strong government was now the sole alternative to chaos.

The war in Spanish Morocco had flared up intermittently for fourteen consecutive years, with minor ups and downs or with disasters as grave as the rout in Annual in the summer of 1921. It was draining the resources of the nation, and the end was nowhere in sight. Strikes and outrages, which since 1917 had made life unbearable in Barcelona, were spreading to other cities, with obvious revolutionary implications. Law and order were becoming mere memories in the larger industrial towns, factories were frequently at a standstill, and production dwindled alarmingly. The nation languished. Whoever attempted to rule it did so without success. The entire machinery of government needed replacement by a system possessing greater authority, less flexibility and more power.

Perhaps the King, like others in Spain, did not consider a military dictatorship an ideal solution. But during the previous fifty years every conceivable system had been unsuccessfully tested. Two liberal Sovereigns, Isabel II and Amadeo de Saboya, had abdicated the throne. A Republic had ended in ignominious failure. One after the other, all possible combinations of Liberals and Conservatives had been tried out democratically under Alfonso XII, the regent Maria Cristina, and their son, Alfonso XIII. Much as they may have favoured democracy, the people needed a chance to work and prosper in peace.

Unlike the national rising against an even graver situation that set off civil war in 1936, General Primo de Rivera's move was a classic *coup d'état*, swiftly and ably executed by a man who did not hesitate to take the entire responsibility on his shoulders. He relied on the partially expressed support of the Army, though not all its leaders backed Primo, nor were they with him unflinchingly until the end. There was no opposition from political parties or labour unions. The majority of the nation resigned itself to a *fait accompli* and hoped for the best, or for something sensational, but there were no street scenes, no riots, no shooting. Objective and far-sighted citizens, without a stake in the political arena and no possibility of gain from turbulence and unrest, heaved a sigh of relief and applauded the *coup d'état*, once its success became evident.

A brief period sufficed to show that the dictator meant business. Instead of persecuting his predecessors or making them responsible for the shortcomings of the regime, Primo de Rivera devoted himself to constructive work. The murder of two postal employees in a railway van, committed shortly after his access to power and punished by a Court of Justice with the extreme rigour of the law, showed that crime was no longer profitable. Plans for military action in Spanish Morocco were revised from bottom to top; in less than three years, the entire Protectorate was pacified and the war was brought to a victorious end. There were no strikes, production attained new levels, private enterprise flourished. A network of roads, properly banked and well-surfaced, spread over the country. At long last, Spain's valuable hydraulic resources began to be harnessed and exploited. Work was carried out in harbours and railways, schools were built, industry and trade registered progress, and national economy soared. Two exhibitions of an impressive character, held in Seville and Barcelona in the year 1929, proved that Spain could thrive rapidly under a system guaranteeing peace, prosperity and the rule of practical law.

PART III

CHAPTER NINE

A Local War at the Gates of Europe

I was again living in London, and it was November 1924. Fourteen months had elapsed since General Primo de Rivera's rise to power. There had been sufficient time in which to plan and start a campaign that would determine the issues in Spanish Morocco, but instead of this, without large scale attacks on either side, Spanish troops were being withdrawn from their outposts in enemy country. The trend was puzzling. Government in Spain had been entrusted to a group of well-chosen Ministers who were running their departments smoothly. Primo had retained the Premiership and was High Commissioner in Morocco and Commander-in-Chief there as well. On the Spanish side every card was in his hands; the moment to play them was drawing near. I obtained a letter of introduction to the General from the Marqués de Merry del Val, under whom I had served at the Embassy, and sailed for Africa to meet the General.

Soon after his arrival in Tetuán, capital of the Spanish Moroccan Protectorate, the conduct of the war had undergone a substantial change. Until then, the capture of new ground had invariably been followed by the establishment of fortified posts known as blockhouses, protected by barbed wire and sandbags and commanding the territory around them. This entailed the need of convoys, to supply the defenders with ammunition and food, and of occasional sorties from the blockhouses, to disperse the enemy that harassed them or to replenish water, invariably scarce on the heights where the outposts were usually perched. The system, not unknown in the classic period of colonial warfare, had been introduced years before in the hope that hostilities would be of short duration. It was supposed to provide the necessary foothold for eventual progress on a wide front, and in any case the vicissitudes of democratic and parliamentary government in Spain, with its endless debates and conflicting views, precluded all possibility of conducting operations in any other way.

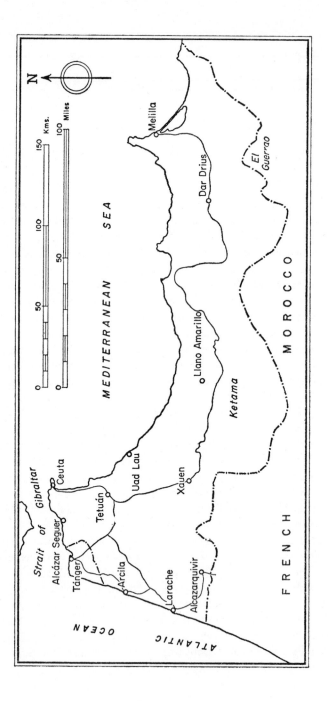

But the campaign had dragged on endlessly, with the enemy attacking blockhouses, the convoys that supplied them from remote or nearby bases, and the fever-ridden garrisons that sallied out to waterholes and wells. At their best, the Moors in Spanish Morocco were masters at this kind of game. They would lie for hours in the prickly-pear scrub or amid the boulders which littered the ground, waiting for a chance to snipe at stragglers or to cut off the rearguard of a retreating column. They rarely wasted a shot. A bunch of dates, a few pats of butter, and some hunks of bread tucked away in the hoods of their *djellabas* would keep them going for days on end. If their opponents deployed to attack them, they withheld their fire to conceal their whereabouts. If hard pressed, they took to their heels and disappeared among the crags and precipices of the surrounding countryside. Artillery was practically useless against a foe not only scarce but invisible, and although the Spaniards rarely lost a major engagement, and won new ground whenever they attacked, the stalemate was bound to continue until a change of plan turned the tide of war in one direction or another.

Primo had a plan and was determined to carry it out despite the advice of some of his subordinates, who could not bear to relinquish the ground so hardly won. The mere talk of surrendering it was in their minds equivalent to an acknowledgement of defeat. But the General added an imaginative touch to the prevalent concept of strategy. To him, fortified posts, costly to supply and to defend, were nothing but targets for the enemy to shoot at. The time had come to abandon them, withdraw their garrisons to a strong line, and prepare a campaign which might prove decisive but in no case would be launched before the whole area allegedly controlled by Spain was finally pacified and firmly held. Opposition to this plan mounted at home and on the field. Younger officers with brilliant records took no pains to hide their disappointment. When Primo arrived at Ben Tieb, a Spanish military camp, to inspect the Foreign Legion, he found a repetitive menu with a hidden meaning, not used in polite society, and a large placard proclaiming that the regiment's watchword was 'Attack'.

The initial phases of the withdrawal were not encouraging. Our troops, assailed as they evacuated their positions, suffered heavy losses. The retreat from Shauen was a nightmare. Shauen, or She-Shauen, as it is also called, is for the Moors a holy city. Notwithstanding its proximity to Europe—it lies barely more than sixty miles from the

Strait of Gibraltar—no European, with the exception of a French missionary, the famous Charles de Foucauld, had entered the town until, in 1920, General Berenguer conquered it for Spain. Ideally situated on the hills below the twin peaks of Kala and Magó, where Barbary apes abound, it is surrounded by narrow gorges filled with rushing water and blessed by a constant breeze that cools the fierce heat in summer. Tiled roofs on its houses, which unlike those of other Moorish towns are not terraced, and the fine woollen rugs woven in its courtyards, have made Shauen famous not only in Morocco but all over Spain. In 1924 there was only one road out of the city and it led to Tetuán, forty miles away, through mountain heights with unlimited observation posts and ideal cover from which to shoot at the retreating Spaniards. Casualties were heavy during the withdrawal, and a General (Serrano), a Colonel (Temprano) and several other officers of high rank were killed. Elsewhere the situation was critical, for when the enemy suspected that a post was about to be abandoned they would invest it or attack, and the orderly retreats originally planned became long and hazardous encounters.

CHAPTER TEN

Muñoz Grandes

I was at dinner in Tetuán two days after my arrival there when I learnt that a young Major, whose name I had never heard before, was due to embark that very night for Wad-Lau with 250 of his native levies to rescue a battalion of the Burgos Regiment which had been surrounded by the enemy as it was about to abandon its camp at a fortified outpost with the Spanish name of San Fernando. Agustín Muñoz Grandes, who commanded an Army Corps in the Civil War, later Captain-General of the Spanish Army, Minister of War under General Franco, and at the time of writing Vice-President of the Spanish Government, was then twenty-eight years old and the youngest major in Spain. He had recently been promoted to this rank for his ability to rescue beleaguered garrisons and escort them to safer positions—a highly specialized job for which he had received some credit and half a dozen wounds. When he appeared at the place in Tetuán where I was dining, I asked if he would take me to Wad-Lau, a valley on the northern coast of Morocco, some miles east of Tetuán. 'You'll find it hotter there than you think,' he said dryly,'and in any case you need written permission from the Commander-in-Chief.'

I rose from the table and went straight to the High Commissioner's quarters. General Primo was at dinner. The day before I had found him cordial and receptive, so I plucked up my courage and sent in a note with an orderly, requesting permission to accompany the Major to Wad-Lau. Five minutes later a tall A.D.C., Lieut.-Col. Monis, came out with one of the General's visiting cards on which Primo himself had written, 'I hereby grant Don Luis Bolin *carte blanche* to move freely with the Spanish troops in the area of our Protectorate in Morocco.'

Moorish units in the Spanish ranks were fighting for their Sultan against the rebellious tribes. Some had been enrolled in regular contingents, officered by Spaniards and native N.C.O.s. They wore fezes,

light khaki uniforms and sashes round their waists, the colour of which
—green, saffron, red, mauve, yellow—varied according to the regiment in which they served. Each of these bore the name of a place or
a town in the Spanish Zone—Melilla, Alhucemas, Ceuta, Tetuán
and Laraiche—and all of them possessed fighting skill and mobility.
Other tribesmen, renowned for their warlike spirit and resourcefulness
in single combat, made up the *harkas*, or irregular levies, with tactics
similar to those of the enemy, whom they fought courageously on
every possible occasion. Like their opponents, they were clothed in
turbans, *djellabas*, and leather babouches, trodden down at the heel. The
manner in which they sped over rough ground and played soccer or
fought while wearing these strapless sandals was something to see.
Subtle distinctions in their attire revealed to the initiated the particular
kabyle to which they belonged. Occasionally it was the same tribe
which they were fighting.

Besides these regular and irregular contingents there was a native
police force, the *Mehalla*, uniformed in dark green and occupied in
police work of the usual kind among their countrymen.

The levies commanded by Muñoz Grandes made up the finest *harka*
in Spanish Morocco. Their leader had found them invaluable for the
type of warfare in which he himself excelled. A Captain and Lieutenant, hand-picked by the Major, completed the officers' cadre. The
Captain's name was Bescansa; he was killed a few months later at the
landing in Alhucemas. The Lieutenant, Menor, also killed at Alhucemas, was then convalescing in Malaga after a leg wound. When I first
met Muñoz Grandes I inquired whether he had recently been in Spain.
'Not for four years,' he replied. 'It's only an hour away. Don't you
ever get leave?' 'Yes,' he answered, 'but there's always something
cooking over here.'

The landing party that sailed from Ceuta that night on the *Atlante*
was made up of four hundred Moors, seven Spanish officers and
myself. A special train collected the *harka* at Tetuán, and the hulla-
baloo set up by its members when Muñoz Grandes arrived, similar to
the shrill cry of their women on appropriate occasions, still rings in my
ears. A company, or *tabor*, of Regulares de Ceuta, three hundred strong,
completed the native contingent. Three Spanish officers commanded
it, and a fourth officer had been detailed to blow up the camp at San
Fernando once the beleaguered battalion got away. The remaining
officer was a gunner who had been sent to replace a casualty.

Firing broke out as we landed from K-boats in the silvery dawn of a fine November morning, not far from the mouth of the river that gives its name to the valley of Wad-Lau. In an instant our Moors had built a parapet, sufficiently thick to protect us from the bullets which were sputtering sand all around, and made with the bales of straw that littered the beach. A detachment of Regulars remained on guard. Muñoz Grandes and his *harkeños* vanished in the scrub, and I soon heard them blazing at their opponents, half a mile or so from us.

The *Atlante* had already left for Ceuta, and, close to the shore, the *Extremadura*, an ancient cruiser with modern 105-mm. pieces, was preparing to shell the enemy. I went on board to watch the fighting, and shortly afterwards Muñoz Grandes turned up, escorted by three of his henchmen and disgusted with his bad luck. A bullet had hit him in the left arm, and his tunic, breeches and leggings were red with blood. Despite his protests—'too much fuss over a little gore'—the doctor packed him off to a nearby hospital ship while his devoted *harkeños* looked on, tears rolling down their cheeks. Bescansa was prey to high fever and had also been ordered to hospital, but somebody had to command the *harka*, and to get him to the place where his men awaited him we both escaped on the cruiser's launch and made for the shore.

Days passed before the battalion could be evacuated, and the *Extremadura* twice ran out of shells. The operation served as a rehearsal for the landing at Alhucemas ten months later. Breguets and Bristol planes observed or bombed the enemy from the air, and I saw a thrilling cavalry charge over a wide, yellow plain against forces entrenched on the fringes of an oak forest. Mounted Regulars fired as they galloped on their Arab steeds, brilliantly led by Adolfo Botín, a young cavalryman famous for his exploits in horse shows who was killed two weeks later while leading a similar charge in Beni Hozmar, almost within sight of Tetuán. Primo de Rivera directed operations from the quarterdeck of the cruiser *Cataluña*, and a fitting curtain was provided by my friend the T.N.T. specialist—he had been with me at school—who blew up the abandoned position with a blast that filled the landscape with thunder and smoke.

When I returned to Madrid a well-known newspaper publisher said to me, 'I liked your stories about Wad-Lau, but don't tell me they were not made up. Not a shot was fired; you know as well as I do that we gave the enemy a million pesetas and ten thousand rifles to pull that battalion out of the mess it had got itself into.' His words provided me with an insight into the devious channels through which opposition to a successful policy occasionally runs; the next day, a politician and historian of high standing expressed himself similarly to me. While the operations lasted I had gone to bed every night with a splitting headache from the incessant roar of cannon. I wondered if the views expressed to me were shared by the rows of corpses which I had seen for a week at the close of battle, lined up in their tight shrouds on the beach at Wad-Lau, the day's work done. Anyhow, I myself told the full story in a series of articles published by the Madrid *A.B.C.* Two weeks later, in London, another of my stories on the battle, illustrated with my own photographs, appeared in the columns of *The Times*.

General Primo de Rivera reviewed every unit in the Protectorate prior to launching his attack against Abd-el-Krim. I accompanied him throughout his tour of inspection, which was exhaustive and thorough. First we visited the camps in the hills and mountains beyond Tetuán, Laraiche and Alcázarquivir; then we sailed east to Melilla and went as far as the Muluya, near the French Zone, driving from there to the heights at Tizzi-Aza, where so much fighting had taken place. The central part of the Spanish Zone was still in the hands of a defiant and unbeaten enemy. No Spaniard, and nobody else, for that matter, had yet penetrated the vast and mountainous expanses retained by the Moors, but Primo had pacified the territory behind his lines, and apart from some desultory shelling on our side I did not hear a single shot throughout the entire journey.

There were no convoys now to blockhouses and outposts exposed on every side to the enemy, no sorties from them in search of water, no killing of soldiers by an invisible foe. Now, when a Moor promised to keep the peace, his assurances remained unheeded until he handed over the only acceptable evidence of his sincerity—a rifle, at least, for every man who swore friendship. The old trick at which the Bakali of Wad-Lau was an adept of proclaiming peace today and revoking the promise—'*ya no estar amigos*'—on the morrow, had been played once too often. So adamant was Primo on this point that the peace he laid down in 1926 remained undisturbed after seventeen years of warfare until the Spaniards left Morocco in 1956.

Whole kabyles flocked from the surrounding countryside to file past the saluting point and pay homage to the General, while military bands played their stirring tunes and the Spanish flag fluttered in the breeze. Some marched on foot, others rode pure-blooded Arab horses with long white tails, firing ancient muskets as they galloped by. Moorish chieftains—some of them, like Amarusen, Mizzian, and Abd-el-Kader, well-seasoned allies of Spain—invited us to sumptuous banquets that stood witness to their loyalty and almost ruined our digestions. It was hard to realize, at these gargantuan repasts, that the twentieth century was twenty-five years old and Europe only an hour away.

For these meals we would make up groups of four and settle ourselves on cushions piled around low tables. Negro attendants from a southern tribe—the Sous—cleansed our hands with orange-water, while gorgeously attired waiters, soft-footed and silent, made a ceremonious entry, carrying round dishes over their heads, the viands we were about to eat hidden from our view by conical, gaily-coloured covers that kept the food hot and heightened our expectations. Below these coloured lids were plates of steaming *couscous*, followed by at least a dozen chickens, roasted, boiled, broiled or fried, all in succession and at the rate of three or four fowls for every guest. The *pièce de résistance*, a lamb, roasted whole, afforded yet another opportunity for one or more of our willing hosts to dig his fingers into the hot meat and offer us some tempting morsel—an odorous kidney, or a piece of heart, still reeking with blood. Spaniards were allowed to drink wine during the meal, of which, to my taste, the best part was the desert—delicious *gacelas*, and the variety of sweets which Arabs prepare so well with almonds and honey.

Our troops were in fine fettle, well-equipped and -uniformed, but there was still some grumbling against the abandonment of outposts in enemy territory. Lunching one day at the big camp in Tenin, east of Laraiche, a young Captain in the Foreign Legion who later lost a leg in the Civil War left his seat at my side, marched up to the Commander-in-Chief, saluted, and requested permission to sing a ditty which reflected the prevailing discontent. When the first verse ended the Captain received a pat on the shoulder from the General and was sent back to enjoy his food.

Part of the Andjera tribe, for long under Raisuni's rule, was maintaining a rebellious attitude in an isolated area on the Strait of Gibraltar.

To subjugate it, Primo planned a landing that was to be the final rehearsal for Alhucemas. The white sands at Alcázar Seguer, east of Tangier and directly opposite Tarifa, are plainly visible on a clear day from the ships that cross the Strait. Those aboard those ships that day must have wondered at the spectacle we provided one fine winter morning, as our cruisers began shelling the African shore while observation planes flew overhead. Soon after our arrival, K-boats detached themselves from the larger ships that had towed them from Ceuta and carried landing parties to the beach, plainly visible through our glasses. There was a show of resistance, but the demonstration put up for their benefit soon cowed the Moors, and their villages and the parapets which they had erected were occupied in a matter of hours.

CHAPTER ELEVEN

The Spanish Foreign Legion

'Let's ride up to the top of the column,' said Lieut.-Colonel Joaquín Ortiz de Zárate. 'I want you to look back and tell me what you think of the sight behind you.'

We had left camp at dawn with a full battalion of the Foreign Legion, made up of warriors with a superb morale, tanned and healthy and magnificently fit, men of a regiment which had known no rest from battle since its creation five years before. Their commander, himself a veteran of a hundred engagements, repeatedly wounded in action and later to be killed near Oyarzun during the advance that led to the capture of San Sebastian from the Reds early in the Civil War, ordered them to halt. We were in hostile territory. The show of strength I was witnessing, carried out to test the aggressiveness of our opponents in that particular area, was more than sufficient to dampen it. Two companies dispersed at the double and their soldiers, heavily equipped and lithe as cats, climbed the slopes before us and disappeared from our view, hugging the ground to render themselves invisible.

The inspired enthusiasm of a lieutenant-colonel, José Millán Astray, brought the Spanish Foreign Legion into being at a critical phase of the Moroccan war. He accomplished his task by firing his men and their officers with a spirit akin to the mysticism which in the sixteenth century carried the Conquistadores to heights of achievement and endeavour wherever they set foot. In no small measure his success was due to the principles that embodied his ideals—aggressiveness in battle, brotherly love and loyalty towards comrades and officers, physical endurance and the will to fight, submission to iron discipline, contempt for death, and *esprit de corps*. To preach this required a special knack and knowledge of men; to instil it into their hearts and minds nothing less than genius was needed. Millán Astray had faith in himself and in his mission, and he was fortunate in the choice of his assistants. One of them, as a youthful Major, had led the first battalion of the

Legion and now commanded the entire regiment with the rank of lieutenant-colonel, to which he had been promoted for his fearlessness and his courage and ability on the field of battle. Francisco Franco was already famous when I first met him in November 1924, at the Commandant's headquarters in Ceuta. The day was chilly. He wore the white-lined cape of the Legion. The searching look in his large brown eyes was as characteristic of him then as it is today.

The men who answered Millán Astray's call were a tough lot, and they came from all parts of the world. What brought them? Millán Astray and Franco, writing of the regiment's early days, have tried to answer this question. One-half of the first four hundred—misfits, gaol-birds, old soldiers—had sailed from Barcelona to enlist. They were a noisy rabble, panting for adventure, and they landed in Morocco with the force of a hurricane, scattering everything before them. Some were idealists, eager to fight for a worthy cause, some wished to atone for past misdeeds, others were hungry. A few had been crossed in love. Many fancied the prospect of a military career in which they could attain the rank of Captain. Former officers, kicked out of their units in different countries, hoped to make good in Morocco; the pick of the bunch were killed there. Sick to death of damp trenches, out-of-work veterans of the First World War joined up to fight under the sun. A candidate with a wooden leg sobbed bitterly on learning that he had been rejected. A young friar, too weak-spirited to live in a convent, discovered that his body was also too frail for the harsh life before him. Members of broken families met again after avoiding each other for years. An elderly recruit, about to salute a lieutenant, recognized his only son and fell into his arms, weeping.

Many stayed on indefinitely, though regimental routine was tougher than most had at first imagined. Impending physical hardships were not hidden from newcomers; on the contrary, they were told that leisure was a thing of the past, that when not fighting they would train to the bone. Brawls would be unmercifully punished—the cramped cells where they might languish in solitary confinement were shown to all. Because the raw material available did not lend itself to anything else, discipline, though stern, was tempered by a sense of humour and an understanding of men's frailties. 'Do you ever get drunk?' an interrogating officer asked recruits. 'Well, sir, since you wish to know, as a matter of fact I do.' 'How often?' The truth would emerge, the officer would continue: 'In future, instead of once a day, you will get drunk once a week, on Wednesdays. The rest of the week you'll stay sober.' After suitable briefings, candidates were given a chance to quit. All they had to do was to tell the doctor they had a sore throat; the door would open silently and allow them to depart, free as the wind. If they passed their medical examination, they signed up for three or five years' service.

A period of intensive training, followed by frequent encounters with the enemy and more training, endowed recruits with qualities few of them suspected. They had to be fit. Eighteen men died of exhaustion while their units, on the way to hard-pressed positions, walked over seventy miles of terrible ground in less than thirty-six consecutive hours. There were daily lectures on behaviour under fire. Well-rehearsed roles were soon acted before the enemy, and the taste which the men acquired for danger became the spice of their lives and ended by embarrassing their officers. A call would go out for volunteers; the assignment was a dangerous one; it meant almost certain death for any who accepted it. At the cry of 'Who steps out?' the whole line would take a pace forward, their eyes looking straight into their leader's eyes, as they had been taught to do. In 1921, twelve months after the regiment was first organized, Corporal Terrero and fourteen others answered the call not far from Melilla and set off towards a post that was in danger of being rushed by the enemy. They reached their goal. Not one of them returned alive.

They did not have to give their real names when enlisting. Nor did anyone ask if they had ever been in gaol. But they were expected to obey orders, to train, march and fight. Well fed, they were provided with incentives that stirred their imagination and fitted in with their love for the romantic and the unusual. Their caps were of a different design and had little red tassels that tickled their foreheads as they walked. They lived in their shirt-sleeves. Shirt collars, open at the neck, were pressed back over their tunics on the rare occasions when they wore these. They had breeches like jodhpurs, buttoned to the ankles, gauntleted gloves, and flowering capes, lined white, with a fur collar and a hood for cold nights. Their straps and belts originally came from England, and were made of webbing, instead of leather, as were others in the Spanish Army. Their uniforms were smartly cut and fitted them. From the first they were well turned out and took pride in their personal appearance; as long as they looked neat nobody frowned at side-burns, whiskers, Hollywood moustachios or even beards. They had billy goats and other mascots, and they were called *Caballeros Legionarios*, 'Gentlemen of the Legion'.

As in the heyday of the Empire, each battalion still boasts its own distinctive banner, which is why they have always been called 'Banderas'—banners—instead of battalions. Every banner evokes an episode, person or symbol famous in the history of Spain—the wild boars of the House of Burgundy, emblem of the first Bandera, adopted later on as his personal pennant by General Franco; the double-headed eagle of the House of Habsburg, lineage of Charles V and Phillip II; the figure of Christ with the image of Our Lady which flew from Don John of Austria's mast-head when he defeated the Turk at Lepanto and saved Europe from the Eastern menace; the coat-of-arms of the great Duke of Alba, whose Tercios set a pattern for the Legion. Because of this, the regiment's badge reproduces sixteenth-century weapons—a bow and an arquebus, crossed over a vertical pike. Its drums and its bugles are longer, and, like its hymn and its marching tunes, sound better than those of any other regiment.

The code of the Legion inspired legionaries without basically altering their personal traits. Sooner or later, in times of stress or under the spell of boredom, their past caught up with some and their real characters emerged. One who called himself 'García' requested a private interview with his commanding officer and confessed that he had escaped from prison while waiting to be hanged after being twice sentenced for murder, once in France and once in Spain. Now he wanted to die fighting. He did. A self-styled Russian prince successively admitted his inability to pay for the hotel where he put up on arrival—'the Bolsheviks had robbed him of everything'—or to control himself in combat. He went home. Cuartillo, a born rebel and a trouble-maker, was a deserter from the regular army who, under fire, would stand up and embrace his Captain to show how much he admired him. He deserted again, was captured and killed by the Moors. So anxious was 'The Page of Death' to meet his master that he wrote one day to the Colonel insisting he could wait no longer. He shot himself. A good soldier, who as a civilian had been a wealthy and successful doctor, refused to speak to his wife when she arrived, gushing, to see him. He had enlisted to lose sight of her. 'M.M.P.' had been ordained a priest; he led an exemplary life and died in battle, tending the wounded. Some ex-officers behaved superbly under fire. One of them, 'Guido Fallieri', fought well, did his duty, refused promotion, and only revealed his name and rank on the day of his departure. He was a Polish Count and a cavalry captain.

On a certain occasion a battalion commander was urgently summoned to a hospital ward, where one of his men lay dying. 'What happened? What did he do?' 'He threw himself out of the window, sir. Every bone in his body is broken.' 'Poor boy, why did you do it?' 'Sir, I know she's bad, but I love her. She said I didn't have the guts to jump from a window . . .' To show a Spanish comrade just how callous to danger he could be, an Italian drew a revolver, inserted a cartridge, spun the cylinder, pointed the weapon to his head and pulled the trigger. 'That's nothing,' said the Spaniard, pulling out the pin from a hand-grenade. 'Watch this!' The blast killed both. A private with a terrible wound in his stomach summoned his friends to his deathbed, expressed his thanks for their kindness, and, after declaring himself a man of substance, bestowed his earthly goods upon them. 'I own considerable funds in Madrid,' he said, 'and a dozen houses in Cuba. I would like you'—the doctor—'and you'—a male nurse—'and you'— an orderly—'to share this, and that, and so much more. My real name is X.X.X.' With that he died leaving not a penny behind him. All he had was a sense of humour.

The Spanish Foreign Legion was founded on 4 September 1920. Six years later, at the conclusion of the war in Morocco, it had taken part in 845 engagements. The total casualties during this time were 116 officers and 1,871 N.C.O.s and men killed, 319 officers and 5,775 N.C.O.s and men wounded. At the outset there had been three battalions, or Banderas; the number soon rose to eight. It increased to twenty in the Spanish Civil War, where some 40,000 of the Legion's officers and men were killed and wounded while fighting.

With the exception of those promoted from its ranks, every officer in the Legion volunteered for service. Pay was higher than in the regular Army, and chances of promotion greater, but in themselves these attractions did not suffice to fill officer's cadres often depleted by enemy bullets. Something else moved those who took the fateful step forward—a spirit of selfless duty, a vocation for constant danger and ceaseless toil. They were young and as fond as any of a joke, a drink and the pleasures of life, but they went through the mill with their men, and always led them in battle. Rigid discipline and the combative spirit of the regiment attracted the best. Home leave was hard to obtain, and death lurked round every corner. They had seen that the crisis which beset Spain when she lost her last colonies in America had come to a head in Morocco and called for a desperate effort, at least from a few. Politicians at home were proving incapable; it was up to the Legion to find a remedy, so far as Morocco was concerned. Long hours between engagements gave them leisure to think, to read, to develop their minds, and to ponder on their nation's future. All they could do was to fight, but they hoped that their sacrifice would help to shape a better Spain. They had learned not only to obey but to lead and to transform human dregs into heroes.

Of all the principles which Millán Astray framed, two were all-important: the principle of comradeship, backed by the oath never to abandon a wounded comrade even if all perished to save him, and the principle of mutual help—at the cry of ¡ A mí la Legión!—'The Legion to my aid'—all must assist a comrade who pleads for help and defend him—with or without justification.

I myself, an honorary Captain of the Spanish Foreign Legion, once gave General Franco, who in peace and in battle had seen these principles applied in action over and over again, an instance of the loyalty with which they were obeyed during the Spanish Civil War. A soldier lay dying in a ward full of wounded men, legionaries like himself. Racked with pain and delirious, he cried out ¡ A mí la Legión! At his call his comrades, as if they had been one and not fifty, bleeding, maimed, too weak to walk, trailing their broken limbs behind them, left their mattresses and, heedless of nurses or doctors, gathered round the dying man and stayed with him till the end. By some who know him little, Franco is reputed to be as cold as ice, but when I told him this one night during the Civil War, in the stillness of his office in Salamanca, though his face remained impassive, tears fell from his eyes.

CHAPTER TWELVE

Alhucemas, and Peace

Primo was planning to deal the enemy a decisive blow. The vital spot to strike at was Alhucemas, in the Riff, where Axdir, the rebel leader's rustic lair, and the kabyles of Beni-Urriaguel and Tensaman, which supplied him with his best warriors, had to be subdued before the struggle could end. Like other rebels in the Central Zone of the Protectorate, those in Axdir were enjoying a false sense of security while maintaining their rebellious attitude.

Perplexed and disconcerted by the apparent lack of objectives on the Spanish side—there were no outposts to shoot at, and the new lines repulsed all attacks—the Moors now directed their activities against the French. They had finally discovered that the weapons which had been smuggled to them could be aimed at different targets. In a series of offensive operations, the Riffis won new ground and almost reached the gates of Fez, an important town in the French Zone, now involved in a threat which so far had only been aimed at Spain.

It was time for France and Spain to join forces and face what was really a common problem. Had this been done before, had it been realized sooner that the protection of Morocco was a joint enterprise in which the participating nations had much to win or lose together, there would have been no Abd-el-Krim, no Annual, no French retreat to the gates of Fez. Primo de Rivera did not indulge in recrimination, and in Marshal Pétain, the defender of Verdun, he found a willing and capable ally. Both leaders drew up their plans. The Spaniards would land in Alhucemas Bay with the support of their own navy and some French vessels. The French would act as a barrier and hold the enemy, once the latter had been routed by their Spanish allies.

My work and a chain of unforeseeable circumstances prevented me from being present when the Spaniards took Alhucemas. But I returned soon to Morocco, and because I followed events there closely and spoke to many participants in the landing I am in a position to reject the version, frequently printed in certain publications, according to which the French did everything to defeat Abd-el-Krim, the Spaniards nothing. Abd-el-Krim was beaten in 1925 as the result of a combined naval, land and air operation jointly executed by the French and by the Spaniards, an operation in which the latter, quite properly, bore the brunt of the fighting. The Moorish chieftain's stronghold, Axdir, was situated in the Spanish Protectorate, facing the Spanish Mediterranean coast and not far from it. While Abd-el-Krim defied Spain, the territories entrusted to her protection could not be subdued or occupied. Hostilities had dragged on for five years between the Spanish troops and the rebel leader's forces. It was up to Spain to beat him, and, because of their common interest in the matter, to do this she concerted an alliance with France, who was being attacked by Abd-el-Krim, and who had been jointly assigned with Spain to maintain peace and order in the Moroccan Empire by the Powers that ratified the Treaty of Algeciras. To destroy Abd-el-Krim, who had trained and equipped a redoubtable contingent of warriors, a landing had to be effected at Alhucemas, Axdir had to be taken, and the territories of the Tensaman and Beni-Urriaguel kabyles had to be occupied.

The naval contingent that supported the landing, a hazardous operation, consisted, on the Spanish side, of 2 battleships, 4 cruisers, 2 destroyers, 6 gun-boats, 11 coastguard vessels, 6 torpedo-boats, 7 auxiliary craft, and 24 merchantmen to transport the troops and to supply them —a total of 62 ships. On the French side, 1 battleship, 2 cruisers, 2 torpedo-boats, 2 monitors, and 1 tug, to which latter was moored a captive balloon, or 8 ships in all. The combined fleets had 241 pieces of artillery. French and Spanish observation planes directed the bombardment from the air.

The Spanish force which landed at Alhucemas on 13 September 1925 consisted of 22,959 men, commanded by 3 generals—Fernández Pérez, Sanjurjo and Saro—69 senior officers and 598 officers of lesser rank. Besides rifles, these forces were armed with 24 cannon, 44 trench mortars, 117 machine-guns and 202 automatic weapons. There were reserve troops in Ceuta and Melilla, ready to embark if necessary, and further reserves available in the Peninsula.

No French troops landed in Alhucemas; seven of their Divisions with a total of 110,000 men covered a wide front far to the south along the River Warga and blocked the access to towns such as Fez, El Gharb and Tazza, all three in the French Protectorate. These forces took no part whatever in the fighting round Alhucemas Bay, but on 3 August, forty days before the landing, they were moved north towards the Spanish Zone for the purpose of pinning down the enemy while the attack from the sea was being launched.

Authoritative sources estimate that Abd-el-Krim had a total of 80,000 men on the field, organized much as a regular army, of which 7,000 *askaris* constituted the most reliable contingent. After their defeat, the rebels surrendered 80,000 rifles, 200 machine-guns and 100 cannon —approximately one-half in the Spanish Zone and the remainder in French territory, which they had succeeded in penetrating.

The operations around Alhucemas lasted a few weeks; the Spanish losses were 33 officers and 381 men killed, and 109 officers and 1,746 men wounded. The French suffered no losses there, apart from a limited number of casualties when their ships were hit by Moorish shells.

The landing, planned by the Spanish General Staff, was a classic of its kind. At first the Moors did not offer much resistance; apparently their plan was to allow their opponents to disembark and to attack them later, on ground previously selected for the purpose. Eventually, resistance became severe. Every inch was disputed by the Riffis, and for some time the outcome was in doubt. Finally the Spaniards won. Alhucemas was a decisive operation, and it put an end to fighting of a serious nature in the Spanish Zone. Eight months later, with the support of the French on and north of the Warga, Spain brought the war to a successful conclusion, two and a half years after General Primo de Rivera had assumed command in Morocco. The whole territory was subdued and opened up to peaceful penetration in a matter of months. Spain soon made fast friends of her former enemies, and the peace which she established with them continued until the Spaniards withdrew from Morocco and has not been broken since.

In May 1926 I returned to Morocco, hoping to accompany Colonel Fernando Capaz on his march through the mountains of Gomara, which were still in enemy hands. But Capaz, who was shortly afterwards promoted to the rank of General, and later shot by the Republicans in Madrid for his refusal to fight on their side at the outbreak of the Civil War, had already left with his men, and on 25 May I called at the High Commissariat to take leave of Primo's successor, General Federico

Berenguer. As we were quietly talking in his office the door burst open and a youthful-looking officer—I failed at first to notice the crossed swords on his epaulettes which in Spain denote a General's rank—dashed in and announced that Abd-el-Krim had surrendered to the French. The officer was General Manuel Goded, Chief of Staff in Morocco, later shot by the Republicans in Barcelona for his part in the national rising against them. He was highly elated by the news. Abd-el-Krim had been a fugitive since his defeat in Alhucemas; he was mainly responsible for the massacre of a large number of Spanish troops, who were cruelly tortured at Annual before being killed. But though Abd-el-Krim's capture by the French incensed the Spaniards, for it meant that he had escaped them, it implied the end of Moorish resistance in Morocco and heralded an era of total peace.

Seventeen months after this, in October 1927, I went from London to Morocco for King Alfonso's visit with Queen Victoria to the principal towns in the Protectorate. Tetuán, its capital, gracefully set against the gentle slopes of Yebel Dersa and the crags and cliffs of the Gorgues range, which for long had been a rebel fortress, was ablaze with festivities in honour of her royal guests. To the flush and ardour of a triumphant army the brilliance of the East was added at the very gates of Europe. Tribes from the surrounding countryside, for years loyal to their Sultan and to the Spanish Crown, were trooping in to swear allegiance together with others lately subdued. The glamour of the events which I witnessed in a few days exceeded my wildest expectations.

The enemy had raided the city only three years before, when it had been dangerous to stay after dusk at *La Hípica*, a country club not far from the sea where people rode and played tennis and *pelota*, for at sundown snipers would start shooting. One night, while visiting a friend in his lovely Moorish house on the outskirts of Tetuán, we hammered on the shutters of a window that refused to close. In an instant a miniature battle flared up, prompted by the belief that our hammering was really rifle fire—from the Spaniards at the natives, or the natives at the Spaniards, nobody knew. Now it was peace, and thousands of Moors with veiled women at their side were filing past the King and Queen of Spain, on foot or on their Arab steeds, to salute their Sultan's ally and present him with every kind of gift. Troops had preceded them—cavalry and infantry units of the Spanish Regular Army, the Foreign Legion, Moorish regulars and *harkas*, more elated even than their European comrades and somewhat at a loss now that their joint success had ended the struggle which constituted their normal mode of life.

Sixteen months had elapsed since the conclusion of hostilities, but in this space of time, with scant means at his disposal, Miguel García de la Herrán, a General in the corps of engineers and one of Primo's principal assistants—he was taken from a hospital bed nine years later in Madrid and shot by the Republicans for his refusal to serve under them—had designed and built a military road from one end to the other of the territory. To prove that it was passable, he planned to drive over its entire length while King Alfonso and Queen Victoria sailed with Primo de Rivera from Ceuta to Melilla. I was thrilled when de la Herrán invited me to accompany him.

It was the first time in history that an overland journey had been attempted between the two extreme points of the Spanish Protectorate in Morocco, and I was about to see a vast expanse of mountainous country no European had ever travelled on. We left Ceuta one day at dawn and reached Melilla early the next morning, without resting on the way. The distance was approximately two hundred and fifty miles, and we would have covered it quicker had we not halted to inspect new camps and road stretches still under construction, some of them cut through the cedar forests of Ketama, where the slopes, thick with the right kind of snow in winter, are ideal for skiing.

The garrisons on the way received us enthusiastically. So friendly were they, and so anxious for news of King Alfonso's reception in Tetuán, that progress was slow. Dusk fell long before we entered the area around Alhucemas, scene of the fighting two years back. Past midnight, a punctured tyre, our only mishap throughout the trip, brought us to a stop on the outskirts of a village—Axdir, Abd-el-Krim's own stronghold and headquarters of the Beni-Urriaguel, fiercest and most warlike of his tribes. By the light of a wan moon I saw the eerie shapes of half a hundred Riffis, ghost-like in their drawn hoods and *djellabas*, advancing silently towards us. We had no escort, and no arms. All the tribesmen wanted was to offer us hospitality and assistance. Primo's victory had indeed been thorough.

We continued through the night. The sun had barely risen when we reached Melilla, our faces caked with yellow dust. Hungry and tired, we narrated to King Alfonso the story of our journey, which I brought to London with me and was published in *The Times*.

PART IV

CHAPTER THIRTEEN

The Fall of the Dictatorship and the Monarchy

In 1928, by royal appointment, I became regional delegate of the Spanish National Tourist Board in Andalusia, the Canary Islands and the Spanish Protectorate in Morocco. My headquarters were in Seville. Entrusted with a wonderful area, for three consecutive years I worked hard to develop it and was also a close observer of the events that changed the history of Spain during a fateful period. It was in Seville, in the spring of 1929, at the opening ceremony of the great Ibero-American Exhibition in the Plaza de España, that I saw General Primo de Rivera for the last time. He made the inaugural speech standing before a magnificent tapestry from the royal collection, one of several set up in a huge open space partly covered with gardens and encircled by stately buildings, their tall red towers rising against a pure blue sky. With him on the dais were the King and Queen, surrounded by Cabinet Ministers, ladies of the Court, Grandees of Spain, the Diplomatic Corps and distinguished guests from the participating nations. The scene was brilliant and the weather perfect. Cavalry squadrons provided the escort, bands played, jewels glittered, decorations shone, and uniforms and flowers were a mass of colour. Eight months afterwards, in January 1930, Primo de Rivera's rule came to an end. Two months later he was dead.

Had he received the support of those most qualified to give it, his mild and efficient dictatorship would have saved the Monarchy and avoided the armed strife that broke out in 1936. The majority were grateful for the benefits which his government brought to the nation. The working classes, content for the most part because strikes and outrages had ended, did not actively oppose Primo. Labour leaders maintained good relations with him, for lack of an alternative, or because it suited their long-term policy to do so. Others were more industrious.

Ousted politicians, certain financial interests, and a small number of Generals whose incompetence in Spanish Morocco Primo's victory had lit up for all to see, never forgave his achievements. That a practically unknown army man should have taken charge of public affairs and accomplished, in a comparatively brief space of time, what others had so signally failed to do, was too much for certain people. Strangely enough, their opposition was encouraged by an influential sector of the aristocracy, too short-sighted or too mindful of their alleged personal interests to abstain from criticism and intrigue.

Together they laid siege to the Crown with demands for Primo's downfall and a return to 'normal' government—the type of government which had been steadily pushing Spain down the slope for years—arguing among themselves that the conclusion of hostilities in Morocco and the improvement in economic affairs discounted a recurrence of labour troubles and covered the risk of mismanagement and stagnation. The capacity for destruction shown by some who are incapable of constructive work is an endless source of wonder, and it was brought to bear upon the situation. Suddenly, those who had supported Primo began to abandon him. He groped for a new footing, and failed to find it. One day, early in 1930, his term of office terminated as quietly as it had begun, without riots, street scenes, or shooting. So filled with accomplishment had it been that few realized the full significance of the event.

'General Primo de Rivera'—and I quote from *The History of Spain, 711–1931*, by Professor Louis Bertrand, a Frenchman, and Sir Charles Petrie, an Englishman, published in London by Eyre & Spottiswoode, 1934—'was very far from being the ruthless military despot of tradition. He possessed all those Andalusian characteristics which have enabled men of the south to play so large a part in the history of Spain. An unfailing courtesy, a power of leadership, and a very sincere devotion to his Church were his most notable qualities.'

Primo loved and trusted the Spanish people. I myself heard him voice his feelings for them on more than one occasion. His whole ambition was to serve them and improve their lot. For his home town, Jerez, he had a special weakness; never did he fail to mention it by name when drinking a toast with his brother officers in Morocco. 'I raise my glass,' he would say, 'filled with a generous wine, wine from Jerez, the land where I had the honour of being born . . .' He liked nothing better than to stroll through the streets of Madrid alone or unescorted, save for a friend, with no thought for the possibility of an attempt on his life, and he would do this even during the carnival season, when the streets were filled with masked people. A born gambler, he maintained the ban on gambling throughout his term of office, during which he never staked a penny on a card or a horse. Yet he would discourse amusingly and with gusto about incidents witnessed at card-tables in his earlier days. He won people easily with his smile, his southern wit and his sincerity, and always had a neat phrase for a pretty girl. His sense of humour and his joy of living were matched with an infinite capacity for hard work. He listened patiently to his visitors, even to those more concerned with private worries than with public business, but once he set his course on an important matter it was hard to make him waver from it. He had the class a man should have to know whether others have it, but the trust he placed in human nature prevented him from forestalling his enemies and countering them before they compassed his ruin.

Though victory in Morocco had proved him an imaginative soldier, at the height of his power he never conceived how rapidly the political errors for which he was responsible would help his immediate successors to reverse his basic policy and open the door to revolution and chaos. He had hesitated between a return to what he himself sometimes called 'a normal form of government', meaning the form of government which he had overthrown and replaced because it had proved inoperative in Spain, and a dictatorship such as his own, essentially constructive despite the fact that, to prolong it, it had been impossible to devise a working system capable of obtaining national support. While his opponents attacked his citadel, he looked for resources to bridge the gaps which opened all around him. Key positions were gradually filled by men whom he could not trust. Editorial firms, the principal chairs in the universities, the top posts in newspapers and news agencies fell into the hands of his enemies. The intellectuals closed their ranks against him. The Spanish press silenced his achievements and forced him to publish official notes which reminded the people of what he had done. Even his victories in Morocco were overlooked, or attributed to the French, thus giving rise to a legend which persists in many countries to this day.

Too busy with the cares of office, at first he did not understand what was happening. He realized it too late, a few weeks after his downfall, and the evidence of what it was bringing about broke his heart. Ten months after the brilliant opening of the Spanish-American Exhibition, on 16 March 1930, he died suddenly one morning, while his daughters were at mass, in a small hotel run by a compatriot in Paris, the Hotel Mont Thabor, in the rue Mont Thabor, where he was staying to escape the strain and pressure of the march of events at home. Don Miguel Primo de Rivera may not have possessed the ability to steer through waters not only turbulent but treacherous, but he was a magnificent administrator, just, generous and fair-minded, a fine soldier, and a great Spaniard.

Instead of bolstering up the Monarchy and defending it with a policy calculated to weather the storm that burst at the end of the dictatorship, Primo's immediate successors pointed to his mistakes and cast some of the blame for them upon the Crown. Primo had set a course to starboard—the thing now was to swing the wheel to port, although port in this case was no harbour. To make it worth while, the break with the past had to be thorough; one after the other, controls were relaxed in quick succession. Little was done by those in power to bridge the gaps between the Dictator and his opponents or between the Dictator and the Throne. There was no attempt to continue the work that had brought Spain to almost unprecedented heights of prosperity and internal peace. Libellous publications blackmailed or threatened the Administration, deriding the dictatorship for its achievements and denouncing it for its zeal to get things done. 'Spain is bankrupt!' shouted a member of the new Cabinet, intent on pouring obloquy on the ablest Finance Minister that Spain had known in a century—Calvo Sotelo. His words dragged the peseta to levels never reached in Primo de Rivera's time.

Nobody tried to discredit the previous government by endeavouring to surpass its accomplishments. While they harped about past responsibilities, the new men did not recognize—they lacked the stature to do so—the identity of those who would most probably benefit by their weakness, and they persisted in this attitude though the crisis called for strength. For the second time in a brief period, others were more active. Republicans and Socialists entered the arena, and in doing so and selecting the right moment for action they gave evidence of an insight that waned progressively once they were in office. The thing to do now was to abuse the past. None would surpass them in this endeavour, nor would any be more generous in formulating promises for the future.

The sky was the limit; the target was the Crown, which did nothing to help itself. Once it came tumbling down, the last barrier would have fallen. A decisive step in this direction was taken when King Alfonso, under pressure from all sides, entrusted the formation of a new Cabinet to Don José Sánchez Guerra, who chose his Ministers from the members of the Republican Revolutionary Committee, then undergoing sentence in a Madrid prison for conspiracy against the Monarchy. Passive for years and almost forgotten, its enemies were not lacking now in diligence. They sealed their pacts stealthily and made secret plans without showing their hand or revealing their power.

For over two centuries, since the House of Habsburg was replaced on the throne of Spain, every deep crisis in Spanish national affairs has been confronted with a choice between authority and dissolution. Once more the dilemma had arisen, and this time the alternative paths could not be more divergent. Only seven years before, democracy within the Monarchy had proved inoperative. Because of its mistakes, though the apathy of the people was more to blame, the dictatorship which succeeded it also vanished into thin air, without leaving a semblance of continuity. Many, with the best of faith and a total lack of acumen, persuaded themselves that the right course now was a complete turn about towards a regime which had failed disastrously when given the chance to prove itself in the 1870's. Isolated outbreaks of a minor character in the military aerodrome at Cuatro Vientos, near Madrid, and at Jaca, a small garrison town in the Pyrenees, showed the Army to be divided in its loyalties and shaped the issues for those who thought that the ideal solution might well be found in a Republic. To clinch the matter, out-and-out demagogues swore that, when they triumphed, they would set up a republic of bankers, professors, bishops and priests.

Municipal elections were held throughout Spain on 12 April 1931. Parties loyal to the Crown carried 22,150 seats; the Socialist-Republican coalition, 5,775. Because the latter had triumphed in the more important cities, their victory was held to be decisive. Not even bayonets could now contain the popular will. To call out the troops, as General Cavalcanti would have done, was out of the question, and there was no possibility of forming a Cabinet under Don Juan de la Cierva, who gallantly offered to defend the Monarchy with colleagues selected specially for this purpose. Though the victors were taken by surprise, and many of their leaders were abroad, their representatives on the spot claimed the day. There were demonstations in Madrid. The rest of the nation remained calm, unconscious of what was happening in the capital and insensitive to its consequences. The Prime Minister, a feeble admiral somewhat more perceptive than most, explained that Spain had gone to bed a Monarchy and woken up as a Republic. He was right. Members of his cabinet, too weak or too undecided to resist, handed over the government when called upon to do so, desirous of avoiding bloodshed and of acting 'in accordance with the will of the people'—though not, incidentally, with the manner in which the people had expressed their will at the polls two days before. On 14 April, the Second Spanish Republic was proclaimed.

That same night Alfonso XIII left his beloved Spain, never more to set foot upon its soil.

CHAPTER FOURTEEN

The First Phase of the Spanish Republic

The downfall of the Monarchy shook Spain to its very foundation. Few had suspected the imminence of the event or realized its gravity, and the first impulse of most Spaniards was to support the regime and await developments. Civil servants, complying with their own inclinations or with the express desire of the King, who wished them to remain in their posts, pledged their loyalty to the Republic. The Church acquiesced to its rule. Army officers were urged by the Government to retire from active service with full pay, and many who were out of sympathy with the new order did so. The Right soon split, into a minority that hoped for a restoration, and a much larger group, potentially formidable but with little influence at the outset, that simply aspired to save religion, the principles of family life, and private property from the fate that had engulfed the Crown. A large part of the country remained neutral. The Left consisted of a small but determined number of Separatists, active Socialists, Anarchists of the nineteenth-century school of Bakunin, and Communists.

The inaugural utterances of the victors contributed little to assuage the misgivings which I shared with many. For over one thousand years Spain had been ruled by Kings. Whenever she had attempted to replace them, the experiment had ended in disasters the magnitude of which was aptly recalled in a moment of sincerity by Emilio Castelar, a politician and flowery orator of the old school, largely responsible for the advent of the First Spanish Republic. In June 1893, Castelar published an article in *La España Moderna*, a review much read at the time, in which, referring to that regime, he wrote: 'Let us evoke the tragic summer of the year 1873, when all idea of legality had vanished and Spain found herself in the throes of dissolution. Some Spanish provinces were attempting to restore the Crown of Aragon, others clamoured for an independent Galicia under English tutelage. Jaén was preparing to make war on Granada, a sister province. Salamanca feared that her famous University might be closed. Small towns were summoning their inhabitants to form part of preposterous constituent assemblies. There were daily riots and revolts. Peaceful citizens were murdered in the streets, there was a demagogic dictatorship in Cadiz, bloody rivalries in Malaga, open strife in Granada, mob rule in Seville and Utrera, arson in Alcoy, anarchy in Valencia and banditry in the Sierra Morena. Murcia and Castellón were a prey to insecurity. Valladolid ran with blood, there was piracy on the high seas, and coastal towns like Alicante and Almeria were frequently bombarded. Ruin, suicide and madness had become rampant all over the country.' This had happened because the Monarchy had fallen and a Republic been set up to replace it. Not without reason has the word *republic*, in idiomatic Spanish, long been synonymous with chaos.

The Second Spanish Republic had everything in its favour, except a resolute will to maintain internal peace no matter from what side the threat against peace might arise, and a measure of statesmanship that would soften the break with the past and steer towards gradual evolution. A fortnight sufficed to show up the new leaders. They had vague notions of their essential duties, even less qualifications for their tasks.

Labour Day—1 May 1931—was the signal for the Socialist demonstrations in Bilbao and Barcelona, where Anarchists and Communists showed signs of restlessness and representative bodies were already flirting with autonomy. On 16 February 1931 *Pravda* had instructed the Spanish branch of the Third International: 'Overthrow the Monarchy,' it had urged, 'and establish a government of peasants and industrial workers. Abandon moderation; what you need now is organized strife.' In August 1927 *La Vague Rouge* had published a brief paragraph informing its readers that according to *La Correspondencia Internacional Communista* of 29 June of that same year, the Spanish Communist Party had been recognized under the Third International. Its Central Committee had met clandestinely on 3 and 4 June, grouped together the delegates of seven different regional federations, and instructed them to campaign against the Dictatorship and the Monarchy, insist on an immediate withdrawal from Morocco, and work for the independence of Catalonia and the Basque Provinces. Vast public demonstrations and strikes were foreseen for the autumn. In *Yo Fuí Ministro de Stalin*—(I was a Minister with Stalin)—(Editorial América, México, 1953), Jesús Hernández, a prominent Spanish Communist who was Minister of Education with Largo Caballero and Negrín during the Civil War, and who turned against Stalinism after living in Russia, where he was a member of the Executive Committee of the Comintern, recalls that in *Europa Entre Dos Guerras*—(Europe Between Two Wars)—Jcaquín Bullejos, Secretary General of the Spanish Communist Party in 1931, revealed that 'The proclamation of the Spanish Republic had soon become a matter of urgent interest to the Communist International, which focused its attention on Spain and its small Communist Party.'

Pravda had no real cause for impatience; events were shaping nicely to its taste. The downfall of the Monarchy was followed by a prison riot in Valencia, where the inmates emerged from gaol after displaying unequivocal signs of their eagerness to share the new freedom. In Bilbao, convicts obtained immediate liberation. In Barcelona a soldier and a night-watchman were murdered, and a number of citizens wounded. In Seville I myself witnessed an outbreak of the same nature close to my house. The opening of the Casa de Campo, a former Crown property on the outskirts of Madrid, was the signal for destruction, perpetrated largely on budding trees and bushes. Magnificent coats of arms, sculpted on marble slabs and emblazoned on public buildings while Ferdinand and Isabella, the Habsburgs, and the Bourbons successively ruled Spain, were demolished, or obliterated with cement when their size and massive weight rendered demolition difficult. The dignified strains of the national anthem, devoid of all words or lyrics, were replaced by an unmelodious jig. Names of streets possessing historical significance or connected in some way with royalty were immediately altered. The colours of the national flag were changed. Principles hitherto considered essential to the peace and welfare of the community were uprooted and discarded as soon as they were denounced.

Opposition, which anywhere but in Spain would have seemed mild, first arose from a small group of Monarchists who met in Madrid to form a private club and elect officials. The meeting was held on 10 May. It took place with full permission of the authorities, and a representative of the Government watched the proceedings. Before its conclusion a large crowd, inflamed by a groundless rumour, forced an entry into the apartment where the meeting was being held and beat up the Monarchists. Whipped to frenzy by extremist propaganda, the rabble declared a general strike and subjected the capital to a night of terror. Similar outbreaks attained an unprecedented pitch of violence in other parts of Spain. They lasted three days, without the Government making the slightest attempt to suppress them. In Madrid the first edifice to go up in flames was the residence of the Jesuit Fathers, situated in a main thoroughfare. An adjoining church, works of art, and a library with 90,000 volumes were also reduced to ashes. Of outstanding passiveness was the attitude of the Minister of the Interior, a 'new Republican' called Miguel Maura who now lives quietly in Barcelona; Maura was responsible for maintaining order and had been warned in advance of what was going to happen. 'Let all the churches burn,' shouted one of his more fiery colleagues. 'They're not worth the life of a single Republican.' The same night ten churches, convents, and colleges, with their libraries, paintings, and sacred images, were destroyed in Madrid alone.

The trail of fire spread through the country with terrifying speed. Before my departure from Seville, four churches were burnt one night, among them the tiny chapel of San José, a jewel of Spanish Baroque art, today wondrously restored. In Cordoba, the Bishop's palace and the world-famous Mosque were attacked and suffered damage. Cadiz lost the Convent of Santo Domingo, one of the finest in the city. Two churches were burnt in Murcia together with Salzillo's masterpiece, an image of the Immaculate Conception. A dozen convents and churches were set on fire or looted in Valencia, and similar outrages shocked the inhabitants of Alicante, Granada, and lesser towns. In Santander the mob vented its spite on the Yacht Club, one of the best run in Europe. No city suffered more than Malaga, where fifty churches and convents were looted or destroyed. I was there shortly after and learnt that the orgy of incendiarism had been largely promoted by the recently appointed Military Governor, General José Caminero, who, acting on instruction from Madrid, had taken command and assumed full powers just before the disturbances broke out.

On 10 May 1931, shortly before midnight, my brother Enrique turned homewards after attending a cinema in Malaga with two close friends, like himself lieutenants in the Army reserve undergoing a period of training. As they left the theatre they heard that mobs were attacking churches in different parts of the town, and on their way home they saw a small group acting suspiciously near the Bishop's residence, a beautiful eighteenth-century building situated in a square next to the Cathedral. The Military Governor's quarters being only a few hundred feet away, they proceeded there to report what they had just heard and seen. General Caminero, a sentry told them, was probably asleep. They found him upstairs, awake and wearing pyjamas. He listened to their story, but declared himself unwilling and unable to oppose the 'will of the people'. The three officers stressed the gravity of the situation and pleaded hard with the Governor for action, arguing that the mob close to the Episcopal Palace was a small one and would disperse before a show of force, however slight. When Caminero maintained that he had no specific orders, my brother requested permission to summon a platoon. He and his friends then helped the General into his uniform and escorted him to the square, where they saw the troops arriving and the rabble taking to its heels. Meanwhile, Caminero had thought things over. Insisting that the people's wish could not be opposed, he dismissed the soldiers and confined them to barracks, whereupon the mob returned and burnt the Bishop's Palace and a seminary adjoining it.

Previous to this, General Caminero had obtained from the Bishop of Malaga a list of all the convents and churches in the city. He needed it, he said, 'to protect them should an emergency arise'. Through an oversight, the name of a small Cistercian chapel was omitted from the list. It was one of three religious edifices that escaped the flames in Malaga on 11 May 1931. The other two were the Cathedral, entirely built of stone, and the Church of La Victoria, which happened to adjoin the Military Hospital. Reduced to ashes in similar buildings were some of the finest religious sculptures in the world, among them Pedro de Mena's masterpieces, the lovely 'Virgin de Belén,' the impressive Christ in Santo Domingo, and the 'Virgin de las Lágrimas'—Our Lady of the Tears—in Los Mártires, before which I had seen an English girl weep with emotion two years before. Because a relative of mine hid it, another fine image of Our Lady, also by Pedro de Mena, exists today in Malaga in the church of La Victoria, but a score of his best works were burnt in the city. A small display of energy would have averted this irreparable loss, but Caminero simply sent a telegram to the Government, saying, 'The burning of churches has started and will continue tomorrow.' He fled the country when fighting broke out, five years later, and has kept himself out of it ever since.

All over Spain the incendiaries were ably directed. Religious buildings do not flare up simultaneously owing to spontaneous combustion. In Madrid their leader was a South American, large-eyed and effeminate, expelled as a Soviet agent from other lands. In Malaga the mob was roused to action by two well-dressed youths, an Argentinian and an Italian, mild-mannered, efficient, polite. Before setting fire to the Convent of the Assumption, where my three sisters had been educated, they called on the Mother Superior and begged her to remove the other nuns and their wards to a safer place. They disliked the idea of anybody being hurt once they started their work. To the Reverend Mother's pleas for help the authorities remained obdurate, and the convent and its school were razed to the ground.

There was a small convent, with a chapel, opposite the house where an uncle of mine, Juan de la Cruz Bolin, lived in Malaga with his family. The night that churches were burnt there, a rabble appeared, took from the chapel altar-pieces, paintings, crucifixes and sacred images, and piled them up in the street. My uncle begged the mob to spare the works of art, which, he insisted, were now the property of the nation. While he spoke, the wife of a local butcher, known as a violent Red, drew near and said, 'You'll regret your words some day.' The dump was duly set on fire; when civil war broke out, my uncle was taken from his home and shot.

I belong to the brotherhood of Our Lady of La Macarena. Her image is one of the loveliest in Seville and was formerly in the church of San Gil, burnt by the Communists in the summer of 1933. The present chapel, built by General Queipo de Llano during the Civil War, stands on the site of a nearby tavern known as Cornelio's Bar, which Republican troops demolished with field-pieces in the course of this same conflict. Not long ago, while La Macarena was being prepared for her annual procession—a dazzling event in Seville's famous Holy Week—I requested the sacristan to tell me how the image had been saved when the Reds burnt San Gil. 'Ask over there,' he said, pointing to an aged charwoman who was scrubbing the floor on her knees. 'When I heard that the Reds were going to burn San Gil,' the char-woman told me, 'I feared greatly for Our Lady. She's not heavy; all the image has is head and shoulders. So I wrapped her in her robes, with the lining on the outside, and took her in my arms and rushed home. I hardly knew what to do, my place is so small, but I made up the bed with a pair of fresh sheets and tucked her inside. She was there quite some time; I didn't tell a soul.' 'And where did you sleep?' I asked. 'Oh,' she said, 'while Our Lady was with me I slept on the floor.'

About this time, many of those who had originally supported the idea of a Republic began to regret their decision. 'I would not have cast my vote for it had I known it was going to win,' said Bergamín, a former Minister of the Crown whose ambitions had been thwarted by the Dictatorship. His feelings were shared by thousands who out of recklessness or bravado had initially sided with the Left. It was too late to repent. In four weeks, their illusions about a conservative republic had vanished into thin air.

The regime needed a Constitution; it repudiated all the teachings of history and sought inspiration from the national charters of Austria, Weimar, Czechoslovakia, Mexico and Uruguay. Three weeks of hurried cribbing and translation sufficed to mould the supreme rules of a new political order. In a land where parliamentary government had failed, a single chamber was entrusted with almost unlimited power; in a profoundly religious nation, the Constitution abrogated religion; in a country with widely different regions, the way was cleared for separatism without a thought for the risks which such a step might imply for the unity of the nation as a whole. The new charter injected a Socialist spirit into labour regulations, recognized the right to expropriate without compensation, and declared that Spain renounced not only religion but also war, adding that her inhabitants were now welded into 'a democratic republic of workers', a statement that provoked hilarity in many quarters, for most workers were now usually on strike.

Before parliament could approve the Constitution, a 'Law for the Defence of the Republic' cancelled the rights and liberties guaranteed by the new charter, empowered the Government to suspend newspapers indefinitely, close meeting-places and clubs, imprison or exile citizens, seize industrial concerns, forbid public meetings, dismiss public servants, or suspend them from the execution of their duties.

Communism spread. Its active membership, 1,800 at the time the Republic was proclaimed, rose rapidly to 12,000, plus another 8,000, enrolled in the party's 'Youth Movement'. Peasants razed farms and outlying buildings, felled olive trees and cork woods, stole crops or burnt them. The expulsion of the Cardinal Primate of Spain, followed by that of the Jesuits, and the closing of the military Academy at Saragossa, the Spanish Sandhurst or West Point, of which General Franco was Director—his farewell address to the cadets there was a model of forbearance and soldierly spirit—stirred deep resentment in two quarters which till then had shown no sign of opposition. Labour troubles, unrest, and a profound mistrust of the new rulers, now shared by all classes, kept the country in a chronic state of panic and stagnation. In twelve months alone there were 776 strikes in Seville, of which the workers won 775. A series of minor riots in the same city culminated in a revolutionary outbreak strongly influenced by Communist agitators.

Genuine Republicans were now perturbed. They had goaded the masses with demagogic speeches, made promises which could not be fulfilled and awakened hostility in a large sector. It was difficult to control public opinion, for their own ranks lacked men with stabilizing power and statesmanship. Azaña, the regime's first Premier, of whom Unamuno once said, 'Beware! He is a writer without readers capable of promoting a revolution simply for the sake of being read,' was noting these facts in his secret diary, stolen from him during the Civil War by one of his more trusted aides. On 9 December 1932 he wrote there: 'How can anybody govern a nation at the head of a pack of imbeciles? Marcelino Domingo'—the Minister for Agriculture—'knows nothing about agriculture; Albornoz'—the Minister of Justice —'is an ignoble creature; de los Ríos'—the Minister for Education, who later enjoyed considerable prestige in the United States, where he represented the Republic—'is a pedant, unreliable and fanatical; Prieto'—a Socialist leader—'belittles everything.'

Other critics were not less severe. Ortega y Gasset, the philosopher, summed up current failings in a speech at the Cortes, when he admonished its members to refrain from acting as 'clowns, tenors, or wild boars', and in an article in *Luz*, 16 June 1932, when he called the new Constitution 'deplorable, devoid of head and feet and lacking the organic matter usually found in bodies between the head and the feet.' Ministers bore the mark of improvisation. The parties to which they belonged had imposed them on the nation, and the mere fact of their holding office, whether representative or executive, in no way reflected the working of a selective process. De los Ríos liked to boast that the regime was working wonders for the progress of education, but two years after the advent of the Republic the need for schools was greater than ever. Many of the best had gone up in flames with their laboratories and libraries, and the kind of teaching which appealed to de los Ríos hardly improved the minds and morals of those who received it.

'Can we allow the masses to think,' cried Azaña on 20 October 1931, 'that the Republic is impotent and inefficient?' The belief was gaining ground, though only six months had elapsed since the proclamation of the new regime. Names of villages hitherto unknown—Feria, Castil-blanco, Arnedo, Magacela, La Coronada and many others—now filled headlines, and newspapers reported riots enacted in them or published pictures of Civil Guards, stretched out in death with working men and peasants. The new leaders seemed to regret that they had won power without a bloody revolution. Public opinion was hesitant about a course of resistance; some felt that force would have to be used to overthrow a government bent on splitting Spain into opposing factions —'Azaña,' Maeztu wrote, 'does something every day to goad the opposing sides against each other'—others hoped for a measure of good sense from the victors once the first flush of triumph had cooled down, or for a decision from the polls, should opportunity arise to contest them.

On 10 August 1932, General Sanjurjo's short-lived revolt broke out. It was a move from the Right, hastily prepared, gallantly supported by a group of high-minded men, and directed solely toward the re-establishment of law and order—the very least a nation can demand from its rulers. To describe his aims, Sanjurjo quoted extensively from the identical manifesto which Republicans and Socialists had jointly signed when they forced the King to leave the throne, with a notable difference: that whereas the charges against the Crown had been prac-tically devoid of substance, these same charges, after sixteen months of Republican rule, reflected real unhappiness and unrest. Moreover, to the original inventory of grievances Sanjurjo added a list of complaints never heard of before in Spain.

The Government, warned in advance, countered the movement in Madrid. Its main source of information was a lady of easy virtue, who told what she knew to obtain a free pardon for her boy-friend, a zealous party to the revolt who had failed to keep his mouth shut. As they advanced at dawn to attack the Ministry of War, the conspirators were met by a hail of bullets; forced to withdraw, they left behind nine dead and twenty wounded. The rebellion triumphed easily in Seville, with Sanjurjo there at its head, but on hearing of its failure in Madrid the General surrendered, was tried and condemned to death, a sentence later reduced to imprisonment for life. One hundred and fifty of his alleged supporters were banished without trial to Villa Cisneros, a bleak settlement on the edge of the Sahara Desert from which, emaciated and starving, they escaped a few months later in an open barque and reached the hospitable shores of Portugal after weeks of hazardous navigation.

All of them were dispossessed of their landed properties, a fate also meted out to 400 members of the nobility who, with hardly an exception, had taken no part in the rising. Some fifty Ambassadors, Ministers and First Secretaries were thrown out of the Diplomatic Service, allegedly for holding ideas to which they had given no expression, probably to make room for others, more pink than themselves. One hundred and fourteen newspapers, among them all the leading dailies, were suppressed for months on end, a measure which deprived me of my pay during an equal period of time—I was now London Correspondent of Madrid's *A.B.C.*—though all I had done was to read about the rising in foreign papers.

Sanjurjo's revolt was not entirely futile, and its lessons were not wasted on those of us who, four years later, rose in arms to overthrow the Republic. After the revolt failed, attempts from the extreme Left became more frequent. Early in 1933 an Anarchist rebellion flared up in several regions, and though it died out quickly for lack of support, the insurgents were well armed—Barcelona provided them with 10,000 bombs, and they had ample supplies of sub-machine-guns and pistols from other sources. The Government, unnerved by these trends, issued orders of unprecedented rigour: 'No prisoners and no wounded! Shoot 'em in the guts!' On 12 January 1933 their instructions were scrupulously carried out at Casas Viejas, a small and isolated village in the foot-hills of Cadiz, where destitute peasants, bewildered to the pitch of frenzy by propaganda of the vilest kind, were preparing to set up a new order known as '*Comunismo Libertario*'. According to the official version, fourteen of these peasants were shot and killed by the police, who also set ablaze a straw hut which burnt to a cinder before its desperate defenders could escape. The Republic was reaping as it had sown. A storm of protests rose through the country, an inquiry was instituted and elicited nothing, and heated debates were held in the Cortes, where Martínez Barrios, a prominent Republican, denounced the regime and declared that it had swamped Spain in 'mud, blood and tears'.

He was not alone in this way of thinking. *La Tierra*, a Madrid Left-wing daily, hailed the Republic's second anniversary—14 April 1933—

with the statement that its first two years constituted an ignominious era—'an era of crime, mass imprisonment, endless persecution, hunger, terror and hate.' Sánchez Román, a distinguished University professor who had played a part in the regime's advent to power, described the situation mildly on that same day in *El Imparcial* by saying that 'citizens lived in constant fear'. *La Vanguardia* repeated this in Barcelona two months later and added that people were being 'continually robbed, shot down or bombed to pieces'. The once prosperous capital of Catalonia had again fallen prey to anarchy. About this time—March 1933—the Economic Federation of Andalusia, an important, non-political body with headquarters in Seville, petitioned the Government with the following words: 'We are victims of perpetual strikes. Every day we are threatened, insulted or attacked. No longer can we suffer such a state of affairs. If our factories are useful, we respectfully demand they be protected. If it is considered necessary to nationalize them under Socialist control, let this be rapidly done.' The Government did nothing. Soon afterwards, on 20 May, Don Pedro Caravaca, the Federation's secretary and in happier years one of the ablest organizers of the Ibero-American Exhibition in Seville—I worked closely with him during that period—was shot dead as he drove to his home in an open carriage.

Five months after the advent of the Republic I arrived in England with my wife and son as London Correspondent of the Madrid newspaper *A.B.C.* I had offered to work for the new regime, but without glancing at my record its rulers had dismissed me from my post in Seville the moment they took over. Our journey from Malaga to the French border, six hundred and fifty miles away, provided me with an insight into the manner in which the temper of the people was being changed. Rabid propaganda had transformed smiling peasants into sullen, scowling boors, who cursed and wished you bad luck. The second stage of their indoctrination was now in progress; they were being taught to hate anybody who appeared to be better off than themselves. When you asked a question the reply was a threat, accompanied as likely as not by a stone or a brick deftly hurled in the direction of your car.

My main concern in London was about events at home. I followed them with passionate interest; every day I received a batch of news-papers from Madrid and another batch from San Sebastian. All attacked the Republic, and when the Government suppressed them I obtained pro-Republican papers from friends in the Embassy and lapped up their contents with equal zeal. Though partial to the regime as such, extremist journals also criticized one or other of the factions represented in the Cabinet, thus providing me with good reading. I saw every Spaniard who came to England and questioned him eagerly. My sources of information were numerous and reliable. I used them to write articles in English newspapers, or for my talks before political clubs and organizations of varied hue, where I was usually listened to and occasionally heckled.

CHAPTER FIFTEEN

A King in Exile

King Alfonso came frequently to London, and I often saw him there. During his years of exile he stayed at Claridge's, usually for brief spells, shopping a little, going to the theatre, of which he was fond, and seeing old friends. My wife's father—a grandson of the Duke of Rivas, the romantic poet and author of *Don Alvaro o La Fuerza del Sino* (*La Forza del Destino*)—had commanded the Húsares de Pavia, a cavalry regiment that took turns in mounting guard at the Royal Palace in Madrid. Don Alfonso would invite us to lunch or dinner, and sometimes we accompanied him to a show or to an afternoon's drive round Richmond or in Windsor Great Park. On these occasions, as always, he talked only of Spain. The affairs of his country obsessed him, and it saddened him to know that conditions there had changed for the worse since his departure. He thought constantly of its people and could hardly resign himself to enforced inaction, yet he was never morose, nor did adversity affect his sense of humour. At no time did I hear him utter a complaint; until the day of his death he acted as a true King of Spain, retaining his dignity and irresistible charm and the warm smile that was one of his chief attractions. No monarch was ever more gracious, more understanding, or more kind.

He was quick to make up his mind, and though he did not object to advice, as often as not he would disregard it. One day, while staying at the Ritz, his favourite hotel in London during the twenties, he summoned a barber to trim his hair. There was a long delay, and finally the manager appeared with a worried expression and the news that the only barber available, a Spaniard, had been an anarchist in his youth. Much as His Majesty's entourage may have opposed any idea of the fellow waiting upon their royal master, the mere fact of his being a Spaniard was enough for Don Alfonso. They parted close friends, the barber with a signed portrait of his new customer, which from that day, suitably framed in silver, occupied a prominent position among the lotions and shampoos that filled a glass case in his shop, the Monarch with an invitation to visit the Spanish Club, an attractive institution of marked bohemian flavour with which his envoy in London would have nothing to do. In due course, despite the ambassador's opposition, Alfonso XIII went to the Club and received a rousing ovation from its members, some of whom, though life-long Republicans, ended by swearing that the best possible candidate to preside over a Spanish Republic was, to their latest way of thinking, none other than the King of Spain.

In his delightful *Laughter in the Next Room* (Macmillan & Co. Ltd., London, 1949), Sir Osbert Sitwell, speaking of the Russian Ballet in the time of Diaghilev, recalls that towards the end of the First World War 'its productions manifested a new accent, a new emphasis, more modern and with a Spanish tang occurring in them as a result of the long sojourn of the Ballet Russe in the Peninsula under the special patronage of the King of Spain, but for whom it would probably have had to be disbanded. (Indeed lovers of beauty owe a great deal to the late King Alfonso for his support of it, and Diaghilev always in subsequent years showed his gratitude by staging a special gala for the King when he paid one of his frequent visits to London).' And, in a footnote, Sir Osbert adds: 'King Alfonso was seldom gratefully used. In the 1914–18 war, in spite of his Austrian blood, he was practically the only friend the allies possessed in Spain. He maintained a private organization for procuring news of Allied officers who were prisoners of war. As many knew, it was most successful, but it cost him the equivalent of sixty thousand pounds a year. Yet the King never received, difficult as it is to believe, a single letter of thanks for his efforts! . . . Similarly, when he came over to England to try and get in touch with Ramsay MacDonald, in his second term of office as Prime Minister, in order to discuss the question of a United States of Europe, he met with nothing but rudeness from the newspapers and neglect from the authorities. I interviewed the King at this time, and was much impressed with his vision and grasp of affairs. When I asked him if I might put him in touch with H. G. Wells—a writer who, being an ardent republican, had attacked him in the past—the King had replied, 'Yes . . . and tell him I am in some ways a much more modern-minded man than he is. I have not stuck fast in 1900!'

King Alfonso's memory for people and their names brought to his mind minor incidents, forgotten by others soon after they had occurred.

One afternoon a chance remark led the conversation between us to the subject of Bravo, Padilla and Maldonado, three Spanish *comuneros* who in the sixteenth century staged a revolt against Charles V and paid for their daring with their lives. To honour Bravo's memory, King Alfonso had gone to Segovia, where a monument to the rebel was to be unveiled. Burgos Mazo, the Minister for the Interior, later an opponent of the Crown, was entrusted with the inaugural address. Somehow the Minister, instead of mentioning Bravo's name, repeatedly cited Maldonado's. Each time this happened the mayor of the city, deeply perturbed, leaned forward anxiously on the dais, cupped his hand to his mouth and corrected the Minister with the words, 'Bravo, sir,' whereupon Burgos Mazo would turn and thank him in a loud voice. King Alfonso found it hard to keep his face.

On another occasion, walking in the forests near Virginia Water, with rhododendrons in bloom and pheasants chucking off in alarm as they had done fifteen years before, when I paced these same woods while cramming Criminal Law and Procedure for an exam at the Inns of Court, the King spoke of his feelings on the fateful day when the Republic was declared and he drove in the dark from Madrid to Cartagena, escorted by his cousin, the Infante Don Alfonso de Orleans, and an A.D.C., the late Pablo Martín Alonso, who had fought well in Morocco, was to achieve distinction in the Civil War and in time became Minister for the Army under Franco. He left his wonderful palace through a secluded gate in the Campo del Moro, the lovely gardens, today beautifully restored, which beneath the building's western façade drop to the level of the Manzanares, Madrid's humble river. Alfonso XIII had been born in that Palace forty-five years before, 17 May 1886, a few months after the death of his father. That same day he had been proclaimed King. Now, at Cartagena, he was to embark for Marseilles, on the first stage of his exile from Spain.

While he drove through the night the notion that he might never return to his country did not even cross his mind. The Republic would fail, and his reign would continue once his supporters rallied round the ideal of a restoration. The tide that was sweeping him away would surely ebb once his people became weary of their new rulers and discovered that the charges levelled against him were trumped up and hollow.

To cast him from his throne, three main accusations were hurled at King Alfonso—that he had used his influence to further his private finances, that he had prolonged the war in Morocco, and that he had failed in his duty as a constitutional monarch. The first was a libel pure and simple; those who spread it had five years and every opportunity, including full access to files and documents, to substantiate their charges, but they did not unearth or publish a single fact to corroborate them. The second, like the first fabricated for consumption by the masses, falls apart as soon as it is scrutinized. The war in Morocco was the direct outcome of an international treaty to which Spain had become a party before the King was twenty-one years old, and when revolt flared in the territories assigned to her protection Spain was forced to act in accordance with her foreign commitments. The blame for the duration of the conflict rested with effete governments, or with the parliaments that controlled their policies. When Primo rendered action easier, the war was quickly brought to a successful conclusion.

The third charge had more substance, for Primo de Rivera's rule was certainly unconstitutional. But the King had little choice in a crisis caused by the inoperativeness of a system which in thirty years tried out 34 Premiers and 402 Cabinet Ministers and consistently failed to work. He had to find a way out or suffer the nation to wither before his eyes. The century that preceded Primo was disastrous for Spain and for its people; Primo's rule had been highly beneficial. Was it fair to blame the King for accepting or maintaining it, when everything else had proved unworkable? Primo de Rivera's greatest shortcoming was his inability to find a formula that would have prolonged his own regime and superseded, once and for all, a system that had brought the nation close to disaster. Had this been done, had a strong government been firmly established, the Monarchy would not have fallen, and there would have been no civil war.

The cruiser that carried King Alfonso next day from Cartagena to Marseilles had been carefully selected by the new rulers, and it was commanded by an officer more worthy of their trust than of the honour now assigned to him, a man who while he sailed across the Mediterranean inflicted every possible humiliation upon his royal passenger. For one who behaved as he did, a former Spanish Naval code prescribed treatment of a drastic nature—that he be lowered into the sea from the bow of his ship, a cannonball weighing down his feet, and hauled up at the stern after the vessel had passed over his body. The officer in question, however, lacked nerve to refuse Don Alfonso's parting request for the cruiser's battle colours. The King wished them for his shroud should he happen to die on foreign soil. His Majesty never parted from this flag; it was wrapped round his body when he died, in Rome, ten years later.

Some maintain that Alfonso XIII should never have left Spain in 1931. Had the issues been fought out then, they hold, countless lives would have been saved. Those who say this probably mean that the King's Ministers should have persuaded him to stay, calling on the armed forces to counter the threat against the Crown, for the King himself was powerless to act or to withstand the pressure brought to bear for his departure. But the spiritual foundations of the Monarchy had been undermined for two hundred years, and the country was morally unprepared to defend the throne from the determined onslaught now launched to complete its destruction. King Alfonso had many friends, the Monarchy few adherents, and those who surrounded the throne believed that all they could do to thwart the impending revolution was to placate its leaders with the evidence of their own weakness, manifested in the desire to please them.

Among the so-called 'forces of the Right', hardly any had opened their eyes to the danger. According to some, all that these forces contributed to support their cause in Madrid during the campaign that led to the Republican triumph was 2,000 pesetas—eighty pounds sterling, or four hundred dollars. There had been ten Leftist posters in the streets for every Rightist poster, at least eight Republican meetings for every Monarchist meeting held. Feigned or real, indifference regarding Spain's form of government or to forms of government on the whole, as expressed by many who should have known better, was of the utmost assistance to the anti-Monarchist, anti-Christian coalition about to seize power. From his pulpit in a fashionable church a well-known preacher, the day the fateful elections took place, addressed his congregation thus: 'One of our leading radicals, asked to choose between a monarchy and a republic, has replied that what Spain needs is a revolution. What it needs, I say, is Christianity!' There was no Christianity on the Left. Liberal slogans had captured many minds, the masses were being lured by Socialism, extremist propaganda was subverting the unwary, and at the eleventh hour Madrid was still a confident and contented city, ignorant of the humiliations and anguish which the new regime was to inflict upon her people and unprepared to oppose the dire threat that was rapidly taking shape.

The will to fight, which in 1936 fired a national rising, had not yet been kindled; it needed years of bitterness and tribulation to come into being. King Alfonso left the country that night because he had no other alternative. 'I do not wish' he said to his advisers and to his family, 'that for my sake a single drop of blood be shed.'

While people in Spain were steeling themselves against the inevitable crisis, in foreign countries an entirely mistaken concept of the Spanish situation was slowly gaining ground. Strengthened by conflicting newspaper reports there was a danger, regardless of what happened, that this false concept might prevail with the passing of time. Leftist tendencies were fashionable, the Republic had friends abroad. Few wished or dared to criticize it, and though it seemed puzzling that a government should be lauded for mismanaging a country, only yesterday Primo de Rivera had been censured for governing it well. The haze around me seemed to thicken; occasionally some light filtered through. Perhaps the praise that was being showered on the Republic had some connection with Spain's enviable strategic position, its proximity to Africa and to the American continent, its endless coasts and safe harbours on the Atlantic Ocean, the Mediterranean and the Strait of Gibraltar. If the fruit ripened till it rotted, Catalonia, the Basque Provinces, the deep Galician fjords, the Balearic Isles, the Canaries or one or other of them might drop into some nation's lap, or to phrase the contingency more diplomatically, into its sphere of influence—a likelihood which, at that very moment, Russia was contemplating with a smirk. As things went from bad to worse, praise for the Republic and for its leaders became louder in foreign circles dominated by the Left.

I spoke of this to the Duke of Alba, an old friend who came frequently to London and had much prestige in England. A great Spaniard, his political tastes—he was a Liberal—did not preclude him from opposing the extreme policies to which Spain was being subjected. Together, with the idea of getting the truth better known, the Duke of Alba and I set about to form a group of English 'Friends of Spain' well fitted to carry out work which could be of equal value to their own country and ours. Until some time after the Civil War began, the composition of this group was limited to its five original members—the Duke of Alba; Douglas Jerrold, director of the publishing firm of Eyre & Spottiswoode, editor of the *English Review* and a distinguished historian;

Sir Charles Petrie, author of widely read books and articles and currently engaged on his contributions to *The History of Spain, 711–1931*, already quoted on another page; Victor Raikes, a Member of Parliament whose presence in the House was an obvious asset; and myself. Soon we developed a not inconsiderable degree of influence in appropriate circles. Later the Marqués del Moral also joined us; he was active, persevering and influential. We met at regular intervals. Often the Duke was our charming and entertaining host. His knowledge of Spain and England, of the history of both countries and of others—he was President of the Spanish Royal Academy of History, an institution which had then temporarily lost its right to use the word 'royal'—was a source of delight to all. In his absence, the rest of us discussed the possibilities of the moment. My English friends were sympathetic and understanding and, when matters came to a head, of real assistance.

Thanks to their help I intensified my efforts to present a fair picture in England of what was happening in Spain. I had no lack of material. Republican papers, though still partial to the regime, were frequently as critical of its failings as were Right-wing publications. Part of what I said at lecture halls appeared to surprise my public as much as their own statements surprised me. At the close of a talk I once gave at Chatham House before the Royal Institute of International Affairs somebody stood up and, with a grieved expression, said, 'Is it not the case that the real cause of the trouble in Spain is the competition which Labour has to face from monasteries and convents?'

In 1933 I wrote a book about Spain. It was called *The Spanish Republic*. Eyre & Spottiswoode published it with the sub-title *A Survey of Two Years of Progress*, suggested by Mr Douglas Jerrold to promote its sale among those who thought that the making of sweets by nuns was a real cause of trouble in my country. The book was signed 'Anonymous', for to append my own name would have been risky. In London, daily, weekly and monthly publications reviewed it extensively, many of them quoting from its pages as did the leading provincial papers in Great Britain and Ireland and others as far away as the *Age*, in Melbourne. When a moderate government took office in Spain, a Spanish version of the book appeared and enjoyed a wide sale.

Had they not been so thick-skinned, the headings under which it was reviewed would have impressed Republican circles. 'Spain's Reign of Terror,' wrote the *Daily Mail*. 'Anarchy and Crime Exposed;

Republic a Fiasco, Spain "Drifting to Anarchy",' said the *Daily Telegraph*, inserting quotation marks for safety, but adding, of its own accord, 'Republic's Record of Oppression; Alleged Police Atrocities' and 'Peasants Massacred'. 'Spain Enjoys Her "Progress",' announced the *Morning Post*. 'Individual Rights Gone.' the *Nottingham Evening Post* drew attention to '500 Deaths in Disturbances Since Alfonso Left,' and the *Manchester Evening News* spoke of 'Spain's Era of Strife' and 'Many Gangsters'. Belfast's *Northern Whig* called the book 'A Scathing Indictment'. The identity of its author puzzled some. 'If he is a Spaniard,' said *The Times Literary Supplement*, '—and an Englishman would be hard put to it to muster the intensity of feeling he displays—either he has a command of the English language that is exceedingly rare among his countrymen, or has been singularly fortunate in his translator.' And, it went on to say, '*The Spanish Republic* contains an immense amount of matter lucidly compiled and set forth, the general exactitude of which cannot be disputed and which constitutes the most serious indictment yet printed in English concerning the Spanish Republic considered as a regime of democracy and liberty.'

CHAPTER SIXTEEN

The Second Phase

Opposition from the Right hardened rapidly during the first two years of Republican rule. It had become articulate within the ranks of Acción Nacional, an organization founded the day after the fall of the Monarchy by Don Angel Herrera, a prominent Catholic layman later ordained, now Bishop of Malaga and a Cardinal. Because, without supporting any specific form of government, it upheld religion, law and order, family life and private property, the right to work and a united Spain, the new group attracted all shades of opinion opposed to the excesses of the Left, including some who would have preferred to hoist a Monarchist banner. A few months later, its name was changed to Acción Popular by a government decree; at the same time, the use of its earlier appellation was prohibited. Señor Herrera resigned in favour of José María Gil Robles, a young and dynamic leader, and Monarchists withdrew from Acción Popular, which had now become acceptable not only to those who cared more for its principles than for a regime well fitted to defend them, but to Republicans of a conservative or near-conservative hue, who speedily reached an agreement with Gil Robles. For the first time since its advent, a Right Wing made its appearance within the Republic. Simultaneously, the possibility of the regime's eventual consolidation began to loom on the political horizon.

On 28 April 1933 municipal elections took place in certain parts of Spain. Leftists in power won 5,048 votes; 4,206 were cast for Republican opposition, henceforth considered as the regime's centre; 4,954 for the Right. Boroughs that voted against him were dismissed as 'rotten' by Azaña, but their verdict was overwhelmingly confirmed at the general elections in November of that same year. Passionately disputed, they were perhaps the only sincere contest of this kind ever held in Spain. Spanish women went to the polls for the first time in history. Their votes decided the issue. Socialists and their Left-wing allies won 98 seats; the Centre, 163; the Right, 212. A Cabinet of moderate tendencies was formed, representing the two major groups in Parliament. The Reds received it with an outburst of rioting, and 120 persons were killed. There had been 15,000 strikes since the establishment of the Republic, practically all of a political and revolutionary character; a new epidemic of strikes broke out, and separatists in Catalonia and in the Basque Provinces intensified their demands for autonomy. By April 1934 all save the more short-sighted could see that the extreme Left was determined to battle against any Cabinet that reflected, even mildly, the composition of Parliament after the polls.

This being apparent, a measure of strength should have been brought into play to maintain law and order and to consolidate the regime. For the failure to do this, three men share full blame: Alcalá Zamora, Lerroux and Gil Robles. Zamora, the President of the Republic, was under the influence of the Left and could not shake off his commitments. Lerroux's radicalism, though weakened by experience and time, still tainted his policy as leader of the Government. It bore the mark of earlier years, when he had dubbed his followers 'Young Barbarians' and addressed them in these terms: 'Pillage and sack this decadent civilization; destroy its churches and its gods, raise the veils worn by nuns and make mothers of them. Burn all title-deeds to private property and elevate the proletariat to judicial rank! Do not hesitate before sepulchres or altars! Fight! Kill!! Die!!!' Gil Robles, though gifted with no mean talents, did not enforce the political rights of his followers or stand up squarely to the growing Red menace.

Socialists seized the initiative. They resorted to strikes and arson, maintained the nation in a state of alarm and encouraged party members to assassinate peaceful citizens, attack buildings of all kinds and snipe at passers-by in public thoroughfares. Red militias were trained to beat up and murder more formidable opponents. They made subversive speeches. Echoing the words which *Pravda* had printed two years before, Azaña said at a meeting in Madrid, in April 1934, 'The time has come to abandon futile talk, party politics and parliamentary tactics! The time for our revolution has arrived!' Peasants were adjured to 'prepare for the struggle of all Spanish workers against the tyranny and terror to which they are subjected!' and told to 'fight under the leadership of the proletariat, follow the example set in the Soviet Union by Bolsheviks and their immortal Lenin,' and 'do as workmen and peasants did in Russia! Organize Soviets in Spain!'

To put this constructive programme into effect an attempt was made to declare a general strike, and though the call went unheeded by most, there were ominous signs in the country. Stocks of arms and ammunition were discovered in Madrid and other cities. Separatism flared again in Catalonia and in the Basque Provinces, where an absurd alliance had been forged between capitalists and Communists, Catholics and atheists. The Grand Orient and the two Internationals used their connections to flood the country with instructions. Nothing was done to counter them, though the Spanish police, with customary efficacy, unearthed not a few of these messages and brought them before the Government. Largo Caballero, an extreme Socialist leader, strove to unite factions hitherto at loggerheads and to establish a federation of republics, based on the Soviet model.

Plans for mass rebellion came to light. It was to have broken out in Madrid, where an unsuspecting newspaper of the Right had been selected to give the signal for its outbreak under the guise of an announcement regarding a funeral service in honour of an imaginary person, supposed to have died in Bilbao. Suitably decoded, the notice contained all necessary information about the date, hour and place of rising. On 11 September, large quantities of arms and ammunition were found in San Sebastian de Pravia, a small port on the coast of Asturias; they had been landed from the s.s. *Turquesa* after being hidden for two years in Cadiz, where the Azaña Government had piled them up to support a frustrated revolt in Portugal. More arms and more explosives appeared at Socialist headquarters in Madrid, also at the University City there, of which the famous Dr Negrin was Secretary. *Renovación*, a Socialist weekly, proclaimed: 'Our revolution is under way, and we need arms and ammunition to destroy the Police. Many death sentences will be signed. The younger members of our party will execute them enthusiastically!' Throughout September, another Socialist newspaper kept repeating 'Watch the Red lights! Next month may well be our Red October.' Meanwhile the Government, this time in the fumbling hands of a weakling called Samper, watched nothing, saw nothing, and took no action whatsoever.

On 4 October 1934, Samper was replaced by Lerroux, and three Cabinet posts out of fourteen were assigned to C.E.D.A., Gil Robles' party. They timidly reflected the composition of the Cortes as determined by the elections held a year before, but the Reds declared a general strike. The Government did not counter this move, nor did 'genuine' republicans, assuming any existed at this juncture, raise a finger to dissociate themselves from its consequences. 'Conservative' Republicans under Miguel Maura and 'national' Republicans under Sánchez Román supported the extremist manœuvre.

That the strike was for the most part a failure spoke highly of the Spanish workman's good sense. In Madrid, two were killed and several were wounded, but Socialists rioted with less zeal than their leaders had thought possible, and citizens awaited anti-Communists' signals to volunteer for public service. On the second day of the strike, a voice came over the radio, saying: 'Alarm clocks mark every hour, especially 4 p.m.' It meant action for the Falange, which José Antonio Primo de Rivera, a son of the Dictator, had founded the year before, for the Youth Movement which Gil Robles had inspired with civic zest, and for all who feared the rule of the Left. The Government called out troops despite the attempts made to subvert them. Were they with or against the Reds? Two companies of a foot regiment set out from their barracks to proclaim Martial Law; the Riot Act was read by an officer while soldiers presented arms. Contemptuous of Red bullets which were whizzing down from the roofs, the people of Madrid flocked to their balconies and cheered.

Catalonia was in a turmoil. Separatist tendencies were thriving there, promoted partly by catch-words like 'self-government' and 'autonomy', partly by the inoperativeness of parliamentary rule, and partly by the proclivity of some, in prosperous areas, to deprive the central government of the fruits of taxation and use them to remunerate lucrative posts, set up for their personal benefit. Local susceptibility to the charms of autonomous rule had waned perceptibly while Primo de Rivera governed with a firm hand, but it was stirred up again by the mixture of Republican misrule and Communism which spread unchecked once the Monarchy fell—Catalonia would have been an ideal area in which to inaugurate a Soviet experiment in Spain. Embittered by his defeat at the polls, Azaña turned up in Barcelona to promote an independent Catalan Republic, the surest way of embarrassing his successors in Madrid. Strangely enough, anarchists in Catalonia were all for national unity. Members of the Party, though not averse to sedition and violence, surprised their employers by offering to defend their factories and persons at the risk of their lives—a worthy gesture which fell short of making these rabid extremists eligible for directing a sound government.

At 8 p.m. on 6 October, the man who headed local rule in Barcelona overcame his trepidations and from a balcony in the lovely Palacio de la Generalidad addressed the crowd in familar terms. The time had come, he said, to break away from 'monarchists' and 'fascists' plotting to betray the Republic in Madrid. At long last the moment had arrived for 'liberal, democratic and progressive' Catalans to proclaim autonomy within their region. Loud and clear, his words resounded over the radio. They were picked up in the nation's capital, from where a state of war was decreed in Barcelona. To suppress the revolt the support of the military was indispensable. Part of the garrison favoured separatism, but the attitude of the remainder, including the General who commanded them, was in doubt. Five hundred soldiers posted themselves at strategic points in the city. A few shells from their field-pieces and some bursts of machine-gun fire sufficed to quench the ardour of the rebels, most of whom chose discretion despite eloquent entreaties from their leaders, who were apprehended before dawn.

Azaña was arrested while hiding on the balcony of a friend's apartment. With few exceptions the people of Barcelona had taken no part whatever in the outbreak, which cost their beloved city 46 dead and 117 wounded, plus structural damage to important buildings and many losses in the field of business. In Bilbao, a half-hearted attempt at autonomy fizzled out before sedition gathered impulse. But in Asturias the situation was extremely grave. As soon as I saw a chance of getting there, I left London for Oviedo, the Asturian capital.

CHAPTER SEVENTEEN

Revolt in Asturias

On the way from León to Oviedo I saw much evidence of recent fighting. Walls were pockmarked with bullet holes, houses had been blown up, destroyed by gun-fire or razed by fire. A column of troops had left León to engage the Reds, who, coming down from the north had met them half way, held their ground, and with machine-guns, well-posted snipers and barrels of dynamite sent rolling down with lighted fuses, inflicted severe casualties on the column until a Foreign Legion commander, General Amado Balmes, cleared the heights before advancing and forced the miners to their villages, where they were no match for his men.

The region of Asturias lies between a broken, wave-pounded shore-line on the Cantabrian Sea and range upon range of high sierras. In October 1934, it was ripe for revolution. Miners in the surrounding areas had been worked up by seditious propaganda and taught to handle dynamite expertly. Large quantities of arms and ammunition had been landed along the Asturian coasts. The gun factory at Trubia was plentifully supplied with shells, there were 20,000 rifles at another factory in La Vega, and a dynamite depot that could be easily looted in the first rush was conveniently situated on the field of action. The Azaña–Socialist Cabinet had passed through the Cortes a series of legislative measures divesting these establishments of their military status and allowing their workers to join extremist syndicates, a device of obvious value should violence be expedient to reverse the verdict of the polls.

Oviedo, a fine city of 100,000 inhabitants and the capital of Asturias, was attacked by an army of 30,000 miners who planned to seize the coalmines and subject the region to Communist rule. They captured the city rapidly, destroying large parts of it as they advanced. Wearing red Socialist shirts or blue Communist jerseys, they spurted from door to door, hugging the walls of the houses, and while they ran they unslung dynamite sticks from their belts, lit the fuses with cigarette-ends, and hurled them into doorways. Others poured petrol on the burning debris. Soon half a hundred buildings were in flames. The extent and nature of the resulting devastation exceeded anything I had seen in France during World War I, or, later, in Spain during the Civil War. Given dynamite and petrol, expert maniacs inflict more damage to edifices specially selected inside a town than an army shelling it from the outside for military reasons. An attacking force does not usually single out art treasures or seats of learning for destruction, nor does it train its guns on official buildings, smart shops or modern blocks of flats. Cannon, however accurate, obliterate their objective totally only after prolonged bombardment.

The havoc perpetrated in Oviedo by Socialists and Communists was thorough. On a single morning they loaded 21 tons of dynamite from stocks piled up in the local Communist centre and exploded dozens of tons in the city, where huge blocks of masonry littered the streets. Three tons were used to blow up the fine Provincial Institute, equivalent to a *Lycée* in France, and the shock that reduced it to rubble shattered a number of private houses in adjacent streets. Eighty buildings, the finest and most important in Oviedo, were demolished or gutted. A principal thoroughfare, the Calle Uría, lost practically every one of its imposing blocks of modern flats, offices and shops. In the oldest sector of the city all the churches and convents were destroyed. Also parts of the fine Gothic Cathedral, with its Holy Chamber, a twelfth-century relic that contained Romanesque statues of the twelve apostles and a priceless collection of jewels, dating from even earlier times, prodigiously restored after being practically pulverized. The seventeenth-century University was lost with its library of 100,000 volumes as were the Bishop's Palace, the old Law Courts, the Campoamor Theatre, the Central Market, a large hospital, and several hotels. Scores of shops, private houses and banks were looted before being set on fire. From one of the latter, Ramon González Peña, leader of the Socialist revolt, personally stole fourteen million pesetas, then worth £700,000. Peña fled from Spain during the Civil War and has not shown himself there since.

Four million cartridges were fired in the city during the revolt; a low daily average of ten rounds, let off by each of the thirty thousand miners who attacked it, would account for three million rounds in ten days. Many of them must have been aimed at the Cathedral's stately tower—the Reds called it *La Loba*, or 'She-Wolf', so fiercely was she defended—considerable parts of which were laboriously and beautifully restored after the Civil War. High up in that tower, a machine-gun manned by policemen poured a withering fire on rebels posted six hundred yards away or more. When they crept nearer, the police used their rifles or made sorties, in one of which their leader, Major Bueno, lost his life. All the houses opposite the tall tower, including the Marqués de Santa Cruz de Marcenado's lovely thirteenth-century home, bore the marks of bullets fired by the men in the Cathedral, some of whom managed to survive. In other parts of the city, handfuls of soldiers, Civil Guards and Police held their own against fearful odds.

The Reds were ruthless. Their mentality was a problem. Some had been led astray by their leaders and forced to choose between shooting others or being shot, but for the most part they were a frenzied horde that murdered soldiers, civilians, nuns and monks, with a ferocity they would not have felt without the incitements to which they had been subjected. Nobody could tell in what manner they planned to organize their future. A man I met, whose name was identical to that of the town's best-known surgeon, was pressed into service as such despite his protestations. He had never been inside a hospital, but it was not long before he found himself performing operations with two rifles pointing at his head. A mine-owner called Pedro Pidal, who was a friend of mine, saved his life thanks to his ability to speak French. The miners used him for imaginary talks over the radio with Monsieur Lebrun, the President of the French Republic, to whom he supposedly gave detailed information about the excesses committed by army planes that bombed 'defenceless miners'. Groups of rebels would burst into a house, order its occupants outside and start shooting at random from the windows. 'It was raining bullets in the streets,' a tobacconist's wife told me, pointing to gaping holes and broken rain-pipes, 'so we remained upstairs, lying on the floor. The walls seemed made of paper.' 'They broke into this convent,' the door-keeper said, 'and ordered the nuns to take away the children. They wanted to shoot at the Cathedral from our balconies.' 'I gave them all they asked for,' a young fellow admitted, 'plus 400 bottles of wine. What could I do? When they were just about to shoot me, one of them said I was a good chap and thus saved my life.' 'Everybody had to sleep in the hall,' said the proprietress of the shabby hotel where I was staying. 'It was the only safe place.' I myself was occupying an inside bathroom with a mattress on the floor. A suspicious odour pervaded it, so I bought a bottle of disinfectant and poured it down the pipes. The day I left somebody told me that the previous tenant had been the Belgian Consul, who had spent a week in the bath, lying in state, after being shot dead in the next room by a stray bullet.

'When I heard that they were after me,' said the still jittery editor of the local Rightist newspaper, 'I disguised myself as a surgeon, swathed my head in bandages and walked straight to the hospital through streets filled with rebels. My first case was a man with a gaping hole in his back, and I dressed it as best as I could, smearing blood over my clothes, as if I had been some time at the job. Almost frantic with the strain, I saw one day through a window four Foreign Legionaries coming towards the hospital, now and then stopping to turn about and fire as they advanced. The ward was full of wounded miners. One of them limped out of bed and screamed, "Comrades! Our revolution has triumphed! The Army is with us!" A burst of cheering went up: "Long live our revolution!" But at that moment the door opened, half a dozen Legionaries covered us with rifles, and the fists clenched by the inmates fell limp on the sheets. I tore off my mask and rushed to join the soldiers.'

The same man who told me this showed me a telegram, received by his paper, with the news that a committee had left England to investigate the Asturian revolution and was due to arrive in Oviedo shortly. The message said nothing about the identity of the committee's members or the precise object of their visit, but next morning, when I left my murky bathroom and descended for breakfast to the Café Peñalba, a glance sufficed to show me that they had arrived. Next to the window, on the left as I entered, sat a sallow-faced middle-aged man and a red-haired woman with a hat that looked Russian, made of sham astrakhan and set jauntily on one side of her head. Their countenances, as much as their attire, revealed the ravages of a sleepless train journey. The man was the Earl of Listowel, the woman's name was Ellen Wilkinson. Years later, both were to occupy prominent posts in a British Labour Cabinet. For the time being they merely represented a 'Committee for the Relief of Victims of Fascism'. In a footnote on page 240 of his book, *The Spanish Civil War*, Hugh Thomas reveals that this Committee was 'one of Muenzenburg's creations', and that Isobel Brown was 'the Communist moving spirit behind it'. (See Appendix IV, pp. 367-8.)

The delegates had set out on their travels under the impression that, in Spain, Red Revolutionaries were mild-mannered men who worked hard to uphold law and order while housewives, Army officers, and other reactionaries ran around throwing bombs, burning other people's homes, and making a general nuisance of themselves. I approached the envoys and questioned Lord Listowel. When he disclosed the nature of his business I begged him to explain its connection, if any, with the events that had taken place in Asturias, where, I pointed out to him, Fascists and Fascism had played no part whatever. This seemed to disconcert the Earl, who somewhat haughtily showed me a letter from the Republican Premier—Lerroux—which in his opinion constituted a safe-conduct. But the document's validity was open to question in a town recently ravished by hordes with which Listowel and his fellow-delegate presumably sympathized. The scars were too fresh for this kind of nonsense.

While Listowel spoke of an appointment with the acting Civil Governor, which he was anxious to keep, our group was joined by a gentleman of fearsome aspect, a harmless lunatic who had read of the committee's arrival in a local paper and whose large face, rapid speech, flaming eyes and voluminous lips made such an impression on the delegates that they set off towards the Governor's office without stopping to finish their breakfast or to investigate anything on the way. Oviedo was still under Martial Law, so I called on the commanding officer and acquainted him with the circumstances of the case. He sized them up speedily and told me that the Governor knew no English, and might like me to act as his interpreter. Our interview with the investigators was courteously and discreetly handled. The Governor listened to his visitors and explained, in great detail, what had really happened in Asturias. Finally he offered them an armed escort, my services as interpreter, and complete freedom to investigate or see anything they might wish. But while he spoke a large crowd had gathered before the building, and though the police were keeping it in check, the mood it was in was nasty. They had no use for foreign busy-bodies, intent on meddling with their affairs. The delegates announced their intention to leave the city with the slightest possible delay.

While we drove through the streets, with Civil Guards in a car behind us, Listowel insisted that he had been unable to discover any trace of the destruction about which newspapers in his country were making such a fuss. 'Didn't you walk through the Calle Uría on your way from the railway station to the Café Peñalba?' I asked him. He had done so, without noticing any damage, though practically every building there was gutted, but he had no inclination to return despite my willingness to escort him. The memory of the crowd before the Governor's office was stronger than his curiosity.

On his return to London, Listowel published an article complaining of his treatment in Oviedo and stating that every night—he was in the city some six hours, from 8 a.m. to about 2 in the afternoon—he had seen long rows of grey carts, carrying the bodies of miners, strangled by Army officers with their own hands. Ellen Wilkinson—'Red Ellen', as in later years she became to be known—protested in the House of Commons against my presence in England in the year 1937, during the Spanish Civil War, and received a perfunctory answer from Sir Samuel Hoare, Home Secretary at the time and in due course Ambassador to Spain.

Listowel's article was the first of a lengthy series about the events in Asturias which appeared in different English periodicals from November 1934 to April 1935, written by people in obvious sympathy with the Spanish Reds and in some cases at least in direct contact with them. Hence the preposterous arguments which served to bolster up their case, a poor one at best. I myself answered these articles, for there was nobody else to do this, and after the controversy had been on for some time 'Beachcomber'—J. B. Morton—had this to say regarding it in his 'By the Way' column in the *Daily Express* of 30 January 1935, where it was published under the heading of 'A Drubbing for the Busybodies'.

'I have been following, in one monthly paper and two weeklies, a correspondence which must be read to be believed. On one side are a number of ignorant busybodies who claim to be humanitarians, and go into screaming hysterics every time any rebel against democratic government is hurt. On the other side is a Spaniard, whose suggestion that, being a Spaniard, he may perhaps know something of his own country is received with howls of derision. But the skilful and vigorous manner in which the Spaniard ties his opponents into lumps and bundles and rolls them about on the ground is something worth watching.'

So many letters did I write to counter the onslaught from the Left that I was not surprised when Kingsley Martin, who, as editor of the *New Statesman*, had already published several, sent one of them back to me with a note to the effect that the discussion was now closed. His decision would have given the last word to one of my opponents. I appealed to Mr Martin's sense of fair play and was grateful when he published my final letter, thus bringing to a satisfactory conclusion—at least for me—a debate, or rather, series of debates, which had dragged on for six months. The rest of the world has much to learn from England regarding the conduct of correspondence columns in newspapers or other periodicals.

Four thousand people were killed in Asturias during the rebellion, many more were wounded; 50 bridges, 26 factories, 58 churches and 313 publicly or privately owned buildings of various kinds were blown up or destroyed by fire, 131,173 firearms, 27 cannon, and many tons of ammunition and explosives were taken from the rebels. The first troops that entered Oviedo found the city littered with corpses. There was no food, no water, no electricity, no telephone service. Hardly a pane of glass remained in the windows, and women and children were still a prey to terror. Yet these people, less than two years later, defended their city against an infinitely more formidable attack which the Reds—the same Reds who, according to Leftists, had been exterminated by soldiers, Civil Guards and police—launched against it as soon as Civil War broke out in Spain. This time the onslaught lasted fifteen months and a far greater portion of the town was destroyed—it has been magnificently rebuilt since—but though there was much tunnelling and mining and hand-to-hand fighting in outlying districts and others, the inhabitants held the city successfully against terrific odds.

The 1934 revolt in Asturias was the principal episode of a Communist-inspired movement which kept the fate of Spain hanging perilously in the balance for two weeks; had it triumphed, a Soviet would have been established in south-western Europe and the whole course of history might have changed. Operations against the Red rebels were directed by General Franco, at the time living quietly in Madrid, with no political contacts and, for once in his life, with sufficient leisure on his hands to visit the Prado or to browse in antique shops, occupations much to his liking. When the tottering Cabinet then in office begged him to become Chief of the General Staff, he accepted the post. It was Franco who encouraged a vacillating General in Barcelona while Catalonia tried to break away from Spain, Franco who ordered two *banderas* of the Foreign Legion and a *tabor* of Native Regulars to embark in Spanish Morocco for Gijón, a port on the coast of Asturias, Franco who directed Lieutenant-Colonel Yagüe, an old Foreign Legion comrade and a magnificent leader in the Civil War, to fly there from León in a Cierva Autogiro—a distance of about 100 miles, most of it over high mountains—and assumed command of the forces from Morocco, and it was Franco who diverted the supporting column from Galicia along a coastal road, eighteen miles north of Oviedo, and thus avoided the bloody fighting that would have resulted had they advanced over steep mountain passes farther south.

Leftists in many countries, sensitive as usual to the rigour with which outbreaks that deserve their sympathy are subdued in other lands, raised an outcry against the use of Legionaries and Native Regulars in Asturias, forgetting that troops similar to these were used in Europe by France and England during World War I. In Morocco, Spain had forces specially trained for this kind of fighting. To employ units lacking experience while combat troops remained idle would have been worse than foolish.

CHAPTER EIGHTEEN

Passiveness and Reaction

Incredibly, the Government continued to act as if the events which had just shocked the nation did not call for some show of energy on its part, forgetting that culprits had to be punished and measures adopted to prevent a repetition of the Asturian tragedy or a recurrence of the Catalan move to cut loose from the rest of Spain. Forty-three death sentences were submitted to the Cabinet's approval. Two were executed, but the ringleaders of both revolts were reprieved and set free after brief spells in gaol. The Left exulted, Alcalá Zamora called for coexistence and appeasement. There was talk of reforming the Constitution. In eight months, four different governments displayed weakness and indecision, and a succession of scandalous affairs lit up their immorality and graft.

Stimulated by violence and inertia, opposition hardened still more. No longer was a moderate group such as C.E.D.A. content to voice its feelings adequately. It needed other outlets. Impatience with the policy of the Republic was growing stronger every day. Now even the humblest knew they had been happier with King Alfonso and Primo de Rivera than under a regime that promised everything and delivered nothing at all. Unemployment increased. Vast programmes initiated by the Dictatorship on roads, railways, reservoirs and ports were denounced and set aside. Strikes halted private enterprise, and workers who refused to join them ran the risk of being shot. Peace and security, at home or in the streets, were memories that belonged to the past.

In October 1933 José Antonio Primo de Rivera, third Marqués de Estella and the Dictator's eldest son, founded the Spanish Falange and captured the imagination of large parts of the working classes and of the youth of Spain by offering them ideals that had no place in a regime devoid of joyfulness or ardour. To a statesmanlike vision and a deep love of his country inherited from his illustrious father, José Antonio added a poetic concept of national affairs. He spoke of an irrevocable faith in the destinies of a united people, of the futility of political parties and of endless strife between them, of the need to replace Liberal catchwords with a profound respect for the liberty of man. He asked for a common belief in the fundamental aims of life, denouncing those who made promises and did not fulfil them. He demanded respect for the religious principles that form the keystone of Spanish history, and encouraged members of the new generation to rekindle their sensitiveness for enterprises of a universal character such as those which had inspired the nation's past. 'The prospect of violence will not intimidate us, should dialectics fail to uphold the cause of Justice.' The Falange, José Antonio insisted, was not a trend of thought, but a way of being —*una manera de ser*. 'We do not beg for crumbs; our place is in the open air, watching our weapons with the stars shining above us. Let others attend festivals while we maintain our vigil and await the dawn with joy in our hearts.'

The party which José Antonio brought to life was born of traditions rooted deep in the soil of Spain and of the circumstances of the moment. From a classic period of imperial Rome, to the splendour of which Spain contributed, the Falange inherited its salute; its crest—the yoke and the arrows, symbols of service and aggressiveness—it took from Rome, and from Ferdinand and Isabella, who had emblazoned it in granite on the monuments which they built. José Antonio was aware that many if not most of his followers would come to him from the extreme Left, disgusted with Socialism and Communism. To draw them to his ranks he used methods on a line with those which his opponents had employed, and was criticized for doing so while his enemies were applauded. His words appealed to the young. Rafael Sánchez Mazas, Eugenio Montes, Ernesto Giménez Caballero, youthful writers in the vanguard of current literary trends, poets like Dionisio Ridruejo, potential rivals in the political field like Onésimo Redondo and Ramiro Ledesma Ramos, all enrolled under his banner or grouped around him.

When rebellion broke out in Asturias the Falange supported the Government, but its newspapers were prohibited, extremists shot down those who printed or distributed them, and any who fired back in self defence were hounded down and killed. The risk of being assassinated, though real, did not seem to worry José Antonio, who was always cool and self-collected. His office was on the ground floor of a building through the windows of which a child could have hurled a bomb. When I saw him there he had a large revolver on his table, ready for use, and occasionally he would change his residence to throw his enemies off the scent. Otherwise he took no precautions, and only enjoyed police protection when he was under arrest. Eventually my meetings with him took place at the home of my wife's sister—he was a distant relative of theirs—where we could talk quietly without being seen. A born leader, his knowledge of his countrymen and his intuitive flair for politics would have made him invaluable in present-day Spain.

Some of his most inspired statements were addressed to his followers from the prison cell which he occupied in Madrid, in March 1936. They are, in parts, as alive today as when he wrote them. 'We are witnessing,' he said, 'a struggle between the Christian, Western, Spanish, individualistic concept of life, with all that it implies in the field of service and self-sacrifice, and an irreligious, materialistic, Russian concept. If the latter should triumph in Spain,' and the issue was then in grave doubt, 'large tracts of our country—Catalonia, the Basque Provinces, Galicia—would break away and submit to the Soviet. We are now in the inept hands of sick men, who out of pure resentment might be capable of handing us over to dissolution and chaos. The Spanish Falange summons all—students, intellectuals, workmen, army officers—to the happy and dangerous task of recapturing our lost heritage.' Nine months later, from his cell in the prison at Alicante, José Antonio Primo de Rivera was taken by the Reds and shot.

One year after the Falange was founded, José Calvo Sotelo launched a new party in Spain. There was no longer room for a genuine Right wing within the Republic's political context. A regime that did not uphold the unity of the nation, nor respect its religious beliefs, nor make a move to maintain law and order, was incompatible with the standards which for centuries had been inherent to Spanish life and people. Its President was too involved with the Left to appoint a Right-wing government, even if it reflected the unimpeachable results of a general election. The mere allocation of three Cabinet posts to C.E.D.A. had been enough to provoke an outburst of violence that imperilled the unity of Spain.

Calvo Sotelo's National Bloc declared itself opposed not so much to parties or policies as to the regime itself, its principles and its basic charter, which large sectors of the population could no longer tolerate or accept. Though José Antonio advocated more advanced views in the field of economics and labour, there were significant coincidences between his programme and the course of action propounded by Calvo Sotelo. Both upheld the fundamental traditions of Spanish life and history; both recognized the failure of parliamentary government as organized in Spain, under the Monarchy as much as under the Republic; both rejected Communism. The publication, in December 1934, of a manifesto announcing the aims of the new party was prohibited by the Government, but the document circulated privately and received widespread support.

Calvo Sotelo had been Finance Minister under Primo de Rivera, and his competence in the field of economics and administrative procedure was unique. He was as much at ease when balancing the budget as when drafting municipal and provincial statutes comparable to the best in any land. The Republic foolishly banished him from Spain. He settled down quietly in Paris, and for two years devoted himself intensely to the study of political science and its practice. Elected to the Cortes by an overwhelming vote in November 1933, he became leader of the Right-wing opposition in Parliament, and the parliamentary immunity he supposedly enjoyed allowed him to attend meetings, make speeches and participate actively in the nation's political life.

I saw him repeatedly in Paris, and again when he returned to Madrid. At first dour and uncompromising, when one broke through his guard he unleashed his thoughts in a torrent of words—as a public speaker he could sweep his audience off its feet—and dazzled his listeners with the depth and clarity of his vision and the firmness of the grounds on which he based it. Calvo Sotelo was only forty-three, ten years older than José Antonio, when the Premier of a Popular Front Government had him taken from his wife and children and murdered at midnight in a street in Madrid.

Simultaneously with the strengthening of the ideals that stimulated the birth of these two new parties, an intellectual renaissance was taking place. Despite the dismal outlook that prevailed, vitality and optimism were the salient features of the movement. Gone were the days when the loss of the last remnants of the Spanish Empire permeated with pessimism or frivolity everything that was published in Spain. *Una manu sua faciebat opus et altera tenebat gladium* was the motto of *Acción Española*, the review which the Marqués de Quintanar, a distinguished engineer and writer and one of my colleagues on the National Tourist Board under Primo de Rivera, had founded in December 1931 to proclaim that whatever the Republic might do to obliterate the past and frustrate the future, Spain possessed a future as well as a past, provided some Spaniards toiled unsparingly with one hand while holding a sword in the other.

Ramiro de Maeztu edited *Acción Española* with the assistance of Eugenio Vegas and Jorge Vigón, later Minister of Public Works and brother of the General who, as Chief of Staff of the Spanish Army, negotiated in 1953 a military agreement with the United States. Maeztu, a brilliant journalist since his youth, was the author of *Defensa de la Hispanidad*, a summary of Spanish civilization and culture and of the ideals that inspired the discovery and colonization of the New World. He and I were in France together as War Correspondents on the British Front, and again with the League of Nations in Geneva where, as a Member of the Secretariat, I helped him in his interviews with Lord Robert Cecil, the Earl of Balfour and other prominent statesmen of the day. We were close friends in London, where he lived for many years, and I respected greatly his intellectual ability and honesty. No contemporary Spanish writer has surpassed his insight and clarity when analysing national problems or interpreting their meaning. The Reds had him shot, with hundreds of others, four months after civil war broke out. Maeztu's mother was an Englishwoman, as was his wife before their marriage. During World War I he wrote countless articles for *La Correspondencia de España*, a Madrid newspaper, and for *La Prensa* of Buenos Aires. All of them defended the British cause. A timely gesture from the influential British quarters in Madrid would have persuaded the Republicans to spare him.

While publicists of the highest rank vindicated their ideals in *Acción Española*, other journalists upheld them in daily papers, published—when not suppressed by the Government—all over Spain. They did so at the risk of their lives, and the journals where their writings appeared braved total destruction to print them. Nor was the danger imaginary. When civil war broke out, scores of writers died for their convictions; in countless cities, newspaper offices or printing presses were destroyed, looted or burnt. Never before or since have defenceless men, anywhere, fought for their ideals more courageously, or with greater consistency and determination.

In the capital, *A.B.C.*, *La Epoca*, *La Nación* and *El Debate* sustained an inspiring battle until overwhelmed or impounded. Year after year José Cuartero wrote his leader for *A.B.C.*, five hundred words long or less, with an exact evaluation of the day's events and their bearing upon the future. But it was not only prominent figures, outstanding men like Cuartero, the finest leader writer Spain has produced, or Juan Ignacio Luca de Tena, who championed the Monarchy in his paper, *A.B.C.*, or José Ignacio Escobar, publisher of *La Epoca*, or Manuel Delgado Barreto, editor of *La Nación*, who risked their lives and sometimes lost them, as did many of their contributors. Among those who wrote for *A.B.C.* or *Acción Española*, Alvaro Alcalá Galiano, Federico Santander, Ramiro Ledesma Ramos, Manuel Bueno, General García de la Herrán, Victor Pradera, Honorio Maura, Pedro Muñoz Seca, Ramiro de Maeztu, José Antonio Primo de Rivera and José Calvo Sotelo were all killed. Every one of those who worked in these papers—typists, printers, messengers, office-boys, lorry-drivers—or in others like them, risked the same fate, and many paid for their courage with their lives.

CHAPTER NINETEEN

The Popular Front

In December 1935 a major crisis arose; the President of the Republic sought counsel, and his decision dumbfounded the nation. Portela Valladares, a man without prestige or personality who led no party or faction and had neither seat nor following in the Cortes, was chosen to head the new Cabinet. Once more Zamora repudiated Gil Robles, who should have been rightfully appointed. His choice incensed the Republic's Right wing and was welcomed by the extremists, for what it meant, and because it heralded a general election.

In July of the same year, Cachin and Dimitroff had addressed the 3rd Communist International's seventh Congress and urged its members to promote the establishment of Popular Fronts in democratic nations. The first duty of such a government in Spain was to distribute landed property among agricultural workers, disarm the Army, arm the proletariat, and liberate 'oppressed nationalities' in Catalonia, the Basque Provinces and Galicia, a region situated in the north-west which had evinced no desire for autonomy. On 16 November 1935, as a prelude to Communist rule, the Comintern instructed Spanish party members to join hands with Socialist and Left-wing Republicans. Without antagonizing the middle classes, they were to intensify their campaign of violence against the Church and the Right and maintain peasants and other workers in constant turmoil and unrest. These instructions were scrupulously executed during the months that followed.

The tactics thus propounded were not new. Lenin had already prophesied that Spain would be the first country after Russia to adopt Communism. Trotsky shared this opinion, and Ivon Delbos, in a book—*L'Expérience Rouge*—which appeared after his visit to Moscow in 1933, spoke of having seen part of a museum there devoted to the future Spanish revolution. Red newspapers like *La Bandera Roja* and *La Palabra* had been brought from Spain and were on view, with pictures of Spanish bolsheviks and turbulent meetings. 'It is obvious,' concluded Delbos, 'that the initial success of their comrades beyond the Pyrenees is discounted by the Soviets.' A Spanish delegate, orating before the congress referred to above, told his listeners that during the revolt in Asturias 'the glorious banner of the Soviets had been hoisted thanks to the initiative, courage, audacity and heroism shown by Communist party members' in Spain.

Many believe that the intrigues leading to Portela Valladares's appointment were prompted by the Grand Orient; be that as it may, Portela spared no effort to establish the Popular Front. An agreement to this end was rapidly subscribed to by Left-wing Republicans, Republican Union, Socialist, Communist and Syndicalist party members, the Workman's Party for Marxist Unification, the General Union of Workmen and the National Federation of Socialist Youths. So-called Conservative Republicans did not sign the pact, but their real feelings showed up in a statement which they published, asserting that the Popular Front's programme was an 'extremely mild' one. More outspoken was Largo Caballero. 'Our first duty was to bring the Republic,' he recalled at a meeting in the Cine Europa, in Madrid, 12 January 1936. 'Our next duty is to establish Socialism, and I mean Marxist Socialism, or Socialism of a revolutionary kind.' Two weeks later, a prominent Communist, Maurín, said this to his Republican allies: 'We shall remain with you while you progress'—towards the Left, needless to say—'but once your objectives are attained we ourselves will continue to advance, and if necessary we will leap over your heads to set up in Spain a Socialist Republic of Workers.'

The book Octubre, published by Socialist Youths, and their weekly paper, Renovación, told enough to enlighten 'conservative' Republicans: 'Our objective is to bolshevize the Socialist party, defeat the middle classes and re-model the international workers' movement on the pattern of the Russian revolution.' In a speech delivered in Madrid six months before it broke out, José Antonio declared that the Reds were now aiming at civil war. Parliament became unworkable. To the extreme Left's great joy, Alcalá Zamora summoned a general election.

The Reds now changed their tactics. Violence was not enough. When at a fateful hour for Catalonia and Asturias their former allies in the

Government called out the Army to oppose them, military discipline had proved stronger than all their efforts to subvert it. They needed not only violence but power. The thing to aim at was a majority in the Cortes, and terror was the best means to secure it.

In January I went to Spain. My wife and son were already in Mallorca, an oasis of quiet in the midst of much turmoil. Our second child was due in mid-February, and the general elections had been scheduled for the 16th of that month. Right-wing parties were showing intense activity, but compared with the incendiary tactics employed by the Republicans their campaign was too sedate and proper, and it made no impression on the masses. The extreme Left clamoured for the dissolution of Parliament and the replacement of the Army, Civil Guards and Police by Red Militia. 'Dimitroff wants direct action; so do we!' thundered the Communist *Mundo Obrero*. At Valencia, on 2 February, Marxist leaders granted an alternative, 'Revolution or Civil War!', but *Pueblo* gave no choice; the Popular Front would fight for Soviet rule. 'No class war; one class!' shouted Jiménez Asúa, a professor in the University of Madrid. The Mayor of Alicante was more drastic: 'Should any vote for the Right, chop off their right hand and force them to eat it!'

We moved to Malaga, and I went to Madrid and Barcelona. Some thought the Right was in for a sweeping victory, others feared it would be overwhelmed, not for lack of enthusiasm or votes, but by deliberate reversal of the results. To campaign against the Reds was becoming increasingly difficult. I attended a meeting in Antequera, thirty-five miles from Malaga, with Right-wing speakers who had come from Madrid for the occasion. When they denounced Red violence, a police official put an end to the proceedings and a band of hooligans forced an entry into the hall and smashed the furniture. Only the speakers were arrested.

At the elections, votes were defiantly cast and recklessly recorded. The Left employed every known means to obtain their much-needed majority. I voted in Malaga, at a little booth in the Camino Nuevo, a stone's throw from the spot where six months later the Reds murdered many residents of nearby houses. Results were not fully known until 1 March. The usual orgy of destruction erupted, this time as a means of confirming the Popular Front's willingness to accept office without delay. Malaga experienced another night of terror. The city's leading newspaper, and a number of private residences, were gutted, looted or destroyed. At noon the following day, while my wife and other members of my family were at my mother's house in the Monte de Sancha, news came that a mob was on its way to our district with the purpose of setting it on fire. My daughter was only four days old. Any idea of resistance was useless, for I had no arms and no possibility of repulsing a band of maniacs intent on arson and plunder. Hurriedly we thought out a plan; we would place my wife on an improvised stretcher, carry her to the hills behind our house, and hide there with some blankets and whatever food we might be able to collect. Even thus, the prospect of watching passively while our home went up in flames was not pleasant.

Fortunately the mob, a small one, got tired of walking or set off in another direction. Nobody interfered with its plans, but the incident, and two others like it, did nothing to reassure my mind. We lived some distance from the city. When I returned home one day I was surprised to learn that my mother was out, shopping. Private cars were unpopular and apt to be stoned, or fired at. 'I took a tram,' she told me later. 'When we passed near the bull-ring they started to shoot and the conductor told us to lie flat on the floor' Shortly after, we discussed the christening of my new-born daughter, but everybody warned us against taking her to our parish church in Malaga—the Sagrario, next to the Cathedral, where altars had been stripped and burnt five years before. 'It might be dangerous,' they said, 'they would shoot or at least stone you.' Neither alternative seemed attractive, so I called up the Bishop and obtained a special licence to have the infant baptized at Miramar, a small chapel not far from our house where the venture seemed less risky. The baby was christened Marisol.

By now, I had had it. In less than forty-eight hours our home had been threatened with destruction, my mother had been sniped at, and we had found it necessary to work out a plan that might prevent our new-born daughter and ourselves from being stoned or shot dead. I slept badly. My waking hours were spent pacing the rooms on the ground floor. I was due in London with my wife and children, but ships of the Orient Line, on which we had return tickets from Gibraltar, were crammed at this time of the year, as were P. & O. steamers, and our departure was further complicated by an incident in which an uncle of mine, named exactly like myself, had just been involved with his wife. Apprehensive of the trends in Malaga, they had left to seek refuge abroad and my aunt had taken her jewels with her. Because the export of valuables was prohibited, they had been arrested at La Línea, while on their way to Gibraltar. I could not help wondering what would happen when I turned up, bearing the same name, at the very place where my relatives had been imprisoned without bail

At last we set off from Malaga, ten days after Marisol's birth. The situation had apparently calmed down, and we had secured a cabin on an ancient Bibby liner, a small vessel with four masts and three funnels that rolled a lot in the Bay of Biscay but otherwise behaved itself. The trip to Gibraltar was uneventful. But I had left with a heavy heart, for Spain was facing a terrible ordeal and close relatives and friends of mine were practically trapped in the country. Little did I realize that soon, so many were to lose their lives.

At the time of which I am writing, March-April 1936, José Antonio Primo de Rivera needed sub-machine-guns to defend his followers from being murderously attacked by the Reds, and he sent me a message asking me to get the guns and somehow smuggle them into Spain. When I informed Douglas Jerrold of my predicament, he reeled off the names of three men who might be in a position to help me. The first one turned me down. The second was Sir Arnold Wilson, then editor of *The Nineteenth Century*; though over fifty-five, at the outbreak of the Second World War he volunteered with great gallantry to fly as an observer and was shot down in the Battle of Britain. There was nothing he could do about the guns. On my third attempt I was luckier. A man who bore a well-known name told me to be at Claridge's on a certain day and hour, wearing a white carnation on my lapel. Someone would in due course appear and work out the deal, but he and I were never again to recognize each other publicly. I kept my appointment. The business was settled in a matter of minutes. The guns were to be purchased in Germany and shipped to Portugal in champagne cases aboard an ocean-cruising yacht. From Oporto, they would be smuggled across the Spanish border in the vicinity of Salamanca. The owner of the yacht would know nothing, nor would any inkling of the nature of the cargo reach his wife, renowned for her beauty the world over, though she was to be on the yacht with a party of friends. Before the guns could be landed, civil war broke out in Spain.

The situation there was deteriorating rapidly. Churches were being burnt to cinders in some places, turned into dance halls in others. Contributions to the Red Relief Fund were unceremoniously exacted from foreign visitors and railway strikes made it difficult for them to leave a country where, because of strikes in restaurants and hotels, they had found it unpleasant to stay. Criminals guilty of the gravest excesses in Asturias were being pardoned, released, and re-installed in their previous occupations. Humble families were forced to re-admit men who had murdered their father or a brother. A local branch of the Bank of Spain was obliged to employ the man who had killed the manager. In Granada, a church, a theatre, a political club and a newspaper were reduced to ashes; Cadiz lost four churches, and similar outrages were committed in Murcia, Palma del Río, Cordoba, Almería, Gamonal, Las Palmas, Cartagena, Montejaque, Barcelona, Toledo, Ecija, Huesca, Badajoz and Jerez de la Frontera. In Santander, Baracaldo, Puebla de Almoradiel, Niebla, Jerez de los Caballeros, San Fernando, Escalona, Aranjuez, Ciaño, Vallecas, La Rúa and Pamplona there was much rioting and disorder. Don Alfredo Martínez, former Minister of a Republican Cabinet, was murdered in Oviedo. Don José María Maura, a well-known industrialist, met the same fate in Bilbao. Four workmen were shot dead in Madrid after joining the Falange. A peasants' riot in Yeste resulted in 25 killed and 115 wounded, and Socialist leaders shed crocodile tears over 'the futile orgy of destruction' which they themselves had set loose. Farmers were beheaded publicly in Yecla, where no religious service could be held because all of its fifteen churches had been burnt. Army officers were insulted, attacked and ordered to remote posts whenever their allegiance to the Left was open to question, officers known for their extremist views being appointed to replace them. To isolate him and keep him under observation, General Franco was appointed Military Governor to the Canary Islands, one thousand miles away.

Moscow dispatched agitators to Spain—Bela Kun, Janson, Lumoviow, Lasvosky were among these new arrivals. Book-stalls were flooded with a wave of Red literature, seditious or pornographic. At a military parade in Madrid, held to commemorate the Republic's fifth anniversary, Socialists shot a young Civil Guard lieutenant. His burial was a mass demonstration against the Left, in which all classes took part; extremists killed several and wounded many more. The previous month two large churches had been burnt in Madrid together with the offices of *La Nación*, an evening paper. When, in the Cortes, Calvo Sotelo listed these outrages and deplored them—in six weeks, he said, 48 private residences, 62 political clubs, 117 private or public buildings, and 142 churches had been looted, destroyed or completely burnt down, and there had been 11 general strikes and 74 persons had been killed and 345 wounded—Azaña, the Prime Minister, rose and said to him, 'You think all this is dreadful; I think it's just silly!'

There was no democratic justification for the exultant excesses of the Left; even after a good deal of cooking, the elections of 16 February had not shown conclusive results—4,570,000 votes for the Right, 4,356,000 for the Left, and 340,000 for the Centre, plus 300,000 abstentions. But these returns, which showed that Spain was splitting up into two extreme parties, were enough for the Left to seize power, appoint a Popular Front Government and draw up a programme which included the ousting of Alcalá Zamora, President of the Republic, to whom a large part of their victory was due, constraint of Army officers, expropriation of real property and nationalization of banks and private industries, destruction of all churches and convents, establishment of a Soviet in Morocco, extermination of the bourgeoisie and of bourgeois newspapers, and creation of armed militias as a first step towards a Red Army and the dictatorship of the proletariat. War against Portugal would be declared before that country was absorbed into the Iberian Soviet. Loyalty to Russia, and free love, were advocated on the side.

Alcalá Zamora was kicked out for dismissing the Cortes unconstitutionally, though he had acted thus—not unwillingly—at the behest of those who ejected him. Azaña was elected his successor. No worthier candidate for the Presidency of such a Republic could have been found. His most unprincipled adherent, Casares Quiroga, was appointed Premier and Minister of War. Other posts in the Cabinet were allotted to Republican Left, Republican Union and Catalan Left, willing pawns of the Red extremists, who, for the time being, directed operations from the wings. Revolt broke out in a dozen towns, and outrages were committed daily in Barcelona, Malaga, Saragossa, Granada, Bilbao and Seville. In Madrid, a riot was caused by a preposterous rumour to the effect that ladies who worked for social welfare had distributed poisoned sweets to children. As a reprisal several churches were burnt and three nuns and two other women, one of them of French nationality, were assaulted and almost lynched by an infuriated mob.

On 7 June, Don Miguel de Unamuno, an opponent of the Monarchy and the Dictatorship who had lined up enthusiastically with the Republic, reported in *Ahora*, a Madrid newspaper of the Left: 'Law courts at Salamanca were invaded the other day by a rabble whose avowed purpose was to lynch magistrates, judges and lawyers. The horde was made up of mere boys who raised clenched fists, and of filthy, toothless harpies carrying a poster with the words "Long Live Free Love!" This grotesque mob paraded the streets under the protection of the authorities. Our revolution is filling up large cities with human dregs no longer tolerated in smaller towns and allowing them to merge with the rottenness that already exists there.' Indalecio Prieto, the Socialist leader, had said on 1 May, 'Spaniards have never, but never, witnessed anything so tragic as the spectacle their country now offers to the world. Spain is totally discredited abroad. Its life-blood is being drained by strife and disorder *devoid of any known revolutionary purpose*'—the italics are mine—'and the resources of government and national vitality are being worn down by a state of chronic unrest which is proving too much for the people.' Thirty days later, in Ecija, Prieto's supporters made an attempt upon his life.

On that same day, 1 May—Labour Day—Socialists paraded in Madrid, and their well-armed militias marched down the Castellana, the city's principal avenue. They represented combat units, 150,000 strong, resistance groups with another 100,000, and syndicates that mustered 200,000 more. They carried pistols, rifles and shot-guns, many of them the legal property of law-abiding citizens who had been dispossessed of their right to hold weapons by order of the Popular Front. Armaments of a more formidable nature had been landed by Russian ships in Seville and Algeciras. Russia also sent instructions, made public at a meeting in Valencia, on 16 May. In an article published in *La Batalla*, on 3 January 1936, Maurin, a Communist leader already quoted, announced that 'the day' was drawing near. 'Our revolution, which began by overthrowing Primo de Rivera,' he explained, 'is now in its seventh year, which may well be a decisive year for all. The Asturias affair was only a prologue, a dress-rehearsal for much that is yet to come.'

In Madrid alone there were 62,000 children without schools, twice as many as there had been when the Republic was proclaimed. Unfulfilled promises, and arson, accounted for the difference. Nine hundred thousand men were workless in Spain, but when Right-wing speakers mentioned this in the Cortes they were denounced as traitors to the regime. Because Falangists defended themselves from their aggressors, the Government declared itself in open belligerency with the Falange. When, on 7 May, a rabid mob attacked and stoned the barracks at Alcalá de Henares, the Government incarcerated the officers and transferred the troops to another town. From his enforced remoteness in the Canary Islands, General Franco, on 23 June, addressed a confidential and persuasive letter to the Minister of War, who was also the head of the Government. As an expression of sound political sense the contents of this letter were beyond reproach. 'The Government's unfairness,' Franco recalled, 'was responsible for the creation of military juntas in 1917; potentially, at least, these juntas exist again today. Certain documents, circulated clandestinely, bear witness to their existence and may, if not taken soon into account, be a herald of civil strife, easily avoidable to my way of thinking if just and considerate measures are adopted in good time. I cannot conceal from Your Excellency the danger that arises when unrest of a professional character adds its weight to the fears which good Spaniards now feel for the future of their country.' Franco's loyal warning remained unanswered and unheeded.

On 16 June, Gil Robles read before the Chamber a list of the outrages perpetrated by extremists during the four months in which the Popular Front had held office. It comprised 169 churches totally destroyed, and another 257 partly burnt down or looted, 269 persons killed and 1,879 wounded, 161 armed robberies, 113 general strikes and 228 local strikes, 381 private or political clubs destroyed, looted or attacked, 43 newspaper offices and printing presses gutted or sacked, 146 bombs exploded and 78 more discovered before they blew up. The events thus listed had been reported in every paper. They were far too well known to be doubted.

Tumult succeeded tumult in the Cortes, where Right-wing deputies swore they would stop at nothing to save their country and Leftist members retaliated with threats of death. When the Prime Minister, Casares Quiroga, warned Calvo Sotelo that he would be held responsible for 'anything' that might happen, the leader of the opposition welcomed the challenge and replied: 'My shoulders are broad! Saint Dominic said to a King of Castile, "Sire, you may deprive me of my life; more you cannot do!" I say as much and accept full responsibility for myself and for those who act with me for the good of Spain. I would rather die than live shamefully. In Russia, Kerensky was the unwitting tool of men more cunning than he. In Hungary, Karoly betrayed a civilization that had flourished for one thousand years. You will never be a Kerensky. Pray God you will never do to Spain what Karoly did to his country!' Before he had finished speaking, La Pasionaria, the Communist woman deputy, was on her feet and shouting 'You have uttered your last words here!'

About a month before this happened, on 8 June, the Wiseman Society had met at Claridge's Hotel in London for a gala dinner at which I was the principal speaker. Hilaire Belloc, Douglas Jerrold and many of my friends were present. There was much interest in Spain, and since my return to England I had given a series of lectures at the Conservative College in Ashridge, the Jesuit College for Novices at Heythrop, near Oxford, and other places. My activities had not been overlooked by the other side. One night at a dreary hall in Bloomsbury I attended a meeting which Spanish Reds, some of them imported for the occasion from Spain, had organized for the benefit of their English friends. Hardly had I taken my seat when my name became the object of violent denunciations. After listening to a few tirades, I got up and left unnoticed, as quietly as I had entered.

That evening at Claridge's the gist of my talk was that a state of latent civil war existed in Spain. A national rising against the imminent threat of Communism might break out any day. Some of those present seemed incredulous. They expressed their inability to understand why the differences between my compatriots could not be settled peacefully. They tended to believe that another general election might provide the necessary solution. In any case, they recalled, English people did not resort to internal strife as a means of unravelling their problems. When I mentioned Naseby, and the Wars of the Roses, and the American Civil War, then only seventy years old, I was reminded that times had changed—even in Spain things had changed, they insisted, to the point of rendering civil war unthinkable.

It exploded forty days later.

CHAPTER TWENTY

The Inevitability of Civil War

The Spanish Civil War was a national movement against five years of misgovernment and oppression without parallel in the history of the country. The immediate objective of all who took part in the rising was to save Spain from disruption, preserve national unity, and prevent the rule of Communism upon its soil. The spark that set off the conflagration was the murder of Calvo Sotelo.

All three of the phases into which the history of the Second Spanish Republic can be divided contributed to its outbreak. The demagogic zeal that fired the coalition of Socialists and Left-wing Republicans which ruled Spain during the first two years of the new regime was responsible for its initial failure. A Cabinet made up of unqualified zealots deliberately stirred up the fury of ingenuous or highly impressionable people, countenanced violence and arson, and renounced the authority with which it had been invested. Further, it used that authority as a cover for its own excesses, ignored the wishes and the inherent rights of a large majority of citizens, and showed utter disdain for constructive work and no respect whatsoever for the principles and the way of life which Spaniards had held sacred for generations. When, at the beginning of the second phase, a general election gave a majority of three to one to the Centre and, more predominantly, to the Right, the President of the Republic scorned the will of the nation, as expressed in the polls, and Left-wing extremists resorted to separatism and violence as a means of preventing their opponents from gaining access to power. During the third phase a government of the Popular Front encouraged violence and terror, planned to split the country into Soviet republics, paved the way for a Communist era, and murdered the leader of the opposition. Throughout these three phases, the failure of the Left-wing intellectuals to analyse, draw conclusions, counsel, and direct, was total and complete. They had been largely responsible for the advent of the Republic. Apart from occasional outbursts, they did little to steer the new regime toward the goals which, they had assured the people, would be attained under its rule.

Constant turmoil, religious persecution, incessant strikes, and economic chaos made civil war inevitable. For a long time, for years, in fact, Spanish people had hesitated before attempting to redress by force the wrongs to which they were being subjected. Peaceful citizens are usually reluctant to employ force as a means of overthrowing their government, though it be tyrannical and incompetent. The American Declaration of Independence reminds us that 'mankind are more disposed to suffer while evils are sufferable than to right themselves by abolishing the forms to which they are accustomed.' But evils may become insufferable; there is a limit to forbearance, especially when force is the instrument selected by the oppressor. 'To force, nothing but force can be successfully opposed,' Lord Melbourne said in 1830, defending his policy as Home Secretary in the English Labourers' revolt. 'All legislation is impotent and ridiculous unless the public peace can be preserved and the liberty and property of individuals saved from outrage and invasion.'* Public peace was only a memory in Spain in 1936. To quote again from the Declaration of Independence: 'When a long train of abuses and usurpation evinces a design to reduce them under absolute despotism'—and a Communist movement would have broken out in Spain in July or August 1936, had the national rising not forestalled it one month before—'it is their right, it is their duty, to throw off such government and to provide new guards for their future security.'

And this is what the Spanish people did in 1936. Three years before, on 31 August 1933, *The Times Literary Supplement* had reviewed my book, *The Spanish Republic*, and said: 'This is obviously written by one who believes that the Spanish Republic is prompted by the Evil Spirit and will at no distant date dissolve into chaos.' Had the returns of the elections held three months after this was published been honoured in accordance with the rules of the democratic game, and a Right-wing government appointed, my forebodings might conceivably have proved wrong. I am inclined to think that the march of events fully bore them out.

**Lord M: the Later Life of Lord Melbourne*, by Lord David Cecil: Constable, 1954.

PART V

CHAPTER TWENTY-ONE

The Death of Sanjurjo

Such was the situation that existed in Spain when the Marqués de Luca de Tena telephoned from Biarritz and asked me to charter a plane in which General Franco could fly from the Canary Islands to Spanish Morocco. For five long years matters in my country had steadily gone from bad to worse. Finally all hope of finding a peaceful solution had disappeared. We had to act, as quickly and resolutely as possible.

The reader will recall that immediately after landing with General Franco in Tetuán I had discussed with him the steps which could be taken to obtain aeroplanes and bombs for the Spanish Nationalist Army. We agreed that I should fly to Rome and endeavour to persuade the Italian Government to give us the help we needed. My own plane was soon in the air. It took Bebb only a few moments to get the Dragon Rapide over the Strait. As we skirted the Moroccan coast and set our course towards Lisbon, I saw the ominous silhouettes of a light cruiser and its accompanying destroyer lying off the harbour at Ceuta, well beyond the reach of land batteries and effectively barring access to the sea from our principal port in North Africa. For the time being our main assets were bottled up, yet in a few hours a small picked force was to break the blockade, and in less than three weeks our best troops in Morocco were to cross the Strait, leave Seville, and begin their march to Madrid.

Musa and Tarik, the ancient Pillars of Hercules one on each side of the Straits, familiar landmarks on the horizon from my home in the hills near Malaga, disappeared in the distance behind us. On our starboard side a dense pall of smoke could be seen rising over Cadiz, tongues of vivid flame occasionally stabbing its grey-black clouds. The flames that licked the smoke implied a possible setback for our cause, in the city and possibly also in San Fernando, the naval base adjoining it. I thought of priceless works by Murillo and Zurbarán, endangered by a holocaust likely to reckon them among its objectives, and recalled the occasion, seven years before, when I had escorted King Alfonso during a visit to the local museum. He had classed it as the finest provincial gallery in Spain. Now it was probably in grave danger.

Some paintings in Cadiz were burnt, including a fine Murillo, but the city itself was saved by a few determined men. General López Pinto, acting under orders issued by General Queipo de Llano in Seville, managed to free General Varela, an officer with a record of courageous leadership in Morocco, who had been imprisoned in Cadiz by the Popular Front. Assisted by a small group of Falangists, the two generals took command of the town after a hazardous night and much sniping in the streets. The timely arrival from Ceuta of the *tabor* of Native Regulars that broke the blockade restored peace and order in Cadiz, but before this happened Arsenio Martínez Campos, a staff officer and grandson of the man who restored the Spanish Monarchy in 1875, devised with Manuel Mora Figueroa, a lieutenant-commander in the Navy and leader of the Falangist Militia in the province of Cadiz, a daring plan that helped to pacify the territory between Algeciras and Seville, a vital bridgehead for the success of military operations in Andalusia.

Reinforcements were needed from Africa. Arsenio owned a fishing fleet and the *almadraba* nets which I had seen from the air as I flew from Lisbon to Casablanca for my meeting with General Franco, and Manolo Mora could contribute a score of volunteers. Supported by these men, they seized at pistol point a couple of trawlers and on the night of 21 July sailed across the Strait of Gibraltar towards Ceuta, which was tightly blockaded by enemy ships. The little trawl boats drifted unseen past several Red warships, but nearer their destination they were swept by a hail of bullets, fired in error from the shore. A few on board were killed; Martínez Campos was gravely wounded. The rest managed to land.

Mora reported at once to Franco and requested permission to take his ships back to Spain, with as many Foreign Legionaries as they would hold. Some condemned the idea as foolhardy, but Franco liked it, and the trawlers left that same night, crammed to the hatchways with troops. Two hundred Legionaries were packed like sardines, their machine-guns on deck, ready to fire. The night was dark and windy. Half way across, the huge silhouette of a Republican battleship, the *Jaime I*, loomed up in the darkness, and the men below were ordered to load their rifles and fix bayonets. All they could hope for was that the look-out on the *Jaime I* would be asleep or mistake them for a couple of fishing smacks, but their vessels were suddenly shrouded in a thick mist and the battleship disappeared. When the fog lifted, day was breaking. As they approached Tarifa, where they were due to land, a low-lying hull was spotted on the surface of the water It looked like a Red submarine about the proximity of which they had been warned, but it turned out to be the keel of a sunken boat, and the Legionaries carried their leader shoulder-high to a neighbouring church, where they fell to their knees and thanked Heaven. In a matter of hours or days this part of south-western Spain was captured and held for Franco. Manolo Mora would have repeated his exploit, but the Republicans had heard of it and threatened to sink fishing smacks on sight, so he organized and led a column that played an important part on various fronts during the ensuing years and was with the forces to which I was attached when we took Malaga. During the war it numbered between 700 and 1,200 men, mostly volunteers from Cadiz and Ronda —peasants, students, fishermen, office workers, and members of well-known families, with a smattering of the *flamenco* singers and dancers in which the region abounds. Its total casualties were 210 killed and 2,300 wounded. Manolo Mora's string of victories made him a legendary hero in Andalusia, where to this day a popular *flamenco* song, an *alegría*, tells of his prowess and records that:

La jaca que montaba Manolo Mora
la mataron de un tiro en una loma.

(The pony ridden by Manolo Mora
was killed by a bullet upon a hill.)

When I reached Lisbon, I found our adherents a prey to doubt. They lacked news of events in Spain, and the possibility of failure in Madrid and other large cities inspired them with dread. At the residence of the Marquesa de Argüelles, General Sanjurjo was being besieged with questions. When he saw me he left a group of which he was the central figure and heard with obvious satisfaction of Franco's arrival in Tetuán. Once more he insisted that the younger man's leadership was essential, and he seemed confident that our forces in Morocco would soon reach the other side of the Strait. When I explained to him the nature of my mission to Italy and showed him the paper which Franco had signed for me in Tetuán that morning, he borrowed my pen and wrote on it, 'I agree with all that General Franco has authorized.' It was probably the last time he ever signed his name. This document, incidentally, is the only one in existence with instructions vital to the outcome of the Spanish rebellion, jointly signed by the man thought by many to be its leader and by the one who eventually directed it to a victorious conclusion.

Two officers drew me aside and inquired if my Dragon Rapide could land Sanjurjo somewhere in Spain. 'Precisely where?' I asked. All I needed was an assurance that the place selected would be under our control, but there was no means of ascertaining this. Nobody knew in which cities we had the upper hand, for the revolt had only just broken out. Salamanca seemed a suitable choice, and so did Burgos; we had good reason to believe that the garrisons in both towns had come out on our side. Pending definite information, however, the one place we could be sure of was a small airstrip at Pamplona, the surface of which, someone said to me, was certain to be rough besides not being very long, a thousand feet or so at most. Bebb would not even consider the idea. His plane needed a longer runway. Those awaiting our decision were not at loss for an alternative: Juan Antonio Ansaldo, a flying officer in Sanjurjo's entourage, volunteered to fly the General to Pamplona in a smaller plane. Meanwhile I would proceed to Biarritz. By now it was 1 a.m. and the date was 20 July.

Bebb and I rose early that morning and set off for the airfield at Alverca. I was eager to reach Biarritz, even more anxious to land in Rome. The Dragon Rapide was ready—our mechanic had seen to that —but for reasons that remained unstated, the Portuguese authorities were delaying its departure. We lunched at the airport. Hours passed by; it was almost two o'clock before we started our flight. In due course I was to learn that earlier that morning Ansaldo's plane had crashed while taking off at Cintra. General Sanjurjo had been killed. His pilot had escaped with minor injuries. Engine failure and the omission to fasten a seat-belt were the causes of this tragic accident.

Of his forty-five years as a soldier, General Sanjurjo spent sixteen fighting in Morocco, where he was seven times promoted for outstanding courage and leadership and awarded a Military Medal and two crosses of San Fernando, the highest decorations in the Spanish

Army, the latter being equivalent to the Victoria Cross or the Congressional Medal of Honor. He rarely wore his medals, and when he did so at a formal function he would hand them to an A.D.C. the moment it was over. The King of Spain had made him Marqués del Rif, but he seldom used the title or responded when addressed thus; he was apt to forget that he was a Marquis. His men loved him, and in Madrid his many friends stood by him staunchly throughout his career. I first met Sanjurjo in the early days of the Moroccan War, when he landed in Malaga at the head of troops that had seen much fighting near Melilla. Those who welcomed him in Malaga were impressed by his shyness and reserve—he did not realize that he had become famous. He always had a twinkle in his eye. At cocktail parties and receptions, which he frequented reluctantly, all that he would drink was a glass of sherry, but he smoked incessantly and always rolled his own cigarettes. On one occasion, while commanding the Civil Guard, a hard-up lieutenant ventured to request a month's pay in advance. The General explained that regimental funds could not be used for loans, adding that he himself would lend the amount on a personal basis, provided it was repaid at the monthly rate of five pesetas. When the grateful officer left, Sanjurjo told an A.D.C. that he had done what he could to prevent the lieutenant from realizing that the loan was a gift. 'I did not want to hurt his feelings,' he said. At the penal settlement of El Dueso, where he was confined as a common convict for his share in an ill-fated revolt against the Republic, his simple manner and his charm impressed the hardened inmates, who volunteered to engineer his escape. The offer was ignored, and the General refused a similar proposal at the Fort of Santa Catalina, near Cadiz, to which he was eventually transferred and where the commanding officer, who turned out the guard to salute him, was arrested and deposed by the Republic. Cervantes would have relished his quick wit. On being asked by the judge who passed sentence at his trial to disclose how many supported him, he replied: 'Now that I have lost, very few; had I won, everybody would have been on my side, yourself included in the first place.'

My four-hour flight from Lisbon to Biarritz was bumpy owing to the heat and to the low altitude at which we flew while searching for unfamiliar landmarks, but it gave me a chance to think about the treatment which the Portuguese had meted out to me on two recent and critical occasions, one at Espinho, near Oporto, on my way to Casablanca, the other at Alverca, near Lisbon. On both I had felt irritated and irked without real cause for complaint, for the Portuguese had merely done their duty, courteously and with the utmost tact. The corporal at Espinho had carried out his orders and acted like a gentleman when, feeling like a worm, I attempted to bribe him with crisp, white English bank-notes worth more than one hundred pounds—a large sum, as I did not fail to point out, if exchanged into local currency. The lieutenant at Espinho had exercised his discretion, intelligently and in a pleasant manner. And the authorities at Alverca had understandably delayed the departure of a plane, chartered by a Spaniard without any clear reason for being in Lisbon at the start of a revolt in Spain, precisely when a tragic accident had befallen a distinguished Spanish General who was enjoying their country's hospitality in somewhat unusual circumstances. In both cases the Portuguese had behaved perfectly and apologized for keeping me on the ground.

Spain feels profoundly grateful towards Portugal for her friendliness and sympathy during a critical period. Long before the outbreak of the Civil War, Salazar, the Portuguese Premier, sized up the realities of the Spanish situation without distorting its salient features. Abundantly equipped to measure the threats that menaced his own country, he framed the policy best calculated to avert them, knowing well that should the larger part of the Iberian Peninsula become a prey to Communism, Portugal would also succumb. To avoid this danger had been hard enough while Spain progressed steadily towards chaos. Now that she was striving to help herself, Portugal could not refrain from giving her a friendly hand.

So, while during the first days of the Civil War, and later, broadcasting stations over most of the world regaled their listeners with insidious reports of a tragic situation, Radio Club Portugal handed out the truth in large doses to those who tuned in with its wave-length at home, and to countless Spaniards in Spain. Some of these heard it unrestrictedly in cities where the Nationalists had triumphed, others toned down their sets to gather wisps of hope, for the Reds slaughtered all they caught listening. Portuguese newspapers published accurate reports of the fighting or exceeded the bounds of discretion in their efforts to encourage the rebels. At no time in Portugal were the Republicans called 'loyalists' by the Press; people there knew as well as their leader that the enemies of all they held sacred were loyal to nothing worthy of respect. When the troops brought by Franco from Morocco left Seville and marched towards Badajoz, they had hazy ideas regarding the precise whereabouts of the border line between the two nations, but if they overstepped it at any time owing to ignorance or to military motives nobody on the Portuguese side troubled to turn them back. A geographical error on the part of Franco's men was preferable to a Communist invasion. Before many months elapsed, the Portuguese were dispatching to their Nationalist friends in Spain convoys of lorries, one hundred units strong or more, loaded with food and clothing, and Portuguese volunteers—thousands of them became casualties—were fighting magnificently on Spanish soil for their ideals, their religion, and their country, as well as for Spain.

By now my plane was flying over Spanish territory. We flew low, and I scanned the landscape for signs of trouble. North of Burgos the clouds thickened as they usually do in that part of Castile, and over Miranda de Ebro they turned again into flames and smoke. Another holocaust was spreading its pall in honour of a short-lived Red triumph. Months afterwards, until reconstruction teams carried out their work of restoration, whenever I drove through Miranda the blackened ruins of Renaissance and Gothic churches there brought back to my mind what I had seen that day from the skies. We flew on. This time Bebb chose to fly low over the railway lines to Bilbao, and I marvelled to see how deftly he piloted his plane through narrow gorges, twisting and turning to avoid the yawning slopes on either side. A stiff gale raged in the Bay of Biscay; trawlers pitched and rolled in the heavy seas, but over Biarritz the weather became clearer and our trusty plane settled easily into the airfield at Parma.

From the villa occupied by the Conde de los Andes, Luca de Tena rushed out to clasp me in his arms. Andes was elated by the news of Franco's arrival in Tetuán, but none of us knew yet of Sanjurjo's tragic end at Cintra, nor did we possess any idea of the progress of our rebellion in Spain. Our chief concern now was to work out a propitious atmosphere in Rome for my attempt to obtain Italian bombers and fighting planes, and Andes undertook to telephone King Alfonso, at that moment in Austria with his family.

Bebb and I flew to Marseilles on the French side of the Pyrenees. Over the Gulf of Lyons a strong Mistral was blowing that almost shook our little craft to pieces. 'Anyone who stands this,' remarked Bebb, 'should never give a thought to air-sickness.' After lunch we said goodbye, and I left for Rome in a huge unpressurized plane which climbed so high over Corsica that for days afterwards my ears were racked with a splitting ache.

CHAPTER TWENTY-TWO

'I Want to See *Il Duce*'

It was mid-afternoon when I arrived in Rome on a hot, damp, typical summer day—21 July 1936. The sun was high. I still had no definite plan for the mission which had brought me to Italy, but there was time, before the day's work ended, to approach one or other of the government circles with which, in all probability, I was going to have to deal. I drove to the Grand Hotel and was shown into a spacious room, where I unpacked my little suitcase and had a bath. While I did so I searched my brains for the best course to take; I had been searching them for the last two days. In Rome I knew nobody who could be of help. The idea of talking to an underling in some Italian Ministry did not appeal to me; there was a risk that I might be forced by the workings of red tape to reveal what I had in mind to a whole chain of officials. My request had to be submitted and considered at higher level. I put on my coat and made my way to the entrance of the hotel.

Before I could jump into a taxi I was hailed by a casual acquaintance from Malaga, anxious to know what was happening in Spain and inquisitive about the reasons for my presence in Rome at such a time. My cab driver could have given him an inkling, for I directed him to the Piazza Venezia. When we arrived there I left the taxi and walked around the wide square. To the tall guard standing below the famous balcony of the Palazzo where Mussolini had his headquarters I said, in my best Italian, 'I want to see *Il Duce*.' The guard smiled good-naturedly—requests of this kind were probably not uncommon—and inquired, 'Are you not a foreigner? In this case you should apply to the Ministry of Foreign Affairs.' Night was falling, and I returned to the Grand Hotel.

A long-distance call awaited me there. It was from King Alfonso. The King's usual anxiety for his country's affairs had now reached a pitch of passionate intensity. I told him that Franco had flown to Tetuán. Repeatedly he questioned me about the situation in Spain, in

Lisbon and in Spanish Morocco. The more I said the more he pressed me for news, and his interest was vehement and insatiable. Finally he announced that the Marqués de Viana, a close friend of his who was his equerry in Austria, had left to help me in Italy. It was the last time that I spoke to King Alfonso; he died in Rome before I ever saw him again, in the same hotel where I was staying.

Viana arrived the next morning. He was a naval officer and a second cousin of my wife's; twelve years before, off the northern coast of Morocco, we had both been with General Primo de Rivera on board the *Reina Victoria Eugenia* for the landing at Alcázar Seguer. Thanks to an influential friend, in a matter of hours he arranged a meeting with Count Ciano, the Italian Minister for Foreign Affairs. Viana's optimism and sound judgement, and the fact that he spoke for King Alfonso, were invaluable during the crucial days that followed.

Galeazzo Ciano received us in his sumptuous office at the Ministero degli Esteri. Quick of mind, warm-hearted and attractive, he had lived in the Argentine for years and his Spanish was fluent and easy. He glanced at my credentials while I outlined the purpose that had brought me to Rome. His reaction was enthusiastic and spontaneous. Without hesitating an instant he promised us the necessary aid. 'We must put an end to the Communist threat in the Mediterranean,' he cried. Then he questioned me closely with regard to the Spanish rebellion. What were its aims? Who was its leader? What made me think it was Franco? Now that Sanjurjo was dead, would not others dispute the leadership of the rising? I did my best to reassure Ciano, who again insisted that Italy would not let us down. Suddenly he pulled himself up. 'You realize, of course,' he said, 'that I must speak to a certain person before giving you a definite assurance. Why not see me tomorrow?'

The next day we were met by Signor Anfuso, the Foreign Minister's *chef de cabinet*. A warm smile and a courteous welcome did not make up for what he had to say. His Excellency had considered our proposals. Deeply as he regretted this, he found it impossible to accept them. When did we plan to leave Rome? 'There must be some misunderstanding,' I interrupted. 'We have no intention of leaving, yet. In any case we cannot leave before seeing Count Ciano a second time. There are certain facts I must submit to him.'

My remonstrances must have sounded childish. If the Minister's decision was final, we had to pack up and go. But Anfuso, under much pressure from both of us, promised to do his best. A day or so later we returned for our second interview with the Foreign Secretary. Ciano assured us that we could rely on his personal sympathy in our courageous struggle against a dangerous enemy—this time he did not speak of a 'common' enemy—but aircraft and men were different. 'Your Excellency can rest assured that in due course we shall not fail to pay for whatever we might receive,' I said. 'Señor Bolin, Señor Bolin,' countered Ciano in a conciliatory tone, 'the question of payment has not even entered our minds. This is not a matter of money, but of the tremendous responsibilities involved in action such as you propose. If we did what you wish we would be taking sides, we would become open belligerents in a civil war.'

'You are belligerents already, even without taking action,' I replied. 'In Spain we are fighting Communism; without planes we are lost. Other countries—Russia and France—will supply them to the Republicans. We ourselves have no equipment. Italy is one of the few nations in Europe that can provide us with what we lack. If we lose, Communism will spread to southern Europe and triumph in Italy as well. We ask for your help because we need it, but the battle we are fighting is your own.'

I spoke passionately, without weighing my words or resorting to the language of diplomacy, nor was there any attempt at bargaining on my part. I had not been authorized to offer anything in exchange for what I requested. Throughout the interview I sensed that to convince Ciano was no real problem. He had been on our side from the start and hated the idea of dismissing us empty-handed. 'Let me have another talk,' he said at last. 'This is something that should be thought over carefully. I shall call you as soon as I have news.'

It was hot in Rome, damp and hot during the day, but the nights were pleasant, and every evening Viana and I would dine at some open-air restaurant, filled with lovely, well-dressed women and good-looking men. My friend's light talk and the sharp wit for which he is famous kept my mind from the matters that weighed on it, but I envied the couples at other tables, who flirted, danced or chatted, carefree and happy. More than once we saw Ciano, wearing a white dinner-jacket and surrounded by attractive companions. He spotted us also but made no sign of recognition. At the Grand Hotel we lunched not far from the Spanish Ambassador; the presence of his family in Madrid was inducing him to remain at his post. Other members of his staff were more forthright. The Military Attaché, Lieutenant-Colonel Villegas, later at General Franco's headquarters in Salamanca, called on me to place on record his allegiance to the National cause. So did Captain Estrada, the Naval Attaché, who was destined to hold high office after attaining the rank of an Admiral. Señor Forns, one of the Secretaries at the Embassy, also resigned his post and declared himself on our side.

Ciano did not keep us waiting long, and this time he received us with a smile. The victory he had scored was as much his triumph as our own. 'Everything is settled,' he told us. 'My Consul in Tangier has seen General Franco. We are sending you bombers and fighters. In due course we may send more.'

'Will they fly straight to Spanish Morocco?' I inquired.

'That is where I understand you want them,' answered Ciano.

'In that case I would like to go with the bombers. It might be as well to have one of us on board.'

Two days later I got my embarkation notice. It told me to be ready at the Grand Hotel at 3 p.m. on Wednesday, 29 July. Punctually at the appointed hour a car drove me to the airport at Ostia, where, anchored in the muddy waters of the Tiber, a seaplane of a brand new type, a Cant-Z, awaited my arrival in a stiff breeze. On board the plane were General Valle, Under-Secretary for Air, and an officer named Ettore Muti who had assumed the name of Valeri. All the officers and men of the squadron I flew with had adopted *noms de guerre* for their Spanish mission. We took off for the air base at Cagliari, in Sardinia, and I was impressed with the performance of our seaplane, a bright red bird, beautifully fitted inside, which conveyed us at great speed to our destination.

At Cagliari, in the course of a brief speech that outlined the purpose of their mission, General Valle presented me to the officers of the twelve Savoia-81 bombers selected to leave next morning for the Tahuima airfield at Nador, near Melilla, our first stop in Spanish Morocco. In the course of his introductory speech he told them that I was one of the leaders of the anti-Communist movement in Spain, an overstatement which I did not trouble to contradict. At dinner I sat with the crew of the plane to which I had been assigned, a pleasant group of fair-headed fellows, full of enthusiasm for their unexpected job and eager for a chance to see another land. Before the first glimmers of dawn lit up the horizon we had shaved, showered and dressed, and were ready for breakfast. I took leave of General Valle. When I got to the field my eardrums were almost shattered by the roar of thirty-six engines, warming up in the grey mist for their flight. Gripping my little suit-case tightly, I started towards a plane at the door of which my companions of the previous evening were waving and beckoning me on. As I placed my foot on the first rung of the ladder, a Major ran up to me and, pointing at another bomber, said, '*That* is your plane, not this one.' I assured him he was mistaken; the plane I was boarding was the right one. 'Our leader wants you with him,' the Major insisted, 'better hurry. It's time to leave.' When I hesitated, he took me by the arm and shouted in my ear, 'This is an order!' I smiled my regrets at my young friends, shrugged my shoulders, and obeyed.

The squadron flew in perfect formation as soon as it became airborne—four rows of three planes each, with the centre one in each row slightly ahead of the other two, my own bomber on the left of the leading machine. From the gunner's turret in the rear I watched the flight maintain its pattern. In four or five hours, our leader reckoned, we would be landing at Melilla. Some time after saying this he pointed out a cape on the Algerian coast, situated, according to him, between Bône and Bougie. A glance at the watch indicated we were on schedule. To relieve the monotony of our flight my plane would occasionally approach the bomber ahead of us and playfully tip a wing in its direction.

We had flown several hours, and the contraption on which I was sitting—a large bomb—was begining to feel less comfortable, when I became conscious of a worried consultation taking place between the pilot and the navigator. Anxiously, or so it seemed to me, they were scrutinizing the instruments before them, shaking their heads and pinpointing positions on a map. 'Is everything all right?' I finally asked. The answer could not have been more reassuring, but we flew on and on, the Algerian coast became endless, six or more hours rolled by and still there was no sign of Melilla. Finally the long, low silhouette of Cape Tres Forcas, west of that city and almost surrounded by blue-green water, revealed its welcome shape on the horizon. We came down. Our machine was the second to land. From the ground I started to count the planes—two had already landed, and one, two, three, four, five, six and seven were in the air. Two and seven made nine. Again I counted. Now there were three on the ground and six in the air. No sign of the remaining three. They had probably lagged behind. They had surely lagged behind if they were not there. Perhaps they had landed elsewhere by mistake. At any rate I could not see them.

Consternation and dismay clouded the faces of my Italian friends, some of whom knew what had happened and were reluctant to reveal it. Hurriedly I discussed the situation with half a dozen Spanish airmen who rushed out to welcome us. Captain Criado, the son of an officer deported to Villa Cisneros after Sanjurjo's rising in 1932, flew off in search of the missing bombers. Much distressed, I called the area commander, who agreed that the loss of three planes was a calamity but found consolation in the fact that the nine bombers which I had brought with me could be put to good use when the moment came to cross the Strait with a convoy of ships, filled to their top decks with troops. I hurried to the Commandant's quarters, placed a call to General Franco in Tetuán and informed him of the situation. Immediately after this I dispatched a cable to London, telling my wife that I had arrived. Two days before I had sent her a message from Rome, saying that I was taking 'the children' to an African beach for a summer vacation. That same night, my wife purchased an early edition of a London paper and learnt that an Italian plane, on its way to join the rebels at Tetuán, had crashed in Algiers with the loss of its entire crew. When she reached home and read my cable she felt better.

One plane had made a forced landing near Oran, and its occupants had been badly shaken. Another had crashed on the right bank of the Muluya River a few yards from Spanish teritory, and all inside it had been killed. A third plane—the one to which I had been first assigned and from which an Italian Major had dragged me, almost by force, a few hours before—had come down in the Mediterranean and the entire crew had been drowned. Head winds and fuel shortage, caused in part by tanks insufficiently filled to facilitate take-off with a heavy load of bombs, had forced three planes down prematurely. The nine others which succeeded in reaching Melilla did so with only a bucketful of petrol in each.

CHAPTER TWENTY-THREE

The Dash Across the Strait

It took two days to enroll the crews of the nine surviving bombers in the Spanish Foreign Legion, which for the first time in its history now boasted a flying detachment. Uniforms for all, smartly cut and handsome, were completed in record time. Officers and men were provided with pistols, Spanish currency, identity papers and identification discs. The same competent Staff officers—Solans, Seguí, Zanón, Gazapo—who had rebelled against the Popular Front on 17 July, twenty-four hours before the day appointed for the rising, solved every problem smilingly and smoothed out difficulties for our new friends. Because I could manage to make myself understood in Italian and was not often at loss to interpret that language, I was appointed liaison officer to the group. My lack of status in the Army was overcome by promoting me to the rank of honorary captain in the Foreign Legion, a distinction which filled me with pride, and which in due course was confirmed by those competent to do so. 'Your hair is so grey,' they told me, 'that we should really have made you a major.'

By dint of much straining and squeezing we scooped out of the other eight planes enough petrol of high-octane quality—*tetraetilo di piombo al 0.56 per mille*, the Italians called it—to fly the squadron-leader's plane to Tetuán. As it was about to leave an officer warned me to keep clear of Cape Tres Forcas. 'We have a battery there,' he said, 'and no means of telling them that you're a friend. They might start shooting if they saw you.' So far out did we fly for safety that soon we were heading for Malaga instead of Tetuán. In the distance, to our left, I saw the little bay of Alhucemas, its perfect shape filled with nostalgic memories of another war. Farther west, as we approached the entrance to the Strait, an argument developed as to whether certain peaks visible in the deepening gloom marked the position of Ceuta, or the exact situation of Gibraltar. Dusk was falling. We had little petrol in our tanks and no time to lose, so I seized the controls and forced the plane towards the landing field at Tetuán, where a fire was smoking in the dusk to show us the approximate direction of the wind.

That same evening I presented my squadron-leader and his officers to General Franco. When the General learnt that the eight remaining Savoias would arrive from Melilla in a couple of days, their tanks replenished thanks to a small tanker which had followed us from Cagliari, their engines overhauled and primed, preparations for crossing the Strait were set afoot. The ships available for the purpose were a mixed lot—a tug, a tramp steamer and two mail-packets. To escort them at sea we had three warships that hardly deserved that name—a gunboat, *Dato*; a small torpedo-boat, known as No. 19; and a converted trawler, *Kert*, then in use as a coast-guard patrol. All three had seen much service in Moroccan waters. All three were decrepit and old. Not far from Ceuta a major part of the Republican fleet lay in wait—a 16,000-ton battleship, the *Jaime I*; two 9,000-ton cruisers, *Libertad* and *Cervantes*; a strong flotilla of destroyers, some of which were capable of doing 35 knots; and several submarines. In the air, until the Italian planes arrived, our effective force had consisted of three old Breguets and a Dornier flying-boat, somewhat the worse for wear. Practically every other machine in the Spanish Air Force was in the hands of the Republicans, to whom France had already sent twenty-five planes. Another twenty-six were on the way from Toulouse to Red Spain.

Against such odds only a man of Franco's mettle could have attempted the crossing, but the risk he took was a calculated one. He knew that the enemy would be thrown off balance by his initiative. Since their nearest base was Madrid, no Republican planes were likely to be around when the convoy sailed from Ceuta, and because their officers had all been murdered or imprisoned, competent men would not be available to direct the movements or the artillery of any Red ships that might try to intercept it. The arrival of my nine Savoias clinched the matter, but even without them the convoy would have sailed. It had to sail, in any circumstances, and though the presence of the Italian planes strenthened our morale and the likelihood of success, it was not a decisive factor. Of far greater weight was Franco's resolute will and his vision.

On 5 August, at 10 a.m., my bomber was the first off the ground. Several Red ships were lurking in the international waters of Tangier Bay, as good a hiding place as any. Our mission was to scout for them and attack, with the object of keeping them at a distance. Should no enemy vessels be in sight, we would proceed to Ceuta and drop smoke bombs in the harbour as a signal for the convoy to leave. The speed at which a fast plane can cover a small, familiar stretch of water remains impressive, at least for me. We flew, instead of sailing, from Ceuta to Algeciras, from Tarifa to Tangier, and from Tetuán to Gibraltar, in a matter of minutes instead of hours. Though the Strait was full of traffic, no warships were at sea, so we dropped our smoke bombs as arranged and remained cruising over Ceuta until the convoy gathered way. At that moment, the *Lepanto*, a Republican destroyer, sailed out from the Bay of Tangier; our Dornier flying-boat soon spotted it and warned the convoy, which turned back to await events. We ourselves also spotted the *Lepanto* and at once began to bomb it. It set off towards Gibraltar, firing wildly at us and carrying the casualties we had inflicted on its crew. One hour later the Governor of Gibraltar received a cable from General Franco reminding him that though a ship engaged in action had every right to land its dead and wounded in a neutral harbour, it also had to sail within a specified period of time, after which, the General added, he would proceed to bomb it, for while *Lepanto* remained where it was the convoy could not enter Algeciras. The Republican ship left its haven. Hugging the coastline, it set course towards Malaga as fast as its engines could take it and disappeared in the midday haze with another of our bombers on its tail.

By half past three the coast was clear, and the convoy sailed again. Swept by heavy seas, the little tug, which was one of the convoy's components, put back a short distance from the harbour. The two mail-boats left the tramp behind and *Dato* had to escort it. Five miles off Algeciras, a look-out on the gunboat saw a Republican destroyer, the *Alcalá Galiano*, heading towards the convoy from the northern shores of the Strait. Outsped and outclassed, *Dato* swung aport to intercept the destroyer, which the three escorting ships immediately engaged. The action lasted half an hour. About one hundred shells were fired, and so close did the *Galiano* sail past the dawdling tramp that those on board had a busy time peppering it with machine-guns and rifles. Finally the Red ship sped by and followed the *Lepanto*'s trail to Malaga. Every man on the convoy landed at Algeciras, an open and unfortified town which the battleship *Jaime*, by way of reprisal, unsuccessfully shelled the next day with her big guns. Little *Dato* suffered heavy damage and defended herself gallantly during the bombardment. Shortly after this, Franco flew from Tetuán to Seville. The forces he had sent from Morocco numbered six thousand men, all of them combat troops destined to make history in Spain. My squadron-leader's bomber also flew to Seville, and, being familiar with the ground beneath us, more than once, during the journey, I pointed out to the pilot that our goal lay somewhere north-west of the course which owing to navigational error he seemed inclined to take. It could have landed us in Madrid.

CHAPTER TWENTY-FOUR

A General at the Radio

Seville was saved for the rebel cause by the resolute action of an imaginative general, Don Gonzalo Queipo de Llano.

During the latter part of King Alfonso's reign, General Queipo de Llano had been an open critic of the Monarchy. When the Republic was established he enjoyed the confidence of its first President, Alcalá Zamora, whose son had married one of his daughters, and whose successors in due course appointed him Inspector General of the Carabiniers, or Coastguards, a post of some importance which he still held when the time came to rebel against the Republican Government. Strongly as Queipo de Llano may have believed that a republic was the best possible solution, when the regime went from bad to worse he joined those who wished to overthrow it. In Andalusia, where he was sent by the leaders of the revolt to investigate the existing possibilities, he found a small minority determined to act and a majority unwilling to do so, but despite the highly pessimistic account which he gave of the situation he was chosen to lead the rising in southern Spain, a decision probably influenced by a widespread confidence in his resourcefulness.

On 16 July he was told to leave Madrid for Seville and organize the rising with whatever means he could collect or improvise. It was due to break out on the 18th. 'All right,' said Queipo de Llano, 'I'll see what I can do.'

No concerted action had been prepared in Seville to combat the Communist menace which was subjecting the city and its inhabitants to revolutionary strikes, arson and murder. The mass of the population longed for law and order, but their opponents were well-led and numerous. Russian ships had landed arms and ammunition along the Guadalquivir River; a Communist *putsch* had been set for the end of July or beginning of August.* The moment Queipo de Llano reached

*See Appendix I, p. 339

Seville he went to Divisional Headquarters and called on General Villaabrille, Commander-in-Chief of the Southern area and a luke-warm Left-winger, explaining that he was on his way to Ayamonte, near the Portuguese border, to present a new banner to the carabiniers. He spent the night of the 17th in Huelva, half-way between Seville and Ayamonte, reading Pericles: 'We should combine audacity and reason in all things; to the prudent and the wise, cowardice is more shameful than death.' Soon he was to escape death by the skin of his teeth.

'I am going to call on the Civil Governor,' he said to his A.D.C. the next morning. 'What for?' 'To put him off the scent.' 'Won't he arrest you?' 'He'll start looking for me if I don't turn up.' The Civil Governor confirmed reports to the effect that an armed revolt was on the point of breaking out against the regime and listened while Queipo de Llano denounced the conspirators and upheld the Government and its policy, after which the General offered his services to the Governor and left for Ayamonte. As he climbed into his car he was stopped by a trustworthy lieutenant, who told him that Don José Cuesta, a staff major and a party to the conspiracy, had telephoned from Seville that Queipo de Llano was urgently wanted there. It is to Major Cuesta, Queipo de Llano's G.S.O.I. during the entire campaign and later Lieutenant-General and Chief of the Spanish General Staff, that I am indebted for this inside information concerning the initial stages of the revolt in Andalusia. Major Cuesta's call to Huelva was well timed; if General Queipo de Llano had continued his trip to Ayamonte he would never have reached Seville. Following instructions from the Minister of the Interior, who had telephoned from Madrid and ordered his arrest, Government Police started looking for him shortly after he left the Governor's office in Huelva. Had he been arrested he would have been shot.

In Seville the bull-fighter Algabeño offered the General his services and the support of a small group of Falangists. Queipo de Llano accepted the offer, donned his uniform, and, escorted by a cap-tain, set off for a plain talk with General Villaabrille. When he arrived at the latter's headquarters he overhead a violent argument between Villaabrille and Cuesta, and without more ado he burst into the office where they were speaking. 'What are you doing here?' asked Villa-abrille. 'Trying to find out whether you are with us or with the Popu-lar Front, which is leading the nation to ruin.' 'I'm with the Government.' 'That's too bad,' said Queipo de Llano. 'Why?' 'Because my instructions are to blow out your brains unless you surrender.' Villa-abrille, another General, two A.D.C.s, and a Staff officer were imprisoned in an adjoining room.

Now the entire garrison had to be subdued or won over, and Queipo de Llano left to harangue the Granada Regiment while Cuesta put the finishing touches to a proclamation declaring a state of war in Seville. But the colonel commanding the Granada Regiment refused to follow Queipo de Llano, and most of his officers did the same. They preferred to obey Villaabrille. Supported only by Major Cuesta, an escorting officer, and his A.D.C., Queipo de Llano won over a young captain who volunteered to take command of the regiment, and locked the remaining officers in a room. They could have overpowered him, but they lacked the moral courage to do this; they knew that Queipo de Llano was right. Some felt inclined to join him, but the memory of General Sanjurjo's failure in the same city, four years before, when all of those implicated in that revolt had been severely punished or cashiered, was too fresh in their minds. Queipo de Llano's disenchantment was great when he found only two hundred men in the barracks; like others in Spain, the regiment had been depleted to make matters easy for the Red Militias when the moment to take action came. But it heartened him to see the soldiers throw their forage caps in the air and cheer his harangue to the echo.

An infantry company marched to the principal squares of the city, where a state of war was proclaimed. Machine-guns were set up to enfilade the main streets. Firing, directed against the troops by Government Police and Marxist Militias, broke out shortly afterwards. A single cannon-shot and a volley subdued two Red armoured cars that had set out to intimidate the population, and, if possible, the rebels. The artillery barracks were occupied, and a battery was dispatched to quell the resistance in the Telephone Building and in the Civil Governor's quarters, both of them situated in the Plaza de San Fernando and occupied by strong detachments of Government Police. A cavalry captain deposed his commanding officer and joined General Queipo de Llano with his squadron. A major in charge of the commissariat reported under a misapprehension to the Civil Governor, who, under another misapprehension, allowed him to depart, dash off to the Municipal building, break the doors open, arrest the Mayor and his councillors, and participate in the attack then developing against the Civil Governor and his police. Because of this major's family ties with a Left-wing Cabinet Minister, nobody had suspected that he would join the revolt.

A call from Madrid was put through to Queipo de Llano's office; it was from the Minister of the Interior, who wished to speak to Villa-abrille. The reply he received must have surprised him. In Tablada, the military airfield, a solitary captain, Vara del Rey, picked up a rifle and by firing a few bullets into its engine grounded a Douglas aeroplane that was leaving to bomb Tetuán. The commander of the air base was deposed and arrested. The next day three more planes, on their way to Madrid from Cape Juby—the same planes which Franco had seen in Agadir—were captured when they landed to refuel. A simple stratagem released sixty-five members of the Falange, imprisoned by the Reds and in danger of being shot. Some of them were detailed to keep an eye on four hundred policemen who had surrendered in the Telephone Building and in the Governor's quarters, after the battery in the Plaza de San Fernando shelled both. A number of these policemen joined Queipo de Llano's effectives under the command of reliable officers. Three hundred more were subdued before they could leave their barracks. A contingent of Civil Guards, fifty strong, offered their services to General Queipo de Llano.

By now, Socialist and Communist Militias were mustering in the outlying districts, advancing towards the centre of the city, and on the way setting fire to churches—San Marcos, Omnium Sanctorum, Santa Marina and San Gil all went up in flames—or burning and pillaging private houses. The sound of gunfire brought from their homes men of different classes, who backed the anti-Republican rebellion and volunteered to fight. All this had taken place in the afternoon and evening of 18 July. To let the people know what was happening, and what could happen unless order was quickly restored, General Queipo de Llano resorted to the radio. It was the first of his many nightly broadcasts. The General had the knack of talking simply to his listeners and knew how to reach their hearts. Soon, tidings of victory flooded the air. Republican reverses were transmitted over varying wave-lengths. A score of Foreign Legionaries, rushed from Tetuán in a plane, dis-guised their appearance repeatedly and changed cars to drive through the streets while, over the radio, Queipo de Llano announced the arrival of whole battalions. Because they had betrayed the nation and let him down, the General flailed his enemies mercilessly, and his sense of humour soon found favour with the people on both sides of the lines. At first his accounts were not always accurate, but the public liked being reassured and did not mind if what they heard was sometimes slightly coloured. He demoralized his opponents by narrating our successes. More than once, his threats cowed the Reds into submission and forced them to abandon positions or cities which might have withstood strong attacks.

During the war and in the years that followed I got to know Queipo de Llano well. I was often with him during his broadcasts. He would start by clearing his throat loudly near the microphone, a habit that distressed the personnel at the radio station as much as it amused his audience. The Reds accused him of drinking, but he was invariably sober, and all that he had at his side while he spoke was a glass of water. Occasionally he would call on me to speak: 'Come on, Captain, say a few words in English to our friends in Gibraltar!' As a boy, Queipo de Llano had spent years in a seminary, studying for the priesthood, but one day he vaulted over a wall and joined the ranks as a gunner. Eventually he became a cadet at the Royal Cavalry Academy in Valladolid and fought in Cuba and in Morocco, where he was repeatedly promoted for his daring. A born rebel, he opposed the Monarchy and Primo de Rivera, though not as determinedly as he opposed the Republic. He was handsome, arrogant and passionate, and he had great human qualities.

Seville, with Saragossa the only large city in Spain to be carried by the Nationalists at the start—Madrid, Barcelona, Valencia, Malaga and Bilbao sided with the Reds—was won by Queipo de Llano thanks to his courage, his audacity, and a series of inspired moves in which luck played a decisive role. It was due to luck that he received the message from Major Cuesta which prevented him from going to Ayamonte and took him instead to Seville. There, less than an hour after his arrival early in the same afternoon, he had the situation well in hand. What would have happened had his opponents attacked him and fought, instead of looting and burning? If Queipo de Llano had lost, who would have urged other garrisons to revolt in southern Spain? His talks over the radio encouraged many and influenced the results in Cadiz, Cordoba, Algeciras, Ecija, and Jerez, vital places all for the triumph of the Nationalist movement in its earliest stages. In Jerez, incidentally, Queipo de Llano's broadcasts and the resolute action of the local military commander, Major Arizón, saved the *bodegas* from losing their priceless stocks of sherry, which would have run to waste had a firm hand been lacking at the outset. The late Cecil Gerahty, in *The Road to Madrid* (Hutchinson & Co., London, 1937), tells us that Mr Carl Williams, a well-known sherry shipper and British Vice-Consul at Jerez de la Frontera wrote the following in *The Wine and Spirit Trade Record*, 16 October 1936: 'When the final clash came, on the 18th of July, the 'Rights' established law and order in most places, but, alas, in several towns, such as Ronda and Malaga, the 'Reds' got the upper hand and the most unbelievable atrocities were perpetrated. In Jerez, for a few hours, the result lay in the balance, but through the prompt action of Major Arizón, of the Remounts, who assumed command of the Town Hall while the Communist Mayor was haggling with the police, the situation was saved, and from that date Jerez has been policed by volunteers, and has remained more normal than probably any town in Spain. If it had not been for the coolness of this gallant officer and his men, there is little doubt that all friends in Jerez would have been murdered and all stocks of sherry gutted.

Queipo de Llano's broadcasts brought hope to countless citizens who were then at the mercy of the Reds and rallied thousands of volunteers to our colours. During the years that followed his power in southern Spain was almost viceregal, but he tempered it with kindness and listened to all. Though at times inclined to overstep the bounds of discretion, the wisdom and prestige of the only man he feared—General Franco—avoided a conflict of authority the results of which would have been disastrous. Don Gonzalo Queipo de Llano died on 9 March 1951, in a country estate near Seville presented to him by the people of a city that owes him lasting gratitude for having saved it from the Red terror.

CHAPTER TWENTY-FIVE

Operations in Southern Spain

In Andalusia, the southernmost region in Spain, and a vital one at the outbreak of hostilities, military operations were directed by General Queipo de Llano, commander of the Army of the South, whose Chief of Staff was Major Cuesta. No two more different men ever worked harmoniously together. Queipo de Llano was, essentially, a politician with a tendency to devote part of his time, even while the war was on, to affairs of a purely administrative and economic character, in itself a form, at least in Spain, of wielding influence in political circles. Cuesta was a realist who stood out for his ability to size up a complicated situation rapidly, even when its component factors were unknown to him. With equal rapidity he would decide the proper course to take, and his judgement rarely erred. When confronted by a problem, the nature of which, as likely as not, was probably alien to his field of work, he would screw up his eyes, bend his head to the right or to the left, and pronounce a decision. But he never did this without listening to those around him, even when their rank was inferior to his own.

Queipo de Llano's initial effectives consisted of 600 officers and men from the local garrison, 100 soldiers from Morocco, as many volunteers, and 50 Civil Guards, reinforced by three armoured trucks captured in Seville from the Reds and by six private planes from the local flying club, manned by volunteers, several of whom were shot down and killed. These amateur pilots 'bombed' their objectives with paving blocks when more suitable missiles were lacking. Volunteers from the Requeté and the Falange submitted to intensive drilling and were dispatched, as battalions, to the various fronts. Hunters, plentiful in a region which abounds in big game, contributed rifles previously trained on wild boars or stags, and horses used to round up fighting bulls, to form a cavalry squadron made up of Spanish grandees, noblemen, land-owners, peasants, artists, gypsies, workmen and street vendors, three hundred and seventeen strong and with sixty-year-old men among its numbers. The unit did good work in open country. Other groups, also heterogeneous, were equally enthusiastic. I remember a fellow who invariably carried his rifle loaded and ready—'just in case, you know'; it went off whenever he beat time with it to his own, or some-body else's, *flamenco* singing. With these forces, if they could thus be called, the principal *pueblos* around Seville were taken and pacified. Huelva, not far from the Portuguese border, was rapidly conquered; the miners at Riotinto, a potential menace, were subdued at the very gates of Seville. Cordoba and Granada were urgently pressing for reinforcements, nowhere to be had, and the presence of a strong Red force at Espejo, a village east of Cordoba, threatened not only this city but the road to Lucena and, more remotely, the main communications from Seville to Antequera and Granada. Queipo de Llano and Cuesta dealt in turn and successfully with each of these problems, but there was something else that worried them as much or more. In every town or village, in the farms and hamlets that surrounded them, citizens were in danger of their lives, for Reds in the area were applying to all and sundry the Bolshevik method of indiscriminate massacre.

Like Manolo Mora, Ramón Carranza, a lieutenant-commander in the Navy, liberated in the true sense of the word many *pueblos* in the country around Seville. When not busy at headquarters or with my Italian friends, I accompanied him on his expeditions—Constantina, Lora del Río, Fuentes de Andalucía. The scenes enacted in each were similar to those witnessed before—corpses lying unburied in the sun; widows and daughters of the victims, weeping before them; desecrated churches and gutted houses; men who loudly protested their innocence and turned out to be guilty. Most of those chiefly responsible for the murders had fled prior to our arrival. Invariably we took along with us some one who knew the *pueblo*; also capable lawyers, accustomed to question witnesses, and a police official or two. Culprits usually con-fessed. When confronted with their guilt, their defence was the same; they had been deceived by Red agitators, made to believe that by eliminating those who disagreed with them, razing their houses to the ground, burning crops, and devoting themselves to wholesale plunder, a new order would be established, all need to work done away with for ever.

A notable event of the campaign in the south was the capture of Ronda by General Varela, two months after the outbreak of the rebellion. I was present at the taking of Ronda, a city of some 30,000

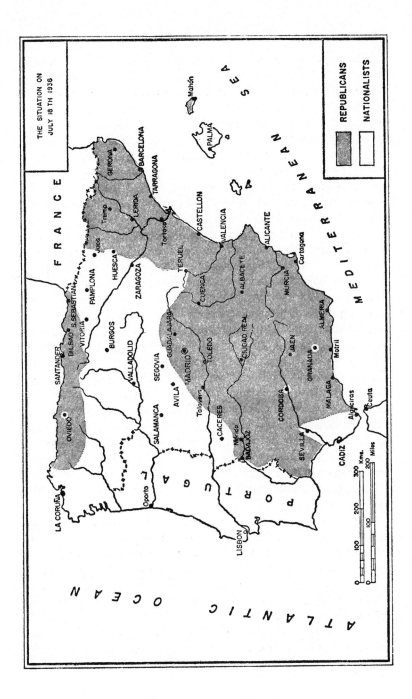

THE SITUATION ON
JULY 18 TH 1936

REPUBLICANS

NATIONALISTS

inhabitants, where there was little fighting; it could have been defended easily, but the Reds took off at our approach. Ronda was the first large town to be captured by our forces in Andalusia. It was famous the world over for its beauty and its unique situation. Six hundred local residents had been dispatched within its walls, and their killers had cloven vertically through all classes without pausing to select aristocrats or landowners, bankers and priests, of which there were certainly less than six hundred in Ronda. Several schoolfriends of mine were murdered there, and I saw with my own eyes the devastation at the beautiful church of Santa Maria la Mayor and at the schools set up twenty years before by the Duquesa de Parcent to educate the poor.

As matters stood, there was a risk of misunderstanding abroad as to the identity of those responsible for these excesses. Despite the difference in principles and conduct between the parties to the struggle, it was not unlikely that articles might begin to appear in other countries, pointing out that there was not much to choose between the two sides. But we had not armed the rabble, nor incited it to plunder and murder. We did not preach destruction or arson, nor condone crimes punishable under the penal code. Distinctions could be drawn, though some abroad might not choose to recognize them. I spoke to General Franco. Unless we acted promptly to establish our case, I said, the blame for what was happening might eventually fall upon us. Why not allow foreign correspondents to accompany the detachments establishing law and order in the *pueblos* then being captured, where they could speak freely with the inhabitants and learn the truth for themselves? Franco acquiesced readily. The horrors that were being enacted were investigated and recorded.

Meanwhile, not all correspondents attached to us were submitting their writings to censorship, as is customary and usual in all wars. In certain cases we could not even find their contributions in the papers they allegedly represented, which were printing stories with the dateline 'Seville' signed with names we had never heard of. It took time to sift credentials, the genuineness of which could not be doubted, from others, undoubtedly false, but we got to know that some of these journalists, after spending a few days with us, were taking advantage of the freedom which they enjoyed to file their pieces under other names in Tangier or Gibraltar, with complete disregard for the rules of fair play. I recalled the restrictions imposed on War Correspondents with the British during World War I. Measures similar to these, though far less strict, were rapidly introduced, and in Seville a Press Office was established, which I directed for a brief period.

Foreign journalists with us were a mixed lot in the early days of the war. They clamoured for interviews with Franco and obtained them when their credentials were in order and the course of events allowed the General a brief respite. The most punctilious and best behaved were those obviously acting for their respective governments; accurate reporting being much to our advantage, their activities met with no objection. One day a special correspondent of the *News Chronicle* turned up at my office. He had just arrived from London, his name was Arthur Koestler, and his credentials were in order, so, partly because he represented a paper inclined to favour our opponents, I gave him every facility and put through his request for an interview with General Queipo de Llano. The request was granted promptly, for Queipo liked talking to journalists. Shortly afterwards, inquiries about Koestler were set on foot by our Intelligence. But Koestler had vanished from Seville, and some months were to elapse before I came across him again.

I was still attached to my Italian friends as liaison officer with General Queipo's Staff. Occasionally I would fly with them or wangle a passage for a friend on one of their bombers. Trips of this kind were at the passenger's risk, for we were at war and the machines were military planes. Moreover, owing to lack of equipment, language difficulties and secrecy in flight, they did not always turn out as planned. One day, Sangróniz, the diplomat who had lent his passport to Franco for the trip from the Canaries, told me that he was leaving for Cáceres, a city in Extremadura, with a Staff Colonel, Don Luis Villanueva. 'How are you going?' I inquired. 'By car, of course,' was the reply. 'Nonsense!' I said, 'the drive is too long, and much too hot. Why not fly? It's only one hour and thirteen minutes by air. I'll fix it for you.' I spoke to my squadron-leader, escorted my friends to the airfield, introduced them to the pilot, who had arrived in Spain the day before, and wished them all a very pleasant journey.

Ten o'clock that same night found me in the hall of the Hotel Cristina, drinking dry sherry with soda and ice. Suddenly the lights went out, and everybody present assumed that an air-raid was in

progress. Seville was an easy target at night, for, despite the presence of Red planes hardly more than a hundred miles away, part of the city was floodlit and the rest illuminated as usual. The lights came back as suddenly as they had been extinguished. Fifteen minutes later Sangróniz and his friend the Colonel appeared at the door of the hotel, pale and somewhat shaky.

'You did not stay long at Cáceres,' I remarked. 'We never got there.' They narrated the events of the day. I had told them that they would take an hour and thirteen minutes to reach Cáceres; when the plane flew on and the Atlantic loomed ahead, miles west of Cáceres, the pilot turned south and proceeded over Portuguese territory for some time. Eventually they again saw water, a large expanse of it—the sea and the estuaries of the Odiel and the Tinto, two rivers that flow into the Atlantic near Huelva, one hundred and fifty miles south-west of Cáceres and fifty miles west of Seville by air. Again the pilot made a turn. Sixty minutes later they saw Malaga and the Mediterranean Sea, one hundred miles south of Seville. Red anti-aircraft guns started shooting. 'Why not return to our starting point?' inquired Sangróniz. 'The trouble,' said the second pilot, 'is that we're short of fuel. You will have to don your parachutes, and jump.' 'But I have never jumped,' protested the Colonel. 'Don't worry, sir. We'll give you a push in the back.' The Spaniards clasped each other tightly and said a prayer, the door of the plane was flung open, the lights of Seville appeared. Before they could give vent to their joy, the city was plunged in darkness. The plane, which had been mistaken for a raider, landed in the dark and came to a stop twenty yards short of a shallow trench situated at the end of the runway.

The Italians who came with me to Spain were a fine group of soldiers. They behaved gallantly and fought well. Some of their fighting pilots were outstanding. Their bombers carried out combat missions with competence and technical skill. Of Galeazzo Ciano and his determination to support us, manifest from the moment I spoke to him, I always think with emotion. In July 1939, at the termination of hostilities, he came to Spain and invited me to visit Italy as Director General of the Spanish Tourist Department and work out a joint plan for American travel in both nations. Soon after this I was appointed Commander of the Order of the Crown of Italy. World War II had already started when I went to Rome in September of that year. Italy was still at peace. 'What about Spain?' asked Ciano. 'She must keep out of this war at all costs.' Ciano wanted Spain and Italy to stay neutral. He meant what he said, and he paid for his sincerity with his life.

In Seville, General Franco had established his headquarters in a private residence opposite the Hotel Alfonso XIII, made available to him by its owner, the Marquéesa de Yanduri, and there he remained a few weeks, working well into the night with a small but efficient staff specially brought over from Spanish Morocco to assist him on problems hard to solve and urgent—recruiting, supplies, logistics, and the strategy involved in the march of his column towards Madrid over three hundred miles of difficult and hostile territory, with much fighting on the way. I saw him often, unflurried, smiling and ready for a chat, working in his shirt-sleeves during the heat of the day, taking everything as a matter of course despite the formidable nature of the issues before him. 'Don't do it,' he said when he heard that I was flying on a private plane to Algeciras, where my mother had arrived after being evacuated from Malaga on a British destroyer. 'You're sure to get killed. We don't even have a runway there.' When I disregarded this advice and my pilot, after losing his way, turned back over the mountains and reached Seville just before dark, I realized that the General had been right.

Franco eventually moved to Cáceres and settled down for more hard work in a sixteenth-century house in the old quarter of the town, occasionally sallying forth to inspect one part or another of a front that had not yet become solid and which changed its shape from day to day. The war had been on for nearly two months; the march from Seville, at first rapid because of scant opposition, was now meeting with stern resistance and a good deal of water as well, according to reports in British newspapers. One day, a foreign Correspondent whose sympathies were with us came to see me in a fluster. Papers in London, he told me, were reporting that most of our advance forces had been engulfed by a wall of water, twenty feet high, released by the Reds from the Alberche dam somewhere in the foothills of the Gredos range. '20,000 Rebels' had been 'Swept to Their Doom' at one point, headlines asserted, and the same torrent of water had 'Submerged 500 Tanks' at another point and '5,000 Lorries' at a third. At the offices of an important Fleet Street daily, I later learnt, a little Scot called Mr McGregor who acted as map man for that paper produced a splendid map with captions showing, 'dams open *there*', '500 tanks submerged *here*', and so on.

The news caused me some concern, for though we had far less than 20,000 men in the area and no tanks anywhere, and, when lucky, counted our lorries by the dozen, never by the thousand, they did indicate that Moses was not yet on our side. The morning the news appeared an Irish friend of mine, Toby O'Brien, who in later years helped me to lure countless British tourists to Spain, was walking up St James's Street on his way to White's when he came across Carlos González Gordon, a mutual friend whose name has already been cited in these pages. Toby said, 'Carlos! The news looks bad!' 'Yes,' answered Carlos, 'and it is even worse than it looks. We are fighting for Church and country, and we had reasonable expectations that Providence would be on our side. But, alas! this clearly isn't so, for only God could make water flow uphill!'

Of the two provinces that form the fertile kingdom of Extremadura, land of conquistadors and pioneers, Badajoz had initially sided with the Republic. A large part of its territory had been easily subdued, but before Mérida and the capital could be taken there was much fighting. Cáceres, from the start, was loyal to the National Movement. After Badajoz, the most decisive battle on the road to Madrid was fought at Talavera de la Reina, a key position on the Tagus and Alberche rivers where the Reds made a stand and were routed. Its name evoked memories of Wellington and the Peninsular War. As it was the only place near the Front where accommodation of a kind could be obtained, the Foreign Press moved there *en masse* and questioned me daily, almost hourly, as to whether the Alcázar at Toledo, or the city of Madrid, constituted Franco's first objective. Anyone capable of reading a map and the heart and the mind of a Spaniard could have guessed the answer.

CHAPTER TWENTY-SIX

The Relief of the Alcázar

According to the first reports that reached Seville about the middle of August, a group of cadets were being besieged by the Reds in the Alcázar. Unless we rescued them soon—and they were three hundred miles away—they would have to surrender or perish. In truth, the cadets in the Alcázar were not many. It was midsummer, holiday time for the Infantry Academy established within its thick walls, and most of them were away. Whoever the defenders might be, to heighten their morale our High Command dispatched planes which at great risk dropped messages, first-aid equipment, and food on the central court-yard of the building, a small target from the air. It was all we could do until our troops managed to reach them. More than once we heard that they had surrendered. Circulated by our enemies, the news invariably proved to be false, but the defenders had slender chances at best. They could only be a handful. Their opponents had the manpower and resources of a capital city like Madrid, only forty miles away. Time was also on their side.

In any case, the Alcázar had to be relieved. It had seen one thousand years of Spanish history; it was the home of the Infantry Academy; its turrets and its ramparts crowned the Imperial City of Toledo. It had become a symbol. The Alcázar had to be relieved and its defenders rescued, for the Reds were sure to slaughter all who fell into their hands. Advancing columns were not pressed unduly, so as not to endanger the whole campaign, but the choice of Madrid or Toledo as a first objective was never a question in Franco's mind. His troops would go first to the Alcázar. After Toledo was captured they might march on the capital and either attack it or invest it, should this be the best course to adopt. From a purely military point of view, Toledo had to be taken before the outskirts of Madrid were reached, if only because the right flank of the advancing column could not be exposed to the risk of onslaught from the south. To the north, Arenas de San Pedro and other towns had been neutralized before the advance from Talavera gathered way. In the same manner, Toledo had to be captured before the march on Madrid could be completed.

One glorious Sunday at the end of September—the 27th of that month —I came upon one of our batteries engaged in shelling a Red position on the outskirts of Toledo. I had motored up that morning with a cavalry officer and a military driver, covering the eighteen miles from Torrijos without seeing a soul and with no idea of where the enemy was until we came on these guns, partly hidden from observation by olive branches. Toledo itself seemed strangely quiet. The Alcázar, for weeks the inspiration of many hopeful prayers, stood erect on its summit. The houses that surrounded it were in ruins and its northern façade had crumbled, but through my glasses I made out the red and gold colours of Spain, fluttering feebly on a turret. The fortress was holding out.

Earlier that day, a gunner told me, a tremendous explosion had again shattered its walls. It seemed inconceivable that anybody could live within them. But the shells occasionally falling on the massive structure indicated that resistance continued; the efforts to abate it had not ceased. There enemy planes—Potez bombers, painted red all over— appeared from nowhere and flew straight towards our battery. I lay on my back in a furrow and watched them while they passed low over our heads and dropped their bombs on an empty field behind us. The performance was repeated a couple of times. Months afterwards, when one of their pilots escaped with another plane and came over to fight on our side, I was ordered by a Staff officer to interrogate him and learnt that the bombs which he was carrying had been deliberately dropped on the vacant field near by. He and a comrade had been forced to fly the Potez planes with pistols prodding their backs, but they had managed to drop their cargo wide of the mark and blamed their sights for the error. The pilot's name was Fernando Rein Loring; he was a native of Malaga and a friend of mine who in subsequent years flew over a million miles for Iberia Airlines of Spain.

Before sunrise next morning I was back at the battery emplacement. There was nothing and nobody there. We drove on, occasionally leaving the car to scout for a likely opponent. I could hear desultory firing; at moments it sounded quite near. The outlying houses of Toledo closed around us. Soldiers and Foreign Legionaries saluted without halting us or stopping our car. Toledo had fallen the previous night. We passed through the Puerta de Bisagra and drove up the hill to the Plaza de Zocodover, one side of which was completely ruined. Standing in the centre of the Plaza were five mules, sole survivors of those which had been in the fortress at the start of the siege, many of which the defenders had sacrificed for food. The slope opposite the Hospital de Santa Cruz was covered with corpses and live hand-grenades. A moment later I entered the Alcázar.

Our troops had relieved it a few hours before. The northern façade was shattered; light poured in through the void where its walls had stood. The great central courtyard, a masterpiece of Spanish Renaissance architecture, was littered with masonry and stones. Pompeo Leoni's contemporary statue of Charles V was torn by shell fragments and surrounded by rubble, but the Emperor's famous words—'If in battle thou shouldst see my horse and my banner fall, first raise my banner, then my horse'—were still legible on the pedestal. To carry out the Emperor's command, I later learnt, a ladder tall enough to reach the second story had been placed against the wall on the western side of the *patio*, beneath a small flag which fluttered with our colours in the breeze. In the scant space available, the defenders of the Alcázar formed a group. They looked like living Grecos, so gaunt and pale were their features, so firm and steadfast their eyes. In the centre, next to General Varela, commander of the relieving column, I saw the impassive, bearded face of the man who had led the defence and inspired it, Colonel Don José Moscardó.

I reported to General Varela. My orders had been to escort journalists to Toledo once the fighting ceased. Isolated Red posts were still being rounded up, but there was a likelihood that the Press would be allowed to visit the city the following morning. To Colonel Moscardó I mumbled a few words. 'The whole world . . .' I said. He would not listen. 'We've simply done what we could.' Others around him thought nothing of their own exploits and were loud in praise of the relieving column. For over two months they had withstood attacks of increasing intensity and fury; they could not understand how our troops had broken through so much opposition and covered so many miles of hostile country. Like true heroes, they were simple, reserved, and unassuming. Women were even more matter of fact. The chief concern of an attractive girl, fair-haired and blue-eyed, was the lack of a suitable substance with which to powder her face. For want of something better she was still using plaster, scraped off the walls. Anything rather than a shiny nose.

I spent the whole of that day in the Alcázar. So did most of its defenders, who had lost the habits of normal life and clung pathetically to the ruins which for weeks had been their home. For hours I spoke to the officers and men and listened to every detail of their epic. In the Alcázar and, later, at the Hotel Castilla, where General Varela set up temporary headquarters from which he directed operations—had an enemy feint from Bargas, a near by village, materialized that day, the situation in Toledo would have become precarious—I talked with Colonel Moscardó. Little by little I pieced up the story of the siege, obtained first-hand from unimpeachable sources, free from histrionics and narrated simply, with no thought for headlines or publicity. I needed it for the journalists at Talavera.

The day that the Nationalist rising broke out, 18 July 1936, had found Colonel Moscardó occupying the post of Director of Physical Training at the Military Academy in Toledo. He sided with the rebels against the government of the Republic, knowing that in the city he could count on 1,150 men, including a small number of officers, all of them professors at the Infantry Academy, seven cadets—the rest were away on their summer vacation—600 Civil Guards, for the most part summoned from small towns and villages in the province, and a few hundred civilians, 120 of whom volunteered to fight. Inside the Alcázar these men were joined by 520 women and 50 children, for the most part members of their families.

The following facts may help one to understand better the nature of the events that followed and the qualities that tempered Colonel Moscardó's character. Before the siege actually started, he received a call from the Republican Under-Secretary for War in Madrid, requesting him to dispatch immediately all available arms and ammunition in the Arms Factory near Toledo. 'I don't seem to recognize your voice,' answered the Colonel, playing for time. 'Don't you trust me?' inquired the Under-Secretary in a grieved tone. 'Let me have your orders in writing,' was the reply. The next call was more peremptory, and it came from Riquelme, a Republican General. 'Can we rely on you? Answer yes or no.' 'You can rely on me to defend Spain, not to betray her.' 'Very good, then. Send us all the cartridges you can collect in the Arms Factory there.' 'I shall deliver nothing to the Red Militias.' 'In that case I myself will take the stuff.' 'That's up to you, sir.' The Minister for Public Education was more cajoling: 'Already you have done enough? Why not abandon your attitude? To maintain it would be childish. You haven't a chance.' Again Riquelme called. 'If the Alcázar is destroyed you will be held responsible.' 'I am doing my duty.' 'Our forces are ready; they will overwhelm you.' 'Let them try.'

On 23 July, Moscardó was once more summoned to the telephone. This time the call came from his twenty-four-year-old son, Luis, but before they could talk a strange voice said, 'As commander of the People's Militias, I enjoin you to surrender the Alcázar. You have ten minutes. Otherwise we shall shoot your son, who is here as my hostage.' 'I readily believe you.' 'Speak to him if you wish. He is at my side.' 'Father!' 'What is it, son?' 'Nothing, Father. They say they're going to shoot me unless you hand over the Alcázar.' 'Put your trust in God, my boy, and die like a man.' 'A big hug, Daddy.' 'A very big hug, my son.'

Luis was cold-bloodedly shot—not then; one month later, in Toledo. I myself learnt the story a few hours after the Alcázar was taken, from the officer who had been present when the conversation took place and who had lacked courage to meet the Colonel's eyes when he told him what had happened. Others showed me the room and the telephone that had been used for the conversation, and suggested that both should be preserved to record their leader's heroism and the sacrifice of his son. Definite news of the boy's death did not reach Moscardó until 28 September, the day I met him in the Alcázar. That same night I gave the story to Spanish and foreign journalists at Talavera. Spanish papers published it immediately in Valladolid and Seville, and *The New York Times* printed it, from an A.P. source datelined Talavera, on 30 September, 1936. In 1957, twenty-one years later, and one year after Colonel Moscardó's death, Mr Herbert L. Matthews, a writer on the staff of *The New York Times*, published a book, *The Yoke and the Arrows*, in which he denied the veracity of this story and stated—on page 201 of his book, to be precise—'Between September, when the Alcázar was relieved, and November, not a word was said about the incident of Moscardó, his son and the telephone. Is this not strange?'

In a later edition of *The Yoke and the Arrows* Mr Herbert Matthews did not mention his version of this incident, but on 20 September 1960, he dispatched the following letter to General Moscardó's widow:

> My dear Señora de Moscardó, I am writing to you at the suggestion of friends of mine, who tell me that the passage in my book called *The Yoke and the Arrows* concerning the Alcázar caused pain to you and your family. This I regret very much, and I ask you and your family to accept my sincerest apologies. I am sure you all realize that I wrote what I did in the original version in good faith. I believe also, that those who furnished me with the information I used, likewise did so in good faith. However, I have become convinced, after reading the evidence published by Manuel Aznar and discussing the matter with other people whom I trust, that I must be entirely mistaken. I am preparing a revised edition of my book to be published next year, and I can assure you that the passage on the Alcázar will not appear in it. If you so desire I would have no objection whatever to you giving whatever publicity you think fit to this letter.

The letter was signed: HERBERT L. MATTHEWS, EDITORIAL BOARD, and dated from *The New York Times* at Times Square, New York 16. Many Spanish newspapers reproduced it in its original form, among them *La Vanguardia*, of Barcelona, with a heading that read: 'This is how Anti-Spanish Campaigns End', and *A.B.C.*, of Madrid, with the caption, 'A Famous Falsehood about Spain'.

Other conversations in the Alcázar prove that Moscardó's spirit did not falter as the odds against him lengthened. On 8 September, after seven weeks of intense bombardment from guns and planes, a voice was heard at nightfall calling for the Colonel or his deputy, Captain (now General) Emilio Alamán, an officer whose anguished thoughts on the day I entered the Alcázar were all for his wife and children, whose lives were in danger in Madrid. The call came from Vicente Rojo, a Major and former professor at the Academy, held in high repute by his colleagues for his military ability, and an able leader on the Republican side throughout the campaign, now living quietly in Spain like countless former opponents of the Nationalists and, like them, regularly drawing his retirement pay from the present Spanish Government.

Rojo wanted to parley. A meeting was arranged for the following morning. Punctually at nine the Major appeared and was led blindfold to the Colonel's office. When the bandage was removed he saluted and was offered a seat. Moscardó addressed Rojo reassuringly; the two men were alone save for Captain Alamán, who had stayed to witness the interview. 'Do not fear. You are among gentlemen. What is it that you wish to tell us?' Rojo handed Moscardó a paper signed by the leader of the attacking column and containing the terms for total surrender. The Colonel bit his lip, glanced at Rojo, took his pen and wrote: 'The defenders of the Alcázar reject any idea of surrender. They will uphold to the last the dignity of Spain.' The two men stood up, and Moscardó said to Rojo, 'If you want the Alcázar you will have to storm it. We would rather it were a cemetery than a dung-heap.' Other officers, former friends and comrades of the Major, entered the room. The conversation became informal, and cigarettes were handed around. 'Why don't you stay with us?' somebody asked. 'I wish I could,' answered Rojo. 'If I did so, this very night my wife and children would be slaughtered in Madrid.' He cried '¡Viva España!' once he was again blindfolded, his heart heavy with the knowledge of his disloyalty to all that he had held sacred throughout his life. As he left, Moscardó entrusted the Major with a message which said that the population of the Alcázar were anxious for the presence of a priest, willing to tend indefinitely to their spiritual needs.

In this request, the Republicans saw a chance to weaken the morale of their opponents. They would send a priest, but they would select him carefully.

Their choice was Don Enrique Vázquez Camarasa, a canon of Madrid Cathedral renowned for his suave and persuasive oratory who, somewhat surprisingly, had so far escaped from being murdered by the Republicans. A truce was called. Camarasa walked up the slope leading to the Alcázar, a large crucifix in his right hand. Two officers bandaged his eyes and led him through passages from which every living being had withdrawn. The canon addressed Moscardó in honeyed terms. 'Think of the women and children, here with you. Why hold out? It is the voice of God that speaks through me!' The Colonel cut him short. 'Are you willing to hear our confessions, say Mass and give us Holy Communion? In that case, do your duty. Time flies, and the truce ends at noon.' Moscardó was the first to confess. An altar was hurriedly erected, and an image of Our Lady was set upon it. When the moment for the sermon arrived, the colonel said to Camarasa, 'Kindly confine your address to religious matters. Do not utter a single word which might lower the morale of my people.' After the service Moscardó beckoned to a woman. 'Are any of you here under duress?' he asked her. 'Not one of us will leave the Alcázar without our husbands and children,' was the reply. Camarasa lowered his head and departed. A few days later, the Popular Front gave him a safe-conduct to France.

All that the defenders had in the way of armaments were 26 machine-guns and repeating rifles, 2 small guns, 3 trench mortars, 500 rifles and one million cartridges—the same cartridges which Moscardó had refused to dispatch to Madrid. The commissariat was stocked with 1,100 lb. of potatoes, 2,640 lb. of white beans, 440 lb. of rice, and 220 lb. of chocolate, plus two sacks each of rice, beans, sugar and salt, the result of a successful raid. Other sorties produced fifty sacks of wheat and 140 tins of condensed milk. A number of horses and mules had to be sacrificed for food. Water was fairly plentiful, but supplies had to be carefully nursed to avoid destruction by enemy fire. Electricity was cut off from the outside shortly after the siege started, and after dark the only light came from a few evil-smelling wicks dipped in horse fat.

Everything was done to protect those within the building. A constant watch was kept on enemy gun emplacements; when those on duty spotted a flash, they cried out 'Fire!' giving time for others to seek shelter. Five Sisters of Charity cared for the chapel, and three of the officers led the religious services. Four doctors, none of them qualified surgeons, performed operations or amputated limbs without surgical instruments, artificial light, or any kind of anaesthetics or antiseptics. One boy and one girl were born in the Alcázar during the siege. Two ladies of advanced age died there from natural causes.

Until 17 August the defenders had no contact whatever with their friends in the outside world. All they heard over the radio were stations controlled by the Popular Front, which, again and again, broadcast news to the effect that the Alcázar had surrendered or was on the point of doing so. But on that day, practically one month after the siege started, an officer managed to tune in to Radio Club in Lisbon. Their joy on learning the progress of Franco's columns in the south and Mola's troops in the north knew no bounds. Five days later, on 22 August, a plane appeared over their heads, dived, and dropped three parcels inside the courtyard. Besides foodstuffs and medicines they contained messages from the Commander-in-Chief of the Armies of Africa and Southern Spain—General Franco. One week later other messages were dropped from planes sent by General Mola, Commander-in-Chief of the Northern Army.

On the night of 15 August underground noises were heard for the first time near the south-western façade of the building. A close watch was kept, and it was concluded that the Reds were digging a mine. One month later, all sounds of digging ceased. The mine, with five tons of T.N.T., was fired at 7 a.m. on 18 September. For some minutes afterwards, a hail of shells fell on the structure. The bombardment was followed by an infantry attack. Wave upon wave of Red militiamen surged determinedly around the Alcázar and stormed the upper floors of the building, hurling hand-grenades at the defenders below. To direct the defence, Moscardó posted himself behind a stone parapet in the south-eastern corner of the courtyard. Machine-guns started sputtering at the raiders, who planted a pole with a red rag emblazoned with the hammer and the sickle. Some of the defending officers volunteered to haul down the pole. To do this they tied together the wooden ladders which I had seen in the courtyard, and, disregarding the hand-grenades that burst around them, climbed up the ladders to the second floor, bombed the invaders, and hoisted the red and gold flag of Spain in the place where the Communist flag had fluttered. Two more mines, with six tons of T.N.T., were exploded under the building, one of them on the morning of 27 September, the day our troops reached the Alcázar. The gaping jaws of the craters left by these mines seemed large enough to engulf the whole garrison.

A careful record was kept. There were eight infantry attacks and thirty bombardments from the air; 15,300 shells, from field-pieces of various calibres, fell on the building. Active defenders numbered 1,100 men, of which 82 were killed, 57 missing, 30 deserters, and 430 wounded. Another 150 were badly hurt and three committed suicide. Five men and two women died of natural causes. No women or children were killed or wounded. Colonel Moscardó may have had this in mind when he greeted General Varela with his famous understatement, 'Nothing to report, sir.'

Night was falling as I left Toledo. Near Cardinal Tavera's Hospital, now restored and furnished by the late Duquesa de Lerma and María Cardona, a volley of bullets from enemy snipers hidden on a nearby

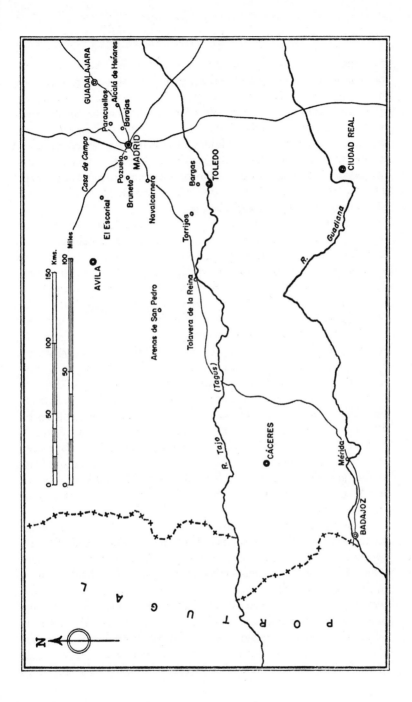

roof spattered the walls behind us as my chauffeur switched on the headlights of our car. I gave the main points of my story to the journalists waiting at Talavera, and accompanied them next morning to Toledo. South of Torrijos, Franco's car was fording the Guadarrama while a company of Foreign Legionaries waded the shallow water, and the men flocked around their leader and listened wide-eyed while he assured them that no forces in the enemy's ranks matched their aggressiveness and stamina. Once in Toledo, newspapermen obtained from Franco, from Moscardó, and from Varela, statements confirming all that I had told them the night before.

Inside the Cathedral a row of packing cases told a story without words. The one nearest the entrance, overflowing with gold and silver ornaments, had the lid leaning against it, ready to be nailed down; the next one was two-thirds full, the one that followed it was half empty. Had our troops been a day late, these treasures would have disappeared as did many others, including the priceless mantle of Our Lady of the Valley, embroidered with thousands of pearls, and a unique manuscript of the Bible, beautifully illuminated, which was later recovered. Stained glass from some of the 750 windows of the Cathedral, shattered by the explosions in the Alcázar, littered the floor. It gave me shivers down the spine to tread on fragments of a work of art lovingly executed five hundred years before, treasured through centuries, now irretrievably lost. I entered the Sacristy, where side by side with paintings by Bassano, Pantoja de la Cruz and Goya, El Greco's 'Twelve Apostles' and the 'Despoilment of Christ', which ranks among his masterpieces, usually hung. The latter was not there, but on leaving the room I saw to the right a small opening in the wall in which several large canvases had been stored. One by one I turned them over, The fourth was the 'Despoilment'.

It was not the only Greco that I recovered that day. I had a sudden feeling that something might have happened to 'The Burial of Count Orgaz', of all of Greco's pictures the most famous. I went to Santo Tomé, the small chapel where it is kept, and where the miracle depicted in the lower part of the painting is said to have taken place. The doors were tightly closed. The sacristan had not yet emerged from his hiding, and it took time to find him. Finally he appeared, disclaiming all knowledge of the picture's whereabouts; with trembling hands he opened the iron railings on the outside, the massive doors within. The 'Burial' was not in its usual place, but in the centre of the church there was a large canvas, rolled up on the floor. When we carefully unrolled it I saw what I was looking for; somebody had planned to remove the picture and lacked an opportunity to do so. Years afterwards I had the privilege of showing it to Lady Churchill. The same sacristan was in charge. I asked if he recalled what had happened to the painting during the war, or how it had been discovered after the relief of the Alcázar. He told the story faithfully, and at the end I inquired whether he remembered the Captain who had helped him unfurl the picture. Only then did he recognize me.

The heroism of the defenders of the Alcázar and Moscardó's sacrifice of his son's life were in keeping with Spanish traditions. Seven centuries earlier a similar episode was enacted in Tarifa, opposite the coast of Africa in Southern Spain, when Alonso Pérez de Guzmán el Bueno, Conde de Niebla and founder of an illustrious lineage, allowed the Moors to kill his son, whom they held as a hostage, sooner than surrender the fortress which he defended for his King. In 1936, while the Alcázar was being besieged, the officers and men of an infantry battalion in Gijón, attacked in the Simancas Barracks by Asturian miners with ten times their numbers and their strength, resisted the onslaught as long as they could and, when the walls that protected them crumbled, flashed a message to the Nationalist cruiser *Cervera*, saying, 'All is lost. The enemy has set foot in our barracks. Train your heavy guns upon us.' The request was not obeyed. During the Civil War, Oviedo, the capital of Asturias, was besieged for over a year by thousands of miners. Backed by the civilian population, a small number of troops and a handful of volunteers beat off the attacks and inflicted 14,000 casualties on their opponents while themselves suffering 2,000 dead and wounded. At the end, to cover a five-mile front, the defending forces numbered 600 stalwarts, of which number 100, though wounded, continued to fight until relieved. The siege of Oviedo, in its most acute stage, lasted three months of hand-to-hand fighting, terror, hunger, hardship and suffering to which the entire population was subjected. A large portion of the city, now admirably rebuilt, was destroyed by shells, fire, and dynamite. The epic has nowhere been surpassed or even equalled in modern times.

Concurrently with these events, Captain Cortés and 1,500 others, civilians and peasants for the most part, were holding out against the Reds in the Santuario de La Virgen de la Cabeza, an isolated monastery, on a peak in Sierra Morena, 2,400 feet high and 100 kilometres from Cordoba. Cortés and many others died, but they held out for nine months against 12,000 men, five batteries, trench-mortars, mine-throwers and machine-guns. Simancas, Oviedo and La Virgen de la Cabeza, together with the Alcázar, should have sufficed to tell the world, in the first months of the Civil War, that so-called 'rebels' were fighting in Spain for something more than the 'political ambitions of a General'.

CHAPTER TWENTY-SEVEN

The Opposing Forces*

From July 1936 to February 1937, while the opposing sides fought each other and recruited and armed their respective forces, the Republicans lost large tracts of territory between Seville, Badajoz, and Madrid and much ground west of San Sebastian and Oviedo and south of Bilbao and Santander. At the same time, the Nationalists advanced on practically every front, their numerical inferiority and scant resources notwithstanding. A comparison between the effective forces engaged at the start of the struggle, their numbers and composition may help us to understand the differences between them.

On paper, when civil war broke out, the Spanish Army consisted of 145,000 men, or one cavalry and eight infantry divisions, two Alpine brigades, artillery in due proportion, and sappers and other auxiliary services. The real figures were different. Some regiments had 150 men or less; their ranks had been depleted to the point where regular army units, the forces in Morocco not included, numbered only 60,230, of whom 37,000 were in Red territory. Automatic weapons were relatively plentiful in Madrid, Barcelona and Valencia, won by the Republicans in the first few days, but in most places the available supplies of arms and ammunition barely sufficed for one week's fighting. Security and Assault Police, the latter created by the Republic to quell disturbances in villages and towns, accounted for 37,500 men, of which 24,000 were also in Red territory, mainly in the more important cities. Under direct orders from the Madrid Government were 9,000 of the 14,790 *Carabineros*, this being the name by which the Coast-Guard and Customs corps was known in Spain, and 20,000 of the 34,230 Civil Guards, a corps first organized by the Duke of Ahumada in 1844, though loose reporting frequently attributes its creation to General Franco. Therefore, during the early stages of the conflict the Republicans had 90,000 trained men at their disposal, the Nationalists

*See Appendix II, page 349

only 56,750, though on this side the balance was made up by the quality of the forces which Franco brought from Morocco, 24,740 strong.

Other circumstances contributed to give the Reds a considerable lead at the start. They had most of the existing supplies, including petrol. They also had 170 planes—60 Breguet 19, 36 Savoia and 5 Dornier seaplanes, 30 Nieuport 62, 26 Vickers, 6 Douglas, 3 Hawker Fury, 3 De Havilland Dragon and 1 La Cierva autogiro, to which should be added a few additional machines in the training schools at Alcalá de Henares and Malaga. The Nationalist had 44 planes—33 Breguet 19, 4 Nieuport, 3 Fokker F-VII, 3 Dornier Seaplanes and 1 De Havilland Dragon. Seven of their Breguets were out of commission, but six light planes from the local flying club at Seville, manned by amateur pilots, rendered signal service during the first weeks of the war.

At sea, the Republicans controlled one battleship, four cruisers, sixteen destroyers, six torpedo-boats, nine submarines, and lesser craft. The Nationalists, one battleship, a cruiser, a destroyer, two gun-boats, and minor vessels.

Not without reason, the Republicans attached great initial importance to their militias, which were armed with automatic weapons, rifles, pistols and hand-grenades and numbered 530,000 men, many of them trained for street fighting in accordance with instructions from abroad. Socialist and Communist units, situated mostly in industrial centres or in large towns such as Madrid, Barcelona, Valencia and Bilbao, were 250,000 strong; Anarchists, who then amounted to about one million in the whole country, contributed 250,000 of their effective forces to the ranks of the Red army; Catalan separatists, known as *escamots*, provided 30,000 more. Together with the regular forces mentioned above, these militias gave the Republicans some 620,000 armed men, an advantage of five to one over the Nationalists, who, counting 12,000 Falangist and 30,000 Requeté volunteers, the latter mostly from Navarre, totalled only 123,500 men at the start.

The Republicans soon proclaimed their capacity to stifle the revolt; they certainly had the means to suppress it. Four days after the outbreak of civil war, Madrid announced that Nationalists in Toledo, Valladolid, Saragossa, and Burgos were 'on the point of being overwhelmed by five powerful columns' which had been dispatched to defeat them. Red planes bombed Nationalist cities. Red warships blockaded Spanish and North African ports in the vicinity of the Strait of Gibraltar. Anarchists

King Alfonso XIII of Spain with Juan de la Cierva, inventor of
the Autogiro, near London in 1935

The Dragon Rapide

The pilot of the Dragon Rapide,
Capt. C. W. H. Bebb

The author's receipt for the
chartering of the plane

OLLEY AIR SERVICE LTD.,
AIRPORT OF LONDON, CROYDON.

TELEPHONE:
CROYDON 5117.

No. 1041   11th July   1936.

Received from L. A. Bolin Esq.

the sum of

One thousand and ten pounds four shillings —

£1,010-4-0

PER. PRO.
OLLEY AIR SERVICE L™

The author's authority to negotiate for the purchase of munitions for the rebel cause. This is the only document in existence signed by both Franco and Sanjurjo after the outbreak of war

Near Nieuport, June 1918. The author (second from left) was at that time war correspondent with the British Forces in France

An ardent supporter of the Second Spanish Republic demonstrates his enthusiasm on the day of its proclamation, April 14, 1931

General Primo de Rivera at work with King Alfonso shortly after his rise to power

A youthful Major Franco, seen at an outpost during the Moroccan War

Generals Primo de Rivera and Sanjurjo at Melilla in 1925

Colonel Franco with a group of Foreign Legion officers
in Morocco in June 1925

The last days of the Spanish Monarchy. King Alfonso and Queen Victoria at the opening of the Ibero-American Exhibition in 1929, with Primo de Rivera (extreme left) and members of the Royal Family and the Court

Don Miguel Primo de Rivera, Marqués de Estella and President of the Dictatorship, a few months before his death

King Alfonso gave this photograph to the author when they met in London in 1932

The cathedral at Sigüenza, near Guadalajara, one of many churches desecrated by Republican extremists

The years before the war produced all too many scenes like this strikers' riot in Valencia in 1933

República de Obreros y Campesinos de Asturias

TRABAJADORES:

El avance progresivo de nuestro glorioso movimiento se va extendiendo por toda España; son muchísimas las poblaciones españolas en donde el movimiento está consolidado con el triunfo de los trabajadores, campesinos obreros y soldados.

Establecidas y aseguradas nuestras comunicaciones interiores, se os tendrá al corriente de cuanto suceda en nuestra República y en el resto de España.

Instaladas nuestras Emisoras de radio, las cuales en onda corriente y en onda extra-corta, os pondrán al corriente de todo.

Es preciso el último esfuerzo para la consolidación del triunfo de la Revolución,

El enemigo fascista se va rindiendo así como se van entregando los componentes mercenarios con su aparato represivo, fusiles, ametralladoras, cartuchería, proyectiles varios (que no podemos señalar) para que no se conozca del material de combate de que disponemos, ha caído en nuestras manos.

Las fuerzas del ejército de la derrotada República del 14 de Abril se baten en retirada y en todas nuestras avanzadillas se van sumando los soldados para enrolarse a nuestro glorioso movimiento,

¡ADELANTE TRABAJADORES, MUJERES, CAMPESINOS SOLDADOS Y MILICIANOS REVOLUCIONARIOS!

¡VIVA LA REPUBLICA INDEPENDIENTE OBRERA Y CAMPESINA DE ASTURIAS! ¡VIVA LA REVOLUCION SOCIAL!

El Comité Revolucionario.

10 - Octobre 1934.

A revolutionary proclamation issued during the troubles in Asturias of October 1934

Calvo Sotelo, whose murder by the agents of the Popular Front Government in 1936 sparked off the Nationalist rising

The menace of communism—Madrid, April 1936

Don Gonzalo Queipo de Llano, the 'Radio General', victor of Seville and commander of the Army of the South

Aid from Russia

The Relief of the Alcázar. General Franco stands between General Varela (right) and the hero of the siege, Colonel Moscardó. Behind Moscardó is the author

A poster issued during the war by the Friends of the Soviet Union. It reads: Russian words were followed by action! Russian action will be followed by our victory!

Largo Caballero, who would have liked to establish a soviet in Spain, with some of his supporters

Basque children arriving in Moscow, where they were sent by
the Separatists shortly before the fall of Bilbao

Christmas Day, 1936—
a Nationalist outpost
in the Guadarrama
Mountains near
Madrid

Men of the Navarre Brigades marching on the Eastern Front

Destruction caused at the Alcázar by Republican mines

Communist officers raising clenched fists and sickles. Below,
Nationalist soldiers advancing on enemy positions

The author as an Honorary Captain in the Spanish Foreign
Legion, during the advance on Malaga in 1937

The International Brigades—prisoners on the Ebro Front

The Teruel front, January 1, 1938, when the temperature was below zero

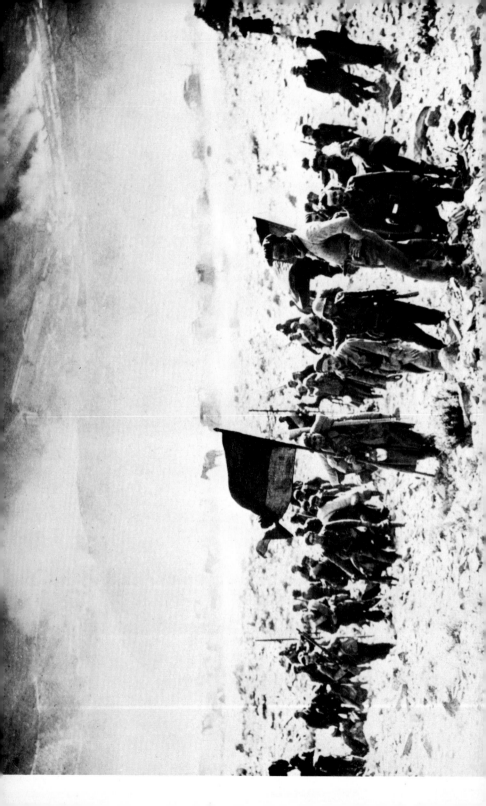

The victors—Nationalist troops in the
Pyrenees, January 1939

Nationalist soldiers distributing
bread after the fall of Tarragona

The last bulletin of the war, and the only one signed by General Franco. It reads: 'Today, after disabling the Red Army and forcing its soldiers to surrender, our victorious troops have achieved their objectives. The war is over.'

CUARTEL GENERAL DEL GENERALISIMO
ESTADO MAYOR   SECCION DE OPERACIONES

PARTE OFICIAL DE GUERRA
correspondiente al día 1º. de Abril de 1939.- III Año Triunf

En el día de hoy, cautivo y desarmado el Ejército rojo, han alcanzado las tropas Nacionales sus últimos objetivos militares.
LA GUERRA HA TERMINADO.

BURGOS 1º. de Abril de 1939
Año de la Victoria
EL GENERALISIMO.

After the war. Left to right: an officer on duty, an A.D.C., Captain Luis Bolin, General Davila (who commanded the Army of the North after the death of General Mola), General Franco, General Queipo de Llano

left Barcelona to invade Aragon with a column ten thousand strong. Six thousand of their comrades marched from Madrid to attack the Guadarrama heights while others advanced towards Avila. Not only did the Reds have a surplus of man-power, but their armament and supplies were far in excess of anything on Franco's side, the reason for this being that they held practically every large city in Spain and the stocks available within them. 'In one month,' they cried, 'we have raised an army the like of which has never before been seen in our country. The people in arms is now organized. Our militias are seasoned troops, with a high morale and plentiful armaments.' All they lacked was discipline, leadership and training.

The Republicans advertised 'twenty thousand vacancies' in the Carabiniers, a favourite corps of Negrín and his Communists, later dissolved by Franco for its terrible record in the field of crime. In Madrid, thirty thousand additional combatants joined Red forces devoid of technicians and professional cadres, and their leaders and junior officers inspired the men with so little confidence that some of the latter assumed command of whole battalions, usually known by flashy names. Even so, the 'Dimitroff Column', the 'Lions', the 'Legion of Steel', the 'Eaglets', and 'La Pasionaria's Regiment' were successfully routed by troops advancing under Franco from Seville, their members killed or made prisoners despite a wealth of supplies and plentiful artillery, most of which was captured by the victors.

Though they sometimes broke and ran, it was not lack of courage that caused Red militias to be overcome so easily during the opening stages of the campaign. Nor was there any lack of enthusiasm on their part; they had been efficiently harangued and filled with the necessary hatred. But they had no real faith in their ideals, and they had been urged to murder and plunder before being taught to fight. In *Homage to Catalonia* George Orwell, a highly sensitive and accurate observer of all that happened around him in the Spanish Civil War, provides a sound explanation for much of what was taking place on the Republican side. 'For the first few months of the war,' he says, 'Franco's real opponent was not so much the Government as the trade unions. As soon as the rising broke out the organized town workers replied by calling a general strike and then by demanding—and, after a struggle, getting—arms from the public arsenals. If they had not acted spontaneously and more or less independently it is quite conceivable that Franco would never have been resisted.' But the state of affairs that prevailed at the Front horrified Orwell. 'How on earth could the war be won by an army of this type?' he asks. 'It was what everyone was saying at the time, and though it was true it was also unreasonable. For in the circumstances the militias could not have been much better than they were.' They had been taught 'nothing about the use of weapons. The so-called instruction was simply parade-ground drill of the most anti-quated, stupid kind. It was an extraordinary form for the training of a guerrilla army to take. Obviously if you have only a few days in which to train a soldier, you must teach him the things he will most need: how to take cover, how to advance across open ground, how to mount guards and build a parapet—above all, how to use his weapons. Yet this mob of eager children, who were going to be thrown into the front line in a few days' time, were not even taught how to fire a rifle or pull the pin out of a bomb. After a few days, though still a complete rabble by any ordinary standard, we were considered fit to be seen in public.' 'Spaniards,' Orwell concludes, 'are good at many things, but not at making war.'

Had Orwell been on the other side, his dictum would have been different. Even on the Republican Front, once they learnt the elemen-tary rules of warfare and after the Spaniard's innate ability to take cover and properly use the ammunition in his cartridge belt was put to pur-pose in action, Red militiamen, though not as well led, were individually every bit as good as their opponents. Though untrained, they fought splendidly on the Jarama River, around La Marañosa, and in the Casa de Campo, when the capital was practically surrounded. On Franco's side at no time during the war were untrained men sent to fight or to line the trenches. A small force, battle-scarred or at least trained, was preferable to an undisciplined contingent, however numerous, and it was invariably commanded by army officers, not by some cock of the walk. People still ask why Franco, with little more than six thousand men who had marched and fought all the way from Seville, did not capture Madrid in October 1936, shortly after the relief of the Alcázar. It might be more appropriate to inquire why 50,000 Red troops in that city, made up partly of militiamen and with one hundred cannon and an International Brigade to support them, failed to overwhelm their opponents. Also, at that moment, an army of 50,000 Basques and as many more Asturian miners could have influenced some issues de-cisively between San Sebastian and Oviedo. They had practically nobody to oppose them. Nor did more than a very few oppose thousands of Reds in Seville, when Queipo de Llano took this city almost alone, or the Rebublican forces around the Alcázar and in the Guadarrama mountains north of Madrid. What happened was that they lacked leadership and the necessary initiative to fight and win.

On the Nationalist side, the infantry which Franco had brought over from Africa was proving its mettle in combat, conquering whole provinces while his ships and planes bridged the distance across the Straits of Gibraltar despite Red efforts to stop them. Veterans of the Moroccan wars were training raw recruits. General Orgaz was setting up the military academies which in due course turned out 50,000 new officers. Cavalry, at first almost non-existent, soon mounted guard on the various fronts. Warships in the slipways were put into commission and manned by amateur sailors and yachtsmen. The same troops which had left Seville with three batteries reached the gates of Madrid with twenty-four, having captured the balance on the way. Foreign Legion battalions and Native Tabors from Morocco reinforced available effectives. But recruits were never called up in excess of minimum requirements, an error to which the Republicans proved partial, mobilizing blindly and transferring armed masses without rhyme or reason from one part of the territory to another. Their raw material was as good as ours but it was the prey of demagogy, and it never quite recovered from the effects of the first days of the war, when possession of a lethal weapon was interpreted as a licence to loot and kill.

Without a false move or a serious set-back, Franco's armies grew in size until they reached a total of one million men, a figure not as considerable as it may at first seem if the extent of the lines that were covered is taken into account—2,930 kilometres, equivalent to approximately 1,818 miles—though, when the front was that long, our effectives were only a third of a million. One of Franco's earliest aims was to reduce its length. In the first fifteen months of the war he shortened it by some 75 miles when he captured Malaga, and, again, by 430 miles when his troops overran the territory between Bilbao and Oviedo and obliterated the entire northern Front. After the Nationalists reached the Mediterranean, their lines were still 2,170 kilometres, or 1,344 miles, long—i.e. 270 miles in Catalonia, from the Pyrenees to the sea; 90 miles from Teruel to the coast; 580 miles from there to the Guadiana river; and 404 miles from this point to Motril, which is sixty-seven miles east of Malaga. A front that long is vulnerable and must be manned effectively to become reasonably safe with only one million men to cover it. Both sides managed to do this, though at the start the Republicans were far more numerous.

Franco thought it wiser to employ a large part of the man-power at his disposal in munitions factories or in agricultural labour, but he spared no effort to bring over the trained reserves available in Morocco. In a few rickety machines which were already in that territory, or in others, hurriedly purchased, 23,393 men were flown to Jerez and Seville during the summer and autumn of 1936—2,063 in July, 8,453 in August, 9,732 in September, 2,300 in October and 845 in November, surely one of the first big airlifts in history. Simultaneously, some 880,000 pounds of supplies were brought from Morocco to Southern Spain by planes which, in their spare time, carried out 475 bombing missions.

Throughout the earlier part of the war Franco retained the initiative, but his resources were scant. In Navarre he had a strong contingent composed of Requetés, who, though trained and fit, lacked equipment. When General García Escámez, a seasoned Foreign Legion commander, ran out of rifle ammunition while holding the Guadarrama heights north of Madrid with a handful of volunteers, his commander-in-chief, General Mola, warned him that only 26,000 rounds remained for the entire northern army. In Andalusia, as we know, General Queipo de Llano set out to subdue the entire region with less than one thousand men; for a time the so-called 'Southern Rebel Army' consisted of little more than a few ill-armed battalions. And, according to Manuel Aznar, author of the *Historia Militar de la Guerra de España*, 'a sense of air power did not exist in Africa'—i.e. in Spanish Morocco—'until, thanks to a successful mission,* nine Savoia bombers landed there on July 30th.' Once this happened the outlook changed, but it should not be forgotten that the Republicans in Barcelona had begun to receive planes from France on 24 or 25 July 1936. Three weeks later, Red combatants from other countries, led by French and Belgian reserve officers, were taking part in the encounters around San Sebastian.

According to a statement in a magazine which the International Brigades published for a short period, their recruits began to assemble in Albacete, in south-eastern Spain, on 12 October 1936, eighty days

*See Chapter 22.

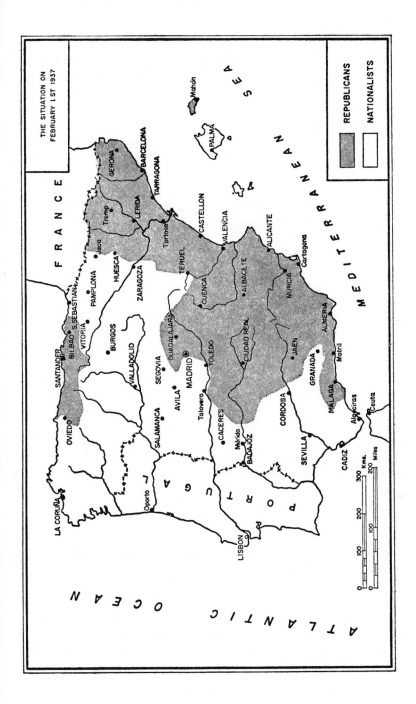

THE SITUATION ON
FEBRUARY 1 ST 1937

REPUBLICANS

NATIONALISTS

after the outbreak of war. Grouped together by nationalities, the Italian, German, French, Polish, Belgian, mixed Slav, and Anglo-Mexican contingents were the first to start training. By 22 October the German, or 'Thaelmann', the French, or 'Commune de Paris', and the Italian, or 'Garibaldi', battalions had formed the First International Brigade, later known as the XIth, which was soon reinforced with the Polish or 'Dombrowski' battalion. On 4 November this Brigade was summoned urgently to Madrid, the Garibaldi battalion remaining at headquarters as the nucleus for the Second International (XIIth Mixed) Brigade, which eventually included a German and Hungarian unit called after Edgar André and a French battalion which bore the name of André Marty, a French Communist leader better known in Spain as 'The Butcher of Albacete'.

Other brigades were made up of either three or four Battalions, each of 800 or 850 men strong. Attached to them were one or two batteries, a cavalry squadron, and auxiliary services, a composition that allowed the brigades to fight as miniature divisions, capable of independent action. The pattern originally established by the Russian High Command was followed in Spain to organize six International Brigades, the XIth, XIIth, XIIIth, XIVth, XVth and LXXXVIth. Recruits from different nations were eventually separated to put an end to the brawls which frequently broke out among them, though in some cases there was not too much friction. In this way, the XIth brigade became a purely German unit; the XIIth was exclusively made up of Italians; the XIIIth was composed of Slavs, but the XIVth was Franco-Belgian and the XVth Anglo-American. Only the LXXXVIth, organized towards the end of the war, when recruits became scarcer and harder to entice, continued to jumble races and nationalities with no regard for the consequences.

Besides the International Brigades, other units, also of foreign composition, were attached to Spanish Republican Divisions or to the command of whole army corps. Documents drawn up at International Brigades Headquarters on 17 December 1937, show that there were practically no Spaniards on the Staff, cavalry, artillery or other services of the 15th, 35th and 45th Divisions of the Spanish Republican Army. This equally was the case as regards the 11th, 13th and 14th anti-aircraft batteries; the anti-aircraft defence training battalion; the 1st and 2nd heavy artillery groups; a railway detachment attached to the International Brigades; the medical service, staff, and administrative personnel at their base; nine more training battalions; one battalion of engineers; and minor organizations. All these units were commanded or staffed by Russians.

In May 1938 the XIth, XIIth, XIIIth, XIVth and XVth Brigades were 37,351 strong, counting not only men but officers and personnel at the Base. If we compare this total to the number—125,000—which until that moment had enlisted in their ranks, we shall better appreciate the importance of the role played by the International Brigades in the Civil War and the reason why so many of their units had to be reconstructed and reorganized during the conflict, some of them repeatedly. Casualties must have been high.

How many Russians joined the Brigades? How many fought in the Spanish Civil War? It is difficult to answer these questions precisely. We know that the XIIIth Brigade was made up of Slavs—Russians, Bulgarians and others—but no record exists of their respective numbers. Many used aliases, and it is not easy to differentiate Russian patronymics from others of the same racial origin. However, bearing in mind that Slavs also formed part of the so-called 'Independent Units', there may have been, in all, not less than 18,000 Slavs in the Brigades, the majority of whom were Russians. There was certainly no lack of Russians in the Soviet Military Mission that supervised the Brigades, commanded by General Ian Berzin, a Russian, who was also *de facto* leader of these contingents.

Together with Russian soldiers in the ranks of the International Brigades, Moscow had in Spain an expeditionary corps composed of 2,000 Russians—staff officers of various ranks, military instructors, gunners, engineers, technicians, radio operators, armoured car and tank specialists, experts in chemical warfare, pilots and mechanics. *Le Matin*, the Paris newspaper, reported at one time the arrival in Spain of 100 officers, 500 N.C.O.s and 300 specialists of the Soviet Navy, sent to replace Spanish naval officers who had been murdered by the Reds or to recommission their ships.

A purely Russian Staff, made up of Generals and colonels, surrounded Berzin and constituted the most important section of the Soviet Military Mission in Republican Spain. Prominent in this body were various Generals—Douglas, commander of the Russian Air Force in the Spanish Civil War; Kuper; Akulof, who directed spying from Catalonia; Petrovich; and Paulof, who planned the operations near La Granja. Among the colonels the best-known were Gans, Kollief,

Alexander, Borisof and Troyecky. Most of these names were apocryphal. The men who used them not only acted as advisers to the High Command of Spanish Red army corps or other large units, but controlled them effectively. Ernest Zund, who fought in the Dimitroff Battalion, wrote in *Revelations* (Brussels, 1937): 'Russian military advisers have been attached to all Spanish Divisions and Brigades; consequently it is Russia, not Spain, that directs the Spanish Civil War on the Republican side.' The statement was true. Russians controlled not only the Red air force, artillery and tanks but ammunition supplies which they constantly threatened to withhold, and the Russian General Staff under Berzin was the real supreme commander of the Spanish Red forces in the Civil War. Nothing comparable to this miserable state of affairs existed or would have been tolerated for a moment on the Nationalist side.

In *A Study of Communism* (Holt, Rinehart and Winston, Inc.; New York, 1962), J. Edgar Hoover, the Director of the U.S. Federal Bureau of Investigation, writes this about the Spanish Civil War: 'One of the first opportunities to exploit political and social upheaval abroad arose in Spain. When a civil war broke out in that country in 1936, the Communists acted in line with the theory that the Soviet Union should be used as the base for the extension of Communist control over other countries. Soviet intervention in the Spanish civil war was twofold in nature. First, in response to directions from the Comintern, the international Communist movement organized International Brigades to fight in Spain. A typical unit was the Abraham Lincoln Brigade, organized in the United States. It succeeded in recruiting about 3,000 men. In all, the Communist parties of 53 countries were represented in the International Brigades with a total fighting strength of approximately 18,000, the first of whom arrived in Spain during the latter part of 1936. Second, the Soviet Union furnished direct military assistance in the form of tanks, artillery, and aircraft flown by Soviet pilots. For two years, Moscow pursued its objectives in the Spanish struggle. However, Soviet intervention ended in the fall of 1938, when the national interest of the Soviet Union forced it to turn its attention elsewhere. In Europe, Hitler's strength was steadily increasing. In addition, Japan's armed invasion of Manchuria posed a direct threat to Soviet territory in the Far East. At the end of 1938, the International Brigades withdrew from Spain. Many Communists throughout the world who answered the Comintern's call to fight in Spain were repaid subsequently by Soviet assistance in their attempts to seize power in their respective countries. Among those identified with Communist efforts in connection with the Spanish civil war who subsequently gained prominence in the Communist movement were Tito (Yugoslavia), Palmiro Togliatti (Italy), Jacques Duclos (France), Klement Gottwald (Czechoslovakia), Erno Gero and Laszlo Rajk (Hungary), and Walter Ulbricht (East Germany).'

In November 1936, when an International Brigade with three battalions was fighting for the Republicans in the outskirts of Madrid and similar units were in the process of formation in Albacete, the Nationalists had with them a handful of Italian volunteers, in all little more than 200 strong, made up of aviators and of 16 officers and 160 men attached to Italian light tanks and 65-mm. batteries which had been recently disembarked in Spain. They had arrived there as instructors, but they volunteered to fight. The Nationalist High Command at Salamanca, aware that foreign combatants were active on the Republican side, allowed Italians to join the Spanish Foreign Legion, which since its creation in 1920 had admitted volunteers of all nationalities into its ranks.* A special unit, composed of the 176 Italian officers and men mentioned above and of a much larger number of Spaniards, was equipped with 15 light tanks, 8 batteries, 3 anti-tank 65-mm. batteries, and a small signalling detachment. This Italian contingent remained at the Front until 26 November, when it was withdrawn and replaced entirely by Spaniards.

It was not until December 1936, by which time four International Brigades with a total of 10,000 men had been fully organized, that headquarters at Salamanca decided to admit additional Italian volunteers to the ranks of the Nationalist Army. Three thousand landed in Cadiz on the 22nd of that month; three thousand more arrived there after a

---

*In this connection it may be recalled the Franco-American Legion of volunteer airmen, which preceded the Lafayette Squadron in the First World War, was enrolled in the French Foreign Legion and took part in active warfare without swearing allegiance to France.

brief interval. On 17 January 1937 these men were drafted into an Italian Volunteer Brigade composed of two regiments with three battalions each, and one with four. Mixed brigades, known as 'Blue Arrows' and 'Black Arrows', with Italian equipment and two-thirds of their effectives Spanish, were also organized shortly afterwards.

One month later, Italian volunteer troops in Spain consisted of 15 battalions, 13 batteries, 3 companies of light tanks, a mechanized company of machine-gunners, three groups of sappers, and other services—in all 18,000 men, who played a part in the taking of Malaga. These units were eventually transferred to the Valladolid–Soria sector, and a corps of 35,000 volunteer troops—'C.T.V.'—was established there with four infantry Divisions, a battalion of light tanks, two companies of mechanized machine-gunners, a company of flame-throwers, and artillery, engineers, and auxiliary services.

By the end of November 1937 the C.T.V. consisted of two Italian Divisions, 'Littorio' and 'XXIIIrd March', and the Blue and Black Arrows. Four months later C.T.V. effectives again totalled 35,000 men, of whom 25,000 were Italian. By this time Franco had 58 Spanish Divisions and approximately one million men in the field.

Early in October 1938 the Nationalist Government decided to repatriate every Italian volunteer with eighteen months' service to his credit, a ruling that applied to the 10,000 men in the 'XXIIIrd March' Division. As a result, and including tanks, batteries, engineers and other services, the C.T.V. consisted henceforth of one Italian Division—'Littorio'—and three mixed Italo-Spanish Divisions—the Black Arrows, Green Arrows and Blue Arrows, commanded partly by Spanish officers and partly by Italians. In December 1938, three months before the termination of the war, the C.T.V. had in Spain some 28,000 men, of which about one-half were of Italian nationality, the remainder being Spanish.

Even if we include Italian aviators with 8 groups of Savoia *81* bombers, 6 groups of Fiat *32* fighters, and a group of *RO37* reconnaissance planes, all of them attached to the Spanish Foreign Legion, the total Italian contingent on Spanish territory never exceeded 40,000 men, a figure that should be compared with the 125,000 foreign combatants who were successively enrolled in the International Brigades, or with the million Spaniards who fought under Franco. Moreover, the Italian forces in Spain were always under the supreme command of the Spanish General Staff and of National Headquarters in Salamanca.

Early in November 1936 the Italian and German contingents with Franco were evenly balanced as regards numbers. Each had little more than 200 men, counting aviators, gunners, tank specialists and signallers. When International Brigades appeared on the Madrid Front, a German expeditionary volunteer corps was formed under the name of 'Condor Legion', members of which, recruited from the Luftwaffe, had landed in Spain in mid-November. They were mainly aircraft pilots and mechanics, anti-aircraft gunners, or specialists of various kinds. They numbered 4,500, or one-tenth of the effectives serving with the Spanish National Air Force.

The Condor Legion eventually consisted of one group of combat planes, one group of scouts, a reconnaissance group, four heavy and two light anti-aircraft batteries, two companies of light tanks, and signalling and transport detachments, with instructors for training purposes. At no time did these effectives surpass a total of 5,000 men.

In an article entitled 'Liberalism and Communism', published in December 1937 in *La Revue de Paris*, and quoted elsewhere in this book, Don Gregorio Marañón wrote the following with regard to the presence of foreign combatants on Spanish soil:

Much is being made at present—1937—of the so-called invasion of Spain by foreign troops, simply because Red leaders, lacking the means to inject a national spirit into their ranks, are trying to make a war of liberation out of a Communist campaign. As might have been expected, the manœuvre is meeting with greater success abroad than at home. Spaniards surrounded by Russians, Czechs, and others of the same hue cannot feel too indignant when they hear that foreigners are also on the opposite side. But no Spaniard, Red or white, entertains the fear that once the war is over a single foreign combatant will be allowed to remain on national soil. Spain has not yet forgotten the war against Napoleon, won with the aid of a powerful English army led by a great General. When that war came to an end, the army in question and its commander packed up and left without claiming any part of Spain. The same happened in France a few years ago, when entire departments were occupied there by English and American troops who retired quietly as soon as victory crowned their efforts. Nobody in Spain believes that the International Brigades or the Italians or the Germans have any territorial ambitions; the possibility of this may cause a flutter in foreign circles, but it leaves Spaniards totally unperturbed. Should any of the nations which now have troops in Spain show the slightest tendency to annex any part of the country, Spanish Marxists and anti-Marxists would join forces to frustrate its plans with the same ardour which they now display to fight each other. No Spaniard worth his salt fails to dream nightly of a piece of Spanish territory [Gibraltar] that fell into English hands two and a half centuries ago, at a time when Spain came close to losing its nationality. What is vital now is that we should retain our spirit of independence. On the Red side, even without Russian soldiers, Spain would be Communist. On the Nationalist side, even if there were millions of Germans and Italians, the spirit of the people would be as Spanish as ever. This alone strengthens one side and weakens the other. Had the Reds chosen 'Arriba España!' as their battle-cry, their chances of winning the war would have been considerably enhanced.

CHAPTER TWENTY-EIGHT

Salamanca, G.H.Q.

Early in October, after the capture of Toledo, Franco moved to Salamanca, where I had a busy time helping others to find a suitable residence for the General, his wife and his daughter, with additional office space for his Staff. We chose the Bishop's Palace, a roomy building opposite the two Cathedrals, which Franco occupied after being appointed on 1 October, at an impressive ceremony conducted in Burgos, Head of the Spanish State and Commander-in-Chief of all land, sea and air forces. He was unanimously elected to these posts by the votes of high-ranking military and naval officers and of the representatives of all the political parties that supported a rebellion of which, in only ten weeks, he had become the undisputed leader. His appointment inspired confidence in those who shared his ideals. His enemies lacked a figure of comparable qualities.

For myself I found an office on the ground floor of the Bishop's Palace and comfortable living quarters in the Duke of Alba's stately Palacio de Monterrey, a boon in winter after my frequent visits to the Front. My task now was to organize War Correspondents and I endeavoured to do this on a pattern similar to what I had seen at the British Front in France during the First World War. Spanish and foreign Press representatives were supplied with passes at Salamanca. Our Press Officers in Avila and Talavera de la Reina spoke a variety of languages, arranged visits to the Front, and escorted newsmen in cars specially assigned for the purpose. The need for these arrangements was obvious despite the protests of a few who would have preferred to roam freely, and it was illustrated by an incident which occurred shortly after I had set up this organization.

In France, a lieutenant, a captain, or a major, acting as Press Officers, invariably occupied a seat—the one next to the driver—in any car that carried correspondents to the Front. These Press Officers showed us what they thought fit and nobody argued with them. In Spain, Press

Officers were at a premium. Practically all of them were civilians, and the best we could do was to have one in the leading car and another in the closing vehicle every time a string of automobiles, filled with newsmen, left on a visit to the lines. The precaution was necessary for military reasons and also because other arrangements or the lack of them might have endangered those whom it was our business to protect. But on one occasion a car containing, besides the driver, three Spanish journalists who had thoughtfully decked themselves out as members of the political parties that backed our movement—Monarchists, Carlists and Falangists—dashed off while other cars waited to have their tanks replenished. Near Pozuelo, a suburb of Madrid, the fleeting vehicle took a wrong turning and ran into a Red platoon. Its occupants were lined up before a firing-squad, but when the subaltern who commanded it glanced at the dejected chauffeur, he threw up his arms and cried, 'He's my brother!' A tender scene followed, and the four prisoners were reprieved, at least temporarily. In Salamanca their comrades soon learnt what had happened and insisted that Franco should intercede with the Republicans, a step which might well have proved fatal had it been adopted. Instead, I suggested that they themselves request the Foreign Press Association at Geneva to demand leniency from the Madrid Government. Publicity, and a message dispatched by members of the Association from the League of Nations seat, did the trick. In due course, the four members of the party were exchanged for an equal number of Reds.

No continuous line of trenches marked the opposing positions in the Spanish Civil War, and a trustworthy guide was therefore an invaluable adjunct to anybody bent on exploration. More than once the commander of an isolated front-line post asked me how I had managed to get there, and his parting words—'Have your pistol cocked and ready in your hand as you walk back'—were not reassuring. The British Acting Military Attaché in Madrid, an American journalist, and two others, were fired upon one day and captured by tanks from our Mechanized Cavalry Division after being told that the road to Andalusia was safe as far as Aranjuez. It had been cut by our troops that morning near Seseña, five miles north of the Tagus. The car in which they were driving overturned in a ditch and its driver was badly wounded, but the rest escaped unhurt. Two days later, in Salamanca, I was detailed to question the whole group. The resulting information did not lack interest, nor was it difficult to obtain. Most of those whom I questioned were glad to tell me what they thought of the Reds.

When a new weapon reached our Front, or an offensive was about to be launched, correspondents from other lands would become restless and evince an urgent need to spend a few days on the other side of the French border. Their wives were going to have a baby, or they themselves required attention from a noted French specialist. About the same time I would get word from the General Staff, cancelling all leave for correspondents. It was invariably cancelled in similar circumstances on the British Front in France during the First World War, and the regulations in force during the Second World War were possibly even more stringent. On the whole, newsmen recognized that military exigencies afford scant leeway to the demands of competitive journalism, but some grumbled, and though we listened to them sympathetically, of necessity their laments had to fall on deaf ears.

Correspondents with us had their difficulties especially during the early months of the war, when it was practically impossible to transmit dispatches to their papers in the minimum time necessary for these messages to see the light in the next issue. The Republican Government in Madrid controlled all telephone communications from Spain with the outside world. This meant that we ourselves, and the correspondents with us, had no means of talking on the telephone with any foreign country, in Europe or elsewhere, a situation which remained unchanged until the war ended in 1939. On the other hand, correspondents in Madrid, Barcelona, and the rest of the Red Zone, in the same way as those attached to Republican troops on the various fronts, had only to raise their receiver and ask for a number; somebody saw to it that no time was lost in establishing the connection.

The lack of telephone communications with the outside world was bad enough for us, but to make matters worse Malaga and Bilbao, two of the three principal cable-heads in Spain, were for a considerable period—until June 1937, as regards the second—also in the hands of the enemy. This left us only with Vigo, the third of the cable-heads referred to above, but telegraph communications with Vigo from the principal theatres of the war were complicated and faulty, and we had no means of improving them; lines were usually jammed, and transmission was slow. Journalists with the Republican forces were invariably first with the news—in London, in New York and in other places, and certain editors preferred their dispatches to those which came from the Nationalist lines, though these would have probably given them a more accurate idea of the situation. When messages from our own side contained versions about some incident or other which differed from those which had already been published, editors found it difficult to print them; they contradicted something that had probably appeared in the previous day's paper. This state of affairs persisted for some time, greatly to our disadvantage. Indeed, it was not until we captured Malaga and Bilbao, where Italcable and Eastern Cable services had their tie-ups, that newsmen attached to us got their reports through fairly rapidly. Even then, our chances of making the headlines remained poor.

Why did we not try to improve them? Perhaps we attributed greater importance to winning the war than to inducing people to believe that we were going to win it. On our side, most of those who might have played a part in persuading others that our cause was a just one preferred to fight, and the far from plentiful funds at our disposal were better employed, we felt, in purchasing arms than in promoting propaganda, an activity to which those who feel certain that they are going to win are not always too prone. We had no foreign currency, and no gold reserves to back our freshly printed money. All the gold we possessed came from the wedding-rings and trinkets which our women willingly gave up to buy arms and ammunition. The Republicans on the other hand, held at the outset the entire gold reserves of the Spanish nation.

At the outbreak of civil war, the Bank of Spain had in its vaults gold bars and coins, minted in Spain or elsewhere, and worth, at the time, some £225,000,000. Today that same quantity of gold would be worth double. It was packed in 10,000 cases, and it belonged, not to the Spanish Republic, as newspapers in other countries sometimes say, but to the Spanish nation—to the two sides engaged at that moment in mortal conflict. A decree jointly signed, on 13 September 1936, by Manuel Azaña and Juan Negrín, respectively President and Prime Minister of the Red Republic in Madrid, empowered the Bank of Spain to ship this gold and send it abroad. The authorization was put into effect the following day. Two thousand two hundred cases, containing 22 per cent. of the total, went to Mont-de-Marsan, in France, and eventually returned to Spain as the property of the Spanish nation. The remainder—seven thousand eight hundred cases, worth £175,000,000—were shipped from Cartagena to Odessa. The gold in these cases, also the property of the Spanish nation, has never been recovered, though, shortly before his death, Negrín very properly handed over to General Franco's government—the government of Spain—the receipts signed by the Russians.

The possession of this vast wealth was one of the reasons for the healthy state of the Spanish national economy before the Civil War; its loss explains some of the difficulties which Spain has had to face in recent years. They might have been alleviated had the gold—sufficient, then and now, to cover the cost of normal Spanish imports during a two-year period—remained in the country that owned it. The date on which it left Spain is in itself highly significant, for it shows that almost immediately—less than two months—after the war started the Reds knew that they were bound to lose. Otherwise the gold would never have been shipped abroad. Part of it was used to deceive public opinion in other lands regarding the vicissitudes of the conflict and the issues at stake in Spain, to the extent that many, after years of reading about 'conclusive Loyalist successes' and endless 'Rebel reverses', must have wondered exceedingly how Franco ever won the war.

During the early part of the war most of the territory behind our lines was governed by a one-man Cabinet made up of Nicolás Franco, eldest of three brothers, each of whom has a place in Spanish history— Ramón, the youngest, hero of the first flight ever made across the Southern Atlantic, was killed in air combat over the Mediterranean shortly after the outbreak of hostilities. A *Junta* in Burgos looked after civil administration; Nicolás submitted matters of exceptional importance to General Franco after collecting the necessary information. A naval engineer, to hear him expatiate on vital problems was a pleasure. His title was that of Secretary-General, and his working hours were unique, as were his waking hours. Rarely at his desk before 1.30 in the afternoon, he would leave it at 4.30, return to his duties between 8 and 9 and adjourn for dinner about midnight; soon after this he would come back and work, articulate and active, until 7 in the morning. When General Franco appointed him Ambassador in Lisbon, Nicolás put his heart into his work and made it the corner-stone of Spain's foreign policy in the years that followed the Civil War.

In the Spanish zone held by the Republicans and their Communist friends people were starving, eating lentils and grain usually fed to cattle and thinking of meat, fish, fruit and milk. They had been promised that once their chosen representatives climbed to power there would be no further need to work. Some of them had not made matters easier by burning crops, razing fruit trees, destroying farms and agricultural implements. They could not blame others for the lack of food, for they themselves no longer cultivated the soil. In unploughed furrows, swarms of locusts nested and bred. They hit the rolled-up windows of my car as I drove south from Madrid shortly after this city was captured, and they would have spread to other parts of Spain had we not exterminated with lightning speed a plague never before known in the country.

While Red territories suffered from famine, food on our side was abundant. Many able bodied men had left their jobs to enlist or been called up, but women and all those too young or too old to fight filled the gaps and toiled unsparingly. Production equalled or exceeded previous levels. Consumption was low, for most large towns were in enemy hands. Markets were glutted. At the Viuda de Fraile, a small restaurant in Salamanca near the Plaza Mayor, where officers from Franco's G.H.Q. sometimes lunched, the fixed price for a midday meal —hors d'oeuvre, eggs with sausages or ham, fish or lobster, a steak or a cutlet, dessert and fruit—remained unchanged at five and a half pesetas, then equivalent to about two shillings and sixpence. After sampling this diet for some days I spoke to the widowed lady who had bestowed her name on the establishment. 'If I charged you one *peseta* less,' she said, misunderstanding me completely, 'there would only be two main courses, instead of three.' We settled for that, thinking more of our waist-lines than our pockets. Menus and prices in our zone were broadcast nightly across the lines, making mouths water and palates pine for peace on the other side. But we had our problems, and one of them was that our available stocks of mineral oil and petrol were running dangerously low.

In September 1936 a young man called José Antonio Alvarez Alonso escaped from Madrid, where his life was in grave danger. He worked for Campsa, the Spanish Government's Oil Monopoly, which had been created in 1927 by General Primo de Rivera and obtained its oil supplies from the Texas Company, an American concern. Alvarez

Alonso was on his way to Burgos; like countless others who fled from the Republican tyranny, he wished to join the forces fighting under General Franco. After leaving Spain he landed in Marseilles, where he rang Mr W. M. Brewster, who represented Texaco in France, and reported his arrival and his plans. Mr Brewster requested him to proceed to Paris, where Alvarez Alonso explained the situation to Captain Thorkild Rieber, Chairman of the Texas Company. Captain Rieber decided to honour his commitments, with the Nationalist Government of Spain. The Texas Company had a long-term contract with the Spanish Oil Monopoly; its chairman maintained the terms of this agreement with those whom he believed to be the real representatives of the Spanish nation. In doing so he showed remarkable foresight. The American company supplied oil to Nationalist Spain under terms identical to those which it had granted to Campsa, and the supplies helped the Nationalists to surmount a crisis which, failing this, would have had to be solved in some other, and probably much more difficult, way.

Apart from the inescapable evidence of war—uniforms, convalescent soldiers, and the like—towns and villages in the territories controlled by Franco had not only the semblance but the substance of normality. In Salamanca, where I lived at intervals for thirteen consecutive months, life was pleasant, safe and calm. Perhaps the beauty of the city helped to make it so. Salamanca stands two thousand five hundred feet high on the plains of Castile; it was cold when the wind from Gredos froze the rain into slippery ice, but the whiteness of the snow against an intense blue sky and the golden-coloured buildings of the city conjured up one of the loveliest sights in Spain. In summer it was even lovelier. The stonework for which Salamanca is famous came to life under a stronger sun and glowed with a roseate hue.

Twice a witness to events which have shaped European history, Salamanca retains a diffident aloofness from public affairs which in itself is essentially Castilian. During the Peninsular War, Spaniards and Englishmen under Wellington fought Junot and Masséna at Fuentes de Oñoro and Ciudad Rodrigo, close by. A third and more decisive battle was named in England 'Salamanca'. In Spain it is called 'Arapiles', as readers of Galdós know well, after two small hillocks that rise south of the city a few hundred feet apart from each other and from which the opposing sides hurled cannon-balls at their enemies until the allies won the day and turned the scales of war against Napoleon. Now the tide of war was being turned against the Reds from Franco's head-quarters in Salamanca, but the city, though involved intensely, re-mained serene. Unamuno's strictures had not disturbed the olympic calm impressed upon it by Fray Luis de León. On summer evenings children held hands and played in the small garden before the Palacio de Anaya, or in the Plaza Mayor. They sang sixteenth-century songs in the large open space adjoining the Dominicans at San Esteban, where a Plateresque façade shimmers with light at sunset, and before the con-vent of the Agustinas, in which an unusual painting by Ribera, a picture of the Immaculate Conception, is reverently treasured by the nuns.

CHAPTER TWENTY-NINE

Madrid in the Grip of the Reds

In June 1937 I spent three weeks' leave in London, during which time I was not altogether idle. My wife was there, working hard to support herself and our children. I had left her with the bare resources to cover their needs for a short period, and my services in Spain were not remunerated. But she had taken up part of my work and was doing it incredibly well, and she was passing on and receiving messages, vital for the success of our cause. When Juan de la Cierva, who at first handled these messages, discovered that his telephone was being tapped from two different sources, my wife took the calls that were pouring in from various European countries. She telephoned back and relayed them, addressing people by mysterious names, using two languages besides her own and seldom knowing to whom she spoke. In Salamanca I introduced her to Lieut.-Col. Barroso, then Franco's Chief of Staff, later a Lieutenant-General and Secretary for War. At once she turned to him and said, 'You are Sánchez!' She had recognized the voice which so often called her from northern Europe, under an assumed name, while she lived alone in London.

One day that summer, while I was lunching at Mrs Ronnie Greville's house in Charles Street, the lady on my left turned to me and said, 'I greatly admire General Franco, but why did he not occupy Madrid last year, after he captured Toledo?' In due course I repeated this question to the General in his office at Salamanca, where he kept very late hours. I would enter and announce that dinner had been on the table for a while. 'Really?' he would answer, a hint of incredulity in his tone. 'What time is it?' 'Getting on to midnight,' I would tell him, whereupon he would smile and say that he had thought it was only eight. Time, compared to what it can bring, has never meant much to Franco. Towards the end of the ten-year drought which Spain suffered in the forties someone expressed the opinion that it was never going to rain. 'It'll rain,' said Franco, all urgency absent from his voice. Long years among the Arabs have taught him that, if you wait, the greenest fruit will ripen and end by falling from the tree.

He knew that Madrid would fall, some day. He was as anxious as any to take it, but soon after his first attacks were launched he realized that to occupy the city then would have been disastrous. Bitter as his disappointment must have been, it was better to wait than to run the risk of losing the war with a rash move. Lieut.-Col. Carlos Asensio— 'Asensio el Bueno', a fine commander, now a Lieutenant-General and late head of Franco's military household—could have captured Madrid with little opposition soon after his troops camped on its outskirts, but the resulting situation would have become untenable in a very short time. Support for the Reds, in the form of arms, planes and ammunition, was pouring in from abroad in large quantities. International Brigades were mustering in Albacete, one hundred and twenty miles from Madrid. Had Franco's men forced an entrance, the city would have been invested and destroyed, and though destruction meant little to the enemy, Madrid was our capital and its inhabitants were Spaniards like ourselves. Franco lacked the military resources to protect Madrid from aeroplane bombs and shells, once he took it. His combat troops only numbered six thousand, and their artillery was scarce. Had they entered the city they would have been pinned down within it and found it hard to defend themselves against superior numbers. Their initiative and mobility would have been lost.

Madrid itself was never an objective for our guns. We resorted to counter-battery fire only when we had to—i.e. when the enemy shelled us from the western outskirts of the town. Because of this, some buildings were demolished or defaced, but most of the city remained untouched until the end. We nursed it carefully, almost tenderly. The damage caused inside it by shells or bombs falling wide of their mark was used as copy by writers of international repute, eager to thrill their editors and readers with visions of danger and destruction, but Madrid itself suffered less in the course of its thirty months' siege than many Allied or German towns in a single night of terror during the Second World War.

From a former royal property, the Casa de Campo, today the Spanish capital's largest park, the city seemed close enough to touch. It remained distant and unattainable for nearly three years. The Foreign Legion dug trenches on the grassy slopes in the Parque del Oeste and in the University City, farther on, and its men shared the watch with

Moorish Regulars who had crossed the Strait with them and whose dwindling ranks, like their own, were constantly being replenished with volunteers. For the Moors, this was a holy war. 'We do not understand why you depose your King,' they had said to me when the Republic was established in Spain and churches began to go up in flames, 'but whoever burns the house of God is an enemy of Allah.' To argue the point adequately, they had enlisted with such zest that in Morocco, during the first days of the Civil War, one could tell at a glance which of them had already been enrolled, which had been rejected, and which remained a prey to anguish while a recruiting sergeant settled the issue. They fought well, but at the outbreak of hostilities it was not easy to make them understand that on principle and in practice the army to which they belonged did not indulge in looting. To their way of thinking, anything or anybody on the other side was fair game. They looked surprised and hurt when ordered to release the goat which they were leading on a string and relinquish the fascinating sewing-machine which, deftly balanced on their head, would have made, together with the goat, a nice present for the wife—*la mujera*—at the termination of the conflict. Likewise, after conquering everything on their way from Seville to Madrid, they reached the conclusion that no place existed which could not be taken. 'Where are you from?' a Moor asked a Dutch friend of mine, Leo van Rhyjn, who lived in Seville and had joined our forces. 'I'm from Holland,' said my friend. 'Holland?' repeated the Moor, somewhat thoughtfully. 'Ah, yes. We took that yesterday!' And, lest on reading this, any should feel inclined to comment on the fact that Moors were employed by Franco in the Spanish Civil War, let me recall that troops from other continents were used in France by the Allies, in the First World War at least.

After the Spanish Popular Front directed its propaganda against the 'outrage' implied by the use of Moorish troops in Spain, Don Gregorio Marañón wrote the following in *La Revue de Paris*, December 1937: 'I myself was then in the country and realized that the outcry against Moorish troops would fail to impress Spaniards, who for centuries have joined forces with the Moors. Those who foolishly believe that history starts today, or that the past counts for nothing, forget that Spanish achievements as genuinely national as the Cid's campaign or as the capture of Granada, which crowned the reconquest of Spain from the Moors, were rendered possible thanks to the assistance of African soldiers. And on the Red side today there is not a man who does not feel closer to the Moors fighting against him than to the semi-Asiatic Russians piling up behind him.'

The Casa de Campo, and even more, the lovely Parque del Oeste and the land around the buildings in the University City, now beautifully restored and well kept, were then a tortuous maze of winding trenches, partly Red and partly ours, so close to one another that to distinguish their tenants in advance was not easy. From the upper floors of the Hospital Clínico the view of Madrid was rewarding, but each turning held the chance of encountering an enemy, complete with hand-grenades and rifle. When thick fogs from the Manzanares River enveloped the ground that banked it, the feeling one had was eerie. One only saw a few yards ahead and soon lost all sense of direction; there was no way of telling which side had fired the shells that rumbled overhead or the bullets that whizzed by.

It was on a day like this that the Duke of Fernán-Nuñez, my next door neighbour in the Palace of Monterrey, left Salamanca for the Casa de Campo. 'I'm carrying a message,' he said to me. 'I'll be back tonight.' Some hours later, a stray bullet hit him on the forehead as he walked through the fog in the former royal park, a mile or two from the house in Madrid where he had spent most of his life. A letter to his wife was found on his body. I have translated it as follows: 'My dear Chita, You will read these lines only if I am killed. I write them to beg your forgiveness for taking an active part in the war against the Reds. This may hurt you, but, after his duty to God, a man's first duty is to his country, and I offer my life for Spain. So far, I have usually been behind the lines, but there is so much destruction, misery and suffering, and so many of our friends are being tortured and killed, that my conscience bids me to do more. I am content and happy to go, regretting only to leave you and the children, whom I love dearly; may it be their lot to see better days. Manolito will live up to our family traditions if he fulfils his obligations, works hard, and chooses his friends wisely. With you, dearest Chita, I have been as happy as a man can be. You are capable and strong. Should it be my fate to die in this crusade, our children, and your Christian training, will give you the necessary strength to carry on. Bringing up Manolito and Mercedes will provide you with a mission in life which you are sure to fulfil. Forgive me, and pray for me. You know how much I love you all.'

The letter, signed 'Manolo', was dated 27 November 1936. Spanish papers published it a few weeks later. A brother of Fernán-Nuñez died as a result of hardships suffered while the Reds ruled Madrid; a second brother—Tristán, Conde de Barajas—was killed fighting near Teruel. Their fate was similar to that of families of all classes on our side during the Civil War, whose men fought and died for high ideals while their relatives were being butchered by those known as 'loyalists' in other lands.

October and November, chilly months that preceded a freezing winter, brought first-hand accounts to Franco's headquarters of conditions in Madrid and other towns, controlled by the Reds. They came from refugees evacuated to foreign countries, or from sources equally reliable and of which we hardly dared to speak. Not until the war was over did we talk freely of the unassuming men and women, members of our Fifth Column in the city, who crossed the lines at frequent intervals, bringing information of the highest value together with terrified citizens who after cheating death by a hair's breadth could scarcely credit their good fortune. The privilege of being furtively escorted out of the town called for courage, and courage was also needed to shelter hunted refugees, to act the role of a dim-witted peasant, or to answer questions at the city's gates. Rural Pimpernels and their wards presented trumped-up passes, spent hazardous nights in friendly farms on their way to the lines, slithered down the steep banks of the Tagus, and swam or rowed across the river at dusk or dawn, hugging the ground when those who they longed to see mistook them for others as they crawled over no-man's-land. But this was better than to lie awake at night listening to the sound of feet climbing the stairway, to a hammering upon the door, or to stories of the Dawn Brigade, a gang that collected its victims at daybreak. When its leader, García Atadell, realized that his friends were not going to win the war, he shipped with his spoils for South America without realizing that the French liner on which he had booked his passage made a call at the island of La Palma, one of the Canaries, where our police helped him ashore. Shrewder than Atadell, members of the 'loyalist' government sent a yacht to Mexico, loaded to the hatchways with valuables which had been looted from private homes and safe deposits. The yacht reached Acapulco, and the treasure was stored as a stand-by for a rainy day in the—then—not too distant future. It has never been recovered.

In Madrid, to have voted against the Popular Front, attended church or worn a tie qualified anyone for a bullet in the neck, Russian style. To harbour a refugee, listen to enemy broadcasts, or fail to clench a fist when others raised theirs in hatred was tantamount to signing one's own death warrant. Women over sixty were shot for having visited the poor or given them comfort and assistance. Married couples were seized from their homes and never seen again. Mothers lost their husbands and their sons in the course of a few hours.

In the Cárcel Modelo, a Madrid prison since razed to the ground to wipe out unspeakable memories, scores of innocent men awaited their fate. From the roofs of nearby houses Red militiamen trained their weapons upon them, killing dozens, wounding more. When prisoners huddled behind the shelter of a wall, their butchers swarmed into the building and mowed them down with machine-guns and pistols. Ministers of the Republic—Rico Avello, Martínez de Velasco, Salazar Alonso, Melquiades Alvarez—known for their Liberal tendencies and their opposition to the Monarchy, perished in the Cárcel Modelo or in the massacres at Paracuellos de Jarama, where hundreds were shot beside the long, shallow grave which had been opened to bury them in the yellow soil that surrounds Madrid's modern airport at Barajas. Depending on the way in which the wind blows when they take off or arrive there, visitors may catch a glimpse of the large cross that now marks the place where they were killed.

With them died General Capaz, a soldier who had opened up large tracts of territory in Spanish Morocco and who was carried to his place of execution from the hospital where he lay gravely ill; Julio Ruíz de Alda, co-pilot with Ramón Franco on the first plane ever to fly across the South Atlantic and founder of the Falange with José Antonio Primo de Rivera, who met his death about this same time in the prison in Alicante; Fernando Primo de Rivera, José Antonio's brother and a soldier like his father, who before being shot knocked one of his murderers flat with his bare fist, saying 'shoot me if you have to, but don't insult me'; the writer Ramiro de Maeztu, who told the firing-squad that faced him, 'You do not know why you kill me, but I know that I die here so that your children and your children's children may be worthier Spaniards than you.'

People sought refuge where they could and spent years in dread of death. Foreign Embassies—not all—took in many, and in due course the Reds allowed some to be evacuated to Mediterranean ports, where, if not recognized, and imprisoned or executed, they boarded a French or British naval ship and eventually reached Gibraltar, Genoa or Marseilles. These were the lucky ones. Others remained in fear of their lives. Throughout the years of mass murder, Republican newspapers published the names and addresses of citizens whose Red sympathies were not beyond question; after they were hounded out and shot, a doctor would take one look at their stiffening corpses and write on a printed form, 'cause of death: haemorrhage'. 'The men on duty at such-and-such a prison,' a paper would say—Madrid was full of chekas —'do not inspire much confidence.' The prison would be emptied and its inmates shot, including the guards. 'Don Antonio So-and-so is living unmolested at such-and-such a place,' another would write, 'we have not forgotten his views about Socialists in the Government.'

If he spotted the item in time, 'Don Antonio' would dash off to an Embassy and plead for admittance, but attempts of this kind were not invariably successful. Sometimes the Embassy was full, or the Ambassador might be away, far from all this unpleasantness in Biarritz or in St.-Jean-de-Luz, where the summer season was in full swing. With the hue and cry at his heels, an agent of a friend of mine arrived panting at the gates of a certain Embassy. He had with him his favourite dog, a thoroughbred of some distinction. The door opened, the agent explained his plight, and became frantic when met with a curt refusal. 'We don't admit refugees. But if you wish to do so you may leave your dog.'

This was an isolated instance. Most Embassies in Madrid behaved splendidly to some of those in grave danger, sheltering them in their own buildings or in others rented specially for this purpose, and though it would be unfair to single out any for special praise, certain representatives of Spanish-American nations carried out at their personal risk a humanitarian work that earned the everlasting gratitude of the Spanish people.

PART VI

CHAPTER THIRTY

End of the Red Rule in Malaga

Early in August 1936, when I arrived in Tetuán with the Italian bombers, my one idea had been to join the troops which, I then believed, were about to free Malaga from the Reds. It was my native town. Part of my family and countless friends and acquaintances lived there. Under the Republic it had suffered the loss of churches, art treasures, and buildings of all kinds. It was now again in grave danger. But my hopes were dashed when General Franco explained to me that, for the time being, any attempt to rescue Malaga was out of the question. We did not have enough men; other objectives were more pressing. Not until February of the following year did the opportunity I longed for arise.

Malaga is a city on the Mediterranean with a coastal highway running west towards Algeciras and Gibraltar, east to Motril and Almería. Other roads branch from it, like fingers from a hand, to Ronda, Antequera and Granada, or to less important towns between those. With the exception of some valleys near the sea and a few flat stretches on the plateau, the entire province is covered with mountains of which the tallest rise to an altitude of six thousand feet or more, while many are not less than three thousand feet high. It should therefore have been easy to organize a strong defence or at least prolonged guerrilla warfare but the mettle of the Red troops around Malaga was as poor as their discipline. When our offensive drew near, Rosemberg, the Soviet Ambassador, and Sourief, his military attaché, urged the Government in Madrid to send reinforcements to Malaga. Three divisions, made up of Socialist militias and International Brigades, were rushed south. They lacked combat experience, preferred city life to the trenches, which they abandoned whenever possible, and had hazy ideas of their new duties.

The forces under the command of General Queipo de Llano were insufficient for an all-out attack, but his disciplined units had a high

SPAIN: THE VITAL YEARS

morale, and the arrival of six thousand Italian infantrymen gave him the necessary man-power, a certain amount of mechanized transport, and an adequate supply of machine-guns, trench-mortars, and field-pieces. With these effectives at hand in January 1937, General Franco decided that the moment to attack Malaga had arrived. Positions held by the Reds were situated on a wide curve from a point on the coast near Marbella, thirty-five miles west of Malaga, to the town of Alhama in a mountainous region south-west of Granada. Reassured by their leaders and lulled by the apparent impregnability of the terrain, our opponents had restricted their efforts to fortifying mountain passes and the heights from which they hoped to repulse our assaults. Their confidence was further strengthened by the possession of a network of roads which fanned out from the city to outlying positions on the plateau, an advantage partly countered by the existence on our side of an outer road which ran parallel to most of the curve described by the front.

Relying on this, our General Staff prepared a simultaneous onslaught on Malaga from four different points—Marbella, Antequera, Loja, and Alhama. A fifth force would attack the enemy near Ronda and march to Malaga along the fertile valley of the Guadalhorce. Warships were to cover our advance along the coast and harass the highway to Almeria, the only means of escape left open. Weather permitting, aeroplanes would also intervene.

In Antequera, where I had arrived to visit our lines, the military commandant quartered me in a comfortable house occupied by a doctor with a large practice, a charming family and a fine cuisine. Part of the city had been burnt by the Reds. They had also murdered many of its inhabitants, among whom were several old school-mates of mine. My tour of the lines was directed first to Alhama, a watering resort with a Moorish name, three thousand feet above the Mediter-ranean and thirty miles from the sea. Most of the troops I saw around Alhama were Italian, and those I spoke with were cheerful and showed confidence in their mission. They were to advance to Zafarraya, whence if all went well they could reach the town of Vélez-Málaga and inter-cept the road to Almeria, or if necessary turn right and threaten the enemy at Venta de los Alazores, a key position on the road from Loja to Malaga.

Loja, where I stopped on my way back to Antequera, was also bustling with Italian troops. Accustomed as I was to the relative scarcity of artillery and mechanized transport on the Madrid front, the displays I saw here were impressive though the forces at hand were not numerous. Soldiers hurried through the streets, and the wide-spread splashes of their dark-green uniforms against the light-coloured soil of a countryside I knew so well left no doubt in my mind as to the effect their impact on the enemy would produce.

Army headquarters in Antequera were thronged with Spanish officers who had come to receive their marching orders for the following day, 5 February. Most of the contingents camped south of the city consisted of volunteers from Malaga itself, who had used every device to escape the Red terror and fight their way back to their home town. The remainder came from nearby places, and were equally aware of what had happened in Malaga and just as eager to win the city back for Spain.

My original plan had been to proceed from Antequera to Ronda and continue to Jerez and Algeciras, following the mountain roads behind our lines. At dusk, however, our sentries barred the way, pointing to evidence of recent fighting and to camp-fires that glowed on slopes a few hundred yards distant from which the enemy sometimes raided our posts and could have easily intercepted a passing car. I was forced to take the longer route though it meant making a wide detour. We drove through the night, stopping twice for a bite, our pace slowed down by an incessant rain that boded ill for the success of the operations next morning. But when we reached Marbella the sun was rising in an unclouded sky.

Two hours later we attacked the Red positions, a mile or so east of the town. The attacking forces in this sector were all Spanish. Their progress was supported by a cruiser and two small gunboats, one of which had driven an enemy ship aground some days before, and their commanding officer was Colonel Borbón, Duke of Seville and a distant relative of the Spanish Royal Family. A fine horseman, given to riding a prancing thoroughbred at the head of his men, the Colonel had set up his headquarters in the western outskirts of the town, where, when I arrived, he sat listening to reports according to which a lightning descent upon our rearguard was being contemplated by a Red detachment quartered in the village of Istán, situated north-west of Marbella on the slopes of Sierra Blanca de Ojén. I knew these mountains, and ventured the opinion that unless the said contingent had occupied Istán before we captured Marbella, and stored adequate supplies of food and ammunition inside the place, could there be any likelihood of its existence. Access to Istán, otherwise than along the road behind us, was not an easy task except for the mountain goats—Spanish ibex—which sometimes peered on the village from the precipitous crags that surround it. My conjectures proved correct.

The enemy before us, on the other hand, was quite real, and soon enough evidence of this reality came hurtling along in the shape of missiles fired by three Russian 12·40 guns, a calibre known among our troops as 'twenty to one'. Our opponents had entrenched themselves on both sides of the road ahead without taking into account that they could be enfiladed from the sea. They had expected too much of their fleet, formidable enough but absent. Shells from Russian pieces fell on Marbella and outlying fields; there were casualties, and an elderly gentleman on a visit to his nephew, a young soldier, was killed by a brick, violently displaced by a Russian missile. For a while our advance was halted. It took shape and progressed after our troops out-flanked the enemy in an encircling movement along the hills and the gun-boat *Cánovas* silenced Red guns and emptied the Red trenches with its raking fire.

Part of the road from Marbella to Torremolinos runs along the shore, and due to this the role of the attendant warships proved decisive. We advanced nearly twenty miles that day, encountering scant opposition, halting only to scour the hills and pine woods on our left and to make sure that no Reds remained behind us. The cruiser *Canarias* did not have to bring her heavy pieces into play; her mere presence was enough to startle the enemy and send him scurrying back to Malaga. Smaller boats were active, and their marksmanship was impressive. More than once they placed a shell through the front door or a window of the tiny houses inside which the Reds were putting up a show of resistance. A few rounds sufficed to blow up a truck loaded with explosives which had made off at full speed.

We occupied Fuengirola that same evening, and at dusk I turned back to Algeciras for a call to Salamanca and a good night's sleep. In the cork-woods east of Marbella I spotted two Republican soldiers, fully armed and walking unconcernedly among the trees. I stopped my car, got out and, pistol in hand, ordered them to lay down their rifles and hold up their hands, but the order had to be repeated, for at first they threw themselves flat on the ground and held fast to their weapons. They were yokels from Gor, a village in the mountains near Granada, with no idea of their ultimate destination and vague notions of what the war was about, so I drove them to Algeciras, questioned them separately, and handed them over with a clean bill of health. Two days later I saw them strutting down a street, wearing our uniform. From the way in which they walked they had obviously concluded that ours was the better club to join.

Early next morning I left Algeciras and rejoined our troops, which had met with little or no opposition as far as Torremolinos and beyond it. Before entering Malaga, however, the hills along the coast had to be cleaned up, supplies replenished and the men given a rest. Our entry into the city had been timed to coincide with that of the columns marching down from the hills. We had no news of their progress, but the ground they had to cover was more difficult. As I crossed the Guadalhorce the next day, a few miles from Malaga, my car was stopped by half a dozen soldiers who had chased about as many opponents into a farm house near the river. We spread out in the sugar cane and fired a few rounds through the windows of the building. Soon the Reds emerged, holding up their hands. Not far from the railway station, just outside Malaga, the vanguard of our column was waiting for the Italians to arrive before occupying the town, but I was anxious to enter the city and after some hesitation the Duke of Seville granted me leave to do so.

My car was flying the Spanish flag, unseen there for nearly six years, it bore the legend of General Franco's headquarters on the windscreen, and on the seat beside me I had a friend called Pim Vázquez and a sub-machine-gun. We drove rapidly through the unprepossessing thoroughfare that gives access to the city from the west, through the old Alameda, a leafy avenue where well-built houses had been gutted by the champions of a new order, through Malaga's lovely park, for once unkempt and dishevelled, through the stately Caleta and the secluded Limonar, where destruction had been rife and wanton. It was early, and few people were about. Perhaps they were staying indoors as a precaution, but those who saw me threw up their arms and cheered.

I was driving straight to a small house behind the Limonar, where, for seven months, a brother and a sister of my late father had been hiding from the Reds with many others. When I arrived there pandemonium broke loose; the joy and emotion to which human beings give vent when reprieved from impending death are pathetic and impressive. An American citizen whom I knew well left his residence and came to see me. He was Edward Norton, a partner in the firm of Bevan and Company, which exports almonds from Malaga, later Acting Consul there for his country. 'I can't tell you what this city has gone through,' he said. His wife threw her arms round my neck and kissed me. 'We've prayed for this day,' she told me. 'You're the best thing I've seen in seven months!'

The house where my relatives had sought refuge belonged to the Mexican Consul in Malaga, Porfirio Smerdou, married to a cousin of mine, Concha Altolaguirre, whose brother Luis had been murdered by the Reds. Porfirio played no part in politics and represented Mexico in an honorary capacity. He lacked all title to diplomatic immunity other than that with which he had invested himself for the occasion, but he admitted any who sought shelter and steadfastly resisted all demands to hand them over.

One of his first refugees was my brother Enrique, three of whose friends—three brothers, Eduardo, Antonio and Carlos Alvarez—had been arrested with him days before and shot. My own brother managed to elude his captors thanks to his quick-wittedness and to the ability to seize a chance when it came by. After hiding at the Smerdous' for a brief spell, he left the house. It was July, and hot. People were taking turns to sleep on the floor, where, for sheer lack of space, they could not all lie at the same time. Sanitary arrangements were unspeakable, it was impossible to have a bath or a shower, and there was barely enough tepid water to drink, a state of affairs which together with the constant risk of death made life there hardly worth living. One day, while Porfirio was absent, Enrique wrote out an imaginary name on a technically valueless safe-conduct, stamped it with a handy seal, hailed a horse-driven, open cab, collected a few things at home, and proceeded to the harbour, where a French destroyer, already packed with refugees, was getting up steam before leaving for Oran. Red militia-men hailed him in the docks, rifles in their hands, guns in their holsters. Recognition meant death, and my brother was well known in Malaga. Two men looked at his pass. When asked for his name, a blank engulfed him; he had forgotten his alias. He recalled it in time, leapt into a waiting boat and hid behind a bunch of gipsy children who were escaping from Malaga with their parents; gipsies, like bull-fighters, *flamenco* dancers

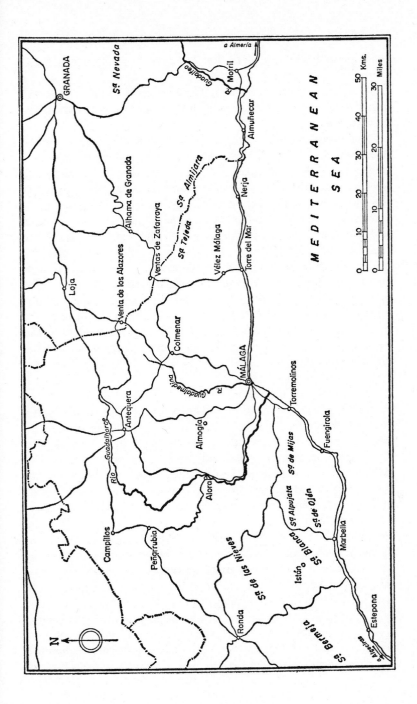

and singers, had little use for the Reds. Once on board, Enrique suffered a fit of hiccoughs that lasted three days. From Oran he dispatched a cable, addressed to me in London, which he omitted to sign. A second lieutenant in the reserve, he was with the troops that entered Malaga from the hills.

What had happened to my parents' home, the house where we had lived for years? Denuded of its contents, it was standing intact when I arrived there. With the exception of a few bookcases and wardrobes, too heavy to move, every piece of furniture had vanished together with the silver, linen, pictures, photographs and books. Crockery and glassware had been smashed to smithereens; a large anarchist poster, framed under glass and displayed prominently in the hall, experienced the same fate at my hands. So-called 'refugees' from the hills had filled the place to overflowing and plundered and looted to their heart's content after being told that all it contained belonged to them. Everything that gives a house the warmth and feeling of a home had disappeared. Of what had meant so much to each of us only the shell remained, but because those dearest to me were still alive, and our house still stood and had not been burnt, and the garden, unkempt and dry, was also there under the same blue sky, with the view over the bay as beautiful as ever, I uttered a silent prayer of thanks.

Others had been less fortunate. A little way off I found the house where my grandmother had lived, gutted and completely ruined. In a similar state was the house next door, built for one of her sons and his wife. A larger house in the Limonar, belonging to the same uncle who had greeted me that morning, had also been reduced to ashes. The home of an aunt of mine in the Alameda had escaped the flames, but every piece of furniture within it had been hurled from the windows and smashed. A house belonging to another uncle, Juan de la Cruz, had been completely sacked. He himself had been flung into prison and shot in reprisal for the bombing of a Republican cruiser by our planes. A fourth uncle owned a large house on a hill, one of the finest in the city. Used by anarchists as a hospital, it had been set on fire when they left. The solidity of its structure prevented it from being gutted.

My uncle Juan de la Cruz, married to the Marquesa de Guirior—the last time they saw each other he had said, 'I know they mean to kill me; if they ask you for a ransom, refuse it'—and two first cousins of mine had been murdered. One had been thrown from a balcony on his third floor apartment in the Alameda and finished off later on the pavement.

Two second cousins had been assassinated by Red N.C.O.s of the warships on which they served as naval lieutenants. The younger of the two had been roped to his comrades and cast into the sea from the battleship *Jaime* The Count de San Isidro, father of one of these officers and director of the harbour in Malaga, had been killed with two other sons after militia-men searched his home in a futile quest for an alleged Falangist. The Count had guaranteed they would find nobody. The Reds had been on the point of leaving when one of them turned and said, 'Wait! This man guaranteed something. He should be held responsible and arrested.' They took him away. Two sons, both of them in their twenties, decided to accompany their father. All three were shot a few hundred yards from their home. Badly wounded, one of them crawled to a clinic near by. A few hours later he was taken out and killed.

The tragic fate of part of my family in Malaga was characteristic of what happened all over Spain during the Civil War. The majority of those murdered by the Reds had little to do with the rebellion, at its outbreak or before. Their principal crime, in the eyes of their killers, was to have voted against the Popular Front or to have sympathized with the parties that opposed it; to have been good Catholics and to have attended church on Sundays; to have worn a collar and a tie, to have lived as millions live today in the Western world, and to believe in the essential dignity of men. For this they paid with their lives, and their homes were burnt over their heads.

Of the 2,579 men and women who were murdered in Malaga and its province, 944 perished in the city. There were not, needless to say, as many priests, bankers, or aristocrats there, but the Reds took their toll from all classes. If a man owned a small cart or a donkey he was classed as a capitalist and shot. Women were shot for having bought much-needed medicines for the poor or supplied them with food. Two close friends of my mother, Soledad Lamothe and the widow of a naval officer named Montero, both over sixty years old, were murdered for having done this. The Reds disapproved of charity.

At the Jesuit college of St Stanislaus, where I completed the courses for the degree that preceded my legal studies in Granada and acquired a more intimate knowledge of the principles impressed upon me since childhood, there had been two hundred boys. Two hundred and six former pupils of the college were shot by the Reds—their names are inscribed on two marble slabs that now hang in the entrance hall of the college—a number approximately equal to that which would have been recorded had all my school-fellows been wiped out together. In ten cases two brothers were shot; in eight cases three brothers were killed at the same time; in one especially appalling instance five brothers were shot. Their name was Fernández de Prada. Later it transpired that their murderers had mistaken them for members of a different family, named Fernández Prida.

What kind of men committed these crimes? What degree of injustice and ill-treatment had they known, that they reacted in such a manner? The majority were probably no better and no worse than other people in the civilized world, then or today. They had behaved as normal human beings under the Monarchy and observed exemplary conduct under Primo's firm but gentle hand. But the Republic promised them everything for their votes and gave them nothing in return. It goaded them against imaginary wrongdoers, taught them to build barricades, stirred up class hatred, and allowed a free hand to agitators. In no case were the murders a result of spontaneous action on the part of large crowds, seething for blood and vengeance. The worst excesses were carried out by a well-trained, ruthless, determined minority.

On 20 October 1936—less than four months before we took Malaga, four months after the Reds seized power—an English visitor, Sir Peter Chalmers-Mitchell, wrote a letter to *The Times* which evoked two interesting replies, the first of which appeared on 22 October of the same year. Signed by Mr J. G. Lockhart at 208 Ashley Gardens, London, S.W.1, it said: 'The picture which Sir Peter Chalmers-Mitchell gives of conditions' (in Malaga) 'does not quite tally with the accounts which some of us have received from our Spanish friends there. The prisoners to whom he refers seem to have numbered many hundred. If they were not "hostages", many were treated as hostages and shot in reprisal for aerial bombardment. Others were murdered on the flimsiest pretexts. One man I used to know was killed because his second name happened to be that of a family with which he was unconnected. A lady I knew, who had done political work for the Right, but was, I believe, entirely innocent of "sedition" was taken out of her house and shot. These are only two examples of numerous incidents which appear to have escaped the attention of Sir Peter Chalmers-Mitchell in his rustic retreat. My friends write that whole families of their acquaintance in the residential district of the Caleta have been murdered. That is my late home, and I last visited it in June, shortly before the rebellion broke out. Although the city was quiet, a few days earlier there had been a street battle between Syndicalists and Communists. Sir Peter's "middle class bourgeois Republicans" were openly threatening to march on the residential suburbs and burn them down. Most of the factories were paralysed by revolutionary strikes. The fields were largely untended. I can well believe that no churches have been destroyed in the present troubles, as with the exception of the Cathedral and two small buildings, every church in the place (some 40 in all), had been burnt long before the troubles began. It is not necessary to be a Fascist or a lover of military dictatorships to feel little regret for a Government which had not only failed to discharge the first of its functions, but in many parts of Spain at least had shown little desire to do so. There are times when rebellion can plead extenuating circumstances.'

Another letter, under the same heading—'Murders in Malaga'—was published by *The Times* on 23 October 1936; dated at Earl's Place, Mark Cross, Tunbridge Wells, it came from Mr S. Burdett-Coutts. 'In an interesting letter which appeared in your issue of October 20th,' it read, 'Sir Peter Chalmers-Mitchell, describing his experiences in Malaga, writes: "But let me say at once that there were no outrages in the ordinary sense of the word, no torturing, mutilations or other horrors." He goes on to describe how some 500 persons, "casually selected", have beeen "taken from their houses, hustled into cars, and thrown out and shot by the roadside". Some of us are sufficiently old-fashioned to regard these nocturnal murders as "outrages in the ordinary sense of the word", and the mental anguish inflicted upon victims, potential victims and their families as the subtlest form of torture.'

These two letters are in a class with countless more which appeared in *The Times* and other English newspapers during the Spanish Civil War. Spaniards can never be grateful enough for the way in which such writings, distinguished by fairness and facts, lit up their problems. Other letters confused the issues, as did Sir Peter Chalmers-Mitchell's, whose sympathies were as obvious as his bias. The opening paragraphs of his letter said, 'Spaniards defending a Government elected by the people were sure that democratic England would be on their side. From the first I tried to disabuse them. I told them that at the mere echo of the word "Communism" the British Government would shrink in horror and that the official Labour Party would acquiesce with professions of reluctance.' The day we entered Malaga, where I knew that Sir Peter had returned, I suspected he might be harbouring some guilty party—a murderer who had convinced him of his gentleness or a spoiler who had failed to get away. He himself would, of course, stay behind as an 'eye-witness' to imaginary excesses, eventually to be described in letters to newspapers which in due course would form the basis of a book. I got into my car with Pim Vázquez and drove to Sir Peter's house. It belonged to an Englishman called Harris and I knew its location well. A brother of Rider Haggard, the novelist, had lived in it years before as British Consul in Malaga, and I had been a friend of his children and frequently gone there to play.

We pulled up some distance from the house and proceeded towards it on foot. If it proved to be empty, save for its tenant, we would bid him good-morning and leave, but a few precautions seemed advisable in the event of my premonitions being correct. I told the driver, who was in uniform but unarmed, to wait outside and intercept anyone trying to escape, asked Pim to cut off all exit through the back door, and walked straight to the front entrance. A gardener met me on the way. 'Who's in the house?' I asked him. 'Sopita,' he said, pronouncing his master's name as if it were the diminutive of the word *sopa*—soup— in Spanish. 'Anybody else?' The man's hesitancy was enough. Alerted by our conversation, Sir Peter showed up on the doorstep. 'There's nobody here,' he assured me, 'and anyhow you can't come in. Don't you see the Union Jack over my front door?' 'The Union Jack puts you under certain obligations,' I told him, 'but it grants you no extraterritorial privileges. Allow me to do my duty.'

As I walked past Sir Peter I heard Pim Vázquez calling out, *!Ahí va la liebre!* which in Spanish is more or less the same as 'yoicks!'. A small-sized man was scurrying up the back stairs like a rabbit. I ordered him to stop. When he did so I recognized Arthur Koestler, who had dis-appeared the previous summer after presenting himself in Seville as special correspondent of the *News Chronicle*, the London newspaper. Of the two, perhaps I was the more surprised, he the more frightened, and rightly so, for I was covering him with a pistol. Like a flash the situation became clear. Koestler had stayed in Malaga to write up whatever he could manage to concoct with Sir Peter and delude foreign opinion still further while achieving 'a sensational scoop'.

'Didn't you tell me there was nobody here?' I said to Sir Peter. 'I am going to take this man into custody and request you to leave with me.'

At that moment an uncle of mine appeared in the doorway; he had lived not far away and, after being arrested by the Reds and spending some weeks in prison, in daily danger of being shot as was one of his brothers, he had been released and, partly thanks to Sir Peter, managed to reach Gibraltar with his family. My uncle told me this, and begged me to see that Sir Peter suffered no harm. Koestler's position was more serious. He had gone over to the enemy after being for some time on our side. I recalled what a Scottish captain, one of my officers on the British Front, had told me during the First World War when I expressed the wish to have a look at the Germans. 'Don't do it,' he said. 'If you went to Germany and we caught you afterwards, we would not hesitate to shoot you.'

Pim Vázquez and the soldier-driver made short work of tying up Koestler with a piece of electric wiring which the gardener had produced. I looked on while Pim chuckled with amusement, whether at the plight of my prisoners or at the expression on my face I never knew. Then we searched the house thoroughly and made off with the fruits of the chase, leaving my uncle on his way to his home, which anarchists had set on fire the previous day. In the Camino Nuevo, where against some rocks within sight of Sir Peter's house scores of my friends and neighbours had been shot during the preceding weeks, we came across a Company of Italian volunteers. 'Who have you got there?' a smiling young captain asked me. I explained the situation in my best Italian. 'Why don't you give them to us? We'll soon settle matters.' But they were my prisoners, and I was determined to deliver one of them to the proper Spanish authorities.

I deposited Sir Peter at a hotel called Hernán Cortés, a few minutes away and the best in the town. There he gave me his word not to move until I returned, but when I arrived the next morning he had left to board a British destroyer, the Commander of which was stepping ashore as I got to the harbour. 'Yes,' he said, 'Sir Peter's here, and I have a message saying that our people are not interested in him. Aren't you well rid of the fellow? If he stays he'll only make a nuisance of himself. Do you really want him?' The Commander, a pleasant fellow with red hair, had sized up the situation adequately. Like other British naval officers, he knew whom we were fighting, and why. Sir Peter remained on board, and I never saw him again. As to Koestler, once the Military Police took over my interest in him ended.*

*See Appendix IV, page 367

A brief tour of the principal streets in Malaga was enough to show me how the city had fared under the Reds. Apart from a small number of impacts on the buildings adjoining the harbour, where Red warships had been bombed at their moorings, the town had not suffered from aerial bombardments, accounts to the contrary notwithstanding. Our enemies made so much capital out of the propaganda possibilities of what was then a new weapon in the art of war that without trustworthy reports we ourselves might have had an excuse for believing that every bomb dropped by our planes had inevitably fallen wide of what, even before the Second World War, were perfectly legitimate targets.

Ninety-nine and a half per cent of the buildings gutted in Malaga were deliberately destroyed by the Reds, who, as usual, selected their objectives carefully. They burnt every church partly rebuilt or restored after the holocaust in May 1931; practically all the blocks of flats in the Calle de Larios, the city's principal thoroughfare, together with the shops and cafés at street level; and as many private houses as they chose in residential quarters such as the Caleta, the Limonar, Miramar and districts farther east.

The cathedral had been desecrated. Of all the sights I saw in Malaga that day, none impressed or shocked me more deeply. A Spaniard, not to speak of an Andalusian like myself, is as proud as any European of living in a cathedral city. Its cathedral—*his* cathedral—is possessed of a special meaning for him throughout his life. 'One's native place is the shell of one's soul,' says Belloc, 'one's church is the kernel of that nut.' As a boy, I had gone every day to the cathedral with my English governess and heard vespers sung to the accompaniment of its fine organ. It was there that the King and Queen of Spain, when they visited Malaga, attended the Te Deum which expressed the city's gratitude for their safe arrival. It was there that citizens rendered special homage to God, with sermons preached before vast crowds and the Bishop in his flowing robes presiding over imposing ceremonies. The Cathedral in Malaga is now entirely restored and better kept than it has ever been. But when I saw it just after we relieved the city it hardly seemed the same place where high mass had been sung for centuries every Sunday, with the officiants in sumptuous white, green, red, mauve or black vestments, according to the occasion, and the attending acolytes in their special attire, canons and choir-boys chanting to the strains of the organ while the smell of incense perfumed the air.

The Reds had not tried to burn the cathedral—they could never have succeeded in doing so, for it is built of stone. Some with great influence among them had walled up all means of access to the choir, and thanks to this, priceless works by Pedro de Mena were saved from destruction. But altars had been divested of their ornaments or pulled down, and the woodwork had been used as fuel. No religious services had been held in the cathedral for seven months, and most of its spacious interior was occupied by an unsightly horde of refugees, camping in squalor and filth, huddled in groups inside the chapels, their miserable mattresses upon the floor. A dead baby was lying near one of the pillars, and a dreadful stench—the stench which the Reds left behind them in every city—pervaded the aisles. On the steps to the high altar, his back towards the baldachino and a hat upon his head, sat a man, oblivious of everything save his thoughts. I spoke to him. When he remonstrated roughly, I seized him by the shoulder and led him out. It was as close as I got to violence the day our troops freed my city from the Reds.

The following day a group of foreign journalists came to Malaga. Mildly impressed, 'Which is the street where you say so many houses were burnt?' one of them asked me after walking by my side through the entire length of the Calle de Larios, where, with one or two exceptions, every house had been set on fire and destroyed. 'The Cathedral is interesting,' remarked a disappointed Dutchman, 'but in the village'— Malaga then had 250,000 inhabitants—'there is nothing.' There was certainly less than there had been when our opponents took the town. 'Are you Red?' an absent-minded journalist asked a negress who was walking down the street. Her reply—'No, sir, I am black'—amused everybody intensely. One thing that surprised newsmen was to find military tribunals already set up and trying those accused of serious crimes against life and property. Correspondents with me were given every facility to attend the hearings.

Later that day I drove to Motril, sixty-eight miles east of Malaga on the road from that city to Almería, which the Reds had followed in their flight. In only three days, our lines had moved eastward one hundred miles or more from the starting point at Marbella. There was no sign of the enemy, but the highway was covered with refugees who had been forced to leave Malaga with them. Terrified by tales of our ferocity—the least we were supposed to do was to cut off women's breasts and slaughter infants wholesale—gullible peasants from half a hundred villages had flocked to the city and fled as our troops drew near, taking with them their possessions, or ours. When possible they had loaded these on little carts, pulled by a donkey or dragged along by their own efforts. When no transport was available they had piled their bedding on their heads and staggered on with babies, sewing machines and odd pieces of furniture, as if moving to another world.

Torn mattresses had spread their contents on the surrounding fields, and the roadside was littered with objects of every kind. Deprived of food and shelter by their own senseless flight, hundreds of refugees lay in the last stage of exhaustion. Some elderly people had died. I spoke to the stragglers, and learnt that all they had eaten were a few bites from the rations shared with them by our soldiers, the day before. I gave them my small stock of provisions, and sped back to inform General Queipo de Llano. That night, a team of doctors and nurses, organized by feminine members of the Falangist Party who during the occupation of Malaga and after carried out much good work in the city and around it, picked up most of the stranded refugees, fed them, and brought them back to their homes or rendered assistance on the spot to those too ill to move.

The Republicans told the world that our warships shelled refugees as they withdrew towards Almería, but nowhere along the coast did I find any evidence of this. Beyond Motril, retreating columns were harassed from the sea, as planned, but the fleeing enemy should have expected this, and any refugees with them had no business to be there. The majority of the latter did not reach Motril, nearly seventy miles from Malaga, for they had no means of transport, nor could they walk that far. No harm would have come to them had they stayed in the city. They were not combatants, and nobody thought of persecuting them. Those that got away with the beaten troops must have had uneasy consciences and the necessary pull to hitch a ride. They were probably implicated in some of the 2,579 murders which had been committed in the province.

As war progressed I learnt to be surprised at nothing which the Reds could think of or do. The extent of the trouble they took in Malaga to carry out tasks devoid of any sense or useful purpose defies description; had we imposed this sort of work upon them we would have been branded as slave-drivers. Across the way from our home they murdered an elderly citizen, the representative of a shipping line, who lived quietly with one or two servants. After this they burnt his house, and after burning it they seized a massive, 2 h.p. electric motor that pumped water from a cistern, hauled it up a crumbling staircase to the third floor of the gutted house, and left it there. More than once they organized an exchange of furniture between two vacant houses, stocking each with the heavy tables, settees and wardrobes which had previously been in the other. They risked their necks repeatedly, and expended immense amounts of energy, to demolish and destroy large altar-pieces before setting on fire the churches in which they stood. More tragically, they killed without rhyme or reason. Most of the people slain in Malaga, and most of those who owned the houses burnt there, had nothing to do with politics, were not concerned with labour conflicts and never in their lives had been industrialists or millionaires—assuming that this constitutes a crime. We had all laughed at home one day, shortly after the Republic was established and the first riots broke out, when after commenting on the mentality of those who fled to Gibraltar or Tangier at the least sign of trouble, my father said, 'I can't conceive the idea of anybody taking the trouble of coming all the way here to murder me.' My father had a sense of humour, but had he not died before the Reds ruled Malaga he would have been murdered, as his brother and his nephews and countless friends of his were murdered, simply because they happened to be alive.

CHAPTER THIRTY-ONE

A Setback in Guadalajara

It was the beginning of March 1937, and we were preparing to attack the Red lines in the province of Guadalajara. Our final objective was Madrid, seventy-five miles south-east of our starting point. Even a partial advance on the city would tighten our hold upon it and help us to encircle it eventually. Encouraged by their success in Malaga, the Italians had volunteered to play the lead in this offensive, their hopes of victory quickened by the arrival of reinforcements and supplies. Other quarters were less confident. The units likely to oppose our allies now—troops seasoned by months of hard fighting against Franco's best men on the Madrid Front, International Brigades from their training camps near Albacete, well armed and ably led—were different from those which had confronted them in the south. Because of this it was decided that no war correspondents, other than those whom the Italians insisted on having with them, would be allowed on the ground until matters took shape, a course of action towards which commanding officers usually incline when the immediate prospects of an impending offensive are not clear; exactly the same happened repeatedly in France during the First World War. I myself would proceed to the field of operations and report as an eye-witness on the day's events, my comments being used to supplement the official bulletin. The eve of my departure from Salamanca, Lieut.-Col. Barroso, who with Colonel Martin Moreno shared the duties of G.S.O.1 under Franco, briefed me concisely on our objectives.

The ground selected for the battle was a stony plateau 3,000 feet high or more, sparsely covered with roads, occasionally intersected by ploughed fields, and creased by valleys along which small streams and three medium-sized rivers, the Henares, the Badiel and the Tajuña, flow south and eventually join the Tagus. The railway from Madrid to Barcelona runs close to the Henares, the most important of the three; north of Guadalajara the main road between those two cities follows

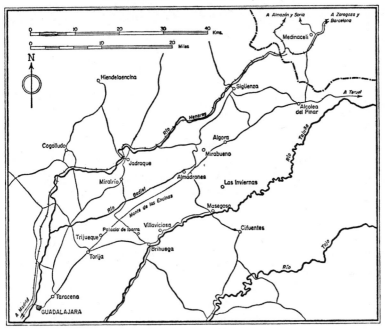

for some fifty miles a course parallel to that of the rivers, at an intermediate distance between the Henares and the Tajuña. The plateau
itself is a vast, unsheltered moor covered with scrub or small deciduous
oak, its monotony broken by a few villages and the remote view of the
eastern summits of the Guadarrama range, among which the most
distinctive is a triangular peak that looms black against the distant
horizon except when whitened in winter by snow.

No more desolate wilderness exists in the whole of the Peninsula, yet
it would not be a part of Spain were it entirely bereft of interest. The
principal town, Sigüenza, is a romantic city with a thirteenth-century
cathedral and much to admire. Scene of encounters between the primi-
tive Spaniards, led by Sertorius, and the legions of Pompey, in 713 it
was captured by the Arabs who overran Spain. Alfonso VI reconquered
it before the end of the eleventh century, when El Cid rode Babieca
over the surrounding plains and the city of Sigüenza successively
belonged to the kingdoms of Toledo, Aragon and Castile and León.
Juan Martín *el Empecinado*, a famous *guerrillero*, fought against Napoleon
in the shadow of its walls. Early in the Civil War Sigüenza was frequently shelled by the Reds, who while they held it caused wanton

destruction to buildings and works of art, since restored. In Brihuega, the second city in the area, ancient walls encircle noble mansions and a famous garden of French design. Remnants of feudal times are Jadraque's ruined castle, once a stronghold of the Dukes of Osuna, and the palace at Cogolludo, built for the Dukes of Medinaceli, whose lineage stems from Alfonso the Wise. Smaller towns and villages, rich in the rust of antiquity—Cifuentes, Taracena, Torija, Trijueque—are not barren of some form of art. In the first decade of the eighteenth century, during the War of the Spanish Succession, the Duke of Berwick set up his headquarters at Jadraque, Stanhope and the English were defeated at Brihuega, and the Duke of Vendôme, at Villaviciosa, won a battle over Stahremberg that helped Philip V, a grandson of Louis XIV, to add fleurs-de-lys to the crown of Spain. On the lesser slopes of the Sierra de las Cabras the castle of Atienza raises its turrets over an empty shell that stands high and dry, like a ship wrecked upon a mountain. In summer, under a torrid sun, the countryside is not lacking in opportunities for walking up quail with a dog.

The configuration of the plateau presented our Staff with a ready-made plan for the battle, of which General Franco was quick to take advantage. The attack would follow three main lines of penetration. In the centre, the highway from Barcelona to Madrid; to the right, the railway to Guadalajara and the roads leading south from Sigüenza and Jadraque; on the left flank, the highway to Brihuega from Almadrones and Masegoso and other roads from Brihuega to Torija and Guadalajara. Spanish forces under Moscardó, who had been raised to the rank of General after his defence of the Alcázar, would attack on the right. The Italians would take the offensive in the centre and to the left. The idea of a mechanized thrust in the direction of Madrid had captured their imagination; they had followed these tactics in Malaga and were determined to apply them now. Given the means and sufficient impetus, they maintained that a break-through was inevitable.

I left Salamanca on the eve of the offensive and with Pim Vázquez drove to Soria and Almazán, where the Douro starts to flow westward and where we found ourselves quartered in a wayside inn, long since abandoned. The weather had been dry and cold on the plains of Castile, but heavy rains began to fall before we reached Soria and continued without a stop for a whole week. Howling winds swept the plateau, which soon became sodden, and the temperature remained steadily below freezing point. More miserable conditions could hardly have been imagined, to fight in or merely to exist in, but the enemy had heard of our plans and the slightest delay would have given him the advantage. The offensive could not be postponed.

Launched on 8 March, to the right and in the centre of our lines, it was successful in both directions. Moscardó stormed the hills around Jadraque, a potential source of trouble, and the Italians took Mirabueno, Almadrones and Las Inviernas and opened up the road to Brihuega. The enemy retreated in good order without leaving much behind, an indication that his movements were being deliberately synchronized to our own. Equally significant was the presence on the battlefield of a considerable number of Russian tanks, which would not have been there had our opponents not thought of counter-attacking at a suitable moment. As the day drew on it became colder, and the rain turned to sleet and hail.

Next morning the Italians advanced some twelve miles from their starting-point in the centre. At divisional headquarters in Algora, a village where one waded ankle-high in mud, junior Italian officers were hopeful—*questa è una guerra di operetta*; 'This is a comic-opera war'— but on the road to Guadalajara an endless line of vehicles was filled with men seeking shelter from the rain if not from the bombs. The downpour was churning adjacent fields into a sea of mud and water where Russian tanks, trapped by the mire before our artillery could disable them, lay deserted by their crews. Any kind of progress was difficult; deployment was out of the question. One side of the highway was occupied by the column of trucks and not enough room remained for two cars to cross each other. Moreover, components of the south-bound Italian convoy had failed to leave sufficient space between them at reasonable intervals for an advancing vehicle to slip in while another passed by. When rash drivers tried their luck on the adjoining swamp, they had to be towed out or left there.

I proceeded as far as I could without finding any line of contact with our opponents. Troops attempting to spread out or dig for cover would have stuck in the mud, but the Italians pushed forward on the highway as the Republicans drew back, firing as they went. Shortly before my arrival, enemy planes had bombed the advancing column without meeting opposition in the air. At Almazán and Soria, where our squadrons waited in vain for the weather to improve, runways made of earth were water-logged to the point that to take off or land was impossible. It was bitterly cold, and a strong wind was blowing. But in

Madrid, one hundred and forty miles south and one thousand feet lower, weather conditions favoured the enemy, who made good use of the airfields at his disposal in Barajas and Alcalá de Henares.

On this second day of the offensive Moscardó and the Italians progressed considerably southwards and an attack against Masegoso and Brihuega took our allies to the outskirts of the latter town. A further thrust in the centre towards Guadalajara saw them twenty miles from their initial starting point. On the right flank the Reds retreated even faster, and to support the Italians should need arise Moscardó moved some of his troops towards the Badiel river, which in this part of the country flows through a deep canyon not far from the main road to Madrid.

Though resistance hardened on 10 March, Brihuega was captured that morning by the 3rd Italian Division, and so rapidly did Moscardó advance that his men left Miralrío behind them and actually saw the Republicans in full flight. After sharp fighting, the 2nd Italian Division took Trijueque on 11 March. Casualties were slight, but the enemy now contested every inch of the ground. Of much value to them was a halt in our offensive, ordered that same evening. This interlude was unavoidable. Fighting had been continuous for four consecutive days, conditions in the open were atrocious, and weariness was beginning to undermine the men's morale. Possibly because of this, the final Italian attack against Torija was repulsed with comparative ease. Had it succeeded, the outcome of the whole battle might have been different.

Prisoners taken by Spanish troops were being questioned as a matter of routine by our own Intelligence officers, but because of language difficulties the Italians occasionally asked me to interrogate doubtful characters who had fallen into their hands, and whose statements they could not make out. The characters in question disclaimed any kind of Red ideology and declared themselves, to a man, devoted adherents to our cause. They were Monarchists, Carlists, Falangists, or prominent members of Catholic Action, fighting against us, according to their explanations, because of unfortunate errors or circumstances unforeseeable and untoward. Never have I known greater liars. Glib, stonyfaced and impudent, concurrent statements from their own fellowprisoners proved them to be political Commissars of their respective

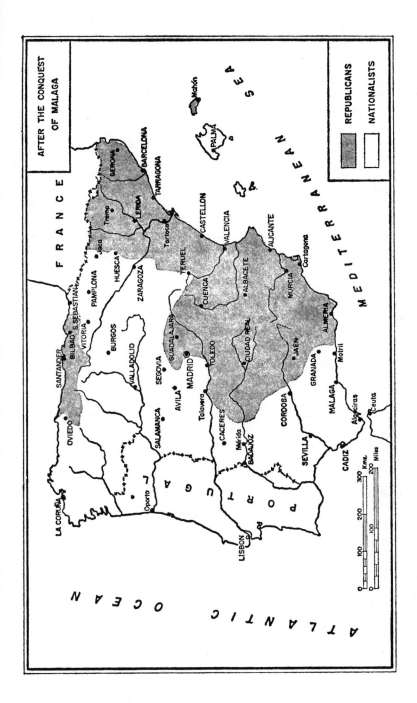

AFTER THE CONQUEST
OF MALAGA

REPUBLICANS

NATIONALISTS

FRANCE

PORTUGAL

ATLANTIC OCEAN

MEDITERRANEAN SEA

LA CORUÑA
OVIEDO
Oporto
SANTANDER
BILBAO S.SEBASTIAN
VITORIA
PAMPLONA
BURGOS
VALLADOLID
SALAMANCA
SEGOVIA
AVILA
MADRID
Talavera
CACERES
Mérida
BADAJOZ
LISBON
SEVILLA
CADIZ
Algeciras
Ceuta
MALAGA
GRANADA
Motril
CORDOBA
JAEN
ALMERIA
MURCIA
CIUDAD REAL
TOLEDO
GUADALAJARA
CUENCA
ALBACETE
Cartagena
ALICANTE
VALENCIA
TERUEL
CASTELLON
Tortosa
ZARAGOZA
HUESCA
Jaca
Tremp
LERIDA
TARRAGONA
BARCELONA
GERONA
Mahón
PALMA

300 Kms.
200 Miles
0 100 200
0 100 200

battalions, a rank imported from Russia and hitherto unknown in the Spanish Army, the holding of which was totally at variance with the hard-luck stories and sentiments they so insistently avowed.

A confused situation and guarded or over-optimistic reports were not helping me to phrase my dispatches. I could see that the cars lined up on the Madrid road were like sitting duck for enemy aircraft, that our own planes could not fly from their drenched runways, and that there was no way of moving infantry over the sea of mud that flanked the highways. In these circumstances I deemed it wiser to keep silent and let official communiques explain the progress of the battle to the world. A scarcity of liaison officers existed, so I offered my services to General Moscardó, who accepted them readily. Thanks to this, I remained on the field of operations in close contact with the Italian and Spanish Staffs, and in due course acquired an idea of the fighting as comprehensive as that possessed by anyone on our side not concerned with its direction.

At a critical stage of the battle Moscardó requested me to ascertain the exact position of our left wing. I went to Algora, where I had consumed slices of smoked ham or invigorating shots of brandy with my hospitable Italian friends, and watched while they took infinite pains to pin-point the required information on my large-scale map. But when I showed it to Moscardó he shook his head. 'They've pulled your leg,' he said, while his second-in-command, Colonel Marzo, looked on with a grin on his face. 'If the Italian vanguard stood where you say, the situation on my left would be easier.' So I went to find out for myself.

My destination was Brihuega, fifteen miles from Jadraque and five miles east of the Madrid–Barcelona road, which I crossed not far from Trijueque, our southernmost point in the centre. To reach Brihuega from Jadraque without making a wide detour I had to drive through a forest of dwarfed oaks known as the 'Monte de Encinas', in the midst of which stood an isolated building, the Palacio de Ibarra. It was there that the battle of Guadalajara was decided. The Italians had captured the Palacio after much fighting and fortified it as strongly as they could, for it was the key to Brihuega and to positions east of Trijueque, near the main road to Madrid. I drove through the wood unaware that, a short distance away, three battalions of the 15th International Brigade lay hidden behind its stocky oaks, the leaves of which, sprouting a short distance from the ground, afforded them ideal cover. It was cold, but I must have sensed something, for I made the route with a sub-machine-gun in my hands, its muzzle peering through the open window of my car.

The capture of Brihuega had been a triumph for the Italians. They had occupied it with great gallantry. When I got there and inquired the whereabouts of their front line, the reply was unhesitating and accurate; it was on the outskirts of the town, they told me, some miles north of the position pin-pointed for me at Algora. I did not take long to find it. Leaving my car in a side street, I walked into open country. Beyond the outlying houses on the southern part of the town I saw Italian artillery, small cannon known as *artiglieria di accompagniamento* of which our allies were rightly proud, ready to fire, with the men grouped near the pieces. A hundred feet or so farther on there were machine-guns, also ready for action. Somewhat farther, infantrymen lay flat, firing at an invisible foe. 'They're all over the place,' an officer told me, 'but so far they're withholding their fire. Perhaps they are waiting for reinforcements. They may be going to attack.' This was our front line. Beyond it lay no-man's-land. It was easier to establish its correct position on the map than to understand why cannon were massed with machine-guns and rifles on such a narrow stretch of ground.

When I returned to Brihuega Don Alvaro de Orleans, son of the Infante Don Alfonso, a first cousin of the late King of Spain, suggested that I spend the night there. 'I'll get you decent quarters,' he said, encouragingly. But my mission was only half accomplished, I had to report to General Moscardó, and there was little to do in a place which, to my mind, was becoming less healthy every minute. I said as much to Don Alvaro and added that unless he had some reason to remain in the town the best he could do was to clear out. We lost Brihuega that night. The road I took back to Jadraque was nearly twenty miles longer than the one I had followed in the first place, and I was well advised to choose it, for the other had already been cut. This time, Moscardó heard my report without question. 'What you tell me now makes sense,' he said. 'The other version didn't.' While we spoke the strongly reinforced Reds were counter-attacking on a wide front from Trijueque to Brihuega.

Moscardó's troops were never hard pressed and could have easily retained the positions they had won, but to avoid being outflanked they fell back in line with those occupied by the Italians. They did so reluctantly, for their thrust had been deep and fruitful, and they hated the idea of withdrawing. A visit to their battle headquarters in Cogolludo, a remote town in the hills west of Jadraque, turned out to be a weird experience. The road from Jadraque to Cogolludo skirts a ravine and runs north for some ten miles, after which it turns sharply south for another ten miles or so. In war, when the whereabouts of the foe are uncertain and there is no unbroken line of trenches, anything that upsets one's bump of locality tends to be disconcerting, especially if after travelling for miles over deserted country one comes across a body of troops attired the same as the enemy. Cogolludo was filled with soldiers, dressed as Reds, and though they saluted instead of shooting I was far from reassured when I got to the commandant's office and found it tenanted by a boorish major, also dressed as a Red. His temper was frayed and his nerves were on edge. When he questioned me sharply I felt as if I had walked into a trap, a constant risk in a war of movement. But his attitude changed when I told him my business. He had just been ordered to give up his hard-won positions on the front line, and he and his men had decided to avail themselves of a brand new stock of Red clothing, captured in Cogolludo. It had come in handy to replace well-worn uniforms, already becoming threadbare.

A political commissar called Hans, attached to the 12th International Brigade, commented in writing on the adverse effect which the 'truly appalling weather' was having on the morale of the Italians. The mud and the rain were preventing their columns from receiving badly needed supplies and ammunition, and the shortage of shells was seriously curtailing their gun-fire. The Reds were better off, Hans says. Sixty Russian tanks helped the International Brigades and other forces to advance, and eighty planes bombed the Italians continuously without meeting opposition in the air. By now the enemy knew as well as we did that our aircraft could not leave their runways, a situation which changed somewhat to our advantage as the weather improved and the battle progressed to its conclusion.

At the Palacio de Ibarra the Italians made a stand and held out. A battalion detailed to support them arrived too late to prevent a detachment of the International Brigades from occupying the building, which was littered with Italian corpses when recaptured two days later. Our opponents fought well, as they had done near Madrid and on the Jarama front for the past six months. They moved their artillery efficiently and used it as well or better than at any other time during the Civil War. Their planes were constantly in the air and hit targets unremittingly on the long, straight roads, though what would have happened had our airmen been able to oppose them we do not know. Their infantry was superb, and its leadership excellent. It was directed by Vicente Rojo, repeatedly mentioned in these pages, by a Hungarian called Kleber, and by a German, Beimler, capable commander of an International Brigade. When the weather allowed, the Italians also fought well, but at a critical stage of their advance they were handicapped by the mud and by a complete lack of air support. Had they been able to spread right and left of the Madrid road and dig trenches until supplies came up and their guns and planes could harass the Republicans, our enemies would have exulted less over the issue.

After two weeks the battle sizzled down to a stop. At the start, the Italians had on the field 31,218 men from their C.T.V. Corps, the Spaniards 8,500 men of the 2nd Brigade, Soria Division, making a total for both of some 40,000 troops. Before the offensive broke out Republican forces on the line consisted of five brigades of the 12th Division, with 10,739 men and 15 field-pieces. To reinforce them, three more Divisions, with a total of eleven brigades and 23,565 men, were brought up together with 40 cannon and the necessary effectives to man these pieces and other equipment. Counting four brigades which made up their reserves, the Republicans must have totalled slightly over 40,000, or a figure equal to our own.

We had 13 bombers and 63 other planes, mostly grounded by foul weather; also plentiful artillery and an adequate supply of tanks. Our opponents had 30 bombers, 90 fighters and observation planes, and 86 Russian tanks. Six Italian planes were destroyed; eight more were damaged. The Republicans lost 20 tanks and 32 planes.

Italian losses included considerable stocks of equipment, among which 16,000 shells, 12,000 hand grenades, and 628 boxes of rifle ammunition. Their casualties, according to C.T.V. headquarters, amounted to 3,000 killed and wounded. In an article published in the review *Ejército*, January 1945, Lieut.-Col. Lago, of the Spanish General Staff, gave approximate figures of the total losses in the battle: Nationalists, 148 killed, 300 wounded; Italians, 1,000 killed, 2,500 wounded, 800 missing. Republicans, 6,500 killed and wounded, 900 prisoners.

Guadalajara was a setback for our side, which failed to attain its objectives. But it was not a disaster, as our adversaries proclaimed. Republican losses offset those suffered by the Nationalists, and the equipment captured by the enemy was rapidly replaced. The twelve miles or so which we finally gained on the road to Madrid lacked strategic value, but this also was the case with the territory re-won by the Republicans. Neither stretch of ground could influence the future conduct of the war or its outcome. Our opponents did not exploit the fruits of their counter-offensive, as they would have done had they seized Alcolea del Pinar and Medinaceli, only twenty-five miles away from the points where they finally established their lines. They did not destroy the morale of our troops nor depress our rearguard unduly. But their victory made an impact on foreign public opinion which time has failed to erase.

On our side the lessons of Guadalajara were not wasted. Before the battle was fought Franco had pointed out that Italian contingents, made up of militias officered by men who were not always professional soldiers, needed reorganization and training. Co-ordination and liaison services had to be established or speeded up to assure a fuller understanding between the respective Staffs, and to keep commanding officers suitably informed. This was done, systematically and fully. Italian brigades and their commanders accepted in due course the idea of being flanked on the field by Spanish effectives. Improvements took place in a situation not unlike that which developed shortly after the first American contingents landed in France to help the Allies win the First World War.

On page 388 of his book, *The Spanish Civil War*, Hugh Thomas recalls what Hemingway wrote about Guadalajara: 'I have been studying the battle for four days, going over the ground with the commanders who directed it, and I can state flatly that Brihuega'—an incidental episode in the general encounter—'will take its place in military history with the other decisive battles in the world.' Herbert Matthews, of *The New York Times*, to quote Mr Thomas again, reported that Guadalajara 'was to Fascism what the defeat of Bailén had been to Napoleon'. The insistence with which our opponents overrated their successes and underrated their enemies in their broadcasts was not copied on our side. During the war, or afterwards, Franco never forgot the mettle shown by the Reds during the drawn-out siege of Madrid, in Guadalajara, in Brunete, in Belchite, or later, on the Ebro front. I heard him refer to it on one occasion, shortly after the conclusion of hostilities, when he addressed a large gathering of workmen at a locomotive factory near Madrid. A distinguished foreign General, he told them, had visited our lines during the Civil War and assured a group of

Spanish officers that our infantry was the best in the world. On hearing this the Spaniards had protested politely that the visiting General's countrymen were second to none. 'Oh no,' said their visitor, 'I have seen them in action, and yours are the best, by far.' 'In that case,' a Spanish colonel ventured, 'your own foot-soldiers must rank immediately after ours.' 'By no means,' answered the visitor, 'the second best soldiers in the world are the men who oppose you now—the Spanish Red infantry.' Most of the workmen present had fought against Franco. When they heard him say this, they cheered.

CHAPTER THIRTY-TWO

Operations in the North

General Franco could not have been much shaken by the setback at Guadalajara, for on 31 March 1937, exactly one week after the fighting there came to a standstill, he launched a powerful offensive against Bilbao, a move he would never have contemplated had his own morale and that of his men, let alone their striking power, been as gravely impaired as his opponents alleged. Indeed, hard as they tried to dissemble, the rapidity with which he struck during the early stages of the conflict must have caused them great concern. Franco had to cope with the serious shortage of troops and equipment already referred to in these pages and with the initial loss not only of Madrid, Barcelona and Valencia, but of Catalonia and part of the Basque Provinces, the two most important industrial areas in Spain. The Asturian coal mines were also in enemy hands. But in only eight months, while the Reds showed no initiative and no disposition to take it, he had landed his troops from Morocco, marched from Seville to Toledo, relieved the Alcázar, invested Madrid and assaulted its defences, captured the province of Malaga, and from the Mediterranean to the Pyrenees and from there to the Bay of Biscay fought a series of actions which evidenced, on his side, the quality of leadership and the capacity to win.

In the early spring of 1937 the various fronts in Spain had a total length of 2,930 kilometres, equivalent to 1,820 miles. Before victory could be achieved they had to be broken up and shortened. The lines around Malaga had already disappeared, but those around Madrid bulged in places, and the Northern Front meandered south of the Bay of Biscay for some 430 miles. A few Nationalist warships and armed trawlers, manned mainly by yachting enthusiasts, were striving to prevent supplies from being landed in ports like Avilés, Gijón, Santander, and Bilbao, all of them distributed along a stormy coast and all of them in Red hands. The Republican North was politically important and industrially resourceful. Rich in iron-ore and coal, with blast

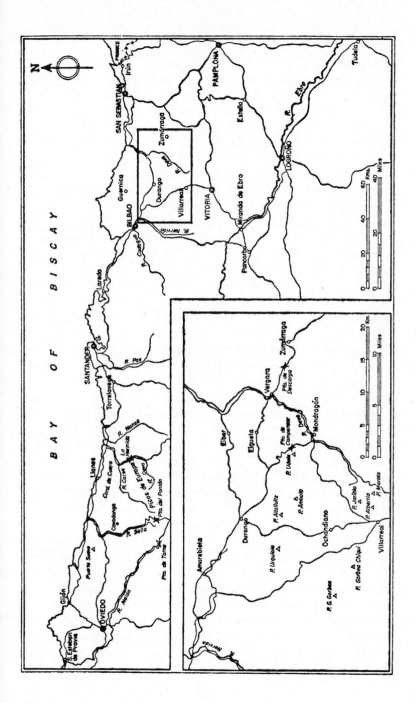

furnaces and steel works of the utmost value for the conduct of war, its deeply religious people had fallen prey to Socialists and Separatists, joined together in an unholy alliance that immobilized and pinned down a large part of Franco's effectives, urgently required elsewhere.

Counting Navarre, there are four Basque provinces in Spain. When civil war started, two of them, Navarre and Vitoria, immediately sided with the Nationalists. The attitude adopted by the other two—Guipuzcoa and Vizcaya—or rather, by a section of their inhabitants and their Separatist leaders, was cleverly exploited by Republican propaganda. It caused much confusion in foreign countries. In an article quoted above on pp. 217 and 229, Gregorio Marañón, an out-and-out supporter of the Spanish Republic at its advent, wrote the following about regionalism and Basque separatism during the Civil War: 'Spaniards, extreme Leftists included, are invariably loaded with a heavy ballast of national qualities even though theirs is an essentially regionalist nation. Spanish regionalism is a genuine and vital manifestation of a strong national spirit, based on regional pride and in itself an amplification of the great family spirit that inflames the Spanish soul and which, instead of weakening, enriches and vitalizes a Spaniard's pride in national unity. Much of the ardour which today'—i.e. 1937—'inspires Nationalist Spain is fired by the idea of national unity as opposed to Basque separatism, a sentiment exclusively backed by the ambitions of a small number of men, who, deplorable as it is to admit this, have allowed themselves to become the pawns of international Communism. Navarre, inhabited by Basques possessed of strong regionalist feelings, has played a leading role in the Nationalist movement. Separatist tendencies also flared up in Spain at the time of the First Republic, but Castelar, a prominent Liberal spokesman for that regime, declared that should they prevail he would renounce Liberalism and Democracy together with the Republican form of government.'

For almost a year, northern cities like Oviedo, practically surrounded on all sides, and Vitoria, at one time seriously threatened from Villarreal de Alava, had lived under the menace of invasion. The Nationalists had to pacify the whole of the northern area before large-scale operations against well-fortified lines, running sinuously from the southern Mediterranean to the central ranges of the Pyrenees, could be carried out successfully. While the battle of Guadalajara was being waged, Franco, working closely with General Mola, laid out the plans for a general onslaught in the North which would be launched in the first place against points situated between San Sebastian and Bilbao, and eventually extended beyond them to Oviedo and Avilés. The entire Northern Front had to be obliterated before the autumn.

Those who when they visit Spain only travel in Castile and Andalusia are unaware, as they leave the country, of how lush and craggy its northern provinces are. Blessed by rains that fall throughout the year, their hills and mountains are covered with forests, a haven for bear, chamois and roe-deer, their rivers are stocked with salmon and trout, and on their slopes milk cows graze. The terrain, ideal for pleasure in summer weather, is also ideal for defence in time of war. Troops advancing against its natural ramparts and abundant cover need stout hearts and strong legs and lungs to scale the heights. Whichever side commands good observation posts has the advantage. Often while on this front the opening lines of a story which I had read in *The Boy's Own Paper* about the Peninsular War came to my mind: 'We looked out like eagles from a crag, seeing everything though seen by none.'

The crag from which my childhood's hero had looked out on northern Spain was situated somewhere in the neighbourhood of Pancorbo, between Burgos and Vitoria. Farther north in the vicinity of Zumárraga, the foothills of the Pyrenees force the railway that runs between Madrid and France to leave the watershed of the Urola and double on its tracks through tunnels before continuing northwards along a wider valley. This same barrier, formed by hills 4,000 feet high and more, opposed our troops as they started on the first stage of their offensive against Bilbao. I came upon them a few miles west of Zumárraga. From my post, ensconced in the Descarga Pass and shared with a group of foreign correspondents, all that one took in at first sight was the size and majesty of the great peaks towering over lesser slopes—Peña Udala, gaunt and stark above Mondragón; Campanzar, a little to the right; farther west, Amboto, Urquiola, Maroto, Albertia, Jarinto, Aitzlluitz and the two Gorbeas, every one of them formidable and imposing, with their tips hidden by the clouds or almost touching them. It was against this barrier that our initial advance was directed. Its bastion formed the framework of the Red Lines. On the other side of the valley below were the triple crests of the Inchortas, an immediate objective, with the village of Elgueta nestling in their folds. To succeed against such obstacles an army needed mountaineers.

The Brigades of Navarre were made up of volunteers known as Requetés, men from these mountains or from others like them, born and bred in a part of Spain where the issues debated in the Spanish Civil War were understood fully from the start. Not in vain did these men descend from those who during the nineteenth century, in these same hills, fought on the Carlist side for the Crown of Spain, disputed by different branches of the reigning dynasty, and also for principles radically opposed to the teachings of the French encyclopaedists which had proved unworkable in the Spanish nation. The hour had once more sounded to fight for God, King and country, for the Catholic faith, for a system of government endowed with sufficient authority to maintain law and order over thirty million individualists—'thirty million kings', as Unamuno once put it—and for the unity of the nation as a whole.

Long before civil war started in 1936 the men of Navarre had prepared for this moment. Their everyday life, spent climbing over hill and crag, had been part of their training; the ideals for which they now fought had been instilled in them from birth. They knew that this war was a crusade, and when it broke out every man in the family, father, grandfather, and son, volunteered to fight. In *Cómo Fuí Ejecutado en Madrid*—'How I was Executed in Madrid'—(Sigiriano Diaz, Avila, 1937), the late Jacinto Miquelarena tells the story of two Nationalist volunteers, a Requeté and a Falangist, who talk together while they advance under enemy fire. The Requeté comes from Navarre, a land of brooks and green mountains. His name is José Maria Hernandorena. His father, his grandfather and his great-grandfather had been Carlists before him. The Falangist is from Castile, where the earth is dry and the sky is like blue satin. He sings,

> How well one goes to the wars,
> how well!
> Without mother or sweetheart to mourn you,
> How well one fights and dies!

The Requeté asks him, 'If you are killed, whom shall I tell?' The Falangist answers, 'Tell nobody. And if you die?' 'Tell my father, José María Hernandorena. He is sixty-five, and he fights for God, King and Spain with the Tercio de Montejurra'—a famous Requeté battalion. 'Should I not find him?' 'Tell José María Hernandorena, fifteen years old, Tercio de Montejurra. He is my son.' In *Spanish Rehearsal* (Hutchinson and Co., London), Sir Arnold Lunn recalls the Carlist widow 'of whose three sons, two enlisted in the first hour of the war.

The third, a boy of sixteen, not unnaturally assumed that he was too young. That evening when he came down to supper he saw that only one place had been laid. "I don't lay places for cowards," said his mother. The boy enlisted next day.' For the men of Navarre, as for many on the Nationalist side, this war was a crusade, nobody too young or too old to enlist and fight on the right side.

General Don José Solchaga led the Brigades. At the start he had with him a small group of officers, also veterans of the Moroccan wars and, to a man, staunch Carlists like their soldiers. General Don Emilio Mola commanded the Army of the North and directed the advance on Bilbao. I had met Mola at headquarters in Salamanca and was glad of a chance to serve under him. Tall, good-mannered, and seemingly aloof and distant, to catch his eye, which was not easy, I devised a ruse that never failed me. The General was passionately fond of photography, and invariably carried a camera slung around his neck. To draw his attention I would stand at a likely corner, a set of photographs in my hand; no matter how busy he might be, he always stopped to look at them, giving me a chance to talk. Unusually perceptive and intelligent, his charm and kindness endeared him to his men. His devotion to duty equalled a political insight of which there is much evidence in his book, *Memorias de mi Paso por la Dirección General de Seguridad*, written before the advent of the Republic after a term of office in the Spanish '*Sureté*', and packed with information on the conspiracies and intrigues that led to the downfall of the Monarchy and, eventually, to chaos and disruption in Spain. Mola was one of the first to realize that to save the country from Communism civil war was the only course, and his share in organizing the rebellion, painstakingly and carefully carried out, was vital for its success.

The offensive against Bilbao started punctually on 31 March. Thirty-five batteries opened fire against the Inchortas and fifty planes, flying low from their bases at Vitoria and Burgos, bombed the enemy before us. Again the weather did not help. It rained in torrents, and visibility was poor; days passed without the enemy being dislodged. In Vergara, where Colonel Don Camilo Alonso Vega, later Minister for the Interior, had established his headquarters, shells fell intermittently, and though part of the inhabitants had left, others took the shelling in their stride, stepping unconcernedly into doorways when missiles came rumbling along. A series of frontal attacks, combined with enveloping manœuvres and strongly supported by artillery and from the air, finally turned the enemy's flank and allowed us to advance beyond Elgueta, leaving the Inchortas in our rear. But many obstacles, all of them imposing, had to be overcome before we came to the 'Iron Belt' that encircled Bilbao, constructed by the Reds, reputed to be impregnable, but easier to overcome than the heights south-east of the city.

During the assault on the Inchortas, Mola's headquarters were on a hill, situated a short distance from the lines just outside Vergara. To see him one walked under fire up a steep path in full view of the enemy— a flimsy curtain set up to camouflage the path and torn to shreds by shells and bullets had finally succumbed to the wind. Mola, when not otherwise occupied, would climb to the summit of this hill and, through his glasses, watch our infantry advance, his light-coloured gloves and raincoat an easy target for snipers, posted in a wood below. He was killed five weeks later, when the plane that carried him to Salamanca crashed near Burgos in a fog. A monument has been erected to his memory near the site of the crash, on a hill half way between Castil de Peones, a village on the road to Madrid, and Belorado, where pilgrims to Compostela halted in the Middle Ages. His remains were interred in the cathedral at Pamplona, close to those of General Sanjurjo. Some have speculated about the future of these two leaders, had they survived the Civil War. Would they have opposed General Franco, and replaced him in due course? What would have happened? The answer is 'nothing at all'. Both would have been appointed to high posts and filled them worthily and with great dignity. Franco would have continued to rule as head of the Spanish State.

Until Mola's death, Franco travelled by air whenever he had a long journey before him, but after that his immediate entourage prevailed upon him to give up flying. He did so reluctantly, for he likes to fly. Never, when I flew with him close to the lines, did he see the need of an escort; to his way of thinking the chances of being intercepted were poor. One day, with two A.D.C.s, he drove to the San Fernando airfield near Salamanca and asked for a plane. A situation had arisen not far from Torrijos, in the vicinity of Toledo, and he wished to speak to General Varela, in charge of operations there, without delay. The only pilot available was a young and inexperienced officer who considered the assignment too much for him, but General Franco was not easily deterred, and finally the plane took off. It was late coming back, and the weather was bad. I was with a group of officers who waited anxiously until he returned. 'There was a storm over the Gredos range, and the pilot lost his way,' Franco explained later. 'We had banked and turned over the peaks for quite a while when I went to the cockpit and said to him, 'Do you know the opening words of the Falange Hymn?' 'Yes sir,' replied the pilot, much surprised. 'Would you repeat them, please.' '*Cara al sol*'—face the sun. 'Fine,' said Franco. 'Let's face the sun and get out of here!' A moment later they were circling over the airfield at Salamanca, the stony crags of Gredos far behind.

CHAPTER THIRTY-THREE

The Guernica Myth

A dispatch from Bonn, published by *The Times* on 6 April 1962, revealed that according to the German Federal Statistical Office 'about 593,000 people died in allied air attacks on Germany during the Second World War and 403,000 dwellings were destroyed. The number of victims is more than threefold that given in the recently published British official history of the bomber raids on Germany. Of the dead 537,000 were civilians, about 15 per cent of them children under 14; 56,000 of them were foreign civilians, prisoners of war, members of the police and the armed forces. The number of wounded for the area now covered by the Federal Republic amounted to 486,000, including 16,000 foreigners and prisoners of war.' A footnote to this dispatch informed us that 'a total of 60,595 civilians were killed by enemy action in Britain and Northern Ireland in the course of the last war.'

The indignation which slaughter from the air arouses among our contemporaries is clearly of a selective nature. Nothing comparable to the recurrent outcry over the alleged destruction of Guernica during the Spanish Civil War has ever been provoked by the terrible havoc which indiscriminate bombing from both sides brought about in the Second World War. But whereas the reality and effectiveness of mass bombardment on both sides during the Second World War cannot be disputed, the story of the wholesale destruction of Guernica by Nationalist bombs during the Spanish Civil War is a myth.

Guernica, a small town of some 3,000 inhabitants situated in the province of Vizcaya near the Bay of Biscay and some twenty miles from Bilbao, owes its fame to the meetings that were held there in the Middle Ages under an oak tree which in time came to be considered as the symbol of Basque liberties. During the advance on Bilbao, Guernica became part of the front line. Even before this happened the town was a military objective. It contained several small factories, one of them engaged in the manufacture of arms and ammunition. It was an important road junction—eight roads meet outside the town—and a depot of substantial size for the massing of reserves on their way to the trenches, or for sheltering combatants after a spell of duty in the lines. It was never, as has been repeatedly alleged, a suitable target for testing the destructive capacity of 'blockbusters' made in Germany. There were no formidable edifices within the city's limits, no imposing blocks of flats or structures of a similar kind.

But the Republicans in Bilbao needed a sensational story to offset their reverses. They dispatched Asturian miners to dynamite Guernica and set fire to its buildings and swore that they had been blown to smithereens by German bombs. Partly bombed previously for sound reasons—around Guernica there were military objectives of the first order—evidence of havoc was not wanting. Foreign correspondents, rushed to the spot from Bilbao shortly before our troops occupied the place and at a loss to distinguish the damage caused around the town by bombs from that wrought inside it by dynamite and arson, concluded that the whole of Guernica had been destroyed from the air and hastened to denounce the outrage. In Spain, during the Civil War, both sides bombed enemy positions while a battle was in progress, or before; they also bombed enemy troops in villages, or in towns and damaged these when there was no alternative. But we ourselves, on the Nationalist side, did not destroy wantonly, nor, it should be noted, did the Reds often bomb cities wantonly from the air. We knew that we would have to rebuild and if only for political reasons we did not wish to antagonize our own people. Much less did we want to slaughter them. Outlying portions of Guernica, like parts of other towns or villages occupied by the opposing forces, were attacked from the air by the Nationalists for military reasons. Most of Guernica was deliberately dynamited or set on fire by the Reds. The report that the town and its inhabitants had been destroyed by German bombs was invented for propaganda purposes. It is one of the myths which our enemies conjured up to deceive public opinion in other countries during the Spanish Civil War.

The real story is contained in a series of routine dispatches summarized in an appendix to this chapter* together with other information; the dispatches referred to exist in their original form in the Historical and Military Archives of the Spanish General Staff in Madrid. The true story is also shown in a detailed analysis of the

*See p. 355

Guernica case, written by Mr Douglas Jerrold, the historian of the Naval Division in the First World War, and author of, among other books, a history of England of which two volumes have appeared. Mr Jerrold, whose name has already been mentioned in these pages, is a writer gifted with the technique of sifting evidence. In an article quoted by Sir Arnold Lunn in *Spanish Rehearsal*, he summed up as follows his own judgement of the Guernica myth:

'Firstly, Guernica is a strategic position of considerable importance. Secondly, it is the centre of an important part of the Basque small-arms industry. Thirdly, by the official admission of the Mayor, in his statement issued by the Bilbao Government and communicated to the Press all over the world, Guernica was full of troops when it was bombed. Fourthly, Guernica was bombed in the proper course of the operations against Bilbao, but it was not bombed on the day it was burnt, and it was burnt by the retreating Basque (or, more probably, by the Asturian) troops, and not by the Nationalist forces.

'Let us examine the evidence for these statements.

'No evidence is required for the first two. The strategic importance of Guernica is obvious to any soldier who looks at the map. That it is surrounded by small-arms factories is also a matter of established fact. The owners of these factories, incidentally, have for years been supplying arms to terrorists and other illegal organizations all over Europe and Asia. But what of the Dean of Valladolid, who was in the town when it was burnt; of *The Times* correspondent, who saw the aeroplanes *en route*; of the two German airmen, whose diaries with military conciseness contained the simple word "Guernica" against the required date?

'As regards the Dean of Valladolid, the ecclesiastical authorities in Valladolid say that the priest in question is not the Dean. Nor is the case for his veracity improved by the discovery that he is the author of another account of the bombardment appearing under another signature, and confirming that which appeared under his own name. *The Times* correspondent was in Bilbao when, like everyone else there, he heard accounts of Guernica. He went to Guernica in the small hours of the following morning. His first excited account began with the statement that the town was completely destroyed, but that the deaths were, fortunately, small. They could hardly have been small if the town had been slowly, systematically, pounded to pieces. They might have been if it was being fired and mined. He was eight and a half miles away from

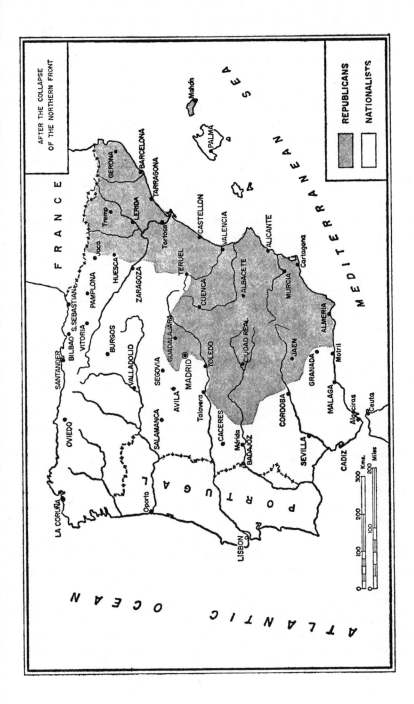

AFTER THE COLLAPSE
OF THE NORTHERN FRONT

REPUBLICANS

NATIONALISTS

Guernica when he "saw" the aeroplanes, and he was certainly in Bilbao when he wrote his despatch. As to the Germans, we have no right whatever to accept the reports of their evidence, but there is no reason to doubt that they bombed Guernica on occasions. It had been bombed intermittently for several days before it was given up.

'On the other side, the evidence is, as near as may be, conclusive. The correspondents of the Havas agency, of *The Times*, and of several other newspapers have affirmed positively that most of the damage which they saw was wrought not by bombing, but by deliberate destruction by fires from the ground. The statements are explicit. There were only a few bomb holes, and the walls of the houses in the quarter most completely destroyed bear no marks of bomb splinters. Nor can the damage done by a bomb and that done by dynamiters and incendiaries be confused by any competent observer.

'And yet, without this testimony from *The Times* correspondent and other neutral journalists, I should feel justified in denying the charge of wanton destruction for quite different reasons. Firstly, I have seen the destruction at Irun, which was admittedly wrought by the same army, under the same leadership, as that which was defending Guernica: a complete street—the principal street of the town—systematically destroyed, house by house, with only the walls left standing, and the interiors completely gutted by fire. A rain of bombs might, in loose journalistic parlance "destroy" a whole street in a town, but it would not destroy it *in that way*. At Guernica, as at Irun, there is hardly a mark in the street. A "rain of bombs" would fall as often in the streets and gardens as on the houses, and must leave traces which could not possibly be obliterated. The roadway would be destroyed, the flowers would be withered. Secondly, people who talk about destruction from the air have no idea of the local effect of a bomb. I have seen, at Malaga and elsewhere, the effect of bombs on a score of houses. A bomb falling from a height will tear its way through a house and explode, leaving half the house standing. That part of the house which it hits, however, will be totally destroyed; the burst will be outwards as well as upwards, and the outside walls will never be left intact. To destroy an entire small town, however, as part of Irun was destroyed, not hundreds, but thousands, of bombs would be required. The resources for such wholesale destruction are entirely lacking to either side in this war. Apart altogether from the question of expediency, such destruction would mean using a month's supply of ammunition for General Franco's entire army, and denuding all fronts of air protection to indulge in an orgy of lunatic folly.

'And again, Eibar was also, and admittedly, burnt. It was never suggested by Bilbao that it had even been severely bombed till two days after the Guernica story had shocked the world. Yet eye-witnesses report that the damage at Eibar is of precisely the same kind as that at Guernica.

'Finally, the question can be cynically determined by reference to that old question "*cui bono?*". When the alleged destruction of Guernica took place it was in process of being evacuated; an advance had taken place on all fronts, and nothing could have saved the town. General Franco had nothing whatever to gain by destroying it. The Basque Government, if they could get their story accepted, had everything to gain. The "incident" would stiffen the resistance of the Catholic Basques. It would influence neutral opinion, strengthen the attitude of the British Government in regard to the blockade of Bilbao, and possibly even lead to its abandonment.'

In his scholarly analysis of the Guernica myth Mr Douglas Jerrold mentions two correspondents of *The Times*. One, Harold Philby, was attached to us; the other was with the Basques in Bilbao, where he covered operations from the Republican side. This second correspondent was the late Mr G. L. Steer, and his blood-curdling accounts to London were partly responsible for the world circulation of the myth. Years later Mr G. L. Steer wrote a book entitled *Sealed and Delivered*; it was published in London by Hodder and Stoughton, and *The Tablet* reviewed it on 26 September 1942. The following paragraphs are extracts from this review.

'At the outbreak of war with Italy, on the grounds that he had formed one of the motley horde of journalists who infested Addis Ababa in the war of 1935–6, Captain Steer was appointed G.3 in Khartoum, in charge of propaganda. In this capacity he saw a great deal of the traffic in desertion which was called the "patriot movement", and was in close touch with Col. Wingate's remarkable column of Sudanese and irregulars which kept disproportionately large enemy forces deployed in the disaffected North-Western provinces and so greatly helped the Indian divisions in their decisive advance to Keren and Amba Alagi. Most of those who interested themselves in the cause of the Emperor Haile Selassie in the years 1935–40 lacked either humour, knowledge or honesty. Captain Steer's humour is boundless, and his knowledge considerable. His honesty may best be judged from his own account (p. 130) "Our next theme was to launch a personal attack on Lorenzini. He was a skunk and a coward. He had run away from Agordat and left his troops in the lurch . . . This of course was not true, for Lorenzini was a very brave man . . . (he) was killed at Keren . . . If I had thought that such a story could have passed a British censorship I would have announced that he had been shot in the back by a deserting Eritrean askari (p. 164). The Emperor did not approve of the particularism of these sheets, and the imperial seal that I put on them was in fact a forgery." The book is full of instances of this kind which Captain Steer records with evident relish. Whether it is prudent at this stage of the war to publish so very frank an account of a propaganda campaign which on many occasions disgusted the fighting soldiers with whom he was associated, is a matter for the higher military authorities to decide. The lay reader may also make a note that this is how Captain Steer treats the truth when he is in a responsible official position. As a free-lance journalist he has written of Abyssinia before, and of the civil war in Spain. We shall know in future how to take the author's statements when his sympathies are engaged.'

In boasting of the lies which he circulated in the world war, Mr Steer is self-convicted as the author of mendacious propaganda.

In *Mine Were of Trouble*, one of the best books written on the Spanish Civil War (Cassell and Company Ltd., London, 1957), the author, Peter Kemp, who was in Spain throughout that war, wrote this about Guernica and its alleged destruction from the air: 'The Republicans were countering the Nationalist offensive against Bilbao with a propaganda offensive of their own; at this time it was concentrated on the famous Guernica incident. It was very cleverly handled, and a great deal of money was spent on it abroad; Botteau'—the correspondent of the Havas Agency with the Nationalists—'was told by his head office that the Republicans spent about six hundred thousand pounds in Paris on propaganda about Guernica alone. The story circulated—and widely believed—was that Guernica, an open town, was destroyed by incendiary bombs dropped by Nationalist aircraft; Cardozo'—this was Harold Cardozo, *Daily Mail* correspondent with the Nationalists—'was indignant at the success it was having in England. He was in Guernica immediately after its occupation by the Nationalists, and so was able to make a pretty thorough examination. It was clear to him, he said, that the Republicans themselves had set fire to the town before leaving, just as they had burnt Irun, Eibar and Amorebieta in the course of their retreat through the Basque Provinces; he himself had witnessed the burning of Amorebieta. Certainly Guernica was bombed by the Nationalists, but it was not an open town at the time it was bombed; it was packed with Republican troops, and was, in fact, a Divisional Headquarters. After watching the burning of Amorebieta, he had entered it next day, and talked to some of the few inhabitants that were left. Before abandoning the town the *milicianos* had come to their houses and taken all their food and clothing, even what they were wearing, so that they were dressed in pieces of sacking; then they had set fire to the town. "We know," these poor people had told Cardozo, "who burned Amorebieta. So we can guess who burned Guernica."

'It seems to me that nothing illustrates better the superiority of Republican propaganda over Nationalist than that the Republican story about Guernica was given immediate and world-wide publicity, and is still generally believed; whereas the Nationalist case scarcely received a hearing.'

When I heard what the foreign press was publishing about Guernica I went to see General Franco. It was a Sunday. He had finished lunch and was sitting in a small leafy garden with his family. In Salamanca, when not busy working, which was seldom, he was always with his wife and daughter. It was a pleasant spring day, and as we paced the shade I ventured the view that it was time we had somebody in London, qualified to speak for us in the right quarters. Only the Reds had diplomatic representatives in England. Juan de la Cierva had been killed there in a plane crash a few months before. One of his wartime associates, the Marqués de Portago, had carried on his work with others and was obtaining results, but we needed someone of greater weight and influence. I mentioned two names, and added that of the two, the Duke of Alba seemed the better choice. As much at home in England as in Spain, he knew everyone in London and had the entrée everywhere. 'Where is he?' asked Franco. 'At Las Dueñas, his home in Seville.' Days later, Alba arrived at Claridge's. Before the end of the year he was our official agent in Great Britain, with Sir Robert Hodgson as his counterpart in Burgos. Eventually, the Duke became Spanish Ambassador to the Court of St James's and accomplished first-class work there under very difficult circumstances.

In London, where as already noted above I spent three busy and pleasant weeks that late spring and summer, I was as much impressed by the warm feelings of our friends as by the venomous acidity with which we were condemned in some circles. We had in general a bad press. Many had not a clue to what was at stake. Years later an English lady told friends of hers in Jerez that she had felt much relieved when Franco 'finally allowed' mass to be said in Spanish churches. 'I was so glad to hear this,' she informed them. We ourselves, I am afraid, did little to clarify the situation; the war kept us busy, and we were intent on winning. Douglas Jerrold, Sir Arthur Bryant, Sir Arnold Lunn, Arthur Loveday, and many others upheld the truth about the war in the face of misunderstanding and opposition. Ian Colvin, the editor of the *Morning Post*, was among the first to clarify the issues, and he did so long before civil war broke out, when people everywhere inclined to believe that the Republic was working wonders in Spain, a belief which Colvin's leading aricles contributed in no small measure to dispel. Hugh Pollard and Cecil Bebb, with Jerrold in the first place, were my invaluable allies throughout the flight which we jointly planned and carried out to bring Franco from the Canary Islands. In every case their reactions were of a personal character; the English are like the Spanish in that they act individually as they think fit. In France, if you knew the party or the nuance of a party to which a man belonged—and in those days the distinction was sometimes a subtle one—you had no trouble in establishing whether its members were for or against you. In England the Catholics were on our side, but the manner in which men and women of different political views and stations in life reacted towards the events then taking place in Spain was unpredictable and occasionally disconcerting.

CHAPTER THIRTY-FOUR

Brunete—Santander—Belchite

The campaign in the north moved rapidly. Bilbao was captured on 19 June, after two and a half months of hard fighting during which we frequently lost what we had won or regained what we had been forced to give up. Both sides suffered many casualties, but the quality of our troops and the manner in which they overcame every obstacle left no doubt as to the ultimate result. The fall of Malaga, a city on the Mediterranean only eighty miles from Gibraltar, had impressed public opinion abroad, especially in England. The fall of Bilbao simplified matters in that country for the Duke of Alba, our official agent in London. Events were moving in our favour, but a reaction from the Republicans was to be expected. Diligently and with great secrecy, using 60,000 men, 150 planes, 20 batteries, and 128 tanks, on 6 July they launched an attack against Brunete, a village lying fifteen miles west of Madrid. Their aim was to capture Navalcarnero, situated five miles farther on the main road to Badajoz and Seville, and thus free the capital from the forces that encircled it on several sides. Had they done so, the besieging troops would have been cut off from their sources of supply and possibly pounded up and destroyed. Our lines were broken in one place, but the resulting gap proved inadequate for enemy contingents to pour through and pivot eastward according to plan.

The battle of Brunete dragged on for nearly three weeks. Both sides fought determinedly. Twenty battalions sorely needed on other fronts were rushed up to replace casualties and bolster up our defence. The advance on Santander had to be halted when it was on the point of being resumed. Franco left Salamanca to direct operations in Brunete, where Varela, who commanded our troops on the field, had a hard time keeping him away from observation posts under gunfire. On one occasion Franco's headquarters were surrounded. The officer who imparted this news—Lieut.-Com. Calderón, a naval A.D.C.—was met with a stony glance from the General, and the words '¿Y qué?'—'so what?' The troops which we brought up as reinforcements were as played out and exhausted as the men whom they replaced. The Republicans lost 25,000 men, our own losses numbered 13,000. Many villages in the area were reduced to rubble by shells and bombs, and rebuilt admirably at the end of a conflict in which Brunete was a vital encounter. Never again did our opponents have a chance as favourable as that which they held in their hands on 6 and 7 July 1937, when they caught us off our guard at Brunete and opened up a breach wide enough to take Navalcarnero and isolate a whole army. But we turned the scales against them and would have demolished their entire front as far as El Escorial and beyond it had not Franco insisted that what mattered now was to advance against Santander before autumn mists, rain and snow combined to postpone operations there until the following spring. At all costs the northern front had to be eliminated while the weather remained fairly steady.

The offensive against Santander gathered way on 14 August, three weeks after the Republican attacks on Brunete ceased. Four Navarre Brigades advanced east from the province of Bilbao, which we had occupied completely. Two more came up from Reinosa, and the Italians attacked in the centre, astride of the road from Burgos and supported on both flanks by Spanish infantry and cavalry squadrons. In all, 106 battalions, with an adequate number of tanks, batteries and planes, took part in the onslaught; 59 Red battalions opposed them, with 50 batteries and 44 planes. Like the attack on Malaga, some aspects of which it recalls, the operation was effectively carried out. On 26 August, twelve days after it started, our soldiers entered Santander and found 17,000 Republican troops patiently awaiting capture in the bull-ring. Many of them would have preferred to fight for us, and were soon given the chance to do so. Two days before Santander fell, the late Rupert Belville, an Englishman whose sympathies were with us and who watched developments from our side, flew his private plane unconcernedly into the local airport, believing the city to be already occupied by our forces. With him was Ricardo González, a close friend of his from Jerez. Seized by the Reds, Rupert was compelled at pistol point to fly a prominent Republican leader to Gijón, from which city he eventually escaped on a British destroyer. Ricardo swore that he was an Englishman lacking all knowledge of Spanish, but his captors suspected something, and though his English was perfect, but for his timely rescue he would have been shot. Both men escaped death thanks to their cool wit and their resourcefulness. They were luckier than others, for the Reds in Santander murdered many people, some of whom they cast into the raging sea from the heights of Cabo Mayor. As usual, they also burnt or looted a number of churches and private houses.

The Republican offensive at Brunete had ended in a failure, so another move was planned farther north. Saragossa, an important city, capital of Aragon in ancient times, lay almost within reach of the enemy, who had already subjected it to a series of fruitless assaults. Operations in this area were now launched on a much larger scale. On 22 August, too late to save Santander, but early enough to try to save Asturias, 80,000 Republicans attacked on a wide front which extended from Huesca, forty-five miles north of Saragossa, to Belchite, thirty miles south-east of that town. Before two of our divisions could be dispatched as reinforcements from the outskirts of Madrid, where they were besieging the city, a strong Republican contingent captured the railway station at Huesca and another closed in around Belchite, where only 2,000 men opposed them. Huesca survived; despite being practically surrounded on several occasions, the garrison there succeeded in repulsing attack after attack until the end of the war. Belchite succumbed. The heat was terrific, the defenders and their opponents were parched with thirst. A strong wind stirred up clouds of dust and almost blinded them. Our troops suffered 1,427 casualties, 58 of them officers. On our side it was reckoned that in the course of their successive assaults on the Aragon front the Republicans lost some 20,000 men without improving their positions or preventing us from capturing Santander.

Nor did the fighting in Aragon stop Franco from attacking Asturias, where our enemies, numerous, determined, well-armed, and strongly encouraged from Madrid, had concentrated every unit within reach. Asturias is a region of sierras some of which rank among the most inaccessible in Spain. They include part of the Picos de Europa, thus called by ancient mariners who espied them as they sailed across the Bay of Biscay near the northern shores of Spain. The peaks and crags that crown them are a favourite haunt of chamois. Other ranges are El Fito, Puerto Sueve and the Cordillera de Cuera. Asturias is separated by mountains from the provinces of Palencia and León. The heights that cut up the country flank canyons and gorges as lovely as El Pontón and La Hermida or riant valleys like Tarna and Burón. It was high in the rocks around Covadonga that King Pelayo defied the Arabs when they overran Spain in the eighth century. Now these obstacles had to be carried against men determined to defend them by troops which had waged war incessantly, in some cases on two fronts, for five exhausting months.

CHAPTER THIRTY-FIVE

Decision in Asturias

For Red leaders, such as those now fighting on its soil, Asturias was the last bastion. They had fought and lost against the Republican Government in the autumn of 1934, and fought and lost again against Franco in the summer months of 1936 and 1937. The miners of Asturias, renowned for their aggressive courage, were not only their mainstay but their last hope. On our side, Solchaga, Muñoz Grandes, and Aranda commanded Navarre Brigades, infantry battalions, Foreign Legion and Moorish units, ideal for mountain fighting and assault. Their advance began on 4 September, nine days after the fall of Santander; it encountered stiff resistance from an enemy which though outwitted and hard-pressed from all directions was determined to hold out till the end. Undeterred by heavy rains, which turned to snow and sleet in the high mountains, or by the slipperiness of the steep paths from which mules were sometimes dashed to pieces on the rocks below, our men advanced and fought while wading across the icy waters of rivers in spate. Fifty-seven hours were needed to hoist the four pieces of a field-battery to the heights of the Sierra de Cuera. Casualties piled up. Colonel Alonso Vega, who led the attack from the east, was seriously wounded in the outskirts of Llanes while his men captured the town. On the first of October, Solchaga took Covadonga. Winter was closing in, and Franco urged his men to occupy Asturias with the least possible delay. When the final onslaught was launched in mid-October, the Brigades from Navarre advanced unopposed. Oviedo, the capital of Asturias, was relieved by our troops on 17 October 1937.

It had been besieged for fifteen consecutive months, of which the hardest were the first three (July–October 1936) when the city was practically encircled and subjected to constant attacks. The defenders numbered three thousand. Eight hundred of them were volunteers, the remainder regular troops, Assault Police, and Civil Guards, with little or no combat experience and insufficiently supplied with ammunition for a drawn-out siege. They had two million rifle cartridges, 2,000 hand-grenades, 3,150 trench-mortar shells, and a sizeable stock of dynamite. A considerable part of the population sympathized with the attacking Reds; practically all the outlying districts of Oviedo were full of Red partisans.

The Nationalist leader, Colonel Don Antonio Aranda, was a capable Staff Officer who could count on a group of men as determined and resourceful as himself. At the start of the siege, to divert part of the forces that opposed him, he had declared himself on the side of the Government and persuaded a large body of Red miners to entrain for the south. Their assistance, he assured them, could be of value to anarchist and communist comrades who were preparing to defend Madrid. Hundreds left for the capital and were routed and defeated on the way. Soon after this Oviedo had to be defended from a series of attacks launched from all sides. A line was established around the city, a mile away from its outlying buildings at some points, two thousand feet or less at others according to the contour of the terrain. Casualties were heavy; not more than two thousand able-bodied men were left to man the trenches that defended Oviedo. Food became scarce, coal was practically unobtainable, there was no electricity, and drinking water had to be rationed for the enemy had cut off the supply. An epidemic of typhoid broke out. The bombardment destroyed many buildings; the defenders were hemmed in. Some houses were occupied partly by Nationalists and partly by Reds who hurled hand-grenades at each other. Whole districts fell into enemy hands, and air raids were frequent.

On 28 August the Republicans announced that Oviedo had fallen into their hands. One week later, the real battle for the city began; it lasted until Oviedo was finally relieved in October 1937. Instead of shelling empty buildings as they had previously done, ten batteries commanded by competent Republican gunners directed their fire against our trenches, and forced the defenders back. Six hundred men, of whom one hundred were suffering from wounds, remained to cover a front that was now five miles long; in support there were four hundred more. They had thousands against them. Sixty per cent of the Nationalist officers and forty per cent of their troops became casualties. Aranda dispatched a telegram to General Mola, the commander-in-chief of the Northern Army, saying, 'All that remains for us now is to die like Spaniards.'

At dawn on 17 October 1936, almost exactly three months after the

start of the siege, the defenders of Oviedo saw Nationalist troops spurting forward on the slopes north of the city. They were the advance guard of a relief column which had left La Coruña weeks before and fought its way into Asturias over mountain heights and passes defended by forces numerically superior. At their head was a colonel, the late Don Pablo Martín Alonso, a veteran of the Moroccan wars and the A.D.C. who escorted King Alfonso on his journey from Madrid to Cartagena the night that the Monarchy fell. With eighteen hundred men under his command he won a decisive victory. The besiegers had attacked the city from every point, dropped upon it as many as fifteen hundred bombs in a single day, shelled it continuously for three months and reduced a large part of it to rubble, causing a destruction which exceeded all that I witnessed elsewhere in the Spanish Civil War; so much of the city was destroyed that it was hard to realize how the population had managed to survive. Before the entire area around Oviedo could be freed, twelve months later, the inhabitants suffered countless hardships, but the life-line to the east which Martín Alonso established allowed many civilians to be evacuated and the remainder to be provisioned and cared for.

When our troops finally occupied the entire province in October 1937, every Red leader in Asturias escaped by plane to France. Twenty-two of their battalions surrendered; 100,000 prisoners were taken. A hostile army, 150,000 strong, vanished into thin air. Franco increased his effectives with a total of 250 battalions, 150 of which, made up of seasoned troops, were soon transferred from the north to other sectors. The remainder resulted from training volunteers and conscripts in the areas just occupied. Many of them were former opponents, willing to fight for us now.

For the enemy, the loss of Asturias was a foretaste of final defeat; for us it was a decisive victory. The Northern Front had disappeared. Though the Reds and their friends abroad denied it, the situation had changed radically in our favour.

CHAPTER THIRTY-SIX

Life Behind the Nationalist Lines

During the Civil War, the three most important cities in Nationalist Spain were Burgos, seat of the provisional Government and of the skeleton civil service that ran the country on our side; Salamanca, where General Franco established his headquarters for the first eighteen months of the war; and Seville, from which General Queipo de Llano commanded the Army of the South and ruled with viceregal authority over most of Andalusia. In all three, as in San Sebastian after its liberation in September 1936, thousands of refugees from the territories occupied by the Reds bided their time until the termination of the conflict, and either worked to support themselves or drew on the credits granted to them by the banking institutions which they had patronized in happier days.

To attract refugees who had escaped from Madrid, Barcelona, and Valencia, the city of Saragossa was too near the front, Malaga too far removed from the scene of political or military activities. San Sebastian and Seville were ideal places to live in, the first because of its cosmopolitan atmosphere and its proximity to the French frontier, which could be crossed fairly easily for a brief stay, the second because of its charm and its mild winter climate. Life was normal in the entire Nationalist zone, peace and order were complete, prices remained low. Though transport facilities were few, Spaniards became better acquainted with other parts of their country, many of them for the first time. To move from one place to another was not easy owing to the lack of cars and fuel or to the disruption of railway communications, for the principal railroads converged on Madrid, and Madrid was in the hands of the enemy. Besides, when a highway ran near the front, a journey by car was not devoid of hazards. Between Seville and Salamanca, for instance, enemy raids were frequent near Mérida, in Extremadura, and in the Sierra Morena, north of Seville. On these stretches, if advisable, traffic would be halted at sundown, and cars sometimes raced to reach their destination before being turned back by a friendly patrol. When this happened it often proved difficult to find a meal or a lodging for the night, and you were never quite sure whether the armed men who stopped your car and while doing so covered you with their rifles were on your side, or the other. But people became accustomed to this, in the same way as they put up with punctured tyres and mechanical breakdowns on the dilapidated vehicles which, filled with luggage, carried them from one end of the country to the other. Strangely enough, they also preferred to run the risk of being bombed while living in cities comparatively near the lines than to set up their quarters in more remote areas such as north-west Spain, where the risk of enemy action was non-existent.

Despite their racial ties with the French and with the Italians, in time of war Spaniards behave far more like the English. During the Civil War all that men on leave wanted was to have the best possible time, and their people helped them to enjoy it. There was no tendency to moroseness on the part of either and little talk about the Front. The optimism and good humour spread around them by those having a respite from fighting and from the constant risk of death or injury contributed to maintain a high morale behind the lines.

General Franco often left his headquarters at Salamanca to direct operations on the field. He later transferred them to Burgos, and, later still, to unspecified places behind the Ebro Front, usually referred to as 'Terminus' and situated near the lines. For a year he had been Supreme Commander of the Nationalist forces and Head of the Spanish State. Six weeks after the war started a vital decision in his favour had been made on these points. Sanjurjo was dead. Besides Franco, two Generals, Mola and Queipo de Llano, were considered as possible candidates for the leadership of the armies on the field and the conduct of national affairs. A similar problem was settled in Doullens, twenty miles north of Amiens, in 1918, when Marshal Foch was proclaimed Supreme Commander of the Allied Armies. To reach a decision in Spain, nine Generals met in a country estate near Salamanca on 12 September 1936. It so happened that I was near Doullens and Salamanca when these decisions were respectively adopted and on both occasions was one of the first to learn about them. In Spain, the promoter of the move was the late General Don Alfredo Kindelán, who commanded the Nationalist Air Force. Franco was reluctant to broach the subject; he feared it might lead to disagreement and argument during a critical phase of the war. Kindelán felt that unity of command was indispensable for victory, and that no time should be lost in selecting a leader. The Generals present at the meeting near Salamanca were Saliquet, Gil Yuste, Orgaz, Mola, Dávila, Cabanellas, Queipo de Llano, Kindelán and Franco. Cabanellas, who presided, thought that the most appropriate solution to adopt was to appoint a Directorate. Orgaz and Kindelán demurred and nominated Franco for leadership. The nomination was accepted, and on 27 September the same group of Generals met again at the same place and elected Franco to the post of Supreme Commander. Six days later, on 3 October, this decision was jointly ratified in Burgos by the commanders of all the Nationalist forces on the field and by the leaders of the three political parties that had rebelled to overthrow the Republic.

The passing of a year had seated Franco firmly in the saddle. Some think of him mainly as a strategic and political commander-in-chief, but throughout the Civil War he was also a tactical leader, as he had been in Morocco. Though he did not physically lead troops in action, he certainly directed their movements, and this explains the prestige he enjoyed. His fellow-officers would hardly have tolerated a perfunctory leader of a more academic type. Wherever he might be he would spend hours poring over large-scale maps pinned on plywood boards and set up on easels under a strong light. Every feature of the ground over which his men fought was noted and taken into account. Minute instructions, issued on the field of battle or transmitted also personally, through long-distance telephone lines, were backed by a knowledge of the terrain equal to that possessed by those who received his orders. That he should issue them in person was taken as a matter of course. Many of his comrades had been with him in Africa, and although when addressing him they used the familiar *tu*, equivalent to calling a man by his first name in other countries, they showed a respect towards him based not so much on his exalted position as Commander-in-Chief and Head of the Spanish State as on the qualities which had raised him to these posts.

In Salamanca, one day, the lights that lit up the large-scale maps used by General Franco were put to another purpose. Averse from publicity, during the first months of the war there had been no way of persuading him to have his picture taken. To comply with requests from journalists and others all that I had was a small set of photographs shaped like postcards and taken in the Canary Islands some time before. The

General was always too busy and had other things to do; his lack of interest in the subject, more than his manner, made it difficult to talk to him about photography as far as it concerned himself. But demands from all quarters became too pressing, and a capable photographer from Saragossa was pleading with us for a sitting. One morning two A.D.C.s and myself, won over to the photographer's cause, cleared up the General's office at breakfast time and brought in the lamps that lit the maps in the dark passage outside. When we told him that the time had come to have his picture taken Franco smiled and shrugged his shoulders. His reluctance to pose has not diminished with the passing of the years. To overcome it now, the prospect of portraying him with his grandchildren is probably the surest lure.

In 1937, for a short period, one of his A.D.C.s in Salamanca was a captain in the Air Force called Carlos Haya. Haya's wife, the daughter of a famous doctor, was a hostage of the Reds in Valencia—they had forcibly taken her with them as they fled from Malaga, her native town, when it was occupied by our troops—and the thought of her and of the anguish which she was enduring was constantly in her husband's mind. He had piloted the planes which dropped messages, provisions, and medical supplies on the courtyard of the Alcázar de Toledo, while the enemy attacked it, and on an even smaller area in the Monasterio of La Virgen de la Cabeza, in Sierra Morena, where it took twelve thousand Reds nearly ten months to subdue five hundred Nationalists and capture the women and children whom they defended. It had been easier for Haya to do this than for him to understand the reason why his wife should be carried off by force and separated from her family. Haya, an intense and passionate man with a cool head for planning and fighting, would sit at his desk with his rosary in his hands, praying for the day when his wife could be set free. Because I came from Malaga and knew her family, he sometimes spoke to me of his hopes and fears. His one idea was to leave Salamanca and rejoin his squadron. Early in 1938, during the battle of the Alfambra, he was shot down in air combat over enemy territory.

The war was producing on our side a fine crop of fighting pilots. Before it started, Captain Joaquín García Morato had piloted planes of various types for 1,860 hours. During the war he flew over 1,000 hours, took part in 511 missions of various kinds and in 144 air combats and shot down 40 enemy planes. Near Madrid, on one occasion, he and his squadron attacked and defeated thirty-six enemy craft. For this action, watched from the trenches by thousands of combatants, he was awarded the Cruz Laureada de San Fernando, a decoration equivalent to the Victoria Cross or to the Congressional Medal of Honor. His squadron was called The Blue Patrol. Its motto was *vista, suerte, y al toro*, which translated inadequately means 'alertness, luck, and decision'. Morato introduced the chain-system of machine-gunning trenches and enemy positions, adopted by others in subsequent wars. He was one of the world's finest airmen, and the qualities he possessed would have been invaluable to organize the Spanish Air Force in time of peace. I was with him frequently in or behind the lines, also in Seville and in San Sebastian, where he usually went when on leave. Good-looking, simple and unassuming, his charm and his keen sense of humour won friends for him all the time. He would talk of air combats or aerial tactics as easily as he carried on a light conversation. In peace and war he had done practically everything that could be done in the air. He was killed near Madrid, accidentally, while flying a single-seater plane, a few days after the conclusion of hostilities.

When Carlos Haya was shot down over Red territory, Joaquin Garcia Morato, his close friend and brother-in-law—Morato's wife and Haya's were sisters—wrote a message to his opponents in the Red air force, and at the risk of his life dropped it on one of their airfields to make sure that it reached its destination. The message said: 'Captain Haya has been killed in air combat on the Teruel Front, not far from the Escandón Pass. His widow requests her husband's body for Christian burial. I beg you to deliver it. This request is not addressed to my friends of yesterday, or to my opponents of today, but to Haya's late comrades in the air. If you grant it, whenever we meet in battle I will salute you in token of gratitude before opening fire.'

The message was never acknowledged.

The Nationalists lost no time in equipping and putting into service two 10,000-ton cruisers that were in the yards at El Ferrol, a naval base, when war broke out. *Canarias* is still in good shape. *Baleares* left Palma de Mallorca shortly after dusk on 5 March, 1938. The night was dark and the sea was smooth. Shortly after midnight, decks were cleared for action. At 1.45 a.m., the cruiser was struck by torpedoes fired from Republican craft. Water rushed through an enormous gap on the starboard side, and *Baleares* was plunged into darkness. Its bulges had been pierced; the ship began to founder. For one brief moment there was a rush to the top deck, but the situation was soon under control.

Two British destroyers appeared out of the void, flooded the darkness with light, and came alongside. One cast a line which was quickly secured but soon had to be severed, for *Baleares* was already going down. Lieutenant Cervera, great-grandson of the Admiral who fought American ironclads with wooden vessels in Santiago de Cuba, addressed his men: "Let us show these English gentlemen how Spanish sailors die." Youthful volunteers sang *Cara al Sol*. There was no panic; those on board faced death with Christian courage. Eleven officers, all under the rank of lieutenant-commander, were saved; Admiral Vierna and others of senior rank, including a number of specialists, were killed or drowned. The two British destroyers lowered boats and picked up many, but at daybreak Red planes appeared and bombed the waters where the swirl left by *Baleares* was visible from the air. So rapidly did the destroyers manœuvre that some of those still floating were sucked down by the force of their propellers.

Out of 1,229 on board, 468 were saved, and 761 officers and men went down with their ship. Their death was felt deeply by the Spanish people. The loss of *Baleares* did not affect Nationalist supremacy at sea.

PART VII

CHAPTER THIRTY-SEVEN

Teruel and the Alfambra

Two months after the conquest of Asturias, on 15 December 1937, while our General Staff was preparing a second onslaught against Guadalajara, part of the 640 battalions which the Republicans had now lined up against us attacked Teruel, one hundred and fifteen miles south of Saragossa on the road from that city to Valencia. From a narrow front, without preparatory bombardments, massed troops were launched against both flanks of a salient on the tip of which Teruel stood. The city lacked strategic importance, but our opponents felt that the capture of a provincial capital was necessary to offset their losses in the north. In their first determined onslaught the enemy swarmed over our lines and almost encircled the town. To prevent reinforcements from being rushed up against them 200 Republican guns opened fire and as many planes bombed the roads and villages behind our lines. Hemmed in on all sides, four thousand Nationalist soldiers withdrew into Teruel and were joined there by about two thousand civilians who had volunteered to defend the city.

A fortnight elapsed without decisive results. Teruel held out, though on two separate occasions the Republicans announced that it had fallen. Erected on a hillock which overlooked the country and surrounded by a natural moat, the product of erosion, its position was ideal for defence, to direct which Franco sent instructions over the radio. Every post, he said, had to be manned and defended; ammunition and supplies were to be rationed. Water was plentiful, for there were wells in some houses and in public squares. Street fighting favoured the defenders, who had roof-tops and windows to shoot from. Tanks could be destroyed with Molotov cocktails and hand-grenades. Hesitant or inept commanders were to be replaced by others endowed with more grit. In no case was the garrison to be intimidated by the loss of one or several buildings. Teruel, Franco insisted, possessed the necessary resources to hold out until relieved.

On 31 December I requested permission from General Franco to leave for Teruel, enter the city through the narrow gap that still linked it to the outside world, and explain the situation to newspaper correspondents with us, who were showing signs of restlessness. 'You'd never get there,' Franco said. 'It has snowed hard for a couple of days and all means of access are cut off. The roads are covered with ice: the temperature is 19 below'—about 2 degrees below zero Fahrenheit. 'Your car would freeze and leave you stranded. If you want to know how matters stand, go upstairs and ask Lieut.-Col. Barroso. You'll see the situation better on a map than if you managed to reach Teruel.'

That day, as the relieving columns approached the outskirts of the city, there was a terrific snowstorm in the area. Truck drivers and soldiers succumbed to the cold and cars had to be dragged by tractors over the frozen roads. On both sides the men sought shelter in the icy snow to avoid being picked out by snipers. Though the outside temperature fell at dawn to forty below zero, airmen dropped bombs and machine-gunned trenches till the blizzard blotted out every shred of visibility. The plains around the city were littered with corpses. One of our divisions, the 84th, suffered 4,308 casualties, and a battalion 720 men strong counted 181 survivors. The heads, arms and legs of dead soldiers emerged stiffly from the snow. Republican guns fired incessantly; 200 Russian tanks cleared the way for the Republican infantry. The commander of another of our divisions, the 13th, reported that his men, after almost dying of thirst in summer, were now perishing of cold and enduring the tortures of hell from frozen feet. They had no protection against the weather; we lacked the money to equip them. A foreign observer wrote: 'Of all my memories of the Spanish Civil War the most vivid and pathetic is the vision of Franco's soldiers around Teruel, thinly clothed, wearing shoes made of canvas and esparto-grass soles, lying silent and unprotesting in the snow, ready to attack or to defend themselves without uttering a word of complaint. I doubt if what I saw could be reproduced anywhere else.'

Teruel fell on 7 January. Its defenders fought desperately, but when the enemy seized building after building the colonel in command of the city ordered the outlying houses to be abandoned and finally expressed his willingness to parley. His opponents treated him disgracefully and a year later, as they fled from Barcelona to France, they riddled his body with bullets a few miles before reaching the French frontier and at the same time murdered the Bishop of Teruel, who like the Colonel was their prisoner.

On 5 February, less than a month after the fall of Teruel, Franco moved forward on the Alfambra river and dealt his enemies a crushing blow. The battle of the Alfambra was one of the war's decisive encounters. It reversed the shape of the bulge which the Reds had driven into our front, with the southern end at Teruel and the northern tip near Vivel del Río, forty-two miles away. Attacked at both ends and pushed back, the Red salient was obliterated. According to our estimates, which at best were only approximate, the Republicans suffered 14,000 dead, 20,000 wounded and 17,000 prisoners. They also lost 20 batteries, 40 tanks, and 500 machine-guns. One hundred of their planes were destroyed in air combat. Fifty *pueblos* and 620 square miles of land were captured, and a gap was opened in the enemy lines wide enough for our troops to reach the Mediterranean shortly afterwards and split the Red front in two. Teruel was retaken on 18 February.

CHAPTER THIRTY-EIGHT

Tourists in Wartime

On 16 February 1938, the formation of Franco's first Cabinet was announced and I was appointed head of the Spanish State Tourist Department. Seven years before, when the Republic was established, after offering my services to the new regime I had been dismissed without explanation from a lesser post in the same field of activity. Spain had much to gain from being known. We had nothing to hide, and there was no conceivable reason why we should not welcome visitors who would pay in foreign currencies for an experience which it had become my business to make pleasurable.

My start was from scratch and my budget was small, but the immediate opportunities for spending money were even smaller. With the exception of five of its members, who had escaped from the Red terror in the capital and who shortly afterwards found themselves fully occupied, most of my staff was in Madrid. In our Zone, the *Paradores* and *Albergues* built in King Alfonso's time or later had continued to serve the public, and Tourist Information offices were also open, but both had to be reconditioned and cared for. Two national hunting preserves, one in Gredos for Spanish Ibex, another in the Picos de Europa for chamois, needed attention. Conditions were different in each. In the Picos there had been much fighting, and some of the keepers there had fought against us. They were prisoners of war; reinstated soon, they fulfilled their duties splendidly. In Gredos, despite their humble status and their aloofness from political affairs, two keepers had been murdered by the Reds, the remainder had taken arms on our side, and none had been paid since the outbreak of hostilities. To this day they have not forgotten how rapidly their troubles were straightened out. When I thanked him for my appointment, General Franco encouraged my plans to organize angling in five of the fifteen salmon rivers that flow along the Spanish coastline between Portugal and France.

The areas behind our lines had been smoothly run. We were beginning to prepare for peace but the task before us was a formidable one, for the most elementary resources were wanting. My Remington Portable was the only typewriter in my office. When Nicolás Franco, the General's brother, presented me with a brand new machine I could hardly credit my luck; no typewriters were being made in Spain and we lacked the wherewithal to import them. I was anxious to prove that war and travel were not incompatible, that foreign tourists were a possibility even before peace had been made. February was still with us when I announced that by 1 July we would have motor-coach tours from the French frontier to Oviedo, with intermediate stops at San Sebastian, Bilbao, Laredo and Santander and a chance to visit battlefields and places on the way as interesting as the remnants of the Iron Belt around Bilbao, the Fito Pass in the Sueve range, Covadonga in the Picos de Europa, and the ruined districts in the city of Oviedo, liberated four months before. The duration of the tour was nine days; the total price, £8 or its equivalent in other currencies, with transport in new buses, hotel accommodation, three daily meals, and the services of qualified guides all included. At the price quoted we could even make money. Approximately 1,000 kilometres, or about 600 miles, would be covered during the round trip, for which different outgoing and incoming routes were selected whenever possible.

When I announced my project nobody believed that it could be carried out. There were no buses and no guides, every bridge on the roads chosen had been blown up, hotels had to be refurbished and supplied. The tours needed organization. But I felt that obstacles could be overcome, and because no country had ever opened its frontiers while fighting a war I knew that my tours would sell themselves the moment they were announced. By the time they started to run, Biarritz and St-Jean-de-Luz, just over the border in France, would be full of summer visitors. Some of them would respond to our appeals, and once they did this the news would spread rapidly. Free publicity would not be lacking. When General Franco approved my plans my confidence in the project increased. He also authorized me to call on the services of an infantry colonel, Don Francisco Vidal Sureda, who before reaching retirement age had opened up Majorca to foreigners, and whose assistance proved invaluable.

The buses were harder to get. I was negotiating for the purchase of twenty vehicles of the type known as 'school-buses' in America. Their price was 660,000 pesetas, equivalent then to some £14,000, and they had to be in Bilbao before the end of June. When the order for the buses was about to be dispatched I received a call from Don Pedro Gárate, the Finance Ministry's Controller, telling me to cancel the purchase. My dollars had been allotted to other purposes, and no more were to be had. I was in San Sebastian; Don Pedro Gárate was in Burgos, 140 miles away. He seemed surprised when I burst into his office three hours later, though perhaps not as much as I was when, after a brief talk, I left with a £14,000 cheque in my pocket. 'You make it difficult to say "no",' was Don Pedro's only comment. The twenty buses were unloaded in Bilbao from an American freighter two days before the end of June.

On 1 July the service started. Our first passengers were three French nuns and a left-wing English journalist who, once home, wrote that our tours were patronized chiefly by nuns, a statement which did not lack truth and helped to recruit a few clients. Even if we only had a single passenger our buses left punctually with twenty-nine empty seats. Soon they started to fill up, and before long they were running at a profit. The tours were called *Rutas Nacionales de Guerra* and each bus was named after a battle—Teruel, Alfambra, Belchite, Oviedo, Santander, Alcázar de Toledo. To simplify matters and sell more tickets we accepted people without visas and did not mind if they lacked passports. Many came to ascertain how Spain was faring under the stress of civil war, some were genuine tourists eager for a bargain, and a few collected background material with which to substantiate lurid accounts, published later abroad, of repression and hunger behind our lines. Stories of this kind were disproved by others whose main argument—'Franco would not have opened up his territories for investigation, if what is alleged were true'—was hard to contradict.

The majority of our passengers were writers, lecturers and preachers, friends of ours and supporters of our cause, in quest of the truth and deeply impressed with what they saw. Led by the Abbé Jobit and M. Pichon, two hundred Friends of Spain came from France and, in seven crammed buses, departed on an extended tour. Maurice Legendre, a distinguished writer and in time of peace the director of the Maison de Velázquez, the French Cultural Institute in Madrid, whose headquarters, at that moment in no-man's-land, were being badly ravaged by the war, met them with me at the border, his eyes filled with tears at the sight of so many of his compatriots, like himself staunch supporters of a free Spain. We took them not only to Oviedo, but to Compostela, and through Galicia and León to a monastery situated near Salamanca on the tip of La Peña de Francia, 5,600 feet high and bitterly cold on a brilliant August day, the feast of the Assumption. From there they went on to Santa Teresa's Avila and practically to the trenches before Madrid. They wanted to meet our soldiers and shake their hands.

Before summer's end the *Rutas* were regularly extended to Galicia, as far as Tuy on the Portuguese border, and their length was more than doubled. When winter came another *Ruta*, appropriate for the season, was opened in Andalusia. It ran from Seville to Jerez, Cadiz, Algeciras, Malaga, Granada and Cordoba, and on two occasions in the last-named cities their participants narrowly escaped from being deliberately bombed by the Republicans, who disliked these excursions. Of the manner in which they tried to discredit them abroad plentiful evidence was forthcoming when, at the conclusion of hostilities, we took over their consulates in Paris, Gibraltar, and other cities. We showed people everything and allowed them to judge for themselves. Our enemies did not like this; they hated the *Rutas*. Nothing comparable could be offered on their side.

The *Rutas Nacionales de Guerra* were the first conducted tours to operate in Spain. All that followed stems from the pattern they set, and the revenues produced by the ensuing business exceeded the most optimistic calculations. When Madrid fell, my buses took people from all parts of the country to see their friends in the capital, or to tour the University City there and the surrounding battlefields. They also brought teams of employees and workers from Seville to Madrid, where they were badly needed. After these emergencies were over my twenty sturdy buses continued to run for ten more years. Transport was scarce, and there were many requests for their services. I recall the look of amazement on the face of a well-known Spanish engineer who had to move the members of a scientific congress from Seville to Santander, and who came to charter eleven buses. It was easy to provide them for him, and I told him this. 'What did you say?' he asked. 'I said that you can have the buses.' 'I am so accustomed to hearing people say "no",' explained the engineer, 'that I could hardly believe my ears when you said "yes".'

Eventually my *Rutas de Guerra* became *Rutas Nacionales de España*. The Second World War had started, there were hardly any foreign tourists, but Spaniards, living in peace, wanted to know their country. Long trips around Spain were organized from Madrid, Barcelona and other cities. In summer the buses covered the north, in winter they toured the south. No private concern wished to undertake a venture of this kind while the rest of the world was at war, but it would have been foolish to lock up our rolling-stock and allow it to rust and rot. The tours were never subsidized by the Government, but the Government received the profits. Added to the receipts, a small working capital of 200,000 pesetas, equivalent at the time to about £4,500, sufficed to pay their way from the start, salaries, petrol, repairs, and every other item included. In this way I kept the bearings greased for the moment when the Second World War ended and international travel could be resumed in Spain. Once this happened, to allow private initiative a free hand I wound up the whole organization. Sixteen of the twenty original motor-coaches were sold by public tender; the others we retained, together with six automobiles purchased with surplus funds from *Rutas*. Total cash profits amounted to over seven million pesetas, almost nine times the money disbursed in the first instance for rolling stock and initial capital. Had Don Pedro Gárate lived, he would have taken into account certain factors which contributed to the success of my endeavours, but he would also have been pleased with the results.

CHAPTER THIRTY-NINE

The Battle of the Ebro

The colonial wars which European nations waged in the nineteenth century and early part of the twentieth were frequently fought without the means for large-scale operations. This was the case in Spanish Morocco, where hostilities dragged on until planning and resources commensurate with the real strength of the rebellious tribes were brought to bear, and it was also the case during the first phase of the Spanish Civil War, when Franco retained the initiative but lacked the means to deal a decisive blow. His successes in the north brought about a radical change. Recently captured factories in Bilbao, Oviedo and Gijón intensified production and delivered to us, instead of to the enemy, sufficient rifles, machine-guns, cartridges, hand-grenades, shells, light artillery, and bombs. Agricultural products and fish became more plentiful. Thousands of recruits were drilled, and war colleges in different parts of Spain trained new officers, many of whom had volunteered for service.

The conquest of the north also released seasoned troops in sufficient quantities for large-scale offensives to become possible in other areas. Until then, only the Republicans had been in a position to launch them; the comparative passivity of our enemies was due to the lack of discipline and unity of command from which they suffered throughout the war. Save for isolated cases—Brunete, Belchite, Teruel—when Red attacks fell short of their objective and eventually turned to our advantage, every significant move—the crossing of the Strait, the march from Seville to Madrid, the relief of the Alcázar, the capture of important cities and whole provinces—had been planned and executed on our side against forces which enjoyed every advantage, including support from the navy. But by November 1937, against 450,000 men, 640 battalions, 200 batteries and 350 planes, Franco had 600,000 men, 650 battalions, a cavalry division, 290 batteries and 400 planes.

The struggle for Teruel began on 15 December 1937. Four months later we had recaptured the city, won the battle of the Alfambra, and advanced eastwards one hundred miles from points between Teruel and Saragossa to Vinaroz and Benicarló, on the shores of the Mediterranean and roughly half-way from Valencia to Barcelona. When Colonel Alonso Vega, at the head of the first column to reach the coast, waded into the sea and made the sign of the cross with his sword upon its waters, the Red front was split in two. Our troops fought their way towards Sagunto, less than twenty miles from Valencia. At Tortosa, near the estuary of the Ebro, they encountered a resistance intended to prevent them from turning the enemy's flank north of the river. Simultaneously, our armies were pressing their opponents in the heart of Catalonia. North of Lérida, Solchaga's Navarre Brigades and the forces led by Muñoz Grandes had progressed as far as Tremp and cut off electricity supplies vital to Barcelona. A French critic, General Baratier, writing in the *Revue Politique et Parlementaire*, said of this manœuvre that it was 'destined to become a classic theme for study and comment in European war colleges', adding that it 'could be cited as a model of the way in which decisive attacks contribute to lower the morale of an opponent, once his own lines have been rent aside and sundered'.

At this stage, real hope of final victory lost, the Republicans should have turned their thoughts to peace and declared themselves ready to surrender. We had no terms to offer them, no possibility of compromise existed between their aims and ours. Incapable of ruling the nation, they had plunged it into anarchy and paved the way for Communism. A large part of the Republican Army was now commanded by Communists. In a footnote to page 550 of his book, *The Spanish Civil War*, Hugh Thomas wrote: 'A secret F.A.I.'—*Federación Anarquista Ibérica*—'circular of September 1938 pointed out that of 7,000 promotions in the Army since May 5,500 had been Communists. In the Army of the Ebro out of 27 brigades, 25 were commanded by Communists, while all 9 divisional commanders, 3 army corps commanders, and the supreme commander (Modesto) were Communists. This was the most extreme case of Communist control, but the proportions for the Anarchists were nearly as depressing elsewhere. In all six armies of Republican Spain the Anarchists believed the proportions to be 163 Communist brigade commanders to 33 Anarchists, 61 divisional commanders to 9 Anarchists, 15 army corps commanders to 2 Anarchists (with 4 Anarchist sympathizers), and 3 Communist army commanders, 2 sympathizers and one neutral. (Peirats, III 230-3.)'

Partly as a result of this the Republicans were becoming subservient tools of Russia. Their incapacity to win, repeatedly proved in the field of battle, was sowing dissension within Republican ranks. Despair, and encouragement from abroad, were prolonging the conflict unnecessarily. Our enemies were being told that Moscow would never allow them to be beaten, that a European war was on the verge of breaking out, that France and her allies were ready to intervene decisively on their side. It was also pointed out to them from abroad that while their armies retained a semblance of power, the possibility of partitioning Spain between the opposing sides would always exist; the Republicans could hold what they had, and Franco could retain the territories occupied by his troops. From the National point of view a more cynical proposal would have been hard to devise, and those fighting for the unity of Spain regarded it as additional evidence of the worthlessness of their opponents. Inadequate intelligence services contributed to deceive the Republicans; an accurate evaluation of the potential on our side would have lowered their morale and their resistance.

Until 1938 was practically over, Franco himself did not believe in the imminence of a Red collapse. The campaign continued. During the spring of that year progress was maintained south of Teruel; also in the Catalonian province of Lérida, where the Republicans lost 30,000 men in a series of futile onslaughts, and in the smiling orange-groves that border the Mediterranean shore, where, on 14 June, our troops occupied Castellón. Deep in the heart of the Pyrenees, a strong Red contingent, after being cornered in Bielsa, sent piteous appeals to their Communist comrades in Toulouse, destroyed every village within reach, slaughtered their inhabitants, and forced the survivors to fly with them to France. Years later, during the Second World War, a band of Spanish Communists left Toulouse, scaled the heights before them, entered Spanish territory, and occupied one of the villages which they had ravaged years before. They had come to 'liberate' it. The villagers waited until the representatives of freedom had eaten and drunk themselves to sleep at their expense. They then bludgeoned their 'liberators' and strung them by their necks from a row of trees.

By 18 July 1938, the second anniversary of the rising, Franco had taken Mérida, Badajoz, Talavera de la Reina, Irún, San Sebastian, Ronda, the islands of Ibiza and Formentera, the entire province of Guipuzcoa, Toledo and the Alcázar. His men had freed Oviedo from

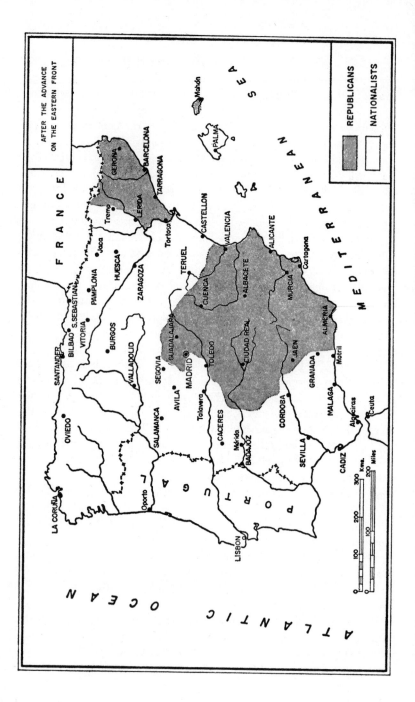

AFTER THE ADVANCE
ON THE EASTERN FRONT

REPUBLICANS

NATIONALISTS

ATLANTIC OCEAN

MEDITERRANEAN SEA

FRANCE

PORTUGAL

Mahón

PALMA

LA CORUÑA

OVIEDO

SANTANDER

BILBAO
S.SEBASTIAN

VITORIA

PAMPLONA

Jaca

HUESCA

ZARAGOZA

BURGOS

VALLADOLID

Oporto

LISBON

SALAMANCA

SEGOVIA

AVILA

MADRID

GUADALAJARA

TERUEL

CUENCA

ALBACETE

Teruel

LERIDA

GERONA

BARCELONA

TARRAGONA

Tortosa

CASTELLON

VALENCIA

ALICANTE

Cartagena

MURCIA

ALMERIA

Motril

JAEN

CIUDAD REAL

TOLEDO

Talavera

CACERES

Mérida

BADAJOZ

SEVILLA

CORDOBA

GRANADA

MALAGA

Algeciras

CADIZ

Ceuta

300 Kms.

200 Miles

100

200

100

0

the forces that encircled it, occupied the Casa de Campo and the University City in the outskirts of Madrid, captured Marbella, Malaga, Motril and Bilbao, retaken Brunete, Teruel and Belchite, and conquered Santander, Covadonga and Gijón in the north, Lérida, Tremp and Balaguer in Catalonia, Bielsa in the Pyrenees, and Vinaroz, Benicarló, Castellón and Nules on the Mediterranean coast, the latter only twenty-seven miles from Valencia. To offset this record the Reds could only list a few isolated successes, none of consequence or real value.

They were now preparing an offensive on the Ebro front, where they had concentrated five army corps with a total of ten divisions, three cavalry regiments, nine companies of tanks, one hundred batteries and a plentiful supply of planes. The initial aim of this offensive was a deep penetration of our lines, which, established on the opposite, or right, bank of the river and adjusted exactly to its course, made a profound dent in enemy territory. If our opponents could overrun this salient, hold, it, and turn south-east towards the Mediterranean, they might cut off the far from inconsiderable forces which earlier in the year had split their front in two and were now situated between Amposta, on the south of the Ebro, and Castellón. Summer would end while all this happened, and on the Republican side it was expected that the coming of the winter would bring with it the evidence of a stalemate, foreign intervention, and outbreaks and riots in the territories under Franco. Red fantasy, at a loss for more solid conjectures, conjured up these figments to prolong the war.

Early in 1938 General Franco had reached the conclusion that the final issues would be decided in Aragon, on the banks of the Ebro and in the sierras that form its last watershed before the river runs into the sea. It was there that the conflict had to be fought out and won. No more appropriate area existed in the whole of Spain to destroy the flower of the Republican armies, open up access to the entire Mediterranean coast, menace Valencia, and march on Barcelona while our troops closed the frontier with France, through which large quantities of arms and ammunition were pouring in for our opponents. The operations in the north had been justified by reasons already explained. An all-out offensive against Madrid, sensational as it could have been had it proved victorious, and much as it might have impressed foreign opinion and damaged the enemy's morale, would decide nothing definite and create many problems. From the start, Franco's main objective had been to seek the enemy and defeat him, wear him out and finally destroy him. Wherever his opponents struck they had found him willing to hit back and all the more determined to do so because they were providing him with the opportunities which he needed to annihilate not only first-line combat troops, but the reserves called up to support them. Relatively speaking all other moves were of less consequence. On our side there would still be hard fighting around Madrid, minor operations in Andalusia and Extremadura, and converging attacks north and east of Lérida and south of the Pyrenees, but compared to the possibilities which existed in the area of the Ebro none of this was important.

The Red onslaught on the Ebro was launched on 25 July. For some time we had known that our opponents were planning to cross the river, but so stealthily was the operation carried out and so well had it been rehearsed beforehand that part of our troops were taken by surprise. Hundreds of boats, built in Barcelona, had been stored near the river in preparation for the attack. The sluggish waters of the Ebro, wide in all places, deep in some, fordable at others, were crossed by the enemy at night. Bridges were rapidly set up. Some of our positions were overwhelmed; others were isolated and surrounded by the triumphant Republicans.

After the first moments of confusion, our troops held fast and stood their ground. The Republican success produced a measure of apprehension behind our lines. People found it difficult to understand how so many Reds had crossed such a wide stretch of water and escaped annihilation in the process. Inclination to criticize without knowledge or reflection is a Spanish trait, and it found an opportunity for expression in clubs and cafés, but General Duval, a French commentator, explained the situation convincingly while the battle was still in progress. 'The Spanish front,' he said, 'is now 1,750 kilometres'—1,100 miles—'long; Franco holds it with only 750,000 men. To understand the significance of these figures let me recall that in 1918 the French front from Nieuport to Switzerland extended over 650 kilometres, equivalent to 400 miles. It was manned by two and a half million French, English, American and Belgian soldiers. Franco, with three times fewer men, is holding a front three times longer. In these circumstances, given the element of surprise and a favourable opening, a few thousand men can easily break his lines and stand fast until troops in sufficient numbers are brought to repulse them. In any case, it is unlikely that the recent onslaught will compel Franco to weaken his positions along the Mediterranean shore.'

The situation, however, was not reassuring, for in a single day our front had been pierced to a depth of almost thirteen miles, but Franco was not too perturbed. He knew that the Red attack was a consequence of the weakness pointed out by Duval. After hearing mass that day—it was the feast of St James, patron saint of Spain and of the Spanish Infantry—he moved to a set of maps on which every phase of the situation had been noted and announced his intention to leave for the Front. The width of the gap was marked on the map as were the positions most suitable to resist the assault and serve as starting points for eventual counter-attacks. 'I feel tempted,' he said, 'to allow the enemy to penetrate as far as they wish while we ourselves hold fast to both ends of the gap. In this way our troops would maintain a stranglehold upon the Red salient and in due course destroy their opponents on the very ground chosen by them.' While preparations were made to leave Pedrola, the Duke of Villahermosa's country seat twenty-five miles north of Saragossa which the Commander-in-Chief was using as temporary headquarters, General Franco picked up a notebook and started to jot down figures. A group of officers around him watched in silence. Finally he spoke. 'It is impossible for a fisherman in Galicia,' he said, 'to live decently on his present rate of pay.'

Besides much ground on the wrong side of the Ebro we had lost most of the heights that overlook the banks of the river. Part of our troops were in a desperate situation, but the 18th *Bandera* of the Foreign Legion gave an indication of its spirit when, after suffering heavy casualties and fighting continuously for twenty-four hours without food or water, its leader dispatched a message to divisional headquarters requesting to be ordered with his men to the place where the struggle was fiercest.

On the battlefield, Franco watched operations or directed them much as a divisional commander would have done. 'Two platoons are fighting it out with hand-grenades on the summit of that hill,' he would say, his eyes glued to his glasses. 'A battalion is deploying on the ground below it. A couple of tanks are advancing towards the hill. Behind the tanks I can see two boys, each carrying a flag. The enemy is firing desperately. Their bullets are kicking up dust around our tanks. Now the flags are half-way up the hill. They've reached the top! Make sure those boys are awarded the Military Medal.' But at night, when the reputedly cold-blooded General read the lists of casualties, he would lean his head on his clenched fists and occasionally break down. Our losses were heavy. One army corps, after five weeks' fighting, reported 2 field-officers, 55 officers and 423 men killed, 4 field-officers, 280 officers and 4,411 men wounded; three weeks later another field-officer, 46 officers and 838 men had been killed, and 9 field-officers, 263 officers and 8,450 men wounded. The last phase of the battle started in October. A large part of the salient opened up on our front had been retaken, but the Reds had dug themselves into the Sierras de Pandols and de Caballs, and before they could be dislodged and forced across the river both ranges had to be carried.

Our opponents fought well, at times outstandingly well, yet there were signs of demoralization in their ranks. Threats of drastic punishments were being circulated to deter their troops from giving way to negligence or cowardice. Any man who lost his rifle would be shot without trial and his name would be published; soldiers who abandoned their posts or inflicted wounds upon themselves would also be executed. Those who failed to hold their ground would be forced to recapture it with their officers marching in front. Though these threats were carried out, the Reds surrendered daily in greater numbers, trusting more in the treatment they hoped to receive from us than in the fate that awaited them should they return defeated and unscathed. Combatants were urged to write to the Government, declaring their will to win or die, but instead of doing this units on their way to the Front complained they were being led to a slaughter-house. Many preferred to desert and fight on our side, a tendency shared alike by raw recruits and hardened veterans, some of whom, at the outbreak of hostilities, had vociferously proclaimed their unshakable abhorrence of all that we stood for.

Including prisoners, the battle of the Ebro cost us 41,414 casualties, the enemy 70,000. The so-called 'Army of Catalonia' was destroyed, International Brigades faded from the picture, and on the enemy side the resultant shortage of man-power was such that convicts were freely pardoned provided they immediately enlisted. Out of a total of 19,653 men captured during this battle, 45 per cent were approximately the same age as our soldiers, 10 per cent were older, the remaining 45 per cent younger. The Reds were also promoting untrained men and threatening relatives of deserters with reprisals of the utmost severity.

Fighting on the Ebro ended on 16 November and General Franco, in an interview with a Spanish journalist, assured the war-weary nation that before long the whole of Catalonia would fall. The end was in sight, he said, and there was no cause for anxiety or impatience. The battle of the Ebro had been a costly and ugly struggle in which the enemy, fighting on a narrow front with excellent observation posts and well-supported flanks, had made good use of his resources to prevent us from manœuvring against him. At first they had gained tactical advantages, but the presence of large masses on the field with a wide river behind them had contributed to their destruction. Day by day our opponents reported casualties 80 per cent higher than our own. Before they recrossed the river most of their effectives were out of commission. They had been badly beaten, but final victory had yet to be achieved.

December 1938 and January 1939 were vital months. On 23 December Franco launched six army corps against 140,000 Republican combatants, plentifully equipped and entrenched on a wide front that extended from the Pyrenees to Tortosa, near the mouth of the Ebro. On its left or northern sector our columns were ordered to march eastwards as soon as they overcame the enemy's initial resistance; on the southern sector they were to advance north along the coast towards Tarragona, which was also to be attacked from the east by forces advancing from Lérida.

The Republican command was meanwhile hesitating between three different moves south of Madrid, all of them intended to counter our offensive. Vicente Rojo, their Chief of Staff, was in favour of an attack on the Andalusian coast, to accomplish which 3,000 men would have had to land near Motril, break our lines there and march on Malaga. But Negrín, the Republican Defence Minister, did not listen to General Rojo. 'The day we abandoned our plans for a landing near Motril,' Rojo wrote later, 'we began to lose Catalonia.'

Fighting in this region was hardest immediately south of the Pyrenees, where the ground is uneven, sierras run in all directions, and some peaks are 6,000 feet high. The enemy fought desperately in the mountains, but on the plains north of the Ebro they abandoned their positions and ran. 'It was a rout,' wrote Rojo, 'one of the many which it has been my lot to witness in the course of these operations.' A half-hearted Republican counter-attack was repulsed, and our opponents suffered heavy losses. Our rate of progress depended on the resistance which we met. We did not force the pace, for we had the situation in hand and our plans were frequently adjusted to the varying conditions of an extremely wide front. Our main concern now was to reduce the number of casualties on both sides. Tarragona was taken on 14 January. Barcelona fell twelve days later.

CHAPTER FORTY

Barcelona

A French military critic, commenting on these events, wrote, 'The Reds have lost not only a series of battles, but their heads and the usefulness of their defensive weapons as well. Their army has been destroyed. No circumstances of any kind, no intervention on anybody's part can save it from complete and unconditional surrender.' Franco, before devoting his attention to the final operations in the south, addressed these words to his adversaries: 'When you possessed all the gold in Spain and practically all the stocks of arms and ammunition and the factories that produced them; when you also had the coal mines and the iron ore and the steel-works and huge supplies of food and raw materials as well as nine-tenths of the Navy, three-fourths of our coasts, hundreds of planes and tanks, a large army supported by 100,000 international combatants and another army in the North, plentifully supplied and equipped; when you had all this, you lost every battle and suffered defeat after defeat. Consider your situation now that you have none of this and that we have gained it all. Without factories, iron or coal, blockaded on the high seas, your warships reduced to impotence, no planes in the air, and a starving population in your cities what hopes can you have of victory?'

The Negrín Government issued a communiqué, stating, 'On the Catalan front, the battle presents its usual features. Our forces are heroically resisting violent attacks launched by Italian troops'—Italian troops, at that time, amounted to less than 4 per cent of Franco's effectives—'supported by Spanish contingents. After suffering great losses, the enemy has compelled us to readjust, slightly, the contour of our lines.' Negrín's communiqué was dated 25 January 1939, one day before the capture of Barcelona. At the time it was issued every Red leader in Catalonia had fled to France, leaving behind them 200,000 men, 242 cannon, 100 planes, 3,500 machine-guns, thousands of rifles, millions of cartridges and every imaginable kind of rolling-stock, including 6,000 lorries, all of which fell into our hands.

I drove up from Malaga and joined our troops before they entered Barcelona. No attempt had been made to defend the city. Its inhabitants were tired of fighting, sick of their rulers, and hungry for food and peace. There had been the usual amount of looting and much senseless destruction. Santa María del Mar, a priceless jewel of Gothic art, had been burnt at the outbreak of war; San Pedro de las Puellas, the earliest Christian monument in Barcelona, had experienced the same fate. The stench was awful. Unswept for years, the streets were full of autumn leaves and garbage, part of the accumulated filth which the Reds bequeathed to every town that they occupied for any amount of time. Near the port, at the eastern end of the Ramblas, I saw houses damaged by bombs which had been aimed at ships anchored in the harbour. Apart from this and from the destruction wrought upon it by the Reds, Barcelona was unharmed.

Large quantities of food, rushed up in endless lines of lorries from happier parts of Spain, were being handed out by smiling, well-scrubbed girls in the blue uniforms of the Falange. My job was to accommodate the legion of civil servants, businessmen, and employees, already in Barcelona and eager to set the city on its feet. Hotels had to be staffed, cleaned up, and supplied with food and all the necessary requisites. The record of their personnel had to be investigated, for it would have been senseless to assign positions of trust to possible devotees of murder, arson, and loot. To have fought against us was one thing; to be a criminal was another. The dust at the Ritz, the best hotel in the town, was inches thick. I told the manager to summon as many charwomen as he could find, for I needed them all. Once they arrived I reviewed them, complete with brooms, mops and pails. 'Has the day at last arrived for us to resume scrubbing floors?' one of them asked me. 'It certainly has,' I replied. 'Thank God for that!' she answered, throwing up her hands to the skies.

I was aware that the Reds, with some coaching from the Russians, had set up a particularly vicious cheka in the Calle Vallmajor, and that same day, in the afternoon, I drove in search of the place. According to my information it was near the centre of the town, but it took time to find it, and finally I inquired its whereabouts from a pleasant-looking fellow who, thin, emaciated, and wearing a threadbare suit, was walking down a deserted thoroughfare. 'If you are looking for the cheka I can tell you where it is,' he said; 'I myself was an inmate there for some weeks.'

The cheka in question had been installed to loosen up the tongues of recalcitrant hostages. It contained cells of two different types. Some were less than five feet high, too small for average-sized persons to stand erect inside them. Nor could they very well sit, for the only place to sit on was a bench, constructed of bricks and slanted from the wall at an angle too steep to be comfortable; those who tried to sleep on the bench eventually rolled off and fell with a thud on other bricks which had been embedded in the floor of the cell, with their corners pointing upwards. The second type of cell was much narrower and less six feet tall. Any fair-sized man who stood inside it would be forced to bend his knees a little. Over a slit in the door of the cell a large, 1,000-watt electric bulb was suspended. Shadeless, it shone bright a few inches from the prisoner's eyes, and to keep them open a thick glass disc, not unlike a monocle, was fixed between his eyelids. A large supply of these discs was still available upon a nearby table. Finally, in a little courtyard or inner patio, exposed to the open air, I saw a large metal globe. The ground on which it stood was paved with small, bumpy cobblestones. The globe, iron-coloured and rusty on the outside, had a spacious door that gave access to its interior. Once inside, the unfortunate inmate sat naked in the dark while the globe was rolled over the cobblestones, banged with a hammer, or heated with boiling hot water in summer. In winter they cooled the metal globe with iced water.

CHAPTER FORTY-ONE

Madrid

Whereas we had fought on every front for the political and territorial unity of the nation, the Republicans had disrupted this unity and attempted to set up separate states in Catalonia and the Basque Provinces. They had championed the doctrines of Marx, Bakunin, and Lenin, all of them alien to our people; we had defended Christian ideals and the principles and traditions of the Western World. They had lost, and we had won. Once more, a minimum of good sense should have sufficed to persuade them that total surrender was now their only possible course. The whole of Catalonia, from the Ebro to the Pyrenees, had been occupied by our troops. The frontier with France, which had been the channel for a regular flow of military supplies, was now tightly closed. Three new Republican attempts to take the offensive, one in Extremadura, one near Cordoba, the third in Brunete, had ended disastrously. Decisively beaten, Republican soldiers had lost their morale and their armaments and all means of re-equipping the fifty divisions which, at least in theory, still faced us in south and central Spain. Their regime had dissolved into chaos. The President of the Republic, Manuel Azaña, had fled to Paris and resigned his post. His Ministers, after meeting in Madrid on 1 February, had vanished into thin air. To prolong the war was an act of criminal irresponsibility, but instead of surrendering, Negrín, the Republican Premier, flew to Madrid to organize a final and futile show of resistance.

Forsaken by their leaders, forlorn and famished, the population of the Red Zone wanted peace. They scorned the blandishments of Negrín and refused to side with either the Communists or the Anarchists, who were now fighting desperately against each other. Fearing Communism more than Anarchy, Colonel Segismundo Casado, a former professor at the War College and leader of the Republican forces in southern Spain—he now lives there—tried to persuade General Miaja, the commander-in-chief of the Red Army and a Communist sympathizer, to delay his flight abroad. Casado wanted Miaja to exert his influence with those who hoped to avoid a final holocaust in Madrid, where the beaten General's Communist friends were planning to liquidate their opponents. A woman member of the Communist party arrived with instructions addressed to the same reliable Red major who two and a half years before had murdered Luis Moscardó, the young son of the defender of the Alcázar, who was held as a hostage and killed. As a result of these instructions fighting broke out in Madrid. It lasted for a week and bloodied the streets of the capital. Meanwhile Casado, though a virtual prisoner of Miaja, dispatched a message to General Franco declaring himself ready to discuss peace.

Casado's envoys landed in Burgos on 20 March and hesitated when informed that surrender had to be unconditional. On the 26th, Franco launched fifty-eight divisions against a huge front extending from Valencia to Motril. Six army corps advanced rapidly. On 28 March our Fifth Column, which for some time had been working openly in the capital, defied the Communists and the Anarchists and took possession of Madrid. The 16th Nationalist Division marched into the city, and that day and the following other forces occupied Valencia, Guadalajara, Alcalá de Henares, Jaén, Sagunto and Albacete, which for years had loomed in the horizon of our military activities as unattainable goals, far beyond our reach. On the 30th they entered Alicante, undefended by 15,000 Reds. On the first day of April, General Franco's headquarters in Burgos issued the final bulletin. It read, 'Today, after disabling the Red Army and forcing its soldiers to surrender, our victorious troops have achieved all their objectives. The war has come to an end.'

In Casablanca, on 18 July 1936, General Franco had said to me, 'We have ideals, faith, and discipline. We shall win.' We had had little more than this at the start but we had won. When Vicente Rojo, Chief of the Red Staff and Franco's most redoubtable opponent on the battlefield, explained the reasons for Franco's victory in *España Heróica* (Buenos Aires, 1942), he resorted to terms far more accurate and to the point than those customarily employed by the victorious General's detractors. 'Military science and the art of war,' wrote Rojo, 'were the guiding principles of Franco's triumph. We lacked resources to continue the struggle, and our technique was faulty in every echelon. Politically, the Republic lacked a purpose worthy of a people striving to determine their destiny. The Red Government did not control the

nation. Our mistakes in the diplomatic field gave the lead to our opponents even before our front began to crumble. Franco's moral stature was higher than ours, at home and abroad. His superiority was the outcome not only of his personal qualities but of the errors committed on our side.' Rojo talked of technique and resources; we, at first, had not been over-burdened with the latter. Indeed, one day, shortly after the war started, the balance in our treasury had barely equalled fourteen hundred dollars. It is true that on the following day this sum was increased by the timely sale of goatskins to a French merchant, but the product of the transaction amounted to only seven hundred thousand francs. Yet so carefully did we nurse our scant means that, soon after peace was established, without a helping hand from anybody, we paid in full for the war supplies and equipment which we had found ourselves forced to purchase in other countries until the conquest of the north liberated the factories and the trained personnel able to produce most of them on our soil.

My orders were to join the column assigned to enter the capital, where, in the same way as in Barcelona, hotels had to be rapidly organized and put to work. Pending the capture of Madrid my offices had been set up in Malaga, a suitable spot from which to prepare the Andalusian region for the flow of visitors which was sure to start some time after the conflict ended, and from where I could also direct the *Rutas de Guerra* services, then operating in the area with substantial numbers of clients. A few days before the fall of Madrid I drove from Malaga to Burgos, situated one hundred and fifty miles north of the capital and one of the three cities—Avila and Toledo were the other two—where the relief column mustered before departing for its humanitarian mission in Madrid. But an anti-typhoid shot, administered by an army doctor as a compulsory precaution to all those about to enter Red territory, presented me with a high temperature and kept me in bed for a brief period. Because of this, I left for Madrid, alone, on the same day that it fell.

To reach Madrid I travelled from Burgos *via* Salamanca and Avila. The direct road over the Somosierra Pass was closed because the Republican troops who defended it had no knowledge as yet of the cease-fire, but some of its features would have given me a foretaste of the pains which our enemies had taken to efface the taint of tradition and history from the names of certain towns and villages. For instance, San Sebastián de los Reyes—'Saint Sebastian of the Kings'—was now neither saintly nor royal; it was merely called 'Sebastián'. Because of the detour which I was forced to make I entered Madrid after three years of war by the same route which I had often followed during the fighting. I could hardly credit my senses when, instead of gunfire and the chatter of machine-guns, a strange, unearthly silence met me at the gates of a great city which despite the strife around it had retained the silhouette rendered famous by Goya when he painted it from the Pradera de San Isidro. Somehow Goya's frescoes in the chapel of San Antonio de la Florida, near the area where the struggle was fiercest, had escaped destruction. Not far from the chapel, a considerable portion of the Barrio de Argüelles, a fine residential quarter, had been partly demolished by our guns. Its buildings faced our positions in the Casa de Campo, and their balconies and roofs had been used as parapets by the Reds. The rest of the city, evil-smelling and dirty, was practically untouched. Only occasionally did one see evidence of damage from a stray shell or a bomb that had dropped wide of its mark.

The shouting and the flag-waving had died out. Tired of milling around, shabbily dressed people lined the thoroughfares and watched with bewilderment in their faces. Republican soldiers, some of them still carrying hand-granades and rifles, stared sheepishly at me, unable to believe their eyes. For years they had been assured that we would never break through— ¡No pasarán!—that victory was for the Reds alone, and now we were here, neither killing nor plundering as some of them had done, but smiling, friendly and happy, handing out bread and tins of milk without asking on whose side the recipients were or inquiring into the nature of the ideas which many of them had favoured politically.

The forces of occupation were in their barracks, the city was quiet, and civilian units, trained and organized months before, were carrying out their allotted tasks. Madrid was emerging from a nightmare. Thousands, some reckon eighty thousand, had been murdered there during the preceding years. The exact number will never be ascertained, for nobody kept a record and there has been no way of establishing the fate of citizens of all classes who disappeared mysteriously and were never seen again. Some of the 227 chekas operating in Madrid alone specialized in methods of torture probably inspired by Soviet sources. Two of the cruellest in Spain, the Baylia and Santa Ursula chekas in Valencia, were run by Peter and Bertha Sonin, a Russian couple who fled the country before the war ended. An imaginary 'Siamese Embassy' established in Madrid enticed people seeking diplomatic protection, despoiled them of their belongings and killed them when their resources came to an end.

Most chekas worked under the direction of a lawless *responsable* who applied the death penalty with Bolshevik thoroughness. Hundreds, including elderly ladies and young girls, were shot for investigating the whereabouts of a relative or a friend. In Valencia, 508 women are known to have been killed; in Madrid, 617. A number of foreign residents were also murdered there, including a Belgian diplomat, Baron Jacques de Borchgrave, son of a former ambassador to Spain, to whose memory a plaque has been installed at the Spanish Ministry of Foreign Affairs. The multiplicity of Red political parties contributed to swell the number of chekas; each party, each shade of a political party, each gang, needed an instrument of execution. This multiplication of groups organized for mass murder was made possible by (a) the direct action of a horde of criminals, released from prison with the express consent of the authorities appointed by the Popular Front, (b) the complicity of a police force that overlooked or countenanced crime, and (c) the passiveness of a so-called 'government', which when not directly responsible was an accessory before and after the fact to every murder that was committed. Some killed to convince themselves of their own power or to eliminate those who might some day accuse them. Their victims came from all classes. Usually of humble status— minor bureaucrats and clerks, petty shopkeepers and their assistants, students and workmen—for the first six months they were given no quarter. The chekas attained their highest degree of lethal efficiency towards the end of that period. Eventually the better feelings of a few granted a new lease of life to many, but some of those who acted thus were members of our Fifth Column, disguised as Reds, who risked their lives every minute of the day. The pace slowed down when remonstrances from abroad, and quaking comments on the Republican side, indicated that matters seemed to be getting out of hand. Later, the dividing line between life and death was drawn still farther to the left. Most aristocrats, army officers, priests, mild liberals, and conservatives had already escaped or been murdered, but thousands who had supported the idea of a moderate Republic were wiped out by cold-blooded chekas that proudly linked their names to the left-wing factions of the now-not-so-Popular Front—Socialists, Anarchists and Communists.

Militiamen, gaolers and members of popular tribunals, however Red on principle, were not always completely ruthless or devoid of human feelings. Some helped their victims to escape, possibly for a consideration; a few had a sense of humour, as may have been the case of the *responsable*, or gaol-keeper, temporarily in charge of two well-known acquaintances of mine, Victor Urrutia and José Cruz Conde. Incarcerated in a cheka, their likelihood of survival was poor. One day the *responsable* told them this and added, 'You are due for trial to-morrow,' the inference being that they would probably be shot the next day. Both captives, after giving thought to this announcement, informed their gaoler that his own chances of a long life were also slender. 'Franco's troops are marching on Madrid. Why not make a deal? Aren't our two heads worth as much as your own?' The gaoler considered the matter and came up with a proposition. Addressing himself to Victor Urrutia, he said, 'When you are brought tomorrow before the Tribunal of the People, somebody will ask whether you are José Cruz Conde. Swear that you are no such person. And when *your* turn comes,' he added, addressing himself to Cruz Conde, 'they will ask if you are Victor Urrutia. Deny this under oath.'

The trial took place as planned and the two men were set free. Cruz Conde sought refuge in an Embassy and died a few days before we captured Madrid. Urrutia escaped from the capital, reached France, crossed the Spanish border near Pamplona and reported to General Mola, who knew him well and had given him up for dead. Mola requested him to carry an urgent message to Fuenterrabía, but the message was never delivered. When Urrutia reached Fuenterrabía, a small town on the Bidasoa opposite Hendaye-Plage in France, the Reds were in possession. He was arrested and marched in the pouring rain by two carabiniers to a small hotel which overlooked the river. 'Get a pretty waitress to vamp these fellows,' he whispered to a friend of his who happened to be there. One of the carabiniers fell for the waitress. The other, insensitive to her charms, led Urrutia to a room and remained on guard inside it. 'I'm drenched to the skin,' Urrutia said. 'I'll take off my clothes and dry them.' When the guard turned his head modestly, Urrutia dived from the balcony straight into the

Bidasoa. A hail of bullets followed. None of them hit Urrutia, but an ebb tide and the swift-flowing waters of the river carried him off to sea.

To this day Victor Urrutia maintains that what saved his life on this occasion was an article in *the Saturday Evening Post* which he had read weeks before, while waiting at his dentist's in Madrid. The article in question recalled that, at sea, a current flowing in a given direction is invariably flanked by a parallel current which flows in the opposite direction. Consequently, a swimmer in the grip of an outgoing current should not attempt to fight it; he should swim slowly across it until an incoming current is encountered. Also, swimmers who find themselves some distance from land should not raise their heads repeatedly in an effort to estimate how far they still have to go; they should swim steadily on until they reach the shore. Urrutia was familiar with the beach at Hendaye-Plage, one of the finest in south-western France. He met the incoming current and swam steadily towards the shore, with his head well down. When his feet scraped the sand he stood up and fell in a dead faint, a few yards from the line where the waves were breaking.

But incidents such as these were few and far between. Death played a part in them, and death was usually the winner. The Republican Government did not show its foreign visitors the Cathedral of San Isidro in Madrid, where their militias had burnt frescoes by Claudio Coello and Goya, robbed paintings by Arellano, Alonso Cano, or Ricci and sculptures by Herrera the Younger and Pedro de Mena. They took them instead to the Monastery of El Escorial, where similar treasures had been preserved, without telling them that fifty-three members of the Augustinian Community in El Escorial had been murdered there or that thirty-seven of their brethren had been assassinated in Madrid, simply because they belonged to a learned Catholic institution. The book *Historia de la Persecución Religiosa en España, 1936-1939—History of the Religious Persecution in Spain, 1936-1939*—by Antonio Montero Moreno (Biblioteca de Autores Cristianos, Madrid, 1961) contains the names and all other relevant particulars of the 4,184 members of the secular clergy, 2,365 members of religious orders, and 283 nuns who were murdered in the 'Loyalist' Zone during the Spanish Civil War. These figures include twelve bishops and one Apostolic administrator, but they do not include army chaplains killed at the Front—on the Nationalist side, needless to say; there were no chaplains with the Republicans—lay brothers who died in action while fighting for us, or others who succumbed in the Red Zone to extreme hardships, such as imprisonment, hunger, and so on.

'One million people,' it is often said, 'died in the Spanish Civil War'—from which it is inferred that the number of combatants who were killed fighting or who died from wounds received in action, added to the number of civilians who were murdered all over the country, amounted to one million. The statement is inaccurate, in its conclusions and in its more subtle implications; the exact total will never be known, but it was certainly not as high.

Statistics on the subject, supplied by the Historical Archives of the Spanish General Staff in Madrid, are reliable but incomplete. Neither side kept a close record of their casualties during the early weeks of the war, when they were sometimes heavy. The Republicans did not list their losses fully; if they did so, the pertinent sources of information have not been brought to light. Taking all this into account, the killed and wounded on both sides must have been well over 700,000; the *total* figure, including prisoners of war and those listed as missing, is probably in the vicinity of one million. This is one reason why one million are said to have died in the Spanish Civil War. A fact which contributed to this figure is that the Reds in Spain, true to the Russian pattern, murdered thousands of civilians, not only men but women; possibly as many as one hundred thousand. Many of their victims succumbed in prison to the sufferings and malnutrition which were rampant in the Red Zone. Also, the fall in the Spanish birth rate during the Civil War was probably commensurate with that usually registered in conflicts of similar proportions. Even so, those who died from all causes in that conflict or failed to be born while it lasted were certainly less than one million.

When Madrid fell there was no food in the city, no light and no warmth. Houses, unheated during the long winter, were bitterly cold. No hotels were open for normal business, but somebody told me that there might be a bed available at Gaylord's, which had served as headquarters for the Russians until a few days before. When I arrived there it was night. A silent caretaker was in sole charge. I chose a room, the cleanest I could find, and obtained fresh sheets for the bed and another to use as a towel, for there were no towels in the hotel. I lit a candle and put my electric torch in a handy place. Then I locked the door, prepared the food I was about to eat and cocked my pistol, for 'Comrade General Staff', otherwise known as the Madrid Delegation of the Soviet Military Mission in Spain, had just left the Hotel Gaylord and there was a possibility that part of this mission might still be around. I had bread, a tin of sardines, a little ham, sausage and a piece of cheese, and I ate without letting my food come in contact with anything inside the room, so great was my repugnance for those it had housed before— Russian members of the O.G.P.U., who had directed the Political Police set up by the Reds and taught them to torture and slaughter.

The place was frozen, but I slept soundly. A cold bath in the morning gave me a chance to discover how hard it is to dry oneself with a flimsy sheet. Hotels had to be thoroughly organized, for people were arriving and had nowhere to stay. Private houses were full of refugees, living in squalor, with two or three families sharing a room, the occupants of which now had to be restored, gently but firmly, to their usual place of residence. The Ritz and the Palace, which for many years had been the two leading hotels in Madrid and now rank among the best in the world, were in a state of utter confusion. To run them, a team of experts led by C. Cortés, the present manager of the Jockey Restaurant in Madrid, travelled from Seville in one of my buses. The Palace Hotel was not in a proper condition to receive guests, for most of the beds were crawling with insects. The Ritz Hotel was cleaner, but had no mattresses. There were plenty of mattresses, however, in one floor of the Palace Hotel, just across the way, brand-new and spotlessly clean, piled high in well-locked rooms. My problem was to get them to the Ritz. I advised the manager there to stand in the street with a fair-sized bank-note in his hand and offer it to the driver of any lorry willing to bring him a truck-load of mattresses. That night the Ritz, scrubbed from top to bottom and with its bedrooms in order, took in its first genuine guests in thirty-two months; it had no hot water, no heating, and no electric light, but it had towels, and the steaming *cocido* served by Cortés tasted better than anything with which he has since regaled his most favoured patrons.

The inhabitants of Madrid set to work with great zest. Provisions were pouring in from all parts of the country except the Red Zone, where production had practically ceased at the outbreak of hostilities. In a couple of days I had a score of hotels working smoothly. Streets were swept and hosed down; the whole aspect of the city underwent a change. Yet had it not been for the tactful manner in which the military commander, General Espinosa de los Monteros, worked with the newly appointed civil authorities to control conflicting interests and direct the rebirth of the capital, many things would have gone wrong.

The flush of triumph and the zeal and ardour that inspired many when Madrid fell were fraught with dangers of a subtle kind. One of them was that available office and housing space might be snapped up by people without any legal claim to it. I was eager to occupy the building which had formerly housed the Spanish Tourist Department, where I hoped to find the necessary equipment to continue my work on a sound basis. According to information received its rooms were unkempt and dirty, but they had not been looted. When I went to take a look at them, though I was in uniform a sentry with fixed bayonet barred the way. The sergeant on duty suggested that I should investigate the situation elsewhere. Three officers of higher rank, with whom I had a friendly talk in another building, advised me to forget the whole matter; the offices in question had already been assigned to another branch of the service—their own. I called my car and directed the driver to Burgos, one hundred and fifty miles away, where I was immediately received by General Martin Moreno, who, as Franco's G.S.O.I, had signed every official communiqué during the war. When I put my case before him he dictated a telegram and told an orderly to dispatch it without delay. The message stressed instructions previously issued, according to which the various departments of the administration were to occupy, in the cities taken from the enemy, the same quarters allotted to them before the war. There would be time for other arrangements should the space available prove inadequate. My offices were evacuated the following morning. I found them in a terrible condition, but the typewriters, files, and general equipment which they contained were a boon after months of penury and want.

Years of strife had come to an end. Not a few of those already in Madrid or just arrived there had suffered the loss of members of their families or friends, murdered by the Reds after being subjected to moral and physical torture. In many cases their own personal belongings had been looted or destroyed. There was a risk that a few might try to take the law into their own hands, an even greater risk that others might attempt to profit in some way from the circumstances of the moment. Bearing in mind the innate individualism of the Spaniard and his inveterate inclination to decide matters for himself, the danger was a real one.

But a new element had come into the picture; there was law and order now. During the war, we had never treated civilians on the other side of the lines as enemies. Now that the war was over, distinctions between the victors and the vanquished were not tolerated. Franco was resolved to unite the country under his rule. Provisions from the Nationalist Zone were rushed to Madrid and other cities in the Red Zone. Food had been abundant on our side; now it became less plentiful and more expensive for those of us who lived in what had been Nationalist Spain. But nobody grumbled because of this. We had to feed our starving countrymen although some of them had fought against us and ceased to produce and work at the behest of their leaders. We were all Spaniards again. No longer did anybody speak of 'Reds' or 'Republicans'. Life in common began to pick up, not where it had stopped three years before, but on an entirely new and more rational basis.

It was made clear to all that justice would be meted out impartially, that those who had held arms against us in legitimate warfare had nothing to fear, though their records would be investigated to ascertain whether they had infringed the penal code in force when war broke out. When the time came to consider the merits possessed by candidates to positions of public trust and responsibility, account would be taken of those who had fought on our side, of their war services and the wounds which they had received, and of arbitrary imprisonment at the hands of the enemy. Anything less than this would have been neither reasonable nor fair. Otherwise no distinction was made between those who had won, and those who had lost. Everybody had to live; everybody was given a chance to work. Victory had been for all. During the thirteen years that followed I directed not only a government department with hundreds of employees, but also a Labour syndicate that counted its members by hundreds of thousands. Apart from weighing the merits listed above, no discrimination was made when it came to assigning a man to a post or to establishing the conditions under which he could be appointed. No one was rejected for having fought against us. What mattered now was that all should work properly and keep the peace.

The end of civil war in Spain was in keeping with the nature of the conflict. A country that defeats another may have some cause for rejoicing—the prospect of territorial conquest, of receiving reparations, or of increased influence in world affairs. In civil strife there is none of this, no matter how great the victory. The only cause for rejoicing is that fighting is finally over. When this happened in Spain we knew that the scars of war had to be healed, that the work of reconstruction would be long and arduous. What we did not know was that during the coming summer a conflict of world-wide magnitude would break out and render our task infinitely more difficult, that while this conflict lasted we would be faced with problems of another kind and almost as great as those which had confronted us in the past years, that when it ended we would be treated in some cases as if we had taken part in that conflict and lost. The people of Spain believed they had nothing to fear on this score. While the World War was being fought they were reassured by a letter which was handed personally to General Franco at nine o'clock on Sunday morning, 8 November 1942, by the American Ambassador in Spain, Mr Carlton J. H. Hayes. The letter was from President Roosevelt, and it said:

DEAR GENERAL FRANCO

It is because your nation and mine are friends in the best sense of the word and because you and I are sincerely desirous of the continuation of that friendship for our mutual good that I want very simply to tell you of the compelling reasons that have forced me to send a powerful American military force to the assistance of the French possessions in North Africa. We have accurate information to the effect that Germany and Italy intend at an early date to occupy with military force French North Africa. With your wide military experience you will understand clearly that in the interests of the defence of both North America and South America it is essential that action be taken to prevent an Axis occupation of French Africa without delay. To provide for America's defence I am sending a powerful army to French possessions and protectorates in North Africa with the sole purpose of preventing occupation by Germany and Italy and with the hope that these areas will not be devastated by the horror of war. I hope you will accept my full assurance that these moves are in no shape manner or form directed against the Government or people of Spain or Spanish Morocco or Spanish territories—metropolitan or overseas. I believe the Spanish Government and the Spanish people wish to maintain neutrality and to remain outside the war. Spain has nothing to fear from the United Nations. I am, my dear General, your sincere friend—FRANKLIN D. ROOSEVELT.

They were also reassured by a statement which Mr Winston Churchill, the British Prime Minister, delivered at the House of Commons on 24 May 1944 (400 H.C. DEB. 5 s.):

If Spain had yielded to German blandishments and pressure our burden would have been much heavier. The Straits of Gibraltar would have been closed and all access to Malta would have been cut off from the West. All the Spanish Coast would have become the nesting-place of German U-boats. [The credit for avoiding this] is undoubtedly due to the Spanish resolve to keep out of the war . . . the critical moment passed. Another very serious crisis occurred in our relations with Spain before the . . . descent of the United States and British Forces upon North West Africa. Before that operation was begun Spain's power to injure us was at its very highest. I can assure the House that the passage of those critical days was very anxious indeed. However, the Spaniards continued absolutely friendly and tranquil. They asked no questions, they raised no inconveniences. I must say that I shall always consider a service was rendered at this time by Spain, not only to the United Kingdom and to the British Empire and Commonwealth, but to the cause of the United Nations. I have, therefore, no sympathy with those who think it clever, and even funny, to insult and abuse the Government of Spain whenever occasion serves. Internal political problems in Spain are a matter for the Spaniards themselves. It is not for us—that is, the Government—to meddle in such affairs. We do not include in our programme of world renovation any forcible action against any government whose internal form of administration does not come up to our own ideas, and any remarks I have made on that subject referred only to enemy Powers and their satellites. There is all the difference in the world between a man who knocks you down and a man who leaves you alone. We speak the same words to the Spaniards in the hour of our strength as we did in the hour of our weakness. I look forward to increasingly good relations with Spain and to an extremely fertile trade between Spain and this country which will, I trust, grow even during the war and will expand after the peace.

The sincerity of the friendship expressed in the above communications was demonstrated when Britain and the United States withdrew their ambassadors from Madrid, leaving their embassies in control of chargés d'affaires. No ambassadors were withdrawn from Russia to mark Western disapproval of dictatorship. The whole episode, which both countries lived to regret, was a striking example of selective indignation.

Those who lived in Madrid were stirred deep in their hearts when they witnessed the Victory Parade, the *Desfile de la Victoria*, held simultaneously in a number of Spanish cities on 19 May 1939. With few exceptions, all the troops which had fought on our side were represented in Madrid, where General Franco took the salute. His indifference to fatigue during the long hours in which he stood at attention with his hand to his cap was noted by those who then obtained their first glimpse of the man who had brought them peace and freedom.

Each of the seventeen Spanish Divisions that marched past had 2,016 men in the parade; each of the various army groups sent 1,008 men to represent them. Cavalrymen on horseback numbered 2,481; sailors, 1,008. Squadrons of bombers and light planes flew low and thundered past in perfect formation. Gunners from the Mechanized Artillery units totalled 9,250; Light Mechanized Columns sent 5,340 men. There were 1,508 engineers and sappers, 600 representing tank-crews, anti-tank guns and machine-guns, and a strong contingent from the auxiliary services. The Italian C.T.V., one-half of its effectives made up of Spanish infantrymen, was present with 7,155 men, of which 2,016 came from the Littorio Division and the remainder from the three Arrow Divisions.

In all, 64,371 men marched that day down the wide Castellana, without a halt or a hitch. Their uniforms were battle-stained, but they sang or they whistled as they marched, and they looked fit and healthy. The day was overcast. At intervals a light drizzle fell, as it often does in Spain during the month of May, but the streets were packed and the crowds stood their ground and clapped wildly. Nobody moved until the parade was over. Madrid had never seen anything to compare with this, and the contrast between these disciplined troops and the Red militias which had terrorized the capital impressed its people deeply. Immediately after the parade, the forces that had marched past withdrew to their barracks or to the camps set up for them in the city. Shortly after this they entrained for the towns where they were quartered until disbanded, which was soon.

Epilogue

The decade that followed the Civil War brought a series of calamities to the Spanish people. A plague of locusts and an epidemic of typhus swept parts of the country and were rapidly checked. Harder to deal with was the shortage of food, from which only the Red Zone had suffered in wartime. Due initially to the absence of cultivation and normal toil under Republican rule—in 1933, by no means the regime's most turbulent year, strikes caused the loss of 14,440,629 working days—the shortage in question now spread all over Spain and was maintained by a ten-year drought and by the scarcity of fertilizers and agricultural machinery. The outbreak of a Second World War hampered foreign trade and retarded the arrival of foreign aid, which some opponents of the Allies were fortunate enough to receive soon after they laid down their arms. Spain had remained neutral in the world conflict, but in due course the United Nations advised its members to withdraw their Ambassadors from Madrid, a course which as already noted most of them adopted, making every excuse for Left-wing dictators and none for Franco. There was no audible outcry for the recall of Ambassadors from Russia and Hungary when the revolt in the latter country was suppressed.

Neither their own war nor the hardships which followed it impaired the vitality of the Spaniards. Deprived of outside help and beset by countless difficulties, they embarked on a programme of reconstruction that included the partial industrialization of a nation which till then had been mainly agricultural. Spain owes much to the United States for its generous assistance in this venture, but without the work that was accomplished with purely inside resources before foreign aid became available the country would not be what it is today. A common aim erased the differences between former enemies; the disillusions of the vanquished strengthened the zest of the victors and a joint resolve to pull through. Some, accused of murder, arson, or theft, were tried and if found guilty punished; those who had incited them to commit these crimes or condoned them were punished as well. When this happened, many who later applauded the Nuremberg trials and still clamour against Nazis in the service of the German Government thought it very wrong of Franco to punish war criminals justly.

The conclusion of civil strife heralded an era of peace without parallel in the history of the nation; never before has a united and sovereign Spain devoted itself peacefully, for at least twenty-five years, to the welfare and progress of its people. To explain this I should recall that though there were periods of peace under the Romans, Spain was not then a sovereign nation. There was little peace after the Visigoths overran the country, and from 711 to 1492 Spaniards fought the Moors upon its soil. Independent kingdoms in Asturias, Castile, León, Navarre, Aragon, and Majorca waged feudal wars against each other or on the invader. Spain was not a united nation until Ferdinand and Isabella expelled the Saracens in 1492. During the next three centuries the Spaniards continued to fight, in other parts of Europe or, more rarely, at home. Their remaining energies were spent in discovering, conquering and civilizing vast territories across the seas. Between 1808 and 1939 they repelled a French invasion, lost an empire, won two wars in Morocco, and were disrupted by internal conflicts of a sporadic nature or by chronic unrest in the political field. In little more than one hundred years they were governed or misgoverned by considerably more than one hundred cabinets, most of which reversed the policies of their immediate predecessors and gave scant attention to constructive work. Sixty years ago, foreign observers classed Spain as a decadent nation, fated to disappear with the last remnants of her empire. Today she is teeming with industry and surprising others with her vitality.

For the stability and peace that have made it possible to enjoy this for over a quarter of a century, even his most relentless opponents grant a measure of credit to General Franco. The night the Nationalist revolt broke out—18 July 1936—in the little room which I shared with him outside Casablanca, Franco spoke with passionate intensity of the need to improve the living standards of the Spanish people. The average wage of an agricultural worker, 2 pesetas fifty years ago, is now 100–172 pesetas (about 12–21s.) per day. In 1935, 2,120,436 children attended schools; over five million attend them now. College attendance has increased from 124,000 in 1935 to 682,226; another 140,723, instead of 32,447, attend labour and industrial colleges;

university students number 78,306 instead of 29,249. Illiteracy, 12·7% in 1960—and over 30% in 1935—now stands at 5%. In thousands of tons, the production of steel has increased from 594 to 3,460; that of coal, from 7,267 to 16,040; nitrate, from 30 to 348; cement, from 404 to 9,950. Total tonnage of ships built in 1935 was 20,000; in 1965, 278,612. Production of electric energy, in thousands of k.w.hs., has risen from 3,272 to 31,650. Reservoirs now have a potential capacity of 27,876,000 cubic metres; in 1935 the figure was 3,500,000. Since 1956, 2,625,000 acres of land have been brought under artificial irrigation; since 1940, reafforestation has been carried out on 4,362,000 acres of land. Against 29,000 houses built in 1935 under State protection, 225,993 were built in 1965. National production is up to 1,126,138,600,000 pesetas, or approximately £67,032,052,000, an increase of 8·2% over 1964. Average *per capita* earnings for the total population rose 7·3% in 1965 to 35,629 pesetas, or £212. The active Spanish population, fourteen years old or more, now amounts to 12,183,600, the percentage of males employed being 60 (64·2% in 1960), that of females 18 (13·5% in 1960). Agricultural workers are now 34·5% of the total, against 41·3% in 1940. Spain had 26,000,000 inhabitants in 1935, and now has 32,000,000; the penal population has fallen during these years from 34,500 to 10,622. The Bank of Spain's reserves, less than $30,000,000 in 1959, are now up to $1,400,000,000.

Not long ago, the representative of an Arabic kingdom had an interview with Khruschev in Moscow. They talked about Spain, and the Soviet leader listened impassively while his visitor praised Spanish infantrymen, whose qualities in battle he had reason to know. 'I refer not only to those who fought on the Nationalist side,' said the Moroccan General, thinking that the expression on Khruschev's face indicated lack of interest, 'but to those who fought against them, to the Spanish foot soldier as a fighting man.' On hearing this Khruschev brightened up and granted that Spanish soldiers had played a distinguished role in military history throughout the ages. The conversation then turned to Franco. Reference was made by the visitor to the Spanish General's best-known qualities, with which he is also familiar. Finally Khruschev smiled and said, 'That fellow and I are the only two who really know what we want.'

Besides becoming better known—it has been visited by nine million foreign tourists in the last sixteen years—Spain is now becoming better understood, especially by those who should be her friends.

In a speech to the British Chamber of Commerce in Madrid on 19 April 1960, the British Ambassador to Spain, Sir Ivo Mallet, recalled that Lord Acton, the English historian, once claimed that there were two hundred definitions of liberty. 'I do not know how many definitions there are of democracy,' Sir Ivo said, 'but I am going to be rash enough to coin another one. Democracy to me is not merely a question of devising a way in which, in different countries of varying histories and different degrees of economic and political development, the individual can best develop his personality. Democracy, in the sense that I have tried to define it, is an essential part of the heritage of Europe which we have to uphold and develop if totalitarian ideas are not to prevail. There are certain persons in my country and other countries abroad who take what is, perhaps, a rather narrow view of democracy, who equate it with certain specific forms, and who regard its rules as absolutes to be applied regardless of existing conditions. It is from these persons that much of the criticism comes which from time to time disturbs relations between Spain and certain other countries. I believe I am right in thinking that what struck you Spaniards'—in the 1930s—'was first, the growing disintegration of the State where freedom was disappearing in anarchy, and later the desperate struggle to save Spain from falling under Communist domination. You were face to face with the threat of Communism in your own towns and countryside. During our war, certain speeches and action seemed to confirm the conception we had formed of the new Spain, and we failed to give due weight to the fact that, although Hitler's Panzer Divisions were at the Pyrenees, the Nazis were not allowed to enter Spain and Spain did not join in the war against us. Nor have we fully realized what might have been the fate of Europe today had the Communists obtained control of Spain in 1939.'

Sir Ivo Mallet had been in Spain five years when he drew that accurate picture of a situation so often misunderstood and distorted; John Davis Lodge had been United States Ambassador in Spain even longer when he said before the American Club in Madrid, on 4 April 1961, 'Nations differ in their talents; largely agricultural nations tend to be more conservative. Those who have sworn to "bury" us are aiming many poisoned arrows at our Spanish friends; they direct a constant stream of propaganda against a people who from bitter bloody experience know what Communism is. Certain legends persist; ignorance and prejudice remain our greatest enemies. Let us try to understand our friends better and to judge them less.'

The Reality of Communism in the
Spanish Crisis

On page 177, mention is made of the Communist *putsch* which was
due to break out in Seville towards the end of July or beginning of
August 1936. The existence of a plan for this *coup de main* has been
questioned or denied in certain circles, but instructions for a Communist rising, entitled *Ordenes y Consignas*—'Orders and Watchwords'—
were in fact issued at high Party level on 6 June 1936. There was
nothing unusual in this. Similar plans had been drawn up befoᴉe in
Spain and occasionally put into effect, the most notable instance of this
being the Communist outbreak in Asturias, in October 1934. In the
summer of 1936, the complicity or passiveness of the government in
power gave likelihood of success to a plot of this kind. Postponed until
mid-August, it was forestalled by the Nationalist revolt. No one on
our side knew of these plans until in August of 1936 they came to light
near Seville, where I myself saw them a few weeks after the start of.our
rebellion. In 1940 they were printed verbatim in Manuel Aznar's
informative *Historia Militar de la Guerra de España* (Madrid, Ediciones
Idea, S.A.).

The instructions in question were tersely phrased. As a first step they
enjoined Communists to denounce to agents of the Popular Front all
prominent members, whether active or passive, of political parties
opposed to extremist aims. All were to be eventually arrested together
with their relatives, employees, and servants, threats being used if
necessary to intimidate them.

Action in army circles was to be preceded by a preparatory phase
during which Communist committees and 'Assault and vigilance'
groups would be set up in barracks whenever possible. Friendly
officers, N.C.O.s and soldiers, besides maintaining contact with the
civilians selected to attack these barracks from the outside, were to

classify the personnel of the garrison into 'enemies, neutrals, sympathizers, and supporters'. At the proper moment, sub-machine-guns would be entrusted to reliable party members, and militiamen would don army uniforms and carry rifles. The committees referred to above would render access to barracks and fraternization within them comparatively easy. 'Neutrals' were to be watched closely, submitted to tests, and if possible won over.

As soon as the Communist rising broke out, 'assault' groups acting under their own responsibility were to shoot down all known enemies, including certain officers, N.C.O.s and private soldiers. Should this order prove difficult to obey, other groups would be called up, officers on duty being told that such groups were reinforcements, arriving to strengthen the defence. In this manner access to barracks would be simplified, after which the leader of the main Communist contingent would take over and see that his orders were scrupulously obeyed, dissenters being summarily executed by two of his followers specially appointed for the purpose.

The instructions were specific as regards the elimination of General Officers, Corps Commanders and Colonels. It was considered preferable to attack them at home, groups of ten men, armed with sub-machine-guns, being assigned to this mission. Generals and Colonels would be shot down by the three most determined members of the group, any persons offering resistance being killed on the spot regardless of sex or age. Officers on leave, or not in active service, were to be eliminated by groups made up of three men, with two more in support. Officers *en route* to the barracks would be attacked by men strategically posted on street corners and armed with sub-machine-guns, such weapons being preferable to pistols, which according to these instructions are better for in-fighting or for personal defence at close quarters.

Machine-gun emplacements, mounted in previously selected positions, would be used to fire on forces attempting a sortie from their barracks, should the plan to overwhelm the barracks fail. Steel plates, held in readiness, were to be assembled on trucks, which, thus protected, would be rushed to defeat resistance wherever it might break out, occupants of these trucks being armed not only with machine-guns and pistols but with hand-grenades as well. Militiamen, while pretending to escort leaders of anti-Marxist political parties, would eliminate them. Capitalists listed by name in Appendix B of these instructions—also known as 'Circular Order No. 32'—would be forced under penalty of summary annihilation to hand over the balance in their bank accounts and all stocks and shares standing to their credit, it being advisable to establish beforehand close relations with domestic servants of these persons, particularly with their chauffeurs and valets. As a warning to all, exemplary punishment would be meted out to some.

Army officers classed as Communist sympathizers or active supporters were to be closely watched, not only because there was a danger that they might be regarded with suspicion by their fellow officers, but because, having betrayed the latter, they might also feel inclined to betray their new allies. Consequently, they were to be treated in the same way as certain officers had been dealt with in Russia, i.e. 'eliminated' after good use had been made of their complicity.

The instructions stressed the need to train militiamen efficiently in the use of firearms and to make them realize that orders were given to be obeyed, and that missions had to be faithfully carried out. Effectives would be trained at night for street-fighting. When hostilities broke out, Communist groups assigned to attack garrison towns were to occupy strategic positions in the outskirts and bring their machine-guns to bear on army units preparing to intercept them, hand-grenades being used for close fighting. To prevent the arrival of enemy reinforcements, other Communist groups, supported by armoured trucks carrying machine-guns, would be posted one kilometre away from any barracks occupied by the former. Automobiles and cyclists would maintain the necessary liaison between these groups and others inside the town, the entire personnel in charge of such services being armed with sub-machine-guns.

Salvador de Madariaga, an Honorary Fellow of Exeter College, Oxford, and an Ambassador of the late Spanish Republic, writes in his *Spain: A Modern History* (Jonathan Cape, London, 1961: p. 457), 'Let no one argue that it was Fascist violence which developed Socialist violence, for leaving aside the fact that a Socialist democracy should have been able to conquer violence not with violence but with the massive power of a nation standing fast on the law, it was not at the Fascists that Largo Caballero's gunmen shot but at their brother Socialists whose crime was that they wanted a Popular Front Government. Much ink has been wasted in discussing whether a rising of the Extreme Left was being prepared when the Army officers rebelled against the State. Largo Caballero never made a mystery of it. It was his avowed, nay, his proclaimed policy to rush Spain on to the dictatorship of the proletariat. Thus pushed on the road to violence, the nation, always prone to it, became more violent than ever.'

Hugh Thomas, in a footnote to *The Spanish Civil War* (Eyre and Spottiswoode, London, 1961, p. 108), writes as follows on the same subject: 'I have come to the conclusion that the three documents alleged to have been found in four separate places after the start of the Civil War, and making plans for a Socialist-Communist *coup d'état* by means of a simulated rising of the Right, are not forgeries. They have often been reprinted, and an English version of the texts, with a facsimile of the document allegedly found at Lora del Río,'—a town near Seville—'is in Loveday, 176 ff. The three documents were (a), a plan to establish Largo Caballero, his followers, and the communists as a "Soviet", between May 11 and June 29; (b) general instructions for revolution'—summarized above in the preceding pages—'and (c), a purported record of a meeting of the Communist party in Valencia, on May 16. The first reference I have found to these documents is in the *Diario de Navarra* of August 7, 1936, a date rather early for clever propaganda forgeries.'

Burnett Bolloten's for the most part well-documented *The Grand Camouflage: The Communist Conspiracy in the Spanish Civil War* (Hollis and Carter, London, 1961), is a book which no student of Spanish affairs should miss. But on one point Mr Bolloten is at fault. On page 97 of his book he tells us that in August 1936, Russia 'anxious not to give body and colour to attacks that pictured her as the open patron of world revolution lest she antagonize the moderate parties in the Western democracies . . . undertook together with other countries participating in the accord not to send arms to Spain,' to which Mr Bolloten adds the following comment in a footnote on the same page: 'This concern for Western opinion ill accords with the charge put forward by rebel sources, to justify the military revolt, that the Communists had been conspiring to set up a Soviet regime in Spain in the summer of 1936 (see Manuel Aznar, *Historia Militar de la Guerra de España*), for it is obvious that had they even attempted to establish such a regime they would have ruined the Comintern's hopes of a rapprochement with the Western powers. For this reason alone, to say nothing of the fact that they certainly did not have the necessary strength, the charge may be safely discounted.'

Mr Bolloten's comments, logical as they may seem, can be dismissed for two reasons: the events of the preceding years amply justified the military revolt; no attempt was made to justify it by publishing plans for a Communist conspiracy. When evidence of the plot summarized above was discovered near Seville, where I heard of it by pure chance, I was in that city as Press Officer in charge of foreign correspondents. I saw the plan, but nobody asked me to release it to the Press, which is what would have been done had it been concocted to justify our rebellion. Equally unwarranted is the assumption that Communists in Spain would have hesitated to act in a manner contrary to the Comintern's policy. Spanish Communists, in July 1936, had yet to be taught discipline and submission to their masters; they did not attach much importance to the Comintern. Lack of the necessary strength would not have deterred them from violence, for to gain their own ends they relied on the strength of others, more foolish than themselves and ready to act as willing tools. And the implication that anybody on our side, in July 1936, would have thought for a moment of faking a conspiracy, complete in every detail and imbued with a genuinely Communist spirit, overlooks the way in which the revolt was launched, with hardly any detailed planning, a total absence of Machiavellian design, and no thought whatever for foreign opinion or for anything else save for the individual conscience of those concerned with its success. No wonder that many abroad, and some at home, never dreamt that it would succeed.

The Nationalists did not have to bolster up their case with imaginary threats from the Left. Such threats were effectively put into force wherever expedient, when the fighting started, or before, by the Communists or by their allies. Calvo Sotelo, the leader of the Opposition, was murdered after La Pasionaria, a Communist deputy, openly threatened him with death in the Cortes, and the Communist plan issued near Seville, though not wholly carried out because the Nationalist rising frustrated it, was put into force to massacre naval officers, many of whom had not even made a move against the regime, and hurl them into the sea from the quarter-decks of their ships, or to torture and kill throughout Spain defenceless men and women who were innocent of all crimes.

The reality of the Communist menace in Spain before the Civil War started, and the rapidity with which this threat materialized after the conflict had been on its way for a short time, were set out in an article, entitled 'Liberalism and Communism', which Don Gregorio Marañón published in *La Revue de Paris*, December 1937. One month later, *La Nación* of Buenos Aires reproduced the same article in its original Spanish version, and in July 1960 it was reprinted in *Punta de Europa*, a Spanish review of literary flavour where I saw it for the first time, months after it appeared. Because of the light which it sheds on the Spanish conflict I have translated and summarized parts of it here.

Don Gregorio Marañón was a doctor, known to students of modern Spain for work in the field of medicine, art, and history which made him the only Spaniard to obtain admittance to the Spanish Royal Academies of Language, Medicine, History, Beaux Arts, and Science. A Doctor *Honoris Causa* of the Sorbonne, of the Universities of Oporto, Coimbra, and Milan, and of the principal universities in Spanish America, Marañón was also a Grand Officer of the Legion of Honour and a member of the British Institute of Science, of the Institut de France, and of the French Academy of Political and Moral Science. He received the Grand Cross of the Argentine Order of Mayo and many Spanish and foreign decorations; his volumes on Antonio Pérez, secretary to Phillip II, and his essay on El Greco have been translated into several languages.

Gregorio Marañón was a friend of King Alfonso and a progressive Liberal who in 1931 decided that, for Spain, the best form of government was a republic. Together with José Ortega y Gasset, the philosopher, and Ramón Pérez de Ayala, the novelist, he founded a group, called *Amigos de la Republica*—'Friends of the Republic'—which contributed to the advent and initial prestige of that regime. Those whose views of the Spanish war were formed by the *New Statesman* in England or by the *New Republic* in America might profit by a study of Marañón's deductions regarding the ultimate causes of that disaster and the conclusions which he reached on the subject.

Marañón, in the article referred to above, wrote that had Spaniards, or others, been asked in 1937 to explain their attitude with regard to the Civil War, few would have answered that they supported the Reds because the Reds were Communists, or that they sided with the Nationalists because the latter opposed Communism. And yet Communism on one side and anti-Communism on the other were the real issues at stake, though even in Spain this was not well understood until the Republic had been established for some time—until, long before civil war broke out, Russia sensed the inherent weakness of the regime's resistance to outside influences and decided to make use of the situation. The Right saw the picture clearly as soon as the Monarchy fell. 'It is beyond a shadow of doubt,' Marañón tells us, 'that the march of events bore out every prophecy made by the extreme Rightists or Monarchists who opposed the advent of the Republic. They foresaw clearly the years of chronic disorder, senseless strikes, burning of convents, religious persecution, exclusion of Liberals from the function of government because they were against class warfare though they had sided with the Republic at first, and denial of fair treatment to citizens of the Right who had accepted the regime in all good faith but were not inflamed with extremist ideas. Whatever may be in store for Spain, politically speaking, it is beyond doubt that in that critical phase of its history it was the reactionaries, not the Liberals, who clearly foresaw the future.'

'One night,' Marañón recalls, 'shortly before the burning of convents in May 1931, I overheard three men discussing politics while walking down a street. They were Communists, and such was their faith in the imminence of a Communist triumph that had I not been convinced that Spaniards on the whole were opposed to Bolshevik tactics, what they said might have impressed me. The burning of the convents proved me wrong. Communist propaganda, although aggressive and intense, had till then been mainly clandestine; the number of known Party members was still small; only one or two Communist deputies had been returned from the polls in the previous general elections. But the smoke columns which at the same fateful hour arose one night towards the sky from hundreds of churches in a score of Spanish towns, with the people at peace and without provocation commensurate to the magnitude of a crime committed with a technical efficiency and a capacity for destruction of which Spaniards had hitherto been guiltless, sufficed to show that a new and totally exotic force had risen in our midst and was making its first concerted effort to destroy organized society. Against this outrage, the only audible protest from Republican ranks was the one which I myself and two illustrious Spaniards signed. Liberals did not join together to denounce the inescapable truth, though many of them turned in disgust from a regime which they had at first supported because it upheld changes later incorporated in the Nationalist programme.

'Henceforth, disturbances in Spain acquired a Communist hue and gradually increased in violence, though the forces which influenced them were subtly concealed to lull public opinion and avoid reaction. The triumph of the Right in a general election served as a pretext for a revolutionary rising in October 1934, engineered by Communists for the purpose of seizing power. This fact may have been forgotten abroad by many unfamiliar with Spanish history, however recent, but Spaniards do not forget it, and they become hilarious when those who rebelled in Asturias against the verdict of a general election hide their heads in pious horror at the thought that part of the nation and the army dared to rebel against government excesses as outrageous as that which brought about the murder of Calvo Sotelo, leader of the opposition in the Cortes. Today's purists are but yesterday's rebels. Let us call them Communists or anti-Communists and forget the word "rebel". It merely stirs up a point of priority.

'The Asturias revolt in 1934 was a Communist attempt to conquer Spain. It failed thanks to a miracle, so another and more formidable attempt was made two years later', i.e. as soon as civil war broke out. 'Nobody who has been in Red Spain, even for an hour,' Marañón wrote in 1937, 'can possibly doubt that this part of the country is today, politically speaking, totally and absolutely Communist, nor can this fact be questioned except by those who insist on viewing it through the artless yet efficient mirages in which liberty is often reflected—the "good of the people"; Democracy; a Constitutional Republic. Militant Communists, once unmasked, never try to conceal their aims. Non-Communists, yoked through the machinations of a relentless fate to the Red cause, persist in talking of a Democratic Republic, possibly because human credulity has no limits, possibly also because, as they often privately admit, personal friendships, party ties and an inescapable urge to keep going and live force them to lay aside the dictates of conscience. My recalcitrant Liberalism does not prevent me from respecting those who sincerely support the Red movement in Spain or merely sympathize with it in the belief that Communism is capable of saving not only Spain but the entire world, but to assert that support and sympathy for Communism are based on love of liberty, universal peace, and democracy, or on a profound respect for other people's ideals, implies bad faith or mental incompetence.

'It is right to say'—in 1937—'that the number of Communists in Spain was, until a short time ago, quite negligible. They still constitute a minority, counting Party members in the trenches and others behind them. But we ourselves and certain European and American countries are guilty of a blatant error when we estimate the importance of an idea —the Communist idea, to be precise—by the number of its adherents. Were we capable of abiding by the teachings of history, it would suffice to recall that the most effective revolution we have known triumphed in Russia through the efforts of an almost insignificant number of Bolsheviks. Exactly this is the case in Spain, where a few determined men have imposed their will on the majority.' Marañón goes on to show that Communists in Spain ruthlessly subjected Socialists, Anarchists, Syndicalists and Republicans, and, after rendering them powerless, exterminated all and any within their ranks who constituted a potential menace, which is something that they could never have succeeded in doing without Liberal support. Liberals feel a weakness for Communism, the most anti-Liberal movement of all time. A characteristic trait of those incapable of distinguishing despotism when it is tinged with red is the fear, akin to panic, of not acting as true Liberals; the fear that others may fail to recognize them as such, rather than fidelity to party principles, constitutes their main preoccupation. Hardened reactionaries are delighted when someone says to them, 'At heart, you yourself are a Liberal,' and Liberals are distressed if their Liberalism is questioned, for according to current thought the failure to be a good Liberal implies lack of intelligence, hostility to the people, and unprogressiveness in the intellectual field. Communism has exploited all this and closed its eyes to the irreconcilability of a school of thought that exalts liberty, and a political system that denies it. 'In Madrid, last November,' Marañón tells us, 'a Communist said to me, "I assume that having always been a Liberal you are now on our side," but that very day the Workmen's Committee vetoed a new edition of one of my books because it contained the following statement, "I, thank God, have always been a Liberal." When I left Spain and said that, to me, this attitude did not seem very liberal, I was declared "an enemy of the people", and an American Communist writer called me "the new Spanish Torquemada".'

Two months before civil war broke out, Marañón wrote an article warning the Popular Front that unless a profound national spirit guided its ideas and its actions, the country would rebel. When he made that statement, non-Marxist Spaniards were reacting in a violently hostile manner to the notoriously Russian-instigated agitation then rampant throughout the land, and ninety per cent of the same University students who had supported the Liberal forces which overthrew the Dictatorship and paved the way for the Republic were clamouring against this agitation, mainly because it was anti-national.

'The conflict before us,' i.e. the Spanish Civil War, 'is a struggle between two ideologies, one of them Communist, anti-democratic and oriental, the other anti-Communist, anti-democratic and European, and the solution must be worked out in accordance with Spanish realities, infinitely powerful and vital. True to her traditions, Spain is contributing the largest part to a victory in which all will share. Spaniards have already taken sides. Others, whose interest in the struggle is more direct and greater than many of them suspect, should line up knowing that the only choice open to them lies between Communism and anti-Communism.'

Nationalist Fighting Strength in the Civil War

A. *Man Power*

A steady growth in man power was a feature of Franco's strategy throughout the war. One hundred and twenty days after it started, i.e. in November 1936, the Army of the North, commanded by General Mola, was composed of 49,897 officers and men, the majority of whom had volunteered for service. In March 1937, this figure had increased to 89,456, and by June of that same year it had grown to 192,052, almost four times higher than it had been seven and a half months before. Eight months after the outbreak of hostilities, the total Nationalist effectives amounted to 289,185 men. In the final stages of the war— i.e. early in 1939—these men made up the following forces:

Infantry (61 Divisions)	840,011
Cavalry	15,323
Artillery	19,013
Auxiliary Services	119,594
Moroccan Troops commanded by Spanish officers, and composed of Spanish and Moroccan soldiers ..	35,000
Italian C.T.V., one-half of which were Spanish	32,000
Condor Division (German Volunteers)	5,000
Total	1,065,941

The above forces were grouped as follows: Army of the Levante, under General Orgaz; Army of the Centre, under General Saliquet; and Army of the South, under General Queipo de Llano. The combined strength of these three armies represented the highest numerical peak attained by the effectives under General Franco in the Spanish Civil War.

B. Arms and Ammunition: The Sources of Supply

At the start of the conflict practically all the existing stocks of arms and ammunition were held by the Republicans, who also possessed most of the factories which produced war material in Spain and soon began to receive additional supplies from France, Russia and other countries. This situation greatly enhanced the chances of a Republican victory. However, the Nationalists managed to pull through, partly by capturing large quantities of equipment on the battlefield and partly by purchasing arms and ammunition from Italy and Germany, the only sources of supply open to them. Such purchases were paid for in full shortly after the termination of the war.

While shipments from foreign lands were vital for the Republicans, on Franco's side they were neither frequent nor considerable. The Nationalists could not afford to pay them, nor did they need them as much as their enemies did. It was the Republicans who supplied them with most of their equipment, and this they did simply by surrendering arms and ammunition on the field of battle, or by losing the factories which produced war supplies in the North. So large were the stocks which the Nationalists captured that a special department was created to classify, repair, and allocate the weapons and munitions which constantly fell into their hands.

In the fifth article of the series 'La Vérité sur la Guerre d'Espagne', Manuel Azaña, who presided over the Spanish Republic during the Civil War, admitted that 70,000 or more rifles, distributed in Madrid to Red Militias in July 1936, 'did not take long to disappear; 17,000 rifles that crossed the Atlantic towards the end of August vanished as a result of the disasters at Talavera.' During the march on Madrid (August–November 1936), when Malaga and its province were taken (February 1937), at the conclusion of the Northern campaign (October 1937), and throughout the offensive in Aragon (1938–9), Nationalist troops seized an immense booty, abandoned by the enemy on the field.

A French writer, Pierre Héricourt, who was frequently with me on the Nationalist Front during the war, published in *Pourquoi Franco a Vaincu* (Editions Baudiniére, Paris, 1939) a list of Republican war supplies captured by the Nationalists which he had personally inspected in May 1937. The list included:

318 French machine-guns
948 Russian machine-guns

565   machine-guns of various origin
954   machine-gun barrels
1,658   French automatic rifles
120,000   cartridge clips
2,600,000   8 mm. Lebel cartridges
12,575   Russian rifles
886   Czechoslovakian rifles
3,582   Mexican rifles
4,875,000   Russian rifle cartridges
24   French (Stokes) mortars
53   French 37 mm. guns
32   French 75 mm. guns
16   French 155 mm. guns
18   Russian 124 mm. guns
52,000   French and Russian shells
110   Russian tanks and armoured-cars

The whole of this equipment was captured in only four months (January–May 1937). Between 1 May and 30 September 1937, according to an account also given by Pierre Héricourt, Franco's troops seized the following:

(a) *Made in France:*

172   Hotchkiss machine-guns
125   Saint-Etienne machine-guns
219   Hotchkiss barrels
43   Saint-Etienne barrels
19,930   8 mm. Lebel rifles
25,098,837   Lebel cartridges
515,440   Lebel clips
62   Stokes mortars
253,152   75 mm. shells
47   75 mm. guns
59,991   Laffite hand-grenades
428,210   hand-grenades of various makes
12,500   gas masks

(b) *Made in Russia:*

283   machine-guns
367   machine-gun barrels

15,952	rifles
20,176,677	rifle cartridges
127,500	shells
49	guns
82	armoured tanks

During the summer of 1938 an exhibition of captured war material was held in San Sebastian. Visitors from foreign lands attended the exhibit and noted its origin and its volume:

200	tanks
700	field-pieces
300,000	rifles
400,000,000	cartridges

Towards the end of the war, after the battle of the Ebro and the conquest of Catalonia, these stocks increased considerably. According to trustworthy statistics, they amounted at that time to:

1,877	guns
25,306	machine-guns
20,000	automatic rifles
576,000	rifles
100,000	bayonets
6,990	mortars
3,683,086	shells
1,136,260,000	rifle cartridges
20,000	aeroplane bombs
17,000,000	hand-grenades
30	anti-aircraft searchlights
3,516,200	kilogrammes of explosives
500	tanks and armoured-cars

Not included in these figures is the equipment utilized against the Reds on the field by the forces that captured it, or the war supplies seized by our troops after the collapse of the entire Republican Front and equivalent to twice the amounts stated above. While fighting was in progress, arms and ammunition factories in different parts of Spain —notably in Seville, from the start of the rebellion, and in and around Bilbao and Oviedo, after the Northern Front collapsed—delivered to the Nationalists war material of all kinds, including guns, rifles, bombs and shells. But the chief source of supply was the enemy.

The information contained in the preceding pages contradicts widely circulated reports according to which Franco's victory in the Civil War was due mainly to Italian and German help. The Italians and the Germans at no time represented more than 4 or 5 per cent of Franco's effectives, potential or on the field, and they provided our troops with war material far less essential to victory, aeroplanes excluded, than that which the Republicans surrendered.

Total equipment of the Nationalist forces at the end of the Civil War consisted of:

(a) Small Arms:

Rifles	.. ..	1,010,648	
Muskets	.. ..	41,078	
Carbines	.. ..	3,049	
Pistols	.. ..	35,532	
Total	.. .. ..	1,090,307	

(b) Automatic Weapons:

Machine-guns	.. .. ..	12,583	
Rifles	.. ..	21,846	
Total	.. .. ..	34,429	

(c) Mortars 7,641

(d) Artillery:

Field equipment (621 batteries) ..	2,453	pieces
37's Anti-tank batteries	375	pieces
94's Coastal batteries	362	pieces
13's Anti-aircraft batteries ..	54	pieces
Total	3,244	pieces

(e) Tanks

35 companies, with about 18 tanks each .. .. 651 tanks

C. *Air Effectives on Both Sides*

The Nationalist purchased during the war 1,079 planes of the following description:

Heinkel *51* (fighters)

Junker 52	(bombers)
Savoia 79	(bombers)
Heinkel 112	(scouts)
Fiat CR- 32	(scouts)
Savoia 81	(bombers)
Heinkel 111	(bombers)
Messerschmidt 109	(scouts)
Cant-Z501	(bombers)

The number of planes purchased during the war by the Republicans was, 1,627. The majority of these planes were Boeing *Y-16* (scouts), Curtis *Y-15* (scouts) and Natacha *204* (bombers).

The total number of planes flown by the Nationalists in the war was 1,122.

The total number of planes flown by the Republicans was 1,807.

These figures include planes respectively in the possession of the opposing sides at the outbreak of hostilities.

The Guernica Myth

Guernica was said to have been destroyed on 26 April 1937. Two days later, Republican and Basque Separatist contingents equal in strength to a full Division reached Guernica from Bilbao with the intention of defending it. Guernica was occupied by our troops on 29 April. At 8 p.m. that same day a liaison officer from General Franco's G.H.Q. sent the following dispatch to Salamanca:

H.Q., 4TH BRIGADE. Destruction at Guernica is greater than at Eibar—a city 26 miles east of Guerniea, also burnt by the Reds before being abandoned.
The enemy offered resistance. Our casualties were 8 dead and 60 wounded. Eight Basque battalions and two battalions from Santander defended Guernica. We captured some wounded soldiers and inflicted heavy losses on the enemy, especially in the heights west of the town where large stocks of supplies were seized.

On the same day, 29 April, the General commanding the Navarre Brigades dispatched two messages to the Commander-in-Chief of the Northern Armies. The first of them said:

The operations for the capture of Guernica continued today and were completed at 11 a.m. Enemy losses were heavy and we took stocks of ammunition and some prisoners, among them two of their leaders. Numerous deserters made their appearance in our lines. The town is completely destroyed and empty; its inhabitants were forced to leave. One of our prisoners is a French journalist who had just landed in Bilbao.

The second dispatch said:

Further to my earlier report of this date we have captured a Cavalry Colonel called Arturo Llarch who commanded the Division defending Guernica and attempted to resist as did two captains and a lieutenant who were killed while trying to lead a counter-attack against our forces. A former provincial deputy from Alava, named Placer, was also taken prisoner; he was an acting artillery major for the Red Army. In all we have taken about 300 prisoners and enemy deserters.

In an article entitled 'Recollections of the Capture of Guernica', published by the review *Ejército* in July 1949, General Martinez Esparza wrote: 'Suddenly, a Red motor-cyclist appeared on the road, some distance before our leading tank. A burst of machine gun bullets, fired into the air to halt him, brought the rider tumbling to the ground, much frightened and with a sprained wrist but otherwise unharmed. On being questioned he stated that he was on his way to Marquina with a message to the forces in that town, ordering them to fall back on Guernica, where the defence was being strengthened by the arrival of a Division from Bilbao. We pushed forward with our tanks, and soon had a fine view of Guernica. A railway train had just arrived, carrying troops to reinforce the Division which defended the town. We drove as far as the church at Ajanguiz, in the outskirts of Guernica, where we were surrounded by retreating Red soldiers who greeted us warmly and laid down their arms when told to do so. Before proceeding towards Guernica we set up two anti-tank pieces with the object of shelling the railway station there and the train which we had seen arriving. No time was lost in doing so, but the engine driver was faster and got away with his train at full speed, escaping a hail of shells from our guns.'

From the above it is evident that until the last moment the Reds considered Guernica to be of military value. As regards its destruction, dispatches from the Nationalist units which occupied Guernica are enlightening. One of them is from the 4th Navarre Brigade, the unit which actually took Guernica on 29 April. It says:

Today our Brigade occupied Uarca, Hill 189, Rentería, Ajanguiz, Guernica, Luno, and Mount Aiserrota. The town of Guernica is destroyed and deserted. All that remains of it at the time of writing is on fire. The Tree and its surroundings have been placed in the custody of a company of Requetés with orders to see that nobody approaches it. We have captured 72 prisoners, among them the colonel commanding the Red troops in the Guernica sector, a Spanish journalist, acting as political delegate of the forces operating in the area, and a French journalist. Numerous peasants and whole families returned to Guernica after learning that it had been liberated, and moving scenes were enacted as they witnessed the destruction and looting wrought in their homes. Our casualties are 5 dead and 28 wounded, among the latter a sub-lieutenant of the Flanders Regiment, Don Juan Antonio García.

A dispatch from the VIth Army Corps, dated 28 April, said:

Our troops have continued their advance and reached a line that extends from Navarriz-Uarca, 2 kilometres east of Guernica, to the town of Durango, which has been occupied after overcoming strong resistance. The enemy was supported by Russian tanks. A thick mist from the mountains blotted out visibility and prevented us from reaching Guernica. Our men were eager to enter the town. They already knew that the enemy had evacuated Guernica after criminally destroying it and was blaming our planes for its destruction, but Guernica itself is free of bomb-craters. The number of Red casualties and of prisoners taken in Durango is not yet known. It must be considerable, in the same way as the stocks seized. Durango was captured at 7 p.m., at which time the fog was very thick. Over one hundred enemy deserters reached our lines today.

The report of the Army of the North on the events that took place on 28 April was as follows:

After hard fighting, the city of Durango was captured today by our troops. Before taking it they occupied the heights around the town, also after much fighting. Enemy attempts to turn Durango into a Red bulwark cost our opponents many casualties and prisoners and the loss of much equipment. Basque fugitives who had reached our lines were terrified by the tragedies enacted in towns such as Guernica, deliberately burnt and destroyed by the Reds while we were not more than ten miles away. There is much indignation among our troops against the Basque-Soviet leaders who blame Nationalist aviators for these barbarous acts. Our planes during the last few days were unable to fly owing to persistant fog and drizzle. The number of prisoners is very high, as is also the number of deserters from the Reds.

None of the dispatches quoted above was written for the public; their contents merely reflected what was seen and heard on the ground. It should be noted, besides, that the destruction, though involving many buildings, spared the Guernica Tree and adjoining structures. Basque Separatists took good care not to damage the Tree, which they —and others on our side—very properly held in special veneration.

357

Had Guernica been bombarded as ruthlessly as these Separatists swore that it had been, the Tree and its surroundings would not have survived.

Two magistrates and two qualified engineers, after hearing the depositions of twenty-five witnesses, came to the following conclusions: (1) Guernica was occupied by Basque troops on 25 April; (2) that day few people attended the market, which was scantily supplied with its usual wares, the inhabitants having been warned that 'destruction was imminent'; (3) planes bombed Guernica intermittently, causing less than one hundred casualties; and (4) Guernica was destroyed by Red incendiaries, who deliberately set fire to the town.

In the article already quoted, General Martinez Esparza refers to the capture in Guernica by Nationalist troops of a deputy of the Basque Separatist Party, a Spanish journalist from Bilbao, and a French journalist, Monsieur Bernard, who belonged to the staff of the Bordeaux newspaper, *La Petite Gironde*. 'We started to roam about, and one of our men informed us that he had come upon two suspicious characters. Near the entrance to a church we found two well-dressed men who identified themselves as a Basque Deputy and a French journalist. They had come to report on the destruction of Guernica with the idea of laying the blame on Nationalist planes, and their report was intended for publication abroad. We requested them to sign a statement admitting that they had witnessed the occupation of the town, that the inhabitants had been well treated by our men, who had posted a guard around the Tree of Guernica and the surrounding buildings, and that Guernica had been destroyed before our effectives reached it. When this was done they were handed over to Intelligence Officers of the 4th Navarre Brigade.'

The above tallies with a dispatch from the 4th Brigade, dated 29 April 1937:

We posted a guard around the Tree of Guernica, and found among the prisoners captured a Basque Separatist deputy called Placer, a journalist from Bilbao and a French war correspondent, who were requested to sign a statement to the effect that they had witnessed the entry of our troops into Guernica, seen how our enemies had destroyed the town before we occupied it, and noted the precautions taken by our leaders to protect the Tree and enforce the laws of war, all of which they did.

General Martinez Esparza's article tells us something about the nature of the destruction in Guernica. 'There was an arms factory there which produced trench-mortars and pistols as well as other weapons. Our planes bombed this factory, and they also bombed the railway station to prevent the arms from being exported. But in Guernica I saw two completely different kinds of ruins. On one side, the bombed arms factory, the railway station and their surroundings; on the other, ruins of a more recent character, the result of arson and dynamite. Because the Reds did not expect us to occupy Guernica as soon as we did, when we entered the town smoke was still pouring out of buildings which had evidently been set on fire. So rapidly did our troops advance that they captured a French journalist and a Basque deputy who was acting as his escort. Both had come to Guernica to concoct a report the purpose of which was to stir up hatred of the Nationalists in foreign lands.'

On p, 279 of *Documents on German Foreign Policy, 1918–1945, Series D, Volume III, The Spanish Civil War* (London, His Majesty's Stationery Office, 1951), there is a dispatch—No. 249—from von Mackensen, the German State Secretary, to the German Embassy in Spain. It is dated in Berlin, 4 May 1937, and it transcribes a telegram from the German Ambassador in London, stating: 'From various quarters the Embassy is receiving communications making German fliers responsible for the bombardment of Guernica, in spite of our denials. In private conversation Franco's denial is still given prominence and is construed to mean that Franco indirectly admits the attack was made by German fliers. The debate in Commons could perhaps be taken as a basis for inducing Franco now to issue an energetic and sharp denial which could not be equivocally construed.'

The denial had already been published. Another document in this same volume, No. 251, reproduces a telegram from the German Ambassador in Spain to the Foreign Ministry in Berlin. Dated 5 May in Salamanca, it explains that 'on April 29 and 30 the Nationalist Government's press bureau' had 'issued dispatches in the form of an article regarding the burning of Guernica. These were also given to foreign press representatives. In the sharpest terms they reject as lies and slanders the Basque Government's report regarding the alleged destruction of the city by German fliers. The interpretation that this denial indirectly admits a German plane attack is malicious and unsupported by the text of the denial. A translation of some of the important passages of the denial of 29 April follows: "Guernica was destroyed with fire and gasoline. It was set afire and reduced to ruins by the Red hordes in the criminal service of Aguirre, the President of the Basque Republic. Aguirre planned the destruction of Guernica with the devilish intention of laying the blame before the enemy's door producing a storm of indignation among the already conquered and demoralized Basques." I request instructions in case a new denial by the Nationalist Government is considered necessary.'

These are the main references to Guernica in the volume cited above. The documents quoted were captured by the Allies when Hitler was defeated. They were secret, and were not meant for publication; there is no apparent reason why these official documents should have disguised the truth or altered it in any way.

The same applies to the dispatches from Nationalist headquarters on the field of battle, dated 28 and 29 April, and transcribed above. Never intended for publication, they corroborate each other. The men who wrote them had no cause and no possible justification for attempting to deceive their superior officers. Had they done so they would have been court-martialled. They simply reported facts as found in the course of the day's fighting, and General Martinez Esparza, when he wrote his recollections for the review *Ejército*, confined himself to reflecting what he saw the day that Guernica was taken.

Sidelights on the Civil War

When Mr Hugh Thomas's excellent book *The Spanish Civil War* was published in London by Eyre and Spottiswoode, I glanced at the index and found several references to my name. One of them, on p. 119, stated that I had chartered a plane to transport General Franco from the Canaries to Morocco, and added that 'there were, apparently, no aircraft in Spain fast enough for so delicate a journey', and that 'the Spanish plotters also considered an English pilot more likely to be trustworthy than one of their own compatriots'. The plane was chartered in England because there were no aircraft in Spain that we could hire capable of flying between Morocco and the Canaries. For numerous reasons it was considered advisable that an English pilot and an English crew should handle the machine; we had to throw dust in other people's eyes. But 'the Spanish plotters', as my readers know, entrusted the entire leadership of the flight to one of their compatriots, i.e. the author of this book (see Part I).

Farther on, in a footnote on p. 165, Mr Thomas writes that during the war, 'journalists were expelled by Captain Bolín, the Nationalist Press chief, with monotonous regularity'. Certain foreign journalists were, in some cases, rightly or wrongly suspected of passing on information to the enemy, and a few were expelled by those with authority to do so. In the same footnote there is a statement to the effect that 'the strict press censorship and limitation of freedom of movement'—both of them, I might point out, far less strict in the Spanish War than they were on the British Front in France during the First World War— 'made news from Nationalist territory hard to come by'. The pertinent facts regarding this situation are explained at some length above, on pp. 219–22.

On p. 214 of his book Mr Thomas writes that on 20 July General Franco sent me to Biarritz, where I took Luca de Tena, editor of the Monarchist paper *A.B.C.*, on board my plane and consulted the millionaire Juan March. None of this is correct. I left Tetuán on 19 July; General Franco did not send me to Biarritz; and in Biarritz I did not see, or speak to, Juan March. Luca de Tena did not fly on to Rome with me 'to approach the Italian Government for the supply of war material'. Nor is it correct to write, as Mr Thomas does on p. 217 of his book: 'Franco's agents, Bolín and Luca de Tena, reached Rome on the evening of 22 July. They immediately saw Count Ciano, the Italian Foreign Minister. To Franco's first emissaries Ciano showed interest and asked about the nature of the Nationalist movement, but did no more.' As already stated, Luca de Tena did not fly with me to Rome, where I arrived alone on 21 July. Regarding what Count Ciano did, or the outcome of my conversations with him, my readers will find a full and detailed version in pp. 167–72 above.

I have not analysed every statement in Mr Thomas's book, but while reading its first edition I have come across a series of inaccuracies which for obvious reasons should be pointed out. For instance, on p. 7 Mr Thomas tells us that Calvo Sotelo, 'prudently spending the first years of the Republic in Paris to escape condemnation as an ally of tyranny, returned to Spain only when the Republic had begun to founder'. Calvo Sotelo was banished by the Republic, not as an 'ally of tyranny' but to get rid of a formidable opponent. He returned to Spain, not when the Republic 'had begun to founder' but as soon as his election to the Cortes invested him with parliamentary immunity—an immunity which did not prevent him from being murdered by the minions of some of those described on p. 3 by Mr Thomas as 'anxious, middleaged, honest men' who abhorred 'violence'. (See pp. 31–2, above).

Mr Thomas also says, on p. 64, that 'for much of the time'—1932— 'the right-wing papers *A.B.C.*, *EL DEBATE* and *INFORMACIONES* were suspended'. He does not disclose that, also 'for much of that time', one hundred and eleven other newspapers were suspended as well. A total of one hundred and fourteen newspapers, suspended for months in a territory smaller than Texas, is not bad for a government which started out claiming to uphold freedom of speech and the liberty of the press, but on this Mr Thomas does not comment. And there were not twenty-six chekas in Madrid—p. 176—but two hundred and twenty-seven. My source for this is the same as Mr Thomas's, i.e. *The Red Domination in Spain: The General Cause*, Madrid 1953.

No sources are quoted by Mr Thomas for stating, in a footnote on

p. 269, that between August 1936 and June 1937, 'popular tribunals', presumably in Madrid, 'judged no less than 46,064 people and imposed 1,318 capital sentences'—many more were certainly executed—or for writing in the text of this same page that by the end of August 1936, steps adopted by the Republican Government 'almost ended illegal killings'. 'Almost' is right; the killings went on.

The distance from Seville to Talavera, p. 276, is not '700 kilometres', but 425; not enough, incidentally, to 'weary the Army of Africa', which took it in its stride while fighting over part of the way. And I differ from Mr Thomas in his evaluation—p. 279—of the members of a foreign committee made up of mistaken busybodies, two secretaries of which were out-and-out Communists, or when he pins a Catholic label—p. 281, footnote—on a radical Left-winger—José Bergamin—who had done nothing to earn it.

No Red militiamen—p. 282—'climbed up on the ruins of the tower'—in the Alcázar—'and fastened there a red flag on the equestrian statue of Charles V in the courtyard' [sic.]: they never set foot in the courtyard, nor was there an equestrian statue there or in the tower (see pp. 194 and 200 above). Mr Thomas's version of this incident is inaccurate and the same applies to his story of the capture of the Alcázar on p. 284 of his book.

Political prisoners in the Model Prison in Madrid—p. 321—were not, as we are cursorily informed, butchered by their guards 'in a moment of alarm'—a state of mind, incidentally, which no sane judge would accept as an excuse for mass murder. The majority were deliberately taken out of the prison, and, with equal deliberateness, massacred in Torrejón de Ardoz and in Paracuellos de Jarama. And the army, 'well equipped but only about 20,000 strong', which on 7 November 1936, 'engaged in a fierce struggle against an ill-armed'—not as regards automatic weapons—'but enormous urban mass' (see p. 322). was far from being '20,000 strong'.

Mr Thomas's information regarding the battles around Madrid is at fault on many points. For instance, the Thaelmann Battalion—a unit of the International Brigades; see p. 328—could not have placed 'bombs in lifts to be sent up to explode in the faces of the Moroccans on the next floor' of the Clinical Hospital in the University City, for the simple reason that there were no lifts there. The building was an empty shell, in process of construction when civil war broke out. Nor could the Moroccans have 'suffered losses' caused by eating 'inoculated animals kept for experimental purposes' in the same Clinical Hospital; there were no such animals in a skeleton building. Men of the Foreign Legion ate with considerable relish a number of inoculated rabbits in the Instituto Llorente, some distance from the University City on the other side of the Manzanares river, between the racecourse and the road to El Pardo, but they proved tougher than the microbes and suffered no ill-effects as a result of their meal.

Little credit should be given to the tales—see p. 329—about 'Franco having remarked before Portuguese journalists that he would destroy Madrid rather than leave it to the "Marxists" '; or about a desire on the part of some 'to see the reaction of a civilian population to a carefully planned attempt to set fire to the city, quarter by quarter'; about 'bombing concentrated as far as possible on hospitals', about the terrible flames that 'caused the capital to appear like some elemental place of torture'; about 'art treasures elsewhere in the Republic' being 'in excellent keeping'—see footnote on this same page; or about 'the Palacio de Liria, the town house of the Duke of Alba', having been 'bombed'. More than nine-tenths of Madrid was never bombed or shelled, nor was there ever an intention to set it on fire or destroy it, much less to blow up hospitals. Madrid was our city, the capital of Spain. And Liria, the Duke of Alba's residence in Madrid, was never bombed. It was deliberately set on fire by the Reds, who, to deceive foreign observers in the capital, kept one of their planes circling above the building while they themselves set it ablaze. 'Elsewhere in the Republic', and, indeed, in Madrid itself, the Reds destroyed or looted a large number of works of art, the property of the Church, the State, or private individuals.

The battle of Malaga—pp. 372 and 373—was not 'inglorious' except for the Reds; the Duke of Seville did not advance on Malaga 'from the Ronda section', nor did others there meet with 'fierce resistance'; the heights of Zafarraya do not dominate 'the escape road to Almería'— they are twenty miles away, and the intermediate country is rugged and mountainous; Malaga itself was never bombed during this battle, nor did the *Canarias*, *Baleares* and *Velasco* ever bombard the city. The port, and the Red naval ships inside it, were bombed from the air some months before the battle started. All the destruction inside Malaga was deliberately caused by the Reds.

Mr Thomas confuses certain issues, but he clarifies others, for he is obviously earnest and sincere. A letter which he published in *The New*

Statesman, on 25 June 1960, speaks for itself. 'Sir,' this letter reads, 'In the spring of 1958 I reviewed in your columns Mr Herbert Matthews' *The Yoke and The Arrows* about contemporary Spain. Mr Matthews threw doubt on the celebrated story of the Alcázar at Toledo in the Spanish Civil War. In particular he alleged that since the telephone wires between the Alcázar and the rest of Toledo were cut, the besieged General Moscardó could not have been rung up by the Republican militia leader and threatened with the execution of his son if the Alcázar were not surrendered within ten minutes. In my review, I accepted Mr Matthews' doubt. However, now, after exhaustive research, including conversations with eye witnesses, I have come to the conclusion that I was wrong to have done this. It is clear to me that the telephone conversation did occur. I wish therefore to offer my profound apologies to the surviving members of General Moscardó's family, including above all his widow Doña María Moscardó.' The letter was signed 'Hugh Thomas', and it was dated at 7 Queens Road, Belmont, Surrey.

A man who owns up deserves respect, and when I read this letter I felt respect for Mr Thomas, who has in any case omitted or corrected in recent editions of his book much of what appeared in the first. *The Spanish Civil War* is a remarkable book, the product of extensive if not exhaustive research, but its reception by serious papers everywhere as a piece of objective history shows that the nature of the conflict which broke out in Spain more than a quarter of a century ago has not yet been properly estimated in all countries. Writing in *The Month*, August 1961, Sir Arnold Lunn, who in *Memory to Memory* and in *And Yet so New* criticized the Franco regime—for its treatment of the Protestant problem, far less acute now than it was—praises highly *The Spanish Civil War* but he also insisted that Mr Thomas, a Left-wing writer and a former Labour candidate for Parliament, 'shares the violent prejudice of his party against General Franco. Nobody with any understanding of the situation in Spain at the beginning of the war could possibly write, as does Mr Thomas, that General Franco on 17 July 1936 had started "on the first stage of a journey which would lead him to supreme power in Spain but which he would almost certainly not have begun had he known how long it would last" (p. 129). It would have been just as perceptive to write "Churchill would certainly not have refused a compromise peace in 1940 had he known how long the World War would last." '

Mr Thomas is too young to remember what happened in the Civil War; he was only five years old at the time. But he does know that for the Western World the conflict was 'a most passionate war'. 'Why,' asks Lunn, 'did the Civil War arouse such passions among the intellectuals of the Left? Not, of course, because they disapproved of *all* attempts to reverse by violence the verdict of a democratic electorate.' Left-wing intellectuals everywhere applauded Socialist and Communist attempts to reverse by violence in 1934 the verdict of the electorate in Spain, but they felt deeply shocked when, in 1936, Spanish Nationalists followed this precedent. The torrents of selective indignation which were then let loose throughout the world are not likely to subside in the foreseeable future.

Sir Arnold Lunn calls Mr Thomas's a 'fascinating book . . . the most comprehensive and best documented' so far published on the Spanish Civil War, an opinion which I wholeheartedly share, but he also notes 'a specious suggestion of scholarly impartiality about any book which is obviously the product of patient and scholarly research. A reader who knew very little about the Civil War would find it easy to accept the publishers' claim that it is the first history of the Civil War that is both objective and comprehensive, but an objective historian would surely begin by discussing what would have been the probable consequences of a Republican victory, and what were the actual consequences of the Nationalist victory to Spain's attitude during the Second World War. There is something uncanny about the consistency with which Left-wing commentators fail to predict the future. Every Left-wing supporter of the Republic insisted that General Franco would fight with Germany when and if the war came.' Some of them still act as if he had.

'In the epilogue to this book Mr Thomas is generous in his recognition of Franco's success in keeping Spain out of the war: "Even his worst enemies"—writes Mr Thomas—"would not deny that Franco's achievement in keeping Spain out of the war was a remarkable one. This is the most obvious way in which Franco differs from the popular image of the imperialist, expansionist Fascist dictator. Hitler and Franco eventually met at Hendaye in 1940. Franco, insisting on his after-luncheon siesta, kept the Führer waiting half an hour—an unprecedented event. And Hitler later said that he found Franco so unyielding that he would prefer to have three or four teeth out than have another such interview" (p. 619).' Hitler should have expected something of this sort. A few months earlier, General Franco's brother,

Nicolás, had kept Ribbentrop waiting in Berlin for almost an hour. It was noon; to an impatient message from the German Foreign Minister, Nicolás had answered that he was in his bath. 'I'll see him as soon as I am ready.' Incidentally, at Hendaye General Franco did not insist on his after-luncheon siesta, a luxury in which he rarely indulges. He merely dallied with his after-luncheon coffee.

Lunn also remarks that 'in his anxiety to discredit the contemporary Church in Spain Mr Thomas does not shrink from quoting sources which are both anonymous and probably tainted. I criticize Mr Thomas for an uncritical acceptance of many attacks both on the Nationalists and on the Spanish Church, and I give him full credit for the objectivity with which he records many facts which are embarrassing to the Republicans or to those who bitterly regret their defeat. Mr Thomas makes no attempt to deny that horrible atrocities were committed in the Republican territory,' but he 'follows the precedents set during the Civil War by arguing that in effect it was a case of six of one and half a dozen of the other; he just could not accept that Republicans were in any respect incomparably worse than the Nationalists. Consequently he welcomed uncritically charges against the Nationalists, for which no adequate evidence is offered. This leads him to forget the role of manufactured atrocities in war propaganda and to reject the principle which objective historians observe, the principle that no atrocity should be accepted which is not supported by weighty evidence. This principle is of decisive importance in the case of accusations made by Communists, fellow-travellers and their dupes. A Communist always has the clearest of consciences when lying on behalf of his cause, for the Communist acts consistently on the principle, falsely attributed to the Jesuits, that the end justifies the means. E. Yaroslavsky in his book, *Red Virtue*, sums up in a few words the guiding principle of Communist propaganda. "What coincides with the interests of the proletarian revolution is ethical." '

On pp. 129–33 of *The Thirties; A Dream Revolved* (London, The Cresset Press, 1960), Julian Symons lights up this situation in a manner which has a direct bearing on the above quotation and also on what I have written on pp. 248–9 of this book about Arthur Koestler's Spanish activities. 'When Arthur Koestler visited Paris a fortnight after the war began, he naturally went to see his friend Willy Muenzenberg, who was at this time the head of "The Comintern's West-European AGITPROP Department". Muenzenberg's propagandist activities were manifold. He had just formed the Committee for War Relief for Republican Spain and the Spanish Milk Fund, and was in process of forming the Committee of Inquiry into Foreign Intervention in the Spanish War. These, and several other Committees, were Communist-front organizations: that is, most of the people who served on them did so in good faith (Philip Noel-Baker, Lord Faringdon, Eleanor Rathbone and other non-Communists were members of the Commission of Inquiry into Alleged Breaches of the Non-Intervention Agreement in Spain), but the organizers were realistic Communists, who knew exactly what they wanted done, and how to do it. Koestler was told that he should make a trip to Franco's headquarters as a newspaper correspondent. He already held a card for the ultra-Conservative Hungarian paper, *Pester Lloyd*, and now Otto Katz, Muenzenberg's second-in-command, made a telephone call to London and arranged within an hour that Koestler should be a *News Chronicle* correspondent also. Would the *Chronicle* pay for the journey? Koestler asked, and learned that the "Committee" would pay.

'So began Koestler's work as a Communist undercover man in Spain, work which is especially interesting because it shows a section of the great Communist honeycomb in the country, with all its members working busily, although sometimes at cross-purposes with each other. Here is Koestler writing *Spanish Testament*, which is to be published as a Left Book Club choice, here is Otto Katz working in the same flat, also on a propaganda book about Spain, here is Muenzenberg criticizing them.

> He would pick up a few sheets of the typescript, scan through them, and shout at me: "Too weak. Too objective. Hit them! Hit them hard! Tell the world how they run over their prisoners with tanks, how they pour petrol over them and burn them alive. Make the world gasp with horror. Hammer it into their heads. Make them wake up!"

'Koestler did his best to make them wake up. He was arrested when Franco captured Malaga, and was sentenced to death. He was saved by an immense propaganda campaign, which had some Communist inspiration but gathered a momentum that had nothing to do with the Communists, but was based on Koestler's position as the presumedly Liberal correspondent of a Liberal newspaper. (Two other *News Chronicle* correspondents in Spain, William Forrest and John Langdon-

Davies, were also Communists at this time.) Fifty-eight Members of Parliament, nearly half of them Conservatives, protested to Franco; authors' and journalists' associations protested also, and so did many political, cultural and religious bodies. The British Government itself addressed representations to Franco on behalf of the Liberal newspaper man. Otto Katz produced some fictitious stories about Koestler's ill-treatment in prison. When at last he was exchanged for the wife of one of Franco's fighter pilots, it was of course necessary for Koestler to go on playing his part. "By the logic of circumstances the fiction of the *bona fide* Liberal journalist had to be maintained," and it was maintained in the *News Chronicle* and elsewhere, in spite of Koestler's increasing distaste for the part he was playing. He made a four weeks' lecture tour for the Left Book Club, to talk about the political and military situation in Spain. Koestler was in a state of suppressed dissatisfaction with Communism, but his heretical answers to questions about the character and fate of the P.O.U.M., which had been suppressed by the Communists in Spain, were regarded merely as proof of an over-tender conscience. "The exploitation of the war by Moscow for its own purposes, the activities of the G.P.U. and S.I.M. behind the front-lines, did not enter the picture. Any mention of these subjects would have met with incredulity and indignation." The Duchess of Atholl, the Conservative who wrote an introduction to *Spanish Testament*, was, Koestler says, the only person who at this time asked him whether he was a member of the Communist Party. "Your word is enough for me," she said, when he denied it.

'In his autobiography Koestler says nothing about the reports he sent back to the *News Chronicle*, but it is obvious that these reports contained just as much truth as the requirements of the Party demanded, and that all the newspaper men or "Liberals" or "impartial observers" who were at this time members of the Communist Party practised a tremendous deception on the British public. Chief among them was the irrepressible Claud Cockburn, who as "Frank Pitcairn" wrote for the *Daily Worker* and in his own identity edited the Communist news sheet called *The Week* which professed to give information about political developments in Europe and America, much of which came straight from Cockburn's fertile brain. As Pitcairn he wrote a book called *Reporter in Spain*, which was accepted by many others besides Communists as a moving and convincing account of conditions in Spain. In *Homage to Catalonia* George Orwell detailed the inaccuracies of which Frank Pitcairn was guilty in dealing with the suppression of the P.O.U.M. in Barcelona, the wholly fictitious account of tanks, scores of machine-guns and thousands of rifles used by the P.O.U.M. in what Pitcairn called a Trotskyist attempt to seize power. Orwell felt nominally compelled to assume Pitcairn's good faith, and to say simply that he was strangely mistaken, but there is no need to make any such assumption today, after the publication of Cockburn-Pitcairn's volumes of autobiography.

'In one of them he tells how he arrived in Paris from Spain, and telephoned Otto Katz at the office of the Spanish Republican Press Agency, *Agence Espagne*. "What I want now," Katz said, "is a tip-top, smashing, eye-witness account of the great anti-Franco revolt which occurred yesterday at Tetuán, the news of it having hitherto been suppressed by censorship." Cockburn-Pitcairn said he had never been in Tetuán, and had not heard of the revolt. "Not the point at all," Katz said. "Nor have I heard of any such thing." He explained that a crucial moment had been reached in the supply of arms to the Republicans. A consignment of arms was waiting on the French frontier, and if a suitable jolt was administered to the French Government, in the form of a hint that Franco's defeat might be imminent, the arms would be let through. What better place for a revolt than Tetuán in Spanish Morocco, which had been the starting place of Franco's rebellion? They set to work.

> Our chief anxiety was that, with nothing to go on but the plans in the guide-books, which were without contours, we might have democrats and fascists firing at one another from either end of an avenue which some travelled night-editor might know had a hump in the middle. The fighting, accordingly, took place in very short streets and open squares.... Katz was insistent that we use a lot of names, of both heroes and villains, but express uncertainty over some of them—thus in the confusion of the struggle outside the barracks it had been impossible to ascertain whether the Captain Murillo who died so gallantly was the same Captain Murillo who, a few months ago in Madrid ... In the end it emerged as one of the most factual, inspiring and at the same time sober pieces of war reporting I ever saw.

'Leon Blum read it and talked excitedly of its significance. The arms got through.'

*

'What is the use of quoting Republican estimates of alleged Nationalist atrocities which even Mr Thomas concedes to be exaggerated?' Sir Arnold Lunn very properly asks. ' "The Madrid Council of Lawyers," Mr Thomas writes (p. 168), "reported that in the first weeks of the war 9,000 workers were killed in Seville (20,000 by late 1937), 2,000 in Saragossa, 5,000 in Granada, 7,000 in all Navarre and 400 in Algeciras. A Catholic deputy and the head of the English Catholic College at Valladolid have separately testified to the deaths of 9,000 persons in that city." Who appointed this Council of Lawyers? What exactly did it consist of? When did it publish its report? How could lawyers in besieged Madrid and cut off from Nationalist Spain form any estimate of the number of executions in Nationalist Spain? Did the Catholic deputy and the head of the English Catholic College at Valladolid independently arrive at the same nice round figure of 9,000 which by a curious coincidence is the same figure as that quoted for the executions in Seville? Has Mr Thomas been in touch with either of these witnesses? Mr Thomas bases his statement on the authority of a private informer whom he does not name. I spent some days in 1950 in the English College in Valladolid, and the Rector described with gratitude the battle in which the Nationalists had saved priests in Valladolid from the same fate as that of the martyrs in Red Spain. Is it not absurd to quote the estimate of a British journalist, the correspondent of a pro-Republican paper who was "unfortunately captured in Madrid", that 100,000 prisoners had been executed by the end of 1939? (p. 607).'

'Mr Thomas states that "nearly all officers of the Republican Army were shot if captured" (p. 607). I remember asking the Infante Don Alfonso de Orleans what happened to officers who fought for the Republicans. What he told me at the time, he has since confirmed in a letter dated 8 May 1961 from which I quote:

I sat on Courts Martial in Madrid when our War ended week after week. We in the Air Force dealt only with Red Air Force prisoners and Air Force activities. Not one single one of those we judged in the Courts I attended was executed though several were condemned to death. All Red Air Force Officers lost their jobs. How could one accept them to command (if of higher rank) our loyal officers? It would have wrecked discipline. The bulk of the condemned received a sentence of three years and one day prison which automatically takes an officer out of the Air Force List.'

Sir Arnold Lunn notes that Mr Thomas is 'equally uncritical in his acceptance of statistics, quoted on p. 367 of his book, of the alleged social progress in Republican territory, statistics for which he offers no corroboration'. There is no evidence for the alleged increase, during the war, in the number of schools and their pupils in Red territory; the war gave the Republicans few opportunities to accomplish what they had left undone in the years of relative peace. Had the amount of land under cultivation risen 6 per cent in the same period, as Mr Thomas asserts on this same page, the inhabitants of the Red Zone would not have been practically starving when we liberated them in 1939. 'In April 1938,' Lunn writes, 'I was attached to press photographers during the Nationalists' advance to the Mediterranean. A Frenchman drew my attention to the contrast between the look of the land in Nationalist Spain and in the territory which had just been reconquered from the Republicans. Peasants in Republican Spain appeared to have lost heart. The impression was reinforced by the hilarious joy with which the liberating army was received. My companion was a war correspondent whose sympathies were with the Republicans, but he made one significant admission. "One thing is certain," he said to me as we entered a village which had just been liberated, "these people are delighted to see the last of the Reds." '

'A minor indication of Mr Thomas's bias,' Sir Arnold says, 'is between his attitude to those who changed sides in the course of the war. Mr Thomas realizes that "thousands of Spaniards first fought on one side or the other entirely because of the accident of where they were in July 1936" (p. 355). From which it follows that it is certainly not objective to criticize a Spaniard as "treacherous" because he seizes the first opportunity to join those with whom he naturally sympathizes, and yet the noun "treachery" or the adjective "treacherous" is applied three times (pp. 401, 445, 446) to a Basque Major who took an early opportunity to join the Nationalists. On the other hand, Antonio Bahamonde "for a year propaganda chief to Queipo de Llano in Seville fled abroad sickened by the job" (p. 168), without being accused by Mr Thomas of "treachery". A book by Jesús Hernández (p. 217, footnote) is described as "this unpleasant work of the leading Communist renegade". The ugly word "renegade" would never be applied by Mr Thomas to a Catholic who attacked the Catholic hierarchy in Spain, Bernanos for instance. My quarrel with Mr Thomas,' Sir Arnold explains, 'does not derive from his obvious bias but from his rash claim to be unbiased. It would be difficult for anybody who was actually involved in the war to be unbiased. I certainly do not pretend to have been.'

A degree of readiness to accept uncorroborated statements may be the cause of much that is inaccurate in what Mr Thomas writes, all of which is the product of research; his youth precludes him from speaking as an eye-witness or a close observer of the events which he describes. His task, in itself formidable enough, has been rendered harder by the circumstances of the case. In Spain it is not easy for a writer, even a writer of Mr Thomas's ability, to carry out research work with complete success. Access to reliable sources is sometimes difficult; compared to the number of books published in certain countries on matters of national or international importance, the available bibliography on a given subject is somewhat limited; the same applies to statistics, which are not always recorded minutely. Many of those who could have shed light on the Civil War have died without writing their memoirs. Others, while writing them, have given a free hand to their imagination. When account is taken of all of this, Mr Thomas's feat is all the more remarkable.

By way of contrast to what is usually written about Spain and the Spanish Civil War I would like to quote from a brief article by Mr Murray D. Kirkwood, an American Rhodes Scholar who after circling the globe in 1937 taught government at Harvard University and during the War received the rank of major in a parachute commando unit for outstanding leadership during the Aleutian campaign of 1943. Mr Kirkwood's article, published in the International Telephone and Telegraph Corporation's *International Review*, January 1949, is entitled 'Spain: Genius, Faith, Glory', and the following are extracts from it.

'The Second Spanish Republic was a prelude to Civil War. Why? Because, while giving expression to and encouraging the development of nearly every divisive force in the Spanish nation, it failed to provide the necessary counterbalance of great leadership and the unifying force of a great ideal. The Left, which dictated the new Constitution and dominated government under it in the first and last phases of its five-year life, was itself united only in what it wanted to destroy; there was no agreement regarding what it wanted to build. How could there be, when it included a Republican Left and a Republican Union, Socialists both moderate and extreme, Marxists loyal to Trotsky and to Stalin, as well as Syndicalists and Anarchists. There were leaders among these

373

men who frankly proclaimed their intention of using the Republic to bring about revolution. But the revolution they sought was for the benefit of their own particular group, or clique within that group; never for Spain as a whole. Probably that is why the Left encouraged regional autonomy for Catalonia, the Basque Provinces and Galicia; a fragmented Spain would be easier to conquer. Certainly, the plague of strikes, riots and assassinations that accompanied the Republic was in accordance with accepted principles of revolutionary procedure. Reaction was inevitable.

'General Franco gave the name of Nationalist to the forces he directed, thereby revealing his sure grasp of the fundamental issue: unity versus anarchy. Much of Spain rallied to his support. It is true that he sought and accepted help from Fascist Italy and Nazi Germany; he did so for the same reason that Great Britain and the United States later sought and accepted help from Communist Russia. And there is this essential difference between the help given by Russia to the Republic, and that given by Germany and Italy to the Nationalists: the Nationalists were strong, but the Republic was weak. Therefore, Nationalist Spain was not at the mercy of her allies at any time; whereas, after 6 November 1936 the Republic was continually at the mercy of the Kremlin. General Franco has expressed the Spanish view of Russia once and for all: Yesterday, today and tomorrow, for the countries of Europe there exists only one danger—Communism. That statement would arouse less unfavourable comment now than when it was made (18 July 1942), but it explains why both the Allies and Hitler found Spain aloof for as long as their alliances with Russia lasted. In point of fact, Spain was a disappointment to both camps during World War II—as any neutral is bound to be. What Allied critics forget is the very different effect of Spanish neutrality upon the Axis and themselves; for the Allies, it meant the possibility of victory; for the Axis, the probability of defeat.

'Notwithstanding material weaknesses, Spain is one of the world's great powers. For greatness is not to be reckoned in material terms alone—by Spain least of all. The great achievements of Spain have always been spiritual, never material. Spain's Golden Age stressed spiritual values even in its material conquests. For that reason, Spain today is the spiritual centre of a great empire that includes all nations to whom she gave her language, her culture and her faith.'

The Gold that went to Russia

Exemplaire N° ...

CONFIDENTIEL.

A C T E.

DE LA RECEPTION DE L'OR ENVOYE EN DEPOT PAR LE GOUVER-
NEMENT DE LA REPUBLIQUE ESPAGNOLE AU DEPOT D'ETAT DES
METAUX PRECIEUX DU COMMISSARIAT DU PEUPLE DES FINANCES
DE l'U.R.S.S. à MOSCOU.

Nous, les soussignés - le Commissaire du Peuple aux Finances de l'U.R.S.S. Grigory Fedorovitch GRINKO et le Commissaire
du Peuple Adjoint aux Affaires Etrangères de l'U.R.S.S. Nikolai
Nikolaevitch KRESTINSKI, d'un côté, et

l'Ambassadeur de la République Espagnole en U.R.S.S.
M. MARCELINO PASCUA, de l'autre côté,

ont dressé le présent Acte afin d'attester que:

PREMIERE PARTIE.

I. Entre le 6 et le I0 novembre 1936 il a été reçu au
Depôt d'Etat des Metaux Précieux du Commissariat du Peuple des
Finances de l'U.R.S.S. à Moscou (désigné par la suite "GOKHRAN")
l'or arrivé d'Espagne, emballé dans 7.800 (sept mille huit
cents) caisses du type standard, appartenant à la République
Espagnole et expédié en dépôt à Moscou par le Gouvernement de
la République Espagnole.

2. Les 7.800 (sept mille huit cents) caisses, contenant
de l'or, mentionnées au paragraphe I, n'étaient pas numerotées
ni accompagnées de factures qui auraient indiqué la quantité,
le poids et le poinçon de l'or; 216 (deux cent seize) de
ces caisses étaient légèrement endommagées.

3. En vue de déterminer la quantité et le poids de l'or,
envoyé en dépôt à Moscou par le Gouvernement de la République

Page 2.

Espagnole, toutes les 7.800 (sept mille huit cents) caisses
contenant de l'or ont été ouvertes et leur contenu compté et
pesé par les fonctionnaires du "Gokhran"; l'ouverture, le compta
ge et le pesage de l'or, contenu dans chaque caisse, étant
effectués en présence et avec la participation d'une des personn
suivantes, qui de l'Espagne avaient accompagné l'or à Moscou:
Arturo CANDELA, Abelardo PADIN, Jose GONZALEC, Jose VELASCO.

Pour chacune des 7.800 (sept mille huit cents) caisses
un acte a été rédigé concernant les résultats du comptage et du
pesage de l'or, cet acte étant signé, d'un côté, par des fonctionnaires du "Gokhran", et de l'autre côté, par une des per-
sonnes enumerées au présent paragraphe et prenant part au comptage et au pesage de l'or par autorisation et sous le contrôle de
l'Ambassadeur de la République Espagnole en U.R.S.S.M.MARCELINO
PASCUA.

4. Les 7.800 (sept mille huit cents) caisses ouvertes
contenaient en tout: I5.57I (quinze mille cinq cent soixante
et onze) sacs avec des pièces de monnaie en or de désignation
et de frappe différente de différents pays, 64 (soixante-
quatre) lingots d'or et 4 (quatre) paquets de copeaux d'or.

Les pièces de monnaie contenues dans les caisses étaient
placées dans les sacs de telle manière que chacun des sacs ne
contenait, comme règle, que des pièces de monnaie d'une seule
espèce. Toutefois, certains sacs contenaient des pièces de
monnaie d'or de désignation différente, mais de la même parité.
Dans ces cas (étant donne la même parité) la désignation
d'une seule monnaie a été adopté au comptage au "Gokhran" pour
exprimer le contenu total d'un sac.

Page 3.

DEUXIEME PARTIE.

Comme résultat du comptage et du pesage de l'or effectués dans l'ordre, indiqué au paragraphe 3 de la Première Partie, il a été constaté que les 7.800 (sept mille huit cents) caisses contenaient en tout:

a) des pesetas espagnoles pour la somme nominale de 313.265.255 (trois cent treize millions deux cent soixante-cinq mille deux cent cinquante-cinq) possédant le poids total d'alliage de I0I.35I.329,55 gr. (cent un million trois cent cinquante et un mille trois cent vingt-neuf grammes et cinquante-cinq centièmes);

b) des francs français pour la somme nominale de 294.299.270 (deux cent quatre-vingt quatorze millions deux cent quatre-vingt dix-neuf mille deux cent soixante-dix) possédant le poids total d'alliage de 94.743.568,05 gr. (quatre-vingt-quatorze millions sept cent quarante-trois mille cinq cent soixante-huit grammes et cinq centièmes);

c) des dollars américains pour la somme nominale de 136.285.348 (cent trente-six millions deux cent quatre-vingt cinq mille trois cent quarante-huit) possédant le poids total d'alliage de 227.698.051, 35 gr. (deux cent vingt-sept millions six cent quatre-vingt-dix-huit mille cinquante et un grammes et trente-cinq centièmes);

d) des marks allemands pour la somme nominale de 401.090 (quatre cent un mille quatre-vingt-dix) possédant le poids total d'alliage de I59.069,2 gr. (cent cinquante-neuf mille soixante-neuf grammes et deux dixièmes);

e) des livres anglaises pour la somme nominale de 10.274.580,5 (dix millions deux cent soixante-quatorze mille

Page 4.

cinq cent quatre-vingts et cinq dixièmes) possédant le poids
total d'alliage de 8I.927.78I,2 gr. (quatre-vingt-un millions
neuf cent vingt-sept mille sept cent quatre-vingt-un grammes et
deux dixièmes);

f) des francs belges pour la somme nominale de 4.300.000
(quatre millions trois cent mille) possédant le poids total
d'alliage de I.383.626,0 gr. (un million trois cent quatre-
vingt-trois mille six cent vingt-six grammes);

g) des lires italiennes pour la somme nominale de 3.600.020
(trois millions six cent mille vingt) possedant le poids total
d'alliage de I.I56.508,4 gr. (un million cent cinquante-six
mille cinq cent huit grammes et quatre dixièmes);

h) des escudos portugais pour la somme nominale de I9.998
(dix- neuf mille neuf cent quatre-vingt-dix huit) possedant
le poids total d'alliage de 35.37I,5 gr. (trente cinq mille
trois cent soixante et onze grammes et cinq dixièmes);

i) des pièces portugaises anciennes possédant le poids total d'alliage de 3I8.603,3 gr. (trois cent dix-huit mille six
cent trois grammes et trois dixièmes);

j) des roubles russes pour la somme nominale de 75.000
(soixante-quinze mille) possédant le poids total d'alliage
de 64.434,0 gr. (soixante-quatre mille quatre cent trente-
quatre grammes);

k) des francs autrichiens pour la somme nominale de
799.990 (sept cent quatre-vingt-dix-neuf mille neuf cent .
quatre-vingt dix) possédant le poids total d'alliage de
257.40I,5 gr. (deux cent cinquante-sept mille quatre cent
un grammes et cinq dixièmes);

378

Page 5.

1) des pesos méxicains pour la somme nominale de 10°.70°
(cent cinq mille sept cent cinq) possédant le poi s total .
d'alliage de 88.027,0 gr. (quatre-vingt-huit mille vingt-sept
grammes);

m) des pesos argentins pour la somme nominale de 4.155 .
(quatre mille cent cinquante-cinq) possédant le poids total
d'alliage de 6.689,8 gr. (six mille six cent quatre-vingt-neuf
grammes et huit dixièmes);

n) des pesos chiliens pour la somme nominale de 100 (cent)
possédant le poids total d'alliage de 59,9 gr. (cinquante-neuf
grammes et neuf dixièmes);

o) des florins hollandais pour la somme nominale de 10 (dix)
possédant le poids total d'alliage de 6,7 gr. (six grammes et
sept dixièmes);

p) des francs suisses pour la somme nominale de 300.000
(trois cent mille) possédant le poids total d'alliage de
96.656,2 gr. (quatre-vingt-seize mille six cent cinquante-six
grammes et deux dixièmes);

q) 64 (soixante-quatre) lingots d'or possédant le poids
total d'alliage de 792.332,65 gr. (sept cent quatre-vingt-douze
mille trois cent trente-deux grammes et soixante-cinq centièmes);

r) des copeaux d'or possédant le poids total d'alliage de
13,0 (treize grammes),
- ce qui correspond aux 7.800 (sept mille huit cents) actes,
dépesés au "Gokhran", concernant l'ouverture et le contrôle des
caisses contenant de l'or.

Les pièces de monnaie d'or, les lingots d'or et les copeaux d'or, appartenant à la République Espagnole, énumérés

Page 8.

dans la présente Partie, possédant en tout un poids total
d'alliage de 510.079.529, 3 gr. (cinq cent dix millions soixante-
dix neuf mille cinq cent vingt-neuf grammes et trois dixièmes),
emballés de nouveau dans 7.800 (sept mille huit cents) caisses
et inscrits dans un livre-régistre spécial, cordonné et cacheté
par les sceaux du Commissariat du Peuple des Finances de l'Union
des Républiques Soviétiques Socialistes et de l'Ambassade de la
République Espagnole en U.R.S.S., sont par le présent Acte reçus
en dépôt par le Commissariat du Peuple des Finances de l'Union
des Républiques Soviétiques Socialistes.

TROISIEME PARTIE.

La remise en dépôt de l'ôr, expedié par le Gouvernement
de la République Espagnole, et sa réception en dépôt ont été
effectuées à Moscou

    - quant à la remise,

par M. MARCELINO PASCUA - Ambassadeur de la République Espagnole
en U.R.S.S.

    - quant à la réception,

par O.I. KAGAN   - Directeur du Département des Devises
                          du Commissariat du Peuple des Finances
                          de l'U.R.S.S.

    J.V. MARGOULIS   - Directeur du Secteur des Métaux Pré-
                          cieux du Commissariat du Peuple des
                          Finances de l'U.R.S.S.

en présence de,

    F.S. WEINBERG   - Représentant du Commissariat du Peuple
                          des Affaires Etrangères de l'U.R.S.S.

Page 7.

QUATRIEME PARTIE.

I. Le présent Acte est le principal et le seul document de
la remise par le Gouvernement de la République Espagnole de
l'or décrit dans la Deuxième Partie, et de sa réception en
dépôt par le Commissariat du Peuple des Finances de l'Union
des Républiques Soviétiques Socialistes.

Par la signature du présent Acte, tous les documents
précédemment rédigés et signés à Moscou, concernant la réception en dépôt de l'or indiqué dans cet Acte, à savoir, les
Protocoles du 5,7 et 10 novembre 1936 et l'Acte de la réception préliminaire du 20 novembre 1936, cessent d'être en vi-
gueur.

2. Au cas où le Gouvernement de la République Espagnole
ordonnerait l'exportation au délà de l'U.R.S.S. de l'or reçu
en dépôt par cet Acte, ou bien au cas où il en disposerait
autrement, la responsabilité assumée par le présent Acte par
le Commissariat du Peuple des Finances de l'U.R.S.S. sera
automatiquement réduite, entièrement ou en partie, en proportion aux dispositions du Gouvernement de la République Espagnole

-----00000-----

Le présent Acte a été dressé à Moscou, en date du 5 février 1937, en langue russe sur 5 pages en trois exemplaires,
qui seront déposés, en un exemplaire, au Commissariat du Peuple
des Finances de l'U.R.S.S., chez l'Ambassadeur de la République
Espagnole en U.R.S.S. M. MARCELINO PASCUA et au Commissariat
du Peuple des Affaires Etrangères de l'U.R.S.S.

Il a été prévu par cet Acte que trois exemplaires de ce

Page 8.

même Acte, devant être déposés auprès des autorités sus-men-
tionnées, seraient rédigés par la suite en langue française
et signés en même date, le texte français ayant le même effet
que le texte russe.

Conformément à quoi, le présent Acte sur 8 pages a été
dressé en date du 5 février en langue française, les deux
textes, russe et français, faisant également foi.

Commissaire du Peuple des
Finances de l'U.R.S.S.

(G.F. Grinko)

Ambassadeur de la
République Espagnole
en U.R.S.S.

(Marcelino Pascua)

Commissaire du Peuple Adjoint
des Affaires Etrangères de
l'U.R.S.S.

(N.N. Krestinski)

Bibliography

Acción Española. Antología, Burgos, 1937

And Yet So New, Sir Arnold Lunn, Sheed & Ward, London, 1958

Avances del Informe Oficial, Estado Español, 1936

Behind the Spanish Barricades, John Langdon-Davies, Martin Secker & Warburg, London, 1937

Campañas en el Rif y Yebala, General Berenguer, Madrid, 1923

Cartas a un Escéptico en Materia de Formas de Gobierno, José Maria Pemán, Cultura Española, Madrid, 135

Cómo Fuí Ejecutado en Madrid, J. Miquelarena (el fugitivo), Sigirano Diaz, Avila, 1937

Death in the Morning, Helen Nicholson, Lovat Dickson, London, 1937

Defensa de la Hispanidad, Ramiro de Maeztu, Madrid, 1934

Dialogue with Death, Arthur Koestler, London, 1937

Diario de una Bandera, Comandante Franco, Madrid, 1922

Documents on German Foreign Policy, Series D, (1937–1945), Volume III, Germany and the Spanish Civil War, 1936–39, His Majesty's Stationery Office, London, 1951

Franco, Joaquín Arrarás, Librería Internacional, San Sebastian, 1937

Franco, Claude Martin, Editions des Quatre Fils Aymon, Paris, 1959

General Queipo de Llano, Antonio y Cuesta Monereo & Teniente General José Oimedo Delgado, Spain, 1957

Guerra en el Aire, Joaquín García Morato, Editoria Nacional, Madrid, 1940

Guerra de Liberación Española, Teniente General Garcia-Valiño, Madrid, 1949

¿Hacia Donde va España?, Arthur F. Loveday, Editora Zig-Zag, Santiago de Chile

Historia de España, Marcelino Menéndez y Pelayo, Madrid, 1934

Historia de la Persecución Religiosa en España, 1936-1939, Antonio Montero Moreno, Madrid, 1961

Historia de la Republica Española, 1931–1936, Melchor Fernández Almagro, Madrid, 1940

Historia Militar de la Guerra de España, Manuel Aznar, Madrid, 1958

History of Spanish Architecture, Bernard Bevan, London, 1938

Incendencias de la Lucha, Revista de Historia Militar, Año VIII, No. 17, 1964

José María Gil Robles: Su Vida, Su Actuación, Sus Ideas, Juan Arrabal, Librería Internacional del Romo, Madrid, 1933

Kings Without Castles, Lucy Herndon Crockett, Rand McNally, New York, 1953

La Actuación de España en Marruecos, Juan de España, Madrid, 1926

La Caida de Alfonso XIII, Julián Cortes Cavanillas, Madrid, 1932

La Cruz de Monte Arruit, Enrique Meneses, Madrid, 1922

La Guerre Civile d'Espagne, Georges-Roux, Fayard, Paris, 1964

La Guerra de Liberación Nacional, Universidad de Zaragoza, 1961

La Legión, José Millán Astray, Madrid, 1923

Laughter in the Next Room, Sir Osbert Sitwell, Macmillan, London, 1949

La Voz de un Perseguido, José Calvo Sotelo, Madrid, 1933

Liquidación de la Monarquía Parlamentaria, Ramiro de Maeztu, Madrid, 1957

Los Valores Históricos en la Dictadura Española, José Pemartín, Editorial Arte y Ciencia, Madrid

Madrid De Corte a Cheka, Agustin de Foxá, Madrid, 1938

Memorias de un Deportado, Andres Coll, Madrid, 1933

Memory to Memory, Sir Arnold Lunn, Hollis & Carter, London, 1956

Mine Were of Trouble, Peter Kemp, Cassell, London, 1957

Monarquía, Sir Charles Petrie, Cultura Española, Madrid, 1935

'No Me Cuente Vd. Su Caso', Javier Martin Artajo, Madrid

Notas del Block, Joaquín Arrarás, Cultura Española, 1936

Nueva Historia de España, M. Legendre, Librería General, Zaragoza, 1951

Obras Completas, Emilio Mola, Librería Santarén, Valladolid, 1940

Por qué cayó Alfonso XIII, Duque de Maura & Melchor Fernández Almagro, Ediciones Ambos Mundos, S.L., Madrid, 1948

Red, White and Spain, Nigel Tangye, Rich & Cowan, London, 1937

Report From Spain, Emmet John Hughes, Henry Holt, New York, 1947

Reporter in Spain, Frank Pitcairn, Lawrence & Wishart, London, 1936

Salud, Peadar O'Donnell, Methuen, London, 1937

BIBLIOGRAPHY

Single to Spain, Keith Scott Watson, Arthur Barker, London, 1937
Spain, Sacheverell Sitwell, B. T. Batsford, London, 1950
Spain and the Defence of the West, Arthur P. Whitaker, New York, 1961
Spain: A Tragic Journey, F. Theo Rogers, The Macaulay Company, New York, 1937
Spain in the Modern World, James Cleugh, Alfred A. Knopf, New York, 1953
Spain in Revolt, Harry Gannes & Theodore Repard, Victor Gollancz, London, 1936
Spain Resurgent, Sir Robert Hodgson, Hutchinson, London, 1953
Spanish Front, Carlos Prieto, Thomas Nelson, London, 1936
Spanish Journey, Halliday Sutherland, Hollis & Carter, London, 1948
Spanish Journey, Eleanora Tennant, Eyre & Spottiswoode, London, 1936
The Alcâzar will not Surrender, Manuel Aznar, New York
The Cid and his Spain, Ramón Menéndez Pidal, London, 1934
The Civil War in Spain, Robert Payne, G. P. Putnam's Sons, New York, 1962
The Cypresses Believe in God, José María Gironella, Alfred A. Knopf, New York, 1955
The Grand Camouflage, Burnett Bolloten, Hollis & Carter, London, 1961
The History of Spain, Louis Bertrand & Sir Charles Petrie, Eyre & Spottiswoode, London, 1934
The Lincoln Battalion, Edwin Rolfe, Random House, New York, 1939
The Origins of Modern Spain, J. B. Trend, University Press, Cambridge, 1934
The Red Domination in Spain, Madrid, 1953
The Reign of King Alfonso XIII of Spain, Mrs Steuart Erskine, Hutchinson, London, 1931
The Road to Madrid, Cecil Gerahty, London, 1937
The Spanish Civil War, Hugh Thomas, Eyre & Spottiswoode, London, 1961
The Spanish Pioneers, Charles F. Lummis, Chicago, 1939
The Spanish Republic, Luis Bolin, Eyre & Spottiswoode, London, 1933 (anonymously)
The Spanish Story, Herbert Feis, Alfred A. Knopf, New York, 1948
The Spanish Tragedy, E. Allison Peers, Methuen, London, 1936
The United States and Spain, Carlton J. H. Hayes, New York, 1951

BIBLIOGRAPHY

The Yoke and the Arrows, Herbert L. Matthews, George Brazillier, New York, 1947

Un Millón de Muertos, José María Gironella, Editorial Planeta, Barcelona, 1961

Un Muerto, F. A. Villarubias & J. F. Lizcano de la Rosa, Editorial Pentágona, S.A., Madrid-Barcelona, 1961

Veinte Años de Política Española, José Cuartero, Prensa Española, S.A., Madrid, 1947

Wartime Mission in Spain, Carlton J. H. Hayes, New York, 1945

Yo Fuí un Ministro de Stalin, Jesús Hernández, Editorial América, México, 1953

Index

1. '*bis*' or '*ter*' after a page reference means that the topic is mentioned twice or thrice *in separate paragraphs* on the page indicated.
2. '*passim*' means 'here and there'.

387

INDEX